Studies in Social and Political Theory

Anthony Giddens has taught at the University of Leicester, at Simon Fraser University, Vancouver, and the University of California. He is currently a Fellow of King's College and lecturer in sociology in the University of Cambridge. He is the author of several works in the fields of social theory and political sociology including *Capitalism and Modern Social Theory* (published in the UK and US by Cambridge University Press, 1971), *Emile Durkheim* (published in the UK and US by Cambridge University Press, 1972), *The Class Structure of the Advanced Societies* (Hutchinson, 1973, published in the US by Harper, Row, 1974), *New Rules of Sociological Method* (Hutchinson, 1976, published in the US by Basic Books), and *Positivism and Sociology* (Heinemann, 1974, distributed in the US by Humanities Press).

Studies in Social and Political Theory

Anthony Giddens
Fellow of King's College
and Lecturer in Sociology,
University of Cambridge

Hutchinson of London

Hutchinson & Co (Publishers) Ltd
3 Fitzroy Square, London W1P 6JD

London Melbourne Sydney Auckland
Wellington Johannesburg and agencies
throughout the world

First published 1977
© Anthony Giddens 1977

Set in Intertype Times
Printed in Great Britain by The Anchor Press Ltd
and bound by Wm Brendon & Son Ltd
both of Tiptree, Essex

ISBN 0 09 129200 X

Contents

Preface

Virtually all of the essays that appear below were written over the past seven or eight years, in conjunction with a number of larger works.* They range over a fairly wide diversity of topics but, as is indicated in the Introduction, they are unified by a concern with a limited number of central problems in the social sciences. Seven of the chapters are followed by fresh appendices. I have written these in order to extend or amplify arguments developed in the main part of the text, and to help to tie together the overall themes of the book. I do not of course claim that these represent comprehensive treatments of the points they raise.

*Capitalism and Modern Social Theory, Cambridge University Press, 1971; Politics and Sociology in the Thought of Max Weber, Macmillan, London, and Humanities Press, New York, 1972; Emile Durkheim: Selected Writings, Cambridge University Press, 1972; The Class Structure of the Advanced Societies, Hutchinson, London, and Basic Books, New York, 1974; New Rules of Sociological Method, Hutchinson, London, and Basic Books, New York, 1976.

Introduction: some issues in the social sciences today

The studies which compose this volume are essentially organized about a critical encounter with European social theory in its 'classical' period – i.e. from the middle years of the nineteenth century until the First World War – and have the aim of working out some of the implications of that encounter for the position and prospects of the social sciences today. The issues involved can be classified broadly under four headings, as relating to the following series of problems: method and epistemology; social development and transformation; the origins of 'sociology' in nineteenth-century social theory; and the status of social science as critique.

Problems of method and epistemology

At the cost of some considerable oversimplification, and with the partial exception of the tradition of the *Geisteswissenschaften* in Germany, it is true to say that nineteenth-century social thought was dominated by the ambition of duplicating, in the sphere of human social life, the successes of physical science in mastering nature intellectually and materially. Nothing exemplifies this outlook more clearly than Comte's hierarchy of the sciences, which both explains the relation between the various sciences, natural and social, and offers an account of the tardy arrival of social physics on the scientific scene. The positive spirit first develops in relation to phenomena of the most general kind, far removed from human control: the objects and events studied in astronomy and physics. From these beginnings science progressively conquers the other realms of nature, moving through the chemical and the biological, to human social conduct itself; sociology is the last in the hierarchy of the sciences to come into being, because man's own social behaviour is the most difficult for him to subject to the objective scrutiny of science.

Comte's 'positive philosophy' has three particular features to which it is relevant to draw attention here, each bearing upon the relation between the natural and the social sciences. First, social science is taken to be *revelatory* in respect of its subject-matter in a manner parallel to that held to be characteristic of natural science; second, in both the natural and social sciences, theories are presumed to be capable of exhaustive or conclusive testing against 'neutral facts'; third, the division between chemical and biological science is treated as being of equal or perhaps greater significance than that between biology and sociology, on the ground that the latter two disciplines deal with organic unities, while chemistry and the sciences below it in the hierarchy are 'non-synthetic' sciences, concerned with aggregates rather than systems. None of these views is peculiar to Comte. Quite the reverse; they have each remained part of the most central traditions in sociology, above all that of functionalism. They have also received strong general support from logical positivism in philosophy, even though the connections between the latter and Comte's 'positivism' were only rather indirect.[1]

The presumption that the social sciences have a revelatory character directly akin to that of natural science depends upon the view that 'common-sense' or lay beliefs are in principle corrigible in the light of scientific findings. In Comte's writing, this appears in the form of an incompatibility between theological and metaphysical thought on the one hand, and the method of the positive sciences on the other. The task of scientific investigation, whether of nature or of society, is one of demystification, the replacement of tradition and prejudice by empirically verified knowledge. Such a view, even purely within the realm of natural science, as Husserl demonstrates in *The Crisis of the European Sciences*, conceals unexplicated premises concerning experience or the 'empirical': the *lebensweltliche a priori*. Positive thought supposedly provides a medium for the principled corrigibility of the world of lay beliefs or the 'natural attitude', but actually accepts implicitly some fundamental elements of the natural attitude which remain concealed and therefore unexplicated.[2] This is, however, distinguishable from the question of the corrigibility of lay beliefs and attitudes within the social sciences specifically. While the *lebensweltliche a priori* may be integral to the 'experience' of the object-world studied in natural science, it does not form part of that object-world as such, which is independent of whatever is believed by human beings. Lay beliefs and the ordinary language in which they are expressed, on the other hand, enter into the constitution of the social world as a series of ongoing practices organized reflexively by their component actors. Actors' knowledge of the practices in which they participate is already an element of those practices. Two aspects of the relation between the social sciences and lay beliefs thus have to be recognized.[3] The 'mutual knowledge', expressed and organized in the practical context of language-use, which lay actors draw upon in the process of the production and reproduction of society, has to be accepted by the observer also as the necessary means of describing social life. But recognition of the significance of 'mutual knowledge' in this sense does not preclude the possibility of subjecting to assessment, in the light of social-scientific findings, 'common-sense beliefs' represented as propositions or statements (about either the behaviour of human beings or natural objects). The potentially revelatory character of social science concerns several types of 'unacknowledged conditions of action': the formalization of the rules and resources used implicitly by actors to generate social interaction; the identification of unconscious or repressed motivational elements of action; and the analysis of discrepancies between intended and unintended consequences of action, in respect of their consequences for the reproduction of structures.[4]

Let us move to the second point mentioned previously, the relation between theories and facts. In recent times, i.e. in the 'post-positivistic' philosophy of natural science that has come to the fore in the past two decades or so, certain basic characteristics of the empirical character of science have been made clear. One is that even in the most developed areas of the natural sciences, theories are underdetermined by facts; another is that all observation statements are 'theory-impregnated'. The implications of these for the natural sciences are controversial, as the continuing debates among philosophers of science show. More important to this volume are the consequences for the logic and method of the social sciences. These, I consider, are as follows: 1) The underdetermination of theories by facts in social science is certainly greater than in natural science. This is one factor (not the only one) explaining the lack of 'paradigms' in the social sciences, the phenomenon which was a stimulus to Kuhn's reflections in *The Structure of Scientific Revolutions*.[5] The reasons for the lower level of underdetermination of theories by facts in the social sciences are not difficult to isolate. They include such difficulties as: the relative absence of controlled experimentation, the intractability of materials to scalar 'measurement', and problems of accurate replication. Of course, the natural sciences also differ between themselves in respect of such characteristics. 2) The theory-laden character of observation-statements in natural sciences entails that the meaning of scientific concepts is tied-in to the meaning of other terms in a theoretical network; moving between theories or paradigms involves hermeneutic tasks. The social sciences, however, imply not only this single level of hermeneutic problems, involved in the theoretical metalanguage, but a 'double hermeneutic', because social-scientific theories concern a 'pre-interpreted' world of lay meanings. There is a two-way connection between the language of social science and ordinary language. The former cannot ignore the categories used by laymen in the practical organization of social life; but on the other hand, the concepts of social science may also be taken over and applied by laymen as elements of their conduct. Rather than treating the latter as something to be avoided or minimized as far as possible, as inimical to the interests of 'prediction', we should understand it as integral to the subject–subject relation involved in the social sciences.

This brings us to the final point mentioned above: that of the proximity of biology and sociology. Nineteenth-century thought, under the influence of evolutionary theory, was preoccupied with biological models and analogies. Functionalist analysis more specifically, from Comte, Spencer and Durkheim through to Merton and Parsons, has been heavily influenced by explicitly or inexplicitly drawn logical parallels between biological and social systems. A major theme underlying the endeavour to specify such parallels is that of the systemic character of biological and social wholes, together with the presumption that these can be analysed teleologically in relation to 'adaptation to environments'. I have tried to identify some of the logical defects of functionalism below. They centre primarily upon the difficulty functionalism encounters in providing a treatment of purposive, reflexively monitored action.[6] Together with the characteristics already mentioned, the significance of mutual knowledge and of the double hermeneutic, this dislocates the social sciences from biology or physiology in much more radical a fashion than these latter are separated from the rest of the natural sciences.

Now Dilthey and others in the tradition of the *Geisteswissen-*

schaften always emphasized such a dislocation between the natural and the 'historical' or 'cultural' sciences. For Dilthey the division between the study of natural occurrences and the study of human conduct corresponded to an opposition between (causal) 'explanation' and 'understanding': *erklären* as contrasted to *verstehen*.[7] Max Weber likewise accepted elements of this contrast, even if, following Rickert, he held that the essential importance of 'understanding' in human conduct does not preclude the causal explanation of action. Dilthey was, however, strongly influenced by Comte and J. S. Mill at the same time as he was critical of their views on the overall unity of the social and natural sciences. In this endeavour, he began within a neo-Kantian framework. Our knowledge of material objects in nature must always be external, since we can never know the thing-in-itself. Consequently explanation in terms of causal laws cannot provide the 'inner' knowledge we have of psychic life. The aim of the historical sciences is to achieve the same kind of reliability in interpretation as the natural sciences have obtained with their 'external' methods of observation and analysis. But this ambition, as Dilthey himself came to recognize in his later work, cannot be realized in the terms in which it is presented; for if *verstehen* involves an intuitive process of 're-enactment' of some sort, it is unable to produce comparable data to natural science, where the character of these data derives precisely from the 'externality' of the objects and events that provide the field of study. We cannot today be content with the traditional division between *erklären* and *verstehen*, and it has indeed come under fire not only from positivistically minded critics, but also from leading hermeneutic philosophers, who have replaced the empathic or 'psychological' notion of *verstehen* by one grounded in a new appreciation of the significance of language in man's 'mode of being in the world'.

A common emphasis upon language as the medium of intersubjectivity brings together the Anglo-Saxon philosophy of language, as influenced by Wittgenstein and Austin, and hermeneutic phenomenology as led by Heidegger, Gadamer and Ricoeur. Both Wittgensteinian philosophy and 'ordinary-language philosophy', on the one hand, and hermeneutics on the other, have been subjected to searching critical attack in respect of their implications for the social sciences. Habermas has developed an elaborate scheme of concepts based upon the notion that a knowledge-constitutive interest in hermeneutic understanding has to be seen as complemented by an interest in prediction and control (and, of course, by that in emancipation through the critique of ideology). But this preserves, albeit in transmuted form, too much of the traditionally established contrast between *erklären* and *verstehen* with which the later hermeneutic philosophers have tried to break. This has unfortunate consequences in Habermas's own theory. One is that social action tends to become identified as merely 'communicative action'; once having abstractly separated the instrumental and 'strategic' from the symbolic, he is unable to reunite them in such a way as to deal with the practical, transformative context of action in terms of the demands of concrete social analysis.[8] I have suggested, therefore, an alternative approach, which treats the process of the production and reproduction of society in relation to a theory of structuration.

This is referred to at various points below.[9] The notions of 'structure' and 'system' are both central to the theory of structuration, but neither is employed in the senses in which they have been applied by most functionalist authors. The latter tend to equate systemic processes, on the basis of a generalized model of organic systems, with homeostatic equilibria, neglecting more complex levels of organization that can be connected directly to rationally monitored action. The idea of 'structure', on the other hand, is used by them in a descriptive way to mean 'pattern' or 'arrangement' of parts, in an anatomical or morphological sense. But there is no 'pattern' in human social life apart from the regularities involved in systems of interaction; hence in the functionalist literature the terms 'system' and 'structure' appear as more or less equivalent, and tend to be used interchangeably. In the theory of structuration, 'structure' is conceptualized as generative rules and resources drawn upon by actors in the production and reproduction of systems of interaction. The key idea linking production and reproduction is that of the duality of structure, by which I mean that structure is both the medium of generating interaction and at the same time the reproduced outcome of it.[10]

Problems of social development and transformation

If I have so far not specifically mentioned Marxism, it is because in some of the main respects relevant to the previous section, the writings of Marx and Engels are either silent or do not express

views that are distinctive enough to single out. Most of the significant contrasts are better illuminated by comparing the views of
authors such as Comte and Mill with the *Geisteswissenschaften*
tradition. Such a comparison certainly does not lose its cogency
when we turn to problems of social transformation, especially if
we regard Weber, with his emphasis upon the significance of
history among the social sciences, as to some extent affiliated with
that tradition. However, if we place the emphasis on theories of
class conflict in relation to social change, as I wish to do here,
Marxism of course enters the picture as the leading strand of
thought in the nineteenth century. At first sight, in fact, it might
appear to have no serious rival, at least in relation to the analysis
of classes and class conflict in nineteenth-century capitalism, and
the potential realization of a classless society. Its major competitor
is not as distinctive as the Marxian theory of classes itself, at least
partly because it is not as immediately affiliated to a particular
political project. But once pieced together, what can be called the
theory of industrial society represents a coherent and internally
consistent alternative to Marxist views in respect of offering a
contrasting typology of society, diagnosis of the origins of class
conflict, and specification of 'classlessness', to those developed by
Marx.

It is of some interest to trace a change in meaning of the term
'industrial society' from its initiation in Saint-Simon to its use by
Aron, Dahrendorf, Lipset, Bell and others in the 1950s and 1960s.
In Saint-Simon's writing the notion of 'industrial society' was
linked to that of *les industriels*; 'industry' preserved the sense that
now only fully survives in 'industrious', and was contrasted to idle-
ness, to unproductive labour in feudalism. As applied in the later
period, the term is used with a more narrowly technological bent,
as contrasted to agrarianism in general.[11] And obviously there are
major elements in Saint-Simon's projection of the emergent industrial society that differ from those of the later theorists, who are
looking back from the perspective of a century and a half of
economic development. None the less, there are still clear lines of
continuity, that run strongly through the work of Comte and
Durkheim also, which come through to the recent period, and
make it possible to identify a consistent theoretical approach
which, while having some common origins with Marxism, has
stood in chronic contrast to it. The theory of industrial society,
first of all, involves a dichotomous typology of society, in contrast

to the threefold conception with which Marxism approaches changes in the modern era (feudalism/capitalism/socialism). The movement of change in modern times is regarded as a transition from 'traditional society' ('*Gemeinschaft*', 'mechanical solidarity', 'status', 'folk society', etc.) to 'industrial society' ('*Gesellschaft*', 'organic solidarity', 'contract', 'secular society', etc.). Of course, the authors who originated these various typologies have not all emphasized the same points in the contrast – and the idea that it is industrial technology, or the social relations that are implied in it, which provides the main basis of the dichotomy only became firmly established among the more contemporary group of writers. However, the use of a twofold rather than a threefold typology inevitably serves to foreclose the possibility that a radically new society (socialism) can be born from the existing order.[12]

Thus in the theory of industrial society, 'capitalism' is not regarded as a generic type of society, as in Marx, but as an historically marginal phase in the emergence of a maturing industrial order. Consequently, while the importance of class conflict is certainly recognized, it is treated as an expression of the strains involved in the break with traditionalism and the formation of industrial society. This is particularly clear in Durkheim (even though he did not favour the term 'industrial society' as such), and his writings may aptly be seen as the pivot connecting earlier versions of the theory of industrial society to the later ones. According to Durkheim, class conflict, and its ideological expression in revolutionary socialism, are symptomatic of an interim period in social development, where most of the features of the old form of society have been discarded, but where the ones that are to replace them in the emergent new order have not become fully consolidated. Class conflict declines as the requisite social changes occur, and as they become normatively regulated.[13] This is a version of what has later come to be called the 'institutionalization of class conflict'; in Durkheim, as in the later authors, the thesis is that as class conflict becomes normatively regulated, it loses its force as a vehicle of social transformation. Implicit in this is a theory of the 'end of ideology', if 'ideology' be understood as either Marxism or revolutionary socialism more generally, or as radical conservatism. For such ideology is held to be the false consciousness of an epoch in transition; in Durkheim's words a 'cry of pain', which dissolves as the conditions giving rise to it become left behind.

The notion of classlessness associated with the theory of industrial society is not concerned, as in Marx, with the transformation of production, but with distributive equality, in respect above all of equality of opportunity. Once more, Durkheim's views presage those expressed in the later generation: as 'organic solidarity' develops, what Durkheim calls 'external inequalities', meaning by this differences in inherited status or wealth, become progressively eliminated. Industrial society is still a differentiated society, in terms of private property and occupational rewards in the division of labour; but the location of individuals within the hierarchy becomes more and more determined by 'internal inequalities', i.e. differences in innate capacities and talents.[14] This is a classless society in a sense similar to that of Saint-Simon's 'oneclass' society (which, however, also influenced the Marxian version of classlessness, achieved through the universalization of propertyless wage-labour): 'class' loses its relevance in a differentiated order marked by fluid mobility. Parsons is one among many authors who have expressed similar views in more recent times.[15]

The disparity between the theory of industrial society and Marxism has provided the main focus of debate over problems of class structure, class conflict and social transformation until quite recently. The writings of Max Weber, who under the influence of others in the *Verein für Sozialpolitik*, was concerned with 'capitalism' rather than 'industrial society', and who was not in the least influenced by the line of thought coming through Saint-Simon and Comte, might appear to cut across this division. On the level of method, and in other respects noted below, this is the case. But certain of the overall themes of Weber's discussion of the development and likely future of the Western economy and society place him close to the theory of industrial society. The rationalization of technology and economic life, consolidated by the general progression of bureaucracy, rather than the class relation of capital and wage-labour, is for Weber the most distinctive feature separating the traditional world from the world of modern capitalist enterprise; and 'rationalization', in Weber's discussion, has the same conceptual consequence as 'industrialization' has in the theory of industrial society, that of minimizing the differences between capitalism and socialism.[16] It is important to point out that several of the main proponents of the theory of industrial society over the past two or three decades, including

Aron and Dahrendorf, have been quite considerably influenced by Max Weber.

It is time today to attempt to transcend the terms of reference within which the debate between the theory of industrial society and Marxist theory has been carried on, which derive from the experience of the European societies in the nineteenth and early twentieth centuries.[17] The underlying character of this experience was expressed, above all in that first and intellectually dominant exemplar of the development of bourgeois democracy and capitalist industrialism, Britain, in the elaboration of the competitive market with the minimal 'intervention' of the state. Several major traits of social thought in the nineteenth and early twentieth centuries have to be understood against this background. The theory of industrial society, and more general theories of social development in non-Marxist social science, have continued to be deeply marked by these traits; Marxism has managed in some part to escape their influence largely by developments subsequent to the writings of Marx and Engels themselves. We may single out here the following as most important: the prevalence of an 'endogenous' or 'unfolding model' of social change; the connected idea that social development can be treated as a matter of the 'internal' evolution of a given society; an underwriting of political influences, such that social change is analysed as determined (in the last instance!) by economic factors; and the related assumption that social development, in the modern era, involves the pacific expansion of exchange relations.

By an 'unfolding model' I mean the view that treats social change as the elaboration or differentiation of a posited 'type' of society which at its inception contains in general form all the main features that come to characterize it when fully developed. This sort of view is most clear in the work of those attracted to biological analogies, treating social development as similar to the maturation of an organism, but is not necessarily associated with a proclivity for such analogies. It is plain that the unfolding view is likely to be associated with a perspective which treats social change as a matter of the internal development of a society. Nor is it difficult to see that each of these emphases accorded fairly well with basic trends of development in Europe prior to the First World War, where these took the form of a progressive transfer from a rural, post-feudal order to an urban, industrialized economy within the boundaries of already established nation-

states. It is not surprising that Max Weber's works, written against
the background of what he saw as the struggle to maintain the
power-position of the newly unified German state encircled by
potentially hostile powers, contain strong disclaimers against the
two views mentioned above. They also diverge from the dominant
trends in social theory in Britain and France in respect of
acknowledging the centrality of political and military power; the
advent of the First World War was an event quite out of accord
with the perspectives of Spencer or Durkheim in a way it was not
with those of Weber.[18]

An endogenous or unfolding conception of social change tends
to be associated with the following assumptions: social development is essentially a unified process, in the sense that the 'parts'
of the society develop in a connected, integrated way, like the
parts of the growing body; development is progressive and continuous, without involving sudden and radical transformations,
unless in pathological cases; and maturation and adaptive advantage are synonymous, so that the progression from the 'less
developed' or 'advanced' to 'more developed' or 'advanced' is
sequential.

A more adequate theory of change relevant to modern times,
by contrast, should acknowledge the significance of the following
notions: 1) *Dependency relations* among societies or nation-states.
It is plain enough that the 'internal' development of nation-
states today is increasingly geared-in to an international system
of economic, political and cultural ties. But this only accentuates
what has always been the case, save perhaps in the most small-
scale and isolated tribal communities: that processes of 'internal'
social development rarely proceed in separation from 'external'
relations of dependency or domination. 2) *The uneven development* of different institutions, sectors or regions within societies.
Social development, even solely economic development, does not
usually take place in a consistent, unified way within a society,
but typically creates dislocations between sectors developing at
different rates and in different ways. 3) *Critical phases* of radical
change, in which the existing alignment of major institutions in
a society becomes transformed, whether or not this occurs through
the agency of political revolution. While the conception of critical
phases encompasses processes of a generic kind, e.g. processes of
industrialization, it also applies to the creation of divergent
'patterns' of development *separating* different societies. A particular

alignment of relations between the labour movement, political parties and the legislatory executive in a modern state, for example, once established, may prove strongly resistant subsequently to major transformation. 4) *A 'leapfrog' idea* of change, whereby what is 'advanced' in one set of circumstances or period of time may later become a source of retardation upon further development; and, vice versa, what is 'retarded' may later become a propitious basis for rapid advancement. This applies even within the limited domain of technological change.

The origins of 'sociology' in nineteenth-century social theory

Two apparently wholly irreconcilable views exist about the origins of modern sociology in the writings of Durkheim, Weber and others in the '1890-1920 generation' of European social thinkers. The polarization of views centres upon the relation between their writings and those of Marx. For many subsequent commentators, not themselves particularly influenced by Marx, or actively hostile to Marxian ideas, the emergence of sociology in the 1890–1920 period was achieved through the supersession of abstract philosophy, and especially the philosophy of history, by empirical science. Such a thesis appears, in highly sophisticated form, in Parsons's enormously influential study, *The Structure of Social Action*. The work is not simply an exercise in intellectual history, but rather an attempt to disclose the emergent foundations of a science of society, as expressed in an immanent convergence of thought of Marshall, Pareto, Durkheim and Weber. A science, Parsons says, obviously involves a concern with empirical fact, but only becomes fully-fledged when the facts are related to a systematic body of theory; the work of the 1890–1920 generation marks the first establishment of the outlines of such a body of theory.[19] Marx's writings are dealt with cursorily in *The Structure of Social Action,* but it is made clear that they are relegated to the limbo of the pre-scientific days of social thought: Parsons has subsequently confirmed and amplified this view. What Parsons has expressed in elaborate technical detail, others have put more brutally.[20]

Authors writing in this vein tend not to attach much particular significance to Marx's writings in the emergence of sociology, because Marx is considered to have compounded a pre-scientific version of social science with a partisan political stance.[21] Those at all strongly influenced by Marx, of course, see things very differently. In their eyes it is precisely Marx's writings that mark the great divide in the history of social thought; 'sociology', as elaborated by the 1890–1920 generation, was developed in the context of a reaction against the claims of Marxism and is (in some sense of that term) an ideological defence of bourgeois society.[22] The ramifications of this controversy extend through to the present day: some of those sympathetic to Marxism see the latter as separated in an irremediable way from 'sociology', while others regard the two as complementary contributions to a common enterprise.[23] Opinions also vary widely as to the scientific status of Marxism. The most coherent and developed thesis representing Marx's writings as the great divide in the history of social thought is that stated by Althusser in his earlier writings. This is in a very real sense a parallel to the case made by Parsons for Durkheim, Weber, and their contemporaries: the 'epistemological break' that is held to divide Marx's mature work from what went before, including his own earlier writings, has some quite close similarities to Parsons's specification of the distinctiveness of 'systematic theory'.[24]

Two problems may be briefly raised here: how important was Marxism in the political background of leading authors in the 1890–1920 generation?; how important were Marx's writings as an intellectual influence, positive or negative, upon such authors? Let us concentrate on Max Weber and Durkheim, as the two writers whose works have been most consequential for the subsequent development of sociology. The view that sees their writings merely as a 'conservative' response to the militant challenge of Marxism can easily be shown to be wrong. Max Weber was bitterly hostile to revolutionary socialism,[25] although he regarded, correctly as it turned out, the SPD orthodoxy as revolutionary in name only. His political concerns and writings were certainly in some part occupied with repudiating the claims of the left; but he was in fact more preoccupied with the right, elements of which he saw as posing the most serious difficulties for the future political and economic development of Germany. He vacillated between right and left in his political views, but the dominant thrust of his concerns is to be understood as an attempt to produce a reworked version of political liberalism in a political context inimical to traditional liberal principles.[26] Marx's writings were certainly a fundamental influence on the intellectual parameters of Weber's thought. Weber is only one of several leading figures in the 1890–1920 generation (Pareto and Mosca are others) to have been called 'the bourgeois Marx'. Salomon's comment that Weber was engaged in a lifelong struggle with the ghost of Marx has become one of the most frequently repeated phrases in the Weber-literature. It is appropriate enough, so long as we remember that it is by no means complete. Marx's work was less important as a polemical foil in Weber's earlier writings than that of some of the prominent representatives of the 'Historical School'; and in his later writings Weber's initial assessment of the intellectual legacy of Marx was intertwined with an ambivalent involvement with irrationalist philosophies, particularly that of Nietzsche.[27] *The Protestant Ethic and the Spirit of Capitalism* was no doubt oriented towards historical materialism, particularly in its cruder and contemporary versions; but the general programme of study of the 'world religions', of which the work was part, is much more broadly connected to Weber's preoccupation with the historical origins of divergent and competing systems of 'ultimate values'.

Marxism was less important in Durkheim's background, both politically and intellectually. Durkheim was no less hostile to revolutionary socialism than Max Weber was; he was deeply affected by the events of the Commune, and by what he saw as the fruitless loss of life which culminated its brief existence. He did not, as Weber did, either write extensively on political events or participate more than marginally in them. His sympathies were with liberal republicanism or reformist socialism, and he was more concerned with resistance to social change from the right than with a possible revolutionary threat from the left. The political development of France, Durkheim believed, was not menaced by the threat of revolution. France was already a society of revolutions; the obstacles confronting the realization of substantial social change derived from the fact that apparent radical transformation signalled by revolutionary activity was confined to superficial phenomena, masking the strongly entrenched power of reactionary groups.[28] In undertaking, in *The Division of Labour* and other subsequent writings, the task of exploring the relation between 'socialism' and 'individualism' within the emerging modern industrial order, Durkheim was posing again, in his own time, similar problems to those tackled by Saint-Simon about a century before. It was the general traditions of socialism, which predate Marxism, with which Durkheim was most absorbed, in relation to their significance for 'industrial society', and in the specific context of the 'French problem' of the bracketing of revolution and stagnation. In so far as he considered Marxism directly, he did so by trying to fit it into the framework he had already elaborated before coming to study Marx's writings in detail.[29]

The implication of what I have said so far is that 'sociology', as elaborated in the writings of the 1890–1920 generation, did not emerge as a reaction to Marxism, nor can it adequately be understood as a conservative defence of capitalism or bourgeois society in the face of a threat from the revolutionary left. To suppose otherwise is to accept the *hubris* of Marxist authors looking back from the context of the world-historical movement which, in the twentieth century, Marxism has become.[30] The point of this last statement should be made perfectly clear. Marxism, as a radical critique of bourgeois society affiliated to the labour movement, played a major role in influencing the political and intellectual form of the works of the leading authors of the 1890–1920 generation. But while their writings provided a rationalization of the critical rejection of the aspirations of revolutionary socialism, this was arrived at in the context of a more general attempt to transcend forms of social theory, including utilitarianism, classical political economy and conservative totalizing philosophies, which Marx also struggled with. From this point of view, sociology, as it was developed in the 1890–1920 generation, can neither be regarded as transcending Marx, nor however just as a reactive antithesis to Marx's writings and the early development of Marxism as a political movement.

At this juncture, we have to separate what Weber and Durkheim meant by 'sociology'. Weber's thought was a mixture of the pessimistic and the progressive, leavening his sombre characterization of the 'steel-hard cage' of the modern social order with some indications of how bureaucratic oppression could be held in check. Sociology was for him secondary to history in the diagnosis of the origins and trend of development of Western capitalism, and his identification of it as a distinct discipline was as ambivalent and qualified as was that diagnosis itself. However significant Weber's thought has been for the subsequent development of the social sciences in modern times, it is not this version of what sociology should strive to be that has been dominant over the past fifty years. Rather than Weber's fractured and tentative subjectivism, it has been Durkheim's confident objectivism which has held the centre of the stage, and which most directly connects nineteenth-century social thought to the modern varieties of functionalism. The term 'sociology' was coined in this tradition, and hence is not an innocent one: it has its origins in the connection between the advocacy of a science of society that will complete the extension of science as a whole, and the formulation of the theory of industrial society as a reformist but progressive account of processes of social transformation. Marx's writings stand opposed to this on both levels, but ambiguously – a phenomenon of crucial importance to the debates which have racked Marxism internally since Marx's death. There are unarguably certain defined positivistic elements in Marx's descriptions of his work as marking the foundation of a science that will deal with class struggles in a manner parallel to the treatment of the development of the species in evolutionary biology.[31] On the other hand, the merging of this standpoint with a radicalized Hegelian inheritance removes it far from the Comtean notion of 'social physics'. Similarly, the analysis of the class relation inherent in the asymmetrical dependence of capital and wage-labour, and its significance for the achievement of a radically new social order, decisively distances Marxism from any version of the theory of industrial society. Nevertheless, both share traits that bear the mark of their partly common origins, and both manifest limitations that reflect the dominant intellectual currents in nineteenth-century European thought.

The characteristic emphasis of Marx, and of the authors of the 1890–1920 generation, was that they were initiating an enterprise which was decisively different from what had gone before: namely, placing the study of human social conduct upon a scientific footing. The proposal for putting an end to philosophy – of achieving the equivalent in the social realm of the replacement of metaphysics by empirically grounded science – is one of the major themes of nineteenth-century social thought, shared by Comte and Marx alike, and by their successors in the generation which followed. The idea that science and philosophy, even metaphysical philosophy, are mutually exclusive endeavours, such that scientific knowledge dispels the need for any philosophy other than that of clarifying the character of scientific method itself, is a positivistic dogma. But it is one that has long dominated in social thought, and has supported the assumption that at *some* point in the nineteenth or early twentieth centuries (perhaps even later) a great divide was established between philosophy and science in the

study of human behaviour. If we look further back however into
the history of social thought, we find that the claim to have
effected a decisive break with the past, to have initiated a science
of social conduct, has repeatedly been made: it is prior even to
Montesquieu's discussion in 1748, in *The Spirit of the Laws*, of the
prospect of discovering the laws governing the organization and
movement of society in the shape of 'the necessary relations that
derive from the nature of things', and Vico's brilliant plan for a
'new science'.[32] The view – formalized in Comte's hierarchy of the
sciences, but implicit in a variety of otherwise divergent schools of
thought up to the present day – that social science is a latecomer
as compared to natural science is an *error*.

To say this, of course, is not to deny either the existence or
importance of discontinuities in social thought, or the occurrence
of major advances in the methodological and theoretical content
of social science – but it is to suggest that we should look at them
in a new light.

The status of social science as critique

The discovery of laws governing natural events reveals causal connections that allow the subjection of such events to human
manipulation. Scientific knowledge here stands in instrumental
relation to technology; the disclosed predictability of the world
is the connecting link between theory and practice. This predictability is the condition of rational human intervention in nature,
but is not brought about by the process of intervention itself.
The instrumental connection between science and technology
was quite correctly seen by Comte and by Marx as the medium
of the expansion of human freedom, in so far as this is manifest
in the subordination of nature to human imperatives; in this
regard the famous maxim that freedom is awareness of necessity holds good. But it was a mistake to extend this reasoning to
social science: a mistake that appears most prominently in Comte,
but which Marx did not manage to avoid in so far as he was unable
satisfactorily to reconcile what he appropriated from classical
German philosophy with his leanings towards a positivistic model
of science.[33] Here the relation between the predictability yielded
by knowledge of causal laws and freedom no longer holds in the
same way, and in one sense even becomes reversed. The knowing
subject, freely undertaking inquiry into the conditions of his own

social existence, rediscovers himself as the outcome of determinate social causes that operate with impersonal force. In such a framework, sociology becomes the science of human unfreedom, rather than the liberative endeavour it is represented as being.[34]

The predictability of human social conduct, unlike the predictability of events in nature, does not happen independently of human knowledge of the social world. Predictability in social life is brought about through the reflexive rationalization of action, although in the context of unacknowledged conditions that are causally relevant both to the initiation of action and to its consequences within social systems.[35] It is in the light of this that we have to try to understand the character of laws in the social sciences, and the differences between them and laws of nature.

Why, in social science, is there not an accumulated set of laws, more or less generally agreed upon by a community of investigators, such as appears to exist even in various of the less developed natural sciences? I have already suggested, in the previous section, that this situation has nothing to do with the 'immaturity' of the social sciences; it is no clarification of the issue at all to appeal to a projected future state in which, either through the cumulative outcome of research or through some sort of Newtonian-like conceptual revolution, the nomological form of the social sciences will more and more approximate to that of natural science. Three considerations are relevant here, progressively more important in distinguishing the nomological character of the social sciences from that of the natural sciences. One I have already alluded to: the lower level of underdetermination of theories by facts in the social than the natural sciences. This obviously varies in some degree in different areas of social science, according to well-known circumstances: the possibility of quantification of data in regard of some type of problems in economics, for example, confers advantages there as compared with other areas of the social sciences. Phenomena of this sort affecting the level of underdetermination of theories by facts in social science are quite well known, and do not differ logically from those involved in differentiating among the natural sciences. If such underdetermination were all that was at issue, we might conclude that social science is merely an inferior cousin of natural science, and leave it at that: the lack of a corpus of agreed laws would simply derive from difficulties involved in the testing of hypotheses. But there are two further, and fundamental, aspects of the social sciences to be considered, each of which is a consequence of the situation that an understanding of the conditions under which social life takes place, and reflection on these conditions, on the part of lay actors, is integral to its orderly or predictable character.

One concerns the degree of 'permeability' of the boundary between the knowledge claimed by professional investigators as the product of esoteric expertise and that applied by lay actors in their day to day lives. The cumulation of nomological knowledge in natural science typically occurs within rather clear parameters separating scientists and laymen, that broadly speaking are accepted by both sides, although there may be some degree of controversy over how far scientific knowledge can or should be 'popularized' and made accessible to the lay population. But the boundaries between 'expert' and 'lay' knowledge in the social sciences are unlikely to be as clear-cut as they have become in natural science (nor is it desirable that they should be so, for reasons I shall come on to immediately). This is because 'expertise' in the world of social relations is not incidental to social life, but is the very medium of its orderliness. The necessary intersubjectivity of the social world makes it 'our world' in a way that has no parallel in the relation of human beings to nature, where knowledge is certainly routinely used in a transformative way, but where that knowledge is not part of the conditions of existence of the universe of objects and events to which it relates. Hence the divisions between what can be sustained by a professional community as acceptable terms of a technical metalanguage, and what is merely redundant 'jargon', i.e. the unacceptable translation of the familiar into the esoteric, are bound to be more diffuse than in the case of the natural sciences. The social sciences are always susceptible to the accusation of 'telling us what we already know' (perhaps wrapped up in technical jargon). This brings us to the third point mentioned above, connecting the permeability of the divisions between expert and lay knowledge with the mutability of causal generalizations or laws in the social sciences. Laws in the social sciences are inherently unstable in respect of the 'environment' to which they refer, i.e. human social conduct and its institutional forms. The circumstances of application of laws in natural science can be altered by the manipulation of their limiting conditions. Except in the case of laws that influence social life from 'outside', e.g. the laws of genetics, laws in the social sciences do not have this form: they are in principle mutable in the very terms they involve, not only in the conditions of their application. They are unstable in respect of new knowledge that comes to be embodied in the rationalization of action of those to whose conduct they refer, including knowledge of such laws themselves.

The latter point is recognized in naturalistic or positivistic versions of social science but only in marginal forms and as something to be avoided or minimized – as 'self-fulfilling' or 'self-negating prophecies', 'bandwagon effect', etc. These appear merely as phenomena complicating the predictive testing of hypotheses, not as elements of a subject–subject relation. Hence no connection is drawn between such phenomena and the practical implications of the social sciences, which are treated in terms of a differentiation between pure and applied science and the dualism of fact and value. These dichotomies rest upon a view of the instrumental connection of science and technology which, even if it provided a satisfactory framework for natural science, could not be sustained in the case of social science, since knowledge produced by the social sciences, especially in so far as it is of a generalizing character, can be reflexively incorporated into the rationalization of action.[36] Social science therefore stands in an inherently critical relation to its 'field of study', human social conduct and institutions, as a potential instrument of emancipation – or of domination. What I have previously described as the double hermeneutic of the social sciences has implications immediately connected to this, on the logical level.[37] Descriptions of social activity are normatively as well as conceptually related to those employed by lay actors; there is no morally separate or transcendentally 'neutral' metalanguage in which to couch the vocabulary of the social sciences. The status of social science as critique has to be elucidated through relating normative implications of social research and theory to reflexivity as the rational basis of freedom. Rejection of the dogma of the absolute logical separation of statements of fact and judgement of value does not compromise the possibility of sustaining such critique objectively; on the contrary, it is the very condition of its realization.

1   Positivism and its critics

'Positivism' has today become more a term of abuse than a technical term of philosophy. The indiscriminate way in which the term has been used in a variety of different polemical interchanges in the past few years, however, makes all the more urgent a study of the influence of positivistic philosophies in the social sciences.

I shall distinguish two main ways in which 'positivism' may be taken, one quite specific, the other much more general. In the more restrictive sense, the term may be taken to apply to the writings of those who have actively called themselves positivists, or at least have been prepared to accept the appellation. This yields two major phases in the development of positivism, one centred mainly in social theory, the other concerned more specifically with epistemology. The earlier phase is that dominated by the works of the author who coined the term 'positive philosophy', Auguste Comte. Although there are obvious contrasts between Comte's positivism and the 'logical positivism' of the Vienna Circle, there are equally clear connections – both historical and intellectual – between the two. Second, the term may be employed more broadly and diffusely to refer to the writings of philosophers who have adopted most or all of a series of connected perspectives: phenomenalism – the thesis, which can be expressed in various ways, that 'reality' consists in sense-impressions; an aversion to metaphysics, the latter being condemned as sophistry or illusion; the representation of philosophy as a method of analysis, clearly separable from, yet at the same time parasitic upon, the findings of science; the duality of fact and value – the thesis that empirical knowledge is logically discrepant from the pursuit of moral aims or the implementation of ethical standards; and the notion of the 'unity of science': the idea that the natural and social sciences share a common logical and perhaps even methodological foundation. Below I shall use the term *positivism* without qualification to refer, in the appropriate context, to the views of Comte and subsequently to those of the leading figures of the Vienna Circle, i.e. to those who have been prepared to call themselves positivists. I shall use *positivistic philosophy* to designate views that embody important elements among those mentioned in the second category. In this sense, positivistic strains are much more widely represented in the history of philosophy, overlapping with empiricism, than would be suggested if attention were confined to self-proclaimed 'positivism'.

I want also, however, to distinguish a third category, which I shall call, for want of a better name, '*positivistic sociology*'. We owe to Comte both the term 'positivism' and the term 'sociology'; in his writings, the two are closely conjoined, since the coming into being of sociology is supposed to mark the final triumph of positivism in human thought. The connection has been a fateful one for the subsequent development of the social sciences, for certain leading traditions in social thought over the past hundred years have been considerably influenced by the kind of logical framework established by Comte in his *Cours de philosophie positive*. As mediated by Durkheim, this framework is closely tied in to modern functionalism. But the influence of positivistic philosophy, as defined above, in sociology (and in Marxism) has ranged much more widely than this. Here sociology is conceived of as a 'natural science of society', which can hope to reproduce a system of laws directly similar in form to those achieved in the natural sciences. In positivistic sociologies, as formulated over the past four or five decades at least, especially in the United States, all three senses of 'positivism' I have just distinguished to some extent recombine. Certain of the prominent members of the Vienna Circle emigrated to the United States, and have exerted a strong influence over the development of philosophy there, particularly in regard of the philosophy of science. Their conception of the philosophy of science has in turn been appropriated, explicitly or otherwise, by many authors writing in the social sciences: and it has proved particularly compatible with the view of those drawing heavily upon the sorts of views expressed by Comte and by Durkheim.

In this essay, I shall begin by discussing the positivism of Comte, and its similarities to and its differences from, the logical positivism of the Vienna Circle. From there, I shall move to a consideration of two partly convergent critiques of positivistic philosophies more generally conceived: one, the so-called 'newer philosophy of science', emanating mainly from within the English-speaking world, the other, 'Frankfurt philosophy' or critical theory, originating primarily in long-established German philosophical traditions.

Auguste Comte: sociology and positivism

In crude summary, we may differentiate several major elements in the intellectual background of Comte's writings. One is the frontal assault on metaphysics undertaken in eighteenth-century philosophy, above all in the works of Hume and his followers in British empiricism, and sustained in different form in Kant's 'critical idealism'. Comte went further than such authors, in not only accepting the success of the destruction of transcendental illusions, but in formally embodying the metaphysical stage in the evolution of humanity as a phase superseded by the advent of positivist thought. In this respect, he accepted one of the fundamental aims of the writers of the Enlightenment, as he did important aspects of the rationalist critique of established religion. In Comte's scheme of history, the theological stage of thought is relegated to a phase prior to the metaphysical – both, to be sure, being regarded as necessary stages in social evolution, but both being dissolved once and for all when positivism triumphs. If Comte himself came to the rediscovery of religion, it was because to his acceptance of these aspects of Enlightenment philosophy was conjoined a deep-rooted aversion to the methodical critique of inherited authority that was basic to the writings of the *philosophes*. Comte rejected the essential idea of Enlightenment itself: that the Middle Ages were also the Dark Ages, whose repudiation opens up the way to revolutionary changes in human intellectual and social life. In place of this Comte substituted a progressivism influenced by the 'retrograde school' of authors – conservative apologists for Catholicism, reacting against Enlightenment radicalism and against the 1789 Revolution which was its heir: Bonald, de Maistre and others. Comte's positivism preserves the theme of progress, but undercuts the radicalism with which this was associated in Enlightenment philosophy. 'Progress' and 'order' are more than reconciled: the one becomes dependent upon the other. Positive thought replaces the 'negative' outlook of the *philosophes*, the perspective that a new dawn can be achieved through the shattering of the past.

Of course, Comte owed many of his ideas most immediately to Saint-Simon, who in turn was considerably indebted to Condorcet and Montesquieu, both of whom had tempered the enthusiasms of the Enlightenment with a rigidly applied version of the subservience of society to natural laws of development. Condorcet assigned to history the same kind of potentialities that Comte was later to allocate to the positive science of sociology, expressed in the famous phrase *savoir pour prévoir, prévoir pour pouvoir*. Condorcet looked to the past to supply the moving principles of evolution whereby the future could be made open to human intervention. Hence he took to task those who arrogantly supposed that it is possible to achieve social change in massive fashion *ex nihilo*. The progress of mankind achieves equilibrium in such a way that, while the pace of development can be speeded or retarded by active human intervention, it has the character of an autonomous force for betterment. I shall not take up the vexed issue of just how directly Comte plundered Saint-Simon's ideas in constructing his own system, a matter of great acrimony in the relations between the two thinkers after Comte broke away from the tutelage of his mentor. Whatever their immediate provenance, it can be remarked without undue simplification that Comte's writings constitute one direction of development out of Saint-Simon, that which gave 'sociology' its name, and established a logical framework for the supposedly new science; the other direction is that taken by Marx, in which elements of Saint-Simon's ideas are reconnected to revolutionary social transformation.[1]

That Comte entitled the first of his two major works *Cours de philosophie positive* should not blind us to the fact that the work actually declares an end to philosophy as previously practised: as an independent enterprise separable from the achievements of science. 'Positive philosophy' is perhaps not, as Marcuse suggests, a contradiction *in adjecto*.[2] But it does reduce philosophy to expressing the emergent synthesis of scientific knowledge. The 'true philosophic spirit', Comte says, incorporates the 'essential attributes . . . summed up in the word *positive*'. These include, first of all, an orientation to 'reality' and to 'utility': the useless endeavours of speculative philosophy to penetrate behind appearances are disavowed. But the term also implies – in all the European languages, according to Comte – 'certainty' and 'precision', attributes which similarly distinguish the intellectual life of modern man from his predecessors. Finally, also suggested by the term are an 'organic tendency' and a 'relativist outlook'. The former of these refers to the constructive character of the positivist spirit: by contrast, 'the metaphysical spirit is incapable of organizing; it can only criticize'. The latter seals the rejection of absolutism, as practised in metaphysical philosophy: the laws that govern the co-variance of phenomena always retain a provisional character, since they are induced on the basis of empirical observation, rather than being posited as 'absolute essences'.[3]

In the *Cours*, the relation between the various sciences is claimed to be hierarchical, in both an analytical and a historical sense, the second being explained in terms of the renowned law of the three stages of human intellectual development. Analytically, Comte makes clear, the sciences form a hierarchy of decreasing generality but increasing complexity; each particular science logically depends upon the ones below it in the hierarchy, and yet at the same time deals with an emergent order of properties that cannot be reduced to those with which the other sciences are concerned. Thus biology, for example, presupposes the laws of physics and chemistry in so far as all organisms are physical entities which obey the laws governing the composition of matter; on the other hand, the behaviour of organisms, as complex beings, cannot be directly derived from those laws. Sociology, at the apex of the hierarchy of sciences, logically presupposes the laws of each of the other scientific disciplines, while at the same time similarly retaining its autonomous subject-matter.

The logical relations between the sciences, according to Comte, provide the means of interpreting their successive formation as separate fields of study in the course of the evolution of human thought. The sciences which develop first, mathematics and astronomy, then physics, are those dealing with the most general or all-enveloping laws of nature, that govern phenomena most removed from human involvement and manipulation. From there, science penetrates more and more closely to man himself, moving through chemistry and biology to its culmination in the science of human conduct – originally labelled by Comte 'social physics', then redubbed 'sociology'. The process is not achieved without struggle; scientific understanding lies at the end of the progression of intellectual life through the theological and metaphysical stages, through which all branches of thought have to move. Human thought as a whole, as well as each science taken separately, progresses through the theological, the metaphysical

B

and the positive stages. In the theological stage, the universe is comprehended as determined by the agency of spiritual beings; this stage, *l'état fictif*, as Comte calls it, is 'the necessary point of departure of the human intellect', and it reaches its climax in Christianity with its recognition of one all-powerful deity.[4] The metaphysical phase replaces these moving spirits with abstract essences, thereby however clearing the ground for the advent of science, *l'état fixe et définitif* of thought. The enunciation of the law of the three stages, Comte says, is enough 'that its correctness should be immediately confirmed by anyone who has a sufficiently profound knowledge of the general history of the sciences'. (Comte later claimed to have achieved personal verification of the law of the three stages in his periods of insanity, which he had experienced, he claimed, as a regression back through from positivism to metaphysics to theology on the level of his own personality, in his recovery retracing these stages forwards again.)

The task of the *Cours* is not only to analyse the transmutation of human thought by science, but also to *complete* it. For man's understanding of himself is still in substantial part in its pre-scientific phase:

> Everything can be reduced to a simple question of fact: does positive philosophy, which over the two past centuries has gradually become so widespread, today embrace all orders of phenomena? It is evident that such is not the case and that consequently there still remains the major scientific undertaking of giving to positive philosophy the universal character that is indispensable to its proper constitution . . . Now that the human mind has founded astronomy, and terrestrial physics – both mechanical and chemical – and organic physics – both botanical and biological – it remains to finalize the system of the sciences by founding *social physics*. Such is, in several capital respects, the greatest and the most pressing intellectual need today . . .[5]

Positivism supplies a general ground-plan for the formation of sociology: that is to say, the new science of society has to share the same overall logical form as the other sciences, as it is cut free of the residues of metaphysics. But since the phenomena with which it is concerned are more complex and specific than the sciences lying below it in the hierarchy, it also has to develop methodological procedures of its own. Like biology, sociology employs concepts that are 'synthetic' in character: that is to say, concepts which relate to the properties of complex wholes, rather than to aggregates of elements as in the lower sciences. The two also share a division into statics and dynamics. In sociology, the first consists in the study of the functional interrelationship of institutions within society, the second in the study of the process of social evolution. The significance of dynamics in sociology, however, is more profound than in biology because – via the law of the three stages – it examines the intellectual development of positive thought as a whole. Sociology relies on three methodological elements, each of which involves features that are particular to it: observation, experiment and comparison. Comte holds that a commitment to the essential importance of empirical observation is not equivalent to an advocacy of empiricism. 'No logical dogma,' Comte says, 'could be more thoroughly irreconcilable with the spirit of positive philosophy, or with its special character in regard to the study of social phenomena, than this.'[6] Consequently, theory is basic to sociological investigations. On the other hand, the context of Comte's discussion makes it apparent that 'empiricism' here is understood in a limited sense; his point is not that all observations of objects or events are (to use Popper's term) 'theory-impregnated', but that 'scientifically speaking, all isolated empirical observation is idle'. 'Scientific and popular observation', Comte says, 'embrace the same facts'; but they regard them from different points of view, because the former is guided by theory whereas the latter is not. Theories direct our attention towards certain facts rather than others.'[7] While experimentation in the laboratory sense is not possible in social physics, it can be replaced by indirect experimentation, i.e. 'natural experiments' whose consequences can be analysed. But this is less important than the comparative method, which is the crucial foundation of sociological research.

Comte always intended sociology to be directed towards practical ends. If it is true that the strange extravagances of the immanent social future envisaged in the *Système de politique positive* are largely absent from Comte's earlier writings, it is still the case that the main elements of his political programme already appear there. These are perhaps stated with greater clarity, in fact, in the *Cours* than they are in the later work. The overriding theme continues that of the intellectual diagnosis of the origins of positive philosophy: the mutual necessity of order and progress. For Comte it is precisely his insistence upon the conjunction of the two that allows positivism to supersede both the 'revolutionary metaphysics' of the *philosophes* and the reactionary connotations of the Catholic apologists. The latter school wanted order, but was against progress; the former sought progress at the expense of order. The 'order' desired by the 'retrograde school' was nothing but a reversion to feudal hierocracy; while the 'progress' aspired to by the revolutionaries was nothing less than the subversion of any form of government as such. The sort of society Comte foresees as guaranteeing order and progress none the less places a heavy enough emphasis upon features that brook large in the writings of the members of the 'retrograde school' – moral consensus, authority, and an antagonism to the 'chimera of equality' – even if stripped of their specific association with Catholicism. At first sight the call to establish a Religion of Humanity seems quite inconsistent with the positive philosophy advocated in the *Cours*, and many commentators have supposed that there is a major hiatus between Comte's earlier and later works.[8] But it is perhaps more plausible to argue that the *Système de politique positive* brings fully into the open the latent substratum of the positive spirit: we see that science cannot, after all, provide its own commitment.

How, even so, can a perspective which insists that the course of human social development is governed by laws akin to laws of nature provide any leverage for rational human intervention in history? Doesn't this imply the adoption of fatalism in the face of the inevitable sweep of social change? According to Comte, the contrary is actually the case. For the rational facilitation of progress is only possible if the limiting conditions of intervention are known; the laws that control the movement of society are subject to considerable margins of variation in their operation, and such variation can be actively influenced by deliberate action.[9]

Comte's influence: the origins of logical positivism

Although his writings had rather little immediate influence in France, Comte's works attracted a considerable following abroad: in other European countries, the United States, and particularly Latin America. In Britain, the *Cours* acquired a notable admirer in John Stuart Mill, and Mill's *Logic* was in important respects its counterpart in English-speaking social thought. Many such followers were alienated, however, by the drift of Comte's thought in the later part of his career, as expressed in the *Système de politique positive*, which Mill called 'this melancholy decadence of a great intellect'. As a social movement, which Comte had all along tried to make it, positivism died with the withering of the groups of disciples who remained to celebrate the Festival of Humanity held in London in 1881. I shall not be interested here in trying to detail in what ways Comte's works were drawn upon by other authors, during his lifetime or after it: some prominent contemporaries, most notably Herbert Spencer, were anxious to claim a greater independence between their ideas and those of Comte than seems in fact to have been the case.[10] I shall consider the influence of Comte only from two aspects: the mode in which his writings were utilized by Durkheim; and the extent to which Comte's views conform intellectually to the philosophical programme developed in logical positivism.

The importance of the line of connection from Comte to Durkheim is easily attested. So far as social science in the twentieth century is concerned, the influence of Comte's writings derives less from their direct impact than from their reworking in Durkheim's version of sociological method. Durkheim's works have provided the proximate source of functionalism in both anthropology and sociology. But Durkheim's work has also had a more broad-ranging and diffuse effect, as a stimulus to those central traditions of contemporary social thought in which the goal of achieving a 'natural science of society' is considered both desirable and feasible.[11]

In Durkheim, the methodological framework of Comte's positivism, which is sustained, is separated from the global theory of historical change, which is largely abandoned. Durkheim makes this quite explicit. Comte regarded Condorcet and Montesquieu as forerunners who established the groundwork of the positivist spirit, but none the less were unable to detach themselves adequately from the speculative philosophy of history. Durkheim has much the same view of the two former thinkers, but lumps Comte along with them as belonging to the pre-scientific phase in the history of sociology. The 'law of the three stages', according to Durkheim, is proclaimed by *fiat* rather than corroborated empirically: a massive research undertaking, well beyond the capacity of any single scholar, would be required to document adequately such a principle of social change.[12] In this respect, Durkheim's comments concur with the judgement of Mill: 'M. Comte, at bottom, was not so solicitous about completeness of proof as becomes a positive philosopher.'[13]

Durkheim's discussions of social evolution, and his diagnosis of the trend of development of modern industrial civilization, owe as much to Saint-Simon and to the German 'academic socialists' as they do to Comte. But the influence of Boutroux and others notwithstanding, it is undeniably the legacy of Comte that looms largest in the methodological scheme of sociology which Durkheim set out. While Durkheim does not endorse the 'hierarchy of the sciences' as such, he insists perhaps even more strongly than Comte upon the autonomy of sociology as a distinctive field of endeavour. Like Comte, he holds that recognition of such autonomy does not imply that the study of human social conduct is logically discrepant from natural science; social facts have a moral dimension that is absent in nature, but have 'to be treated as things' in the same manner as natural objects. The aim of sociology is to arrive at the formulation of principles that have the same objective status as natural scientific laws. In Durkheim, a Baconian version of scientific method is perhaps more apparent than in Comte. Every science, Durkheim says, including sociology, advances only slowly and cautiously, through the patient inductive generalization on the basis of observed regularities in social facts. This is, indeed, why he is critical of Comte's claims to have established a positivist account of history. When Durkheim refuses the designation 'positivist', in favour of 'naturalism', he seeks to dissociate his general position from that of Comte, while reaffirming the character of sociology as a natural science of society. Durkheim's account of the emergence of the scientific spirit, although not elaborated in anything like the historical detail attempted by Comte, actually follows the outline of Comte's discussion very closely. All thought, Durkheim holds (and tries to explain concretely how this is so in *Les formes élémentaires de la vie religieuse*), originates in religion; it can be demonstrated that even the Kantian categories are first of all religious concepts.[14] The key differences between pre-scientific and scientific thought are methodological; 'thought and reflection are prior to science, which merely uses them methodologically'.[15] As religious concepts become secularized in the form of metaphysical philosophy, they become more precise, but they are finally rendered scientific only by being anchored in empirical observation, and thereby transformed.

It is clear that Durkheim derives his conception of functionalist method from Comte and not from Spencer. Durkheim follows Comte closely in separating out functional explanation (statics) from historical explanation (dynamics), although he criticizes Comte along with Spencer for reifying 'progress': treating the impetus to self-betterment as if it were a general cause of the evolution of society. As in Comte's writings, and of course in those of many other nineteenth-century writers also, Durkheim's stress upon the significance of functional explanation in sociology comes fairly directly from the model of biology, as does his acceptance of 'holistic' concepts as basic to sociological analysis. The biological parallel also provides, however, another very important element in Durkheim's works, bearing immediately upon the practical implications of social science. In claiming that the scientific study of society can offer the means of distinguishing what is normal from what is pathological, in any particular type of society, Durkheim upholds the most intrinsic part of Comte's programme for positivism. For just as natural science shows us that the development of knowledge can only be achieved incrementally, so sociology shows us that all truly progressive social change occurs only cumulatively. The mutual dependence of progress and order is as much a theme of Durkheim's writings as it is of those of Comte. Durkheim's antagonism to revolution continues that of Comte, and is likewise held to be grounded scientifically: political revolution expresses the inability of a society to generate progressive change, rather than itself providing a possible instrument of securing social transformation. However, while the form of the account is similar, the content is not wholly the same: that is to say, in identifying what is normal, and what is pathological, in contemporary society, and thus specifying the immanent trend of social development, Durkheim moves away substantially from Comte.[16]

In mentioning these respects in which Durkheim was indebted to Comte, I do not, of course, want to claim that Durkheim's works can be regarded as little more than an extension of those of the earlier thinker. But I do want to hold that Durkheim's writings have been more influential than those of any other author in academic social science in the spread of 'positivistic sociology', as I have defined that term previously. Through them, Comte's 'positivism' has had a major influence upon the more diffuse development of such positivistic sociology. This is one line of filiation leading from Comte through to twentieth-century thought. The other is less direct, and is that connecting Comte to the logical positivism of the Vienna Circle.

The principal mediator between Comte's positivism and the positivism of the Vienna Circle is normally held to be Ernst Mach, the physicist and physiologist. Mach, like Durkheim, rejected the label 'positivist' and, unlike Durkheim, was not directly influenced by Comte save in minor respects.[17] The importance of Comte in relation to Mach is really in helping to further the intellectual currents that were in the background of Mach's work as a natural scientist. The following elements in Comte's thought are relevant in this respect: 1) The reconstruction of history as the realization of the positive spirit. In this scheme of things, religion and metaphysics have a definite place, but only as prior phases of mystification, to be broken through by the advent of science. With the development of the scientific outlook, the 'pre-history' of the human species is completed; the positive stage of thought is not a transitional one, like the others. 2) The final dissolution of metaphysics, closely linked to the idea of the supersession of philosophy itself. In Comte's positivism, science replaces philosophy: 'positive philosophy' is the logical explication of the canons of scientific method. Metaphysics is not accorded the status of being open to philosophical discussion in its own right: it is consigned to the lumber-room of history on the basis that the questions posed in metaphysical philosophy are empty of content. 3) The existence of a clear and definable boundary between the factual, or the 'observable', and the imaginary, or the 'fictitious'. Comte does not provide an ontological justification of what counts as factual, but rather a methodological one.[18] It is in this regard, his disavowals notwithstanding, that Comte adopts the standpoint of empiricism. Systematic observation supposedly distinguishes positive science from other types of claim to knowledge, and such observation, according to Comte, depends upon the evidence of sense-perception; this is the ground of certainty in science. The rationalist features of Comte's thought do not enter in at this level, but only at the level of the selective organization of facts within theories: theories provide for the *connection* of facts to universal propositions or laws. 4) The 'relativism' of scientific knowledge. 'Relativism' here is not used in the sense which it has subsequently come to acquire: the acceptance, in some form or other, of multiple worlds of reality. That is to say, it is again not an ontological term, but refers to the thesis that science confines itself to explaining the interdependence of phenomena: it does not claim to discover essences or final causes. Scientific knowledge is never 'finished', but constantly open to modification and improvement. 5) The integral tie between science and the moral and material progress of mankind. Comte's adoption of the Baconian formula that the foreknowledge yielded by science makes possible technological control, the integration of *prévoir* and *pouvoir*, expresses this exactly. This not only unifies science and technology, but extends the realm of the technological to human social development itself; as Comte says quite explicitly, technology will no longer be exclusively associated with the physical, but will become 'political and moral'.[19]

Each of these views reappears in Mach's writings, although not of course in identical form to their expression in Comte's works. There is nothing in Mach comparable to Comte's massive endeavour to synthesize scientific knowledge within a scheme that is simultaneously historical and analytical. But Mach was directly influenced by theories of evolution, and saw in Darwin and Lamarck a basis for explaining the emerging hegemony of scientific thought from the entanglements of metaphysics. For Mach, the scientific outlook triumphs historically, and finds its moral justification in facilitating the survival and welfare of the human species.[20] Mach uses the term 'philosophy' in the same dual connotation as Comte. When he writes that he is not a philosopher, and that science does not rely on any particular type or system of philosophy, Mach echoes Comte's theme of the abolition of philosophy. 'Philosophy' here is used to mean transcendental or 'metaphysical philosophy': both Comte and Mach proclaim an end to philosophy in this sense. Where Comte and Mach speak of the retention of philosophy, on the other hand, it is as '*philosophie positive*': philosophy here is the logical clarification of the basis of science. 'There is above all *no* Machian philosophy', Mach emphasizes, there is at the most 'a natural-scientific methodology and a psychology of knowledge'; these latter 'are like all scientific theories provisional, incomplete attempts'.[21] Mach's dismissal of metaphysics is as complete as that of Comte, although linked to a more thorough-going phenomenalism than Comte ever adopted:

I should like the scientists to realize that my view eliminates all metaphysical questions indifferently, whether they be only regarded as insoluble at the present moment, or whether they be regarded as meaningless for all time. I should like then, further, to reflect that everything that we can know about the world is necessarily expressed in the sensations, which can be set free from the individual influence of the observer in a precisely definable manner . . . Everything that we can want to know is given by the solution of a problem in mathematical form, by the ascertainment of the functional dependency of the sensational elements on one another. This knowledge exhausts the knowledge of 'reality'.[22]

For Mach, scientific knowledge is 'relative' in Comte's sense; the object of science is to discover relations between phenomena. According to Mach, however, this carries the implication that theory has a purely heuristic role in scientific investigations. The precise identification of the mathematical functions that express the dependencies between phenomena in nature renders theory obsolete. In Mach's phrase, theories resemble dead leaves which fall away when the tree of science no longer has a need to breathe through them. Although this is distinct from Comte's view, it is not as far removed from it as may seem the case at first blush. In his discussion of the positive method of science, Comte commingles empiricism and rationalism: as I have already mentioned, however, he does so by treating theory as the mode of organizing fact in a way relevant to scientific procedure.

In Comte's positivism, no place is found for the reflexive subject; psychology does not even appear in the hierarchy of the sciences, and the notion of subjective experience is regarded as a metaphysical fiction. In this regard, Comte stands in direct line of descent from Hume. But this is a standpoint that is taken for granted in Comte's writings rather than defended in detail. Mach, however, confronts the issue directly, and his stand upon it is quite unequivocal. The self or ego does not exist as a unity; it is merely an aggregate of sensations. According to Mach, if this is accepted, it disposes of the accusation of solipsism that is frequently made against phenomenalism; since the self does not exist, there can be no question of the isolation of the self in the universe. Mach saw no discrepancy between this view and either the existence of morality or the role of science in furthering the betterment of humanity. It is anti-religious in so far as it has the consequence that there can be no survival of the soul after death, since 'I' has no unitary existence anyway – although in the latter part of his career Mach came to see affinities between his standpoint and the world-view of Buddhism. Mach believed that his view, far from rejecting the ethical value of the individual personality, enhances it by preventing an over-evaluation of the 'self'; it places the emphasis on the moral welfare of mankind as a whole. This links back to Mach's

conception of the relation between science and human progress: the triumph of the scientific spirit provides both a technological and a moral basis for the evolutionary advancement of
man.

Mach's writings and teachings both helped to foster a climate of
opinion in Vienna propitious for the development of what came
to be known as logical positivism or logical empiricism (the latter
being the term preferred by Schlick), and also directly influenced
ideas of the most prominent members of the Vienna Circle.[23] But
the logical positivists drew heavily upon other sources also, and in
certain respects their work contrasts quite clearly with that of
Mach. Beginning with the group formed in 1907 around Frank, a
physicist, Neurath, an economist, and Hahn, a mathematician, the
logical positivists sought to develop a view of science which would
recognize the vital significance of logic and mathematics, as
systems of symbolic representations, in scientific thought. This led
them to acknowledge the central importance of language: a theme
which connects their writings to the major thrust of development
of philosophy as a whole in the twentieth century. One line of
thought leading in this direction within the philosophy of science
was that provided by Poincaré's conventionalism, sometimes
referred to as the 'new positivism'. Schlick and others were critical
of conventionalism, but recognized the force of the claim that
scientific theories embody linguistic conventions. The thesis that
theories are languages for the representation of facts, stripped of
some of the sceptical features of conventionalism, was taken over
as a key element of logical positivism.

But in their approach to the mode of analysing the content of
such languages, the logical positivists were indebted to British
philosophy. What has been called the 'revolution in British
philosophy',[24] led by Moore and Russell, was initiated by them as
a reaction to the Hegelianism of Bradley, McTaggart and others.
It was both a return to the traditions of British empiricism and a
new departure. Russell himself did not set out to discredit metaphysics; rather, he believed that philosophy should become
rigorous and precise, and that the way to achieve this goal lay
through the logical elucidation of the language in which scientific
theories are couched. Philosophy is to reveal the logical structure
which underlies the superficial play of appearances. Russell's
object was not, like that of Husserl's transcendental reduction,
eventually to recover the everyday world of common sense or of

the 'natural attitude', but to provide an account that would conform to established scientific knowledge. Russell's 'logical atomism' had a strong influence on the young Wittgenstein, and it was partly through Wittgenstein's personal contacts with some of the Vienna Circle, and through his *Tractatus*, that these ideas were communicated. Wittgenstein's impact upon the members of the Circle has been so frequently emphasized, however, that it is worthwhile pointing out that Carnap, ultimately the most influential of the group, has acknowledged Frege and Russell as having had the strongest effect upon his philosophical development. He attended Frege's lectures in Jena, and through them was introduced to the *Principia Mathematica*; Hahn had independently acquainted the members of the Circle with the latter work.[25]

In retrospect, it has become clear that the logical positivists read Wittgenstein's *Tractatus* against a Machian background which led them to disregard crucial features of it. The book is not an exposition which as a whole could be said to exemplify the traditional tenets of empiricism; it is rather, as Wittgenstein remarked subsequently, a sort of 'Platonic myth', a metaphor in its own right. This undoubtedly separates the early Wittgenstein decisively from the main line of development of logical positivism, even if Schlick and his associates saw themselves as continuing along the path Wittgenstein had opened up.[26] The *Tractatus* influenced the growth of logical positivism particularly in respect of the argument for the distinction between the analytic and the synthetic. There are no synthetic *a priori* judgements. Systems of logic or mathematics, deductively derived from axioms, are essentially tautological; any other general claim to knowledge is synthetic, which means that it can be counterfactually shown to be false.

Logical positivism and modern empiricism

The members of the Vienna Circle, in its early days, saw themselves as the enthusiastic progenitors of a new Enlightenment: as Feigl has described it, as carrying on 'in the spirit of Hume and Comte, but equipped with more fully developed logical tools'.[27] In the writings of the logical positivists the differentiation of what is scientific and what is not became convergent with what is meaningful and what is meaningless. What came to be called the 'Verification Principle' went through numerous versions, as the inadequacy of Schlick's original formulation, that the meaning of (synthetic) statements consists in the method of their verification, became very rapidly apparent. In these later versions, 'testability' was substituted for 'verification'. Obviously it would be mistaken to hold that a statement is meaningful only when we have managed to test its validity: otherwise, with improvements in empirical techniques of validation, previously meaningless statements would suddenly become meaningful ones. So the Verification Principle was altered to hold that a statement is meaningful if there is some means of potentially testing, or 'confirming', it. But various major difficulties still remained evident, the most-debated being the status of the Principle itself. For if it cannot be subjected to the criterion of testability, if it cannot itself be tested, it should seemingly be dismissed as meaningless.

To attempt to get around this difficulty, the Verification Principle was declared to be a procedural rule, not itself a statement. This helped to indicate that what was at issue was, in some part, a problem of the nature of statements: of what constitutes a statement. This can be illustrated by reference to another dilemma in the early formulations of the Verification Principle, concerning the breadth of its application. If taken as a criterion to be applied very generally to all kinds of moral prescriptions or aesthetic judgements, it has the consequence of eliminating these as meaningless, along with metaphysics and theology. But if it concerns only the meaningfulness of 'statements', the implication could be drawn that it supplies a criterion for distinguishing statements from other kinds of judgements, commands, etc. The first, more 'radical', version of logical positivism gradually became abandoned in favour of the second, more 'liberal' one – especially in the hands of Carnap.[28] The view that the 'pseudo-sentences' of metaphysics are meaningless came to be supplanted by the more sophisticated notion that metaphysical doctrines lack cognitive meaning, although they may have emotive meaning. To borrow an expression of Ayer's, originally applied in a slightly different context, the metaphysician is treated less like a criminal than like a patient.[29]

The logical positivists initially classified most of the traditional ontological and epistemological dilemmas of philosophy as belonging to metaphysics, and hence as outside the scope of rational discussion. The disputes between phenomenalism, realism, idealism, and so on were dismissed as meaningless, since there is no way that they can be made to submit to any characterization of the Verification Principle. However, they believed that certain issues relevant to these long-established debates could be sustained, and resolved, if they were treated as debates about appropriate philosophical languages. In this way the back door was left ajar for the incorporation of features within the writings of the logical positivists that were denied public admittance at the front. Carnap's earlier work sets out a version of phenomenalism, although he claimed to be discussing only the relevance of 'a phenomenalistic language' to scientific procedures. His major work in the first part of his intellectual career, *Der logische Aufbau der Welt*, pursues the theme that the aim of philosophy is to express knowledge as a logical structure of basic certainties. Here Carnap advocates a phenomenalistic grounding of such certainties. The only sure knowledge is that which is immediately given as sense-data; our knowledge of material objects is secondary and derived.[30] Neurath was mainly instrumental in persuading Carnap to abandon this position, the first of several substantial alterations the latter was to introduce into his views over the course of the years. In order to skirt the suggestion that he was again becoming involved in the sorts of epistemological debates that were prohibited, Carnap referred to his shift from phenomenalism to physicalism as a change of 'attitude', and not one of 'belief', since this would require a theoretical defence of the falsity of the first and the truth of the latter. However, it is clear enough that there was an underlying theoretical justification of the change which both Neurath and Carnap accepted: that whereas phenomenalism leads to solipsistic paradoxes, physicalism provides more readily for an intersubjective language in which reports of observations are communicated between observers.[31]

Neurath and Carnap developed their physicalist thesis in some part in direct opposition to the tradition of the *Geisteswissenschaften*, which insisted upon the existence of logical and methodological differences between the natural and the social sciences. Everything, Neurath held, occurs in nature, as part of the physical world. Carnap attempted to express this as a thesis about language: that is, to show that all knowledge can be reduced to the propositions of a physicalist language. This applies as much to our knowledge of minds as to that of happenings in nature. All statements in psychology, according to Carnap, whether they are about mental states of one's own or of others, can be translated into a

language which refers to physical events in the body of the person
or persons concerned.

On these grounds, psychology is a part of the domain of unified
science based on physics. By 'physics' we wish to mean, not the system
of currently known physical laws, but rather the science characterized
by a mode of concept formation which traces every concept back to
state-coordinates, that is, to systematic assignments of numbers to
space–time points. Understanding 'physics' in this way, we can rephrase
our thesis in a particular thesis of physicalism – as follows: psychology
is a branch of physics.[32]

The members of the Vienna Circle were already divided quite
considerably among themselves prior to their enforced scattering
into exile and Schlick's death in 1936. Hahn, Neurath and Carnap,
the so-called 'left wing' of the Circle, were the main figures in the
shift away from the dogmatic views of the earlier days, whereas
Schlick and Waismann were more inclined to hold fast to their
established ideas. In later times, the core of the movement was
continued in the United States, and to a lesser extent in Britain.
'Logical positivism' lost the clear-cut identity that it previously
had, and devolved into a more general stream of positivistic philosophy, finding ready contacts with, and having a great deal of
influence upon, the traditions of empiricism and pragmatism
already strongly engrained in Anglo-Saxon philosophy. Among the
members of the Vienna Circle, Carnap, Neurath, Frank, Gödel
and Feigl went to the United States, as did Reichenbach, von
Mises, and Hempel from the Berlin group of philosophers who
shared much in common with them, and the Polish logician
Tarski, whose ideas have influenced both Carnap and Popper (who
came to Britain after a spell of time in New Zealand). The sway
of these authors over the development of certain core areas of
analytic philosophy in the English-speaking world has been very
considerable indeed, although tempered in Britain particularly by
the influence of 'ordinary-language philosophy' and the later
Wittgenstein. I shall be concerned with two principal, connected
aspects of the influence of the former group of authors: in respect
of the philosophy of natural science, the dominance of what has
been variously called (by Feigl) the 'orthodox' or (by Putnam) the
'received' model of science; and the elaboration, in the light of
these views, of the thesis of the unity of science in respect of the
logic of the social sciences.

The orthodox model of science derives from the liberalization of the original logical positivist doctrines, especially as led by Carnap; but it also preserves features that stretch back through to Mach's writings. Mach wanted to reduce experience to relations between simple elements. These elements are sensations, not statements about sensations, such as appear in scientific theories. Hence Mach failed to recognize the difference between 'formal' and 'material' modes of speaking. Statements are frequently couched in such a form that they seem to concern experiences, while in fact they are assertions about other statements: these are called by Carnap 'syntactical sentences'. Mach's positivistic philosophy was transformed into logical positivism by the treating of Mach's 'elements' syntactically, as components not of experience but of a formal language in which experience is described. Mach's elements became 'elementary sentences' or 'protocol sentences': the simplest sentences, not further reducible, in which the formal language is expressed.[33] A protocol sentence, as in legal transcription of protocols, is supposed to be a statement of experience, immediately recorded. Carnap regarded the problem of the form of protocol statements as the basic issue in the logic of science, and his attempts to grapple with it provide the key to some of the major changes in his ideas from his early phenomenalist viewpoint onwards. The original view of most of the Vienna Circle was that scientific knowledge rests upon a bedrock of indubitable fact, expressed in the immediacy of sensations as specified by Mach: this is the theme of the *Aufbau*. But just as Neurath rejected phenomenalism, he never accepted the existence of the bedrock of certainty as ordered by protocol statements. In his famous analogy, knowledge is like a ship that has to be continually rebuilt even while it remains afloat. Carnap was influenced by this, and also came to acknowledge that the thesis that scientific theories could in a fairly simple sense be 'reduced' to protocol statements had to be revised and made more elaborate.

Carnap was thus led to place a much greater emphasis upon the role of theoretical concepts in the advancement of scientific knowledge than in his very early work, upon the incompleteness of such concepts, and upon their differentiation from the language of observation protocols. Theoretical concepts, one part of the system of scientific knowledge, cannot be directly derived from, or reduced to, the other part, the language of observation. The theoretical language and the observation language however are connected by 'correspondence rules', whereby observations may be interpreted in the light of theories, and vice versa. This conception is the core of the orthodox model. A science such as physics is conceived to be a calculus, whose axioms are the fundamental physical laws. The calculus is not directly interpreted, but is a 'freely floating system', in relation to which other theoretical terms are defined. Some of the latter can be interpreted by semantic rules that relate them to a groundwork of observable fact; but interpretation of the theoretical terms is never complete. The theoretical cohesion of the system is provided by its hypothetico-deductive character, in which theorems can be deduced from the axioms and hence, via the rules of correspondence, particular observations can be 'explained'. This is some way from the original emphases of logical positivism in so far as the criterion of 'testability' only applies in an immediate way at the level of the observation language – although in the final works of his career Carnap still expressed the belief that a means could be found for differentiating cognitively meaningful theoretical terms from meaningless ones.

The precise nature of correspondence rules has proved a controversial matter among positivistically minded philosophers. The usual general picture of the relation between the observational and theoretical languages is something akin to Braithwaite's analogy: correspondence rules are the 'zip' that fastens together theory and observation; the fastener progressively pulls the two elements of a system of knowledge together as uninterpreted theorems are transformed into observation statements, expanding the empirical content of the theoretical constructs.[34] The allowing of a detachment between theoretical concepts and observation statements, representing the abandonment of the Verification Principle in anything at all close to its original form, has the virtue, Carnap claims, of allowing for the creative scope of scientific innovation and the wide explanatory power that abstract theory can possess.[35] On the other hand, since it has become generally recognized that observation statements are not unchallengeable, the implication might be drawn that the claimed differentiation between the theoretical and the observation language cannot be drawn clearly at all. For, as Feigl says, most positivistically inclined authors today, even those involved in or close to the original Vienna group, recognize that observation-statements cannot be entirely 'theory-free'.[36]

The dominant account of scientific explanation developed in modern empiricism is that given clearest shape in a famous article by Hempel and Oppenheim.[37] It has stimulated a wide-ranging debate, and a very large literature, in response to which Hempel has modified and elaborated upon his views as first set out. I shall only summarize its main features briefly here; since its possible application to the social sciences and history has provoked as much discussion as its relevance to natural science, it provides an appropriate transition-point to move to an appraisal of the influence of positivistic philosophy in sociology. The core idea is that the most precise, although not only, form of scientific explanation is 'deductive-nomological' (this has also, following Dray, come to be called the 'covering-law model' of explanation). Explanation of an event here involves reference to information supplied by two types of statements, which are brought together. These are, first, general laws; and, second, statements that specify particular circumstances in which those laws have application. The statement referring to the event or phenomenon to be explained (the 'explanandum') is deduced as a necessity from the conjunction of these two.[38] The objective testing of a scientific explanation hence involves empirical confirmation of the statement describing the initial or 'boundary' conditions; empirical confirmation of the laws in relation to which the explanandum is deduced; and logical confirmation of the deduction made. According to Hempel, there is a symmetry, or a 'structural equality' between explanation and prediction, since the logical form of the two is the same: a prediction consists in deducing a statement about a future rather than a past event. Deductive-nomological explanation is held to be integral to all 'empirical sciences', save that in the social sciences and history it is often less clearly manifest than in natural science. Hempel offers two reasons for this: the universal laws in question are frequently common-sense ones, that are taken for granted implicitly rather than formulated as explicit statements; and, partly because of this, not enough is known about the empirical basis of such laws for us to be able to state them with precision. Historians mostly offer what Hempel calls 'explanation sketches', in which the relevant laws and boundary conditions are only vaguely hinted at: explanation sketches can be made more complete, and thus more 'scientifically acceptable', in Hempel's words, through being filled out by empirical testing of the laws and conditions on which they are based.

This theory of explanation in social science is affirmed by Hempel in conscious contradistinction to the tradition of 'interpretative understanding' of the *Geisteswissenschaften* – thus echoing one of the persistent themes of logical positivism. *Verstehen,* or what Hempel refers to as 'the method of empathic understanding' is admitted as a component in the method of the social sciences only as a mode of suggesting hypotheses. It is not indispensable for social or historical explanation, and any hypotheses arrived at empathically have then to be established in deductive form, and tested empirically. Hempel makes it clear that an empiricist criterion of cognitive meaning has to be applied in the same way here as in the natural sciences. Interpretations of 'meaning' that are made in sociology and history

consist either in subsuming the phenomena in question under a scientific explanation or explanation sketch ; or in an attempt to subsume them under some general idea which is not amenable to any empirical test. In the former case, interpretation clearly is explanation by means of universal hypotheses ; in the latter, it amounts to a pseudo-explanation which may have emotive appeal and evoke vivid pictorial associations, but which does not further our theoretical understanding of the phenomena under consideration.[39]

Positivistic philosophy and modern sociology

Of the members of the Vienna Circle, Neurath wrote most extensively on social issues, and made the most sustained attempt to apply logical positivist views to sociology, which he approached from a self-professedly Marxist standpoint. While Neurath was a strong supporter of, and a major influence upon, the thesis that the 'scientific way of thinking' in philosophy marked the way ahead in the evolution of human thought, he was more inclined than the other members of the group to emphasize the importance of the social context of particular philosophical traditions in explaining the hold that such traditions may have over their adherents. Neurath was the main figure who kept logical positivism tied to the general interest in the promotion of social progress characteristic of Comte and of Mach. His Marxism however was unobtrusive theoretically, save in respect of his advocacy of physicalism; he rejected dialectical logic, the Hegelian legacy in Marx, no less completely than did his colleagues.[40]

For Neurath sociology is regarded as one segment of the

division of labour in the totality of unified science: like every other science, it is 'free of any world view'.[41] He envisages the coming into being of a system of the sciences in which the laws of each particular science, such as sociology, will be connected with the laws of all the other sciences in a uniform logical structure. Laws, Neurath says, are abstract means of passing from observation statements to predictions; the concept of observation is in turn analysed in terms of physicalism, as involving a 'social behaviourism'. Neurath's behaviourism bears close affinities with operationalism, which of course has in various general respects run parallel to logical positivism as a whole. In deciding whether a term such as 'religious ethos' may be legitimately employed in sociology, according to Neurath, we have to infer the sorts of observation statements it presupposes, as concrete modes of behaviour. 'Let him [the sociologist] not speak of the "spirit of the age" if it is not completely clear that he means by it certain verbal combinations, forms of worship, modes of architecture, fashions, styles of painting, etc.'[42]

Neurath's writings seem to have had little direct influence in sociology as such. The influence of the writings of the logical positivists has been assimilated into sociology in a much more important and pervasive way through a general acceptance of the model of scientific explanation developed in the phase of the devolution of logical positivism into positivistic philosophy. Since this is so diffuse, it would be out of the question to inquire into it in any detail here. I shall therefore indicate some of the connections between positivistic philosophy and positivistic sociology by illustration. Such illustration is easy to find. One aspect of the broad influence which positivistic philosophy has enjoyed within the social sciences, in the English-speaking world at least, is reflected in the replacement of the term 'method' by 'methodology'. The latter has come to mean nothing more than the analysis of procedures of research; it has little explicit relation to the broader process of reflection on the form and concerns of sociology, which is hived off as the proper task of the 'philosophy of the social sciences'. Methodology is often presumed to involve no particular philosophical commitments; but most of the leading texts offer a few positivistic trimmings to the package. Thus Lazarsfeld and Rosenberg, for example, quote Bridgman and Hempel with approval, accepting the positivist programme of effecting the substitution of a precise, formal language of observation for everyday language as the first demand of a scientific sociology.[43]

Rather than attempting to multiply such examples, I shall concentrate upon indicating the direction of emphasis of three authors whose work has been widely adopted within the mainstream of contemporary sociology. First, Ernest Nagel, whose book *The Structure of Science* has served as a stock reference for innumerable sociological texts and discussions; second, Zetterberg's *On Theory and Verification in Sociology,* a representative and influential discussion of the methodology of social science; and third, Hempel's analysis of functionalism, which connects functional explanation to the deductive-nomological model, thereby re-establishing direct contact between 'positivism' in its modern form and 'positivism' in the tradition of Comte and Durkheim.

Nagel's book is explicitly indebted to Carnap and Frank (as well as to M. R. Cohen).[44] The work follows something of a Comtean outline: the discussion proceeds from mechanics through physics to biology and the social sciences. The account is anchored in terms of an exposition of deductive-nomological explanation, and the differentiation of languages of observation and theory connected by correspondence rules; biology and the social sciences are distinct from the rest of natural science in so far as the former may make use of teleological or functional explanations. Nagel denies that 'teleology' is specifically dependent upon the activities of conscious, reasoning agents, or that teleological explanation involves a presumption of final causes. The question of the 'subjective' or 'meaningful' character of human conduct is taken up at some length. 'Interpretative understanding', according to Nagel, involves two characteristics: the assumption that one or more particular individuals are, at a certain time, in certain psychological states; and the assumption of a general principle or law stating the ways in which such states are related both to each other and to 'overt behaviour'. Observational evidence is required for both of these, rather than any kind of emphatic identification with the actors whose conduct is to be explained:

We can *know* that a man fleeing from a pursuing crowd that is animated by hatred towards him is in a state of fear, without our having experienced such violent fears and hatred or without imaginatively recreating such emotions in ourselves – just as we can *know* that the temperature of a piece of wire is rising because the velocities of its constituent molecules are increasing, without having to imagine what it is like to be a rapidly moving molecule.[45]

Like Hempel, Nagel accepts that empathy may play a part in the derivation of hypotheses; but such hypotheses have then to be tested by 'controlled sensory observation'.

Most of the generalizations in the social sciences, Nagel says, are statistical uniformities rather than universal laws. This is not, however, because of any specific features of human behaviour as such, but is primarily because of the relatively youthful stage of development of sociology, which has not yet developed the conceptual and observational precision necessary for determining exactly the limiting conditions of its generalizations; although he has strong reservations about existing functionalist theories in the social sciences, Nagel apparently believes that such precision may be achieved in principle, although there are various factors likely to prevent its full realization in practice. In any case statistical, rather than universal, laws are typical of many areas of natural science. Statistical generalizations are complemented in the social sciences by functional ones, the latter explaining the maintenance of system states through regulative feedback. The advance of functional explanations in sociology and anthropology is, as in the case of deductive explanations, hindered by the as yet diffuse character of most social scientific concepts.

In Nagel's view, the fact that human beings can modify their conduct in the light of their knowledge, including potentially their knowledge of generalizations made by sociologists, is not a major source of 'difficulty' for social science. It is not in fact something which is unique to the social sciences: in natural science also the observation of a phenomenon can alter the character of that phenomenon. The very statement of the latter implies some awareness of the extent to which what is observed is altered by the process of observation; hence the effects produced by the interaction will either be small, and can be ignored, or if large can be calculated and corrected for. The logical character of the 'interference' is the same in nature and society, although the 'mechanisms involved' are different.[46] The possibility of self-fulfilling and self-negating predictions in the social sciences similarly finds direct analogy in natural science. A computer, for example, which guides the firing of a gun, may be defective such that it just misses the target; however, the oscillations produced by the transmitting of the (erroneous) calculations could cause the gun to in fact hit the target just because it was originally aimed wrongly.

Nagel's work is consciously directed to a spelling-out of 'liberalized logical positivism'; that of Zetterberg, on the other hand, is more concerned to describe the conduct of research in sociology, and the connection between such research and what he calls 'theoretical sociology'.[47] It is an attempt, the author says, to complement the insistence of authors such as Lundberg that sociology should match the scientific rigour of the natural sciences with a fuller appreciation than Lundberg expressed of the basic importance of theory in science. Zetterberg makes due obeisance to the 'humanistic content' of the social sciences, but the main emphasis of his argument is upon the continuity between physics, biology and sociology. Explanation in sociology, if at any rate it is to advance beyond lay knowledge or lay beliefs, must assume the same deductive-nomological form which it has in natural science. 'Theory' in sociology is often used very broadly, as virtually equivalent to 'social thought', Zetterberg says; in his usage however, it means a set of deductively connected laws, to which any particular event, within boundary conditions, can be referred. Zetterberg's description of the formalized language which sociology needs if it is to meet the demands of being an empirical science, in which he draws upon Hempel's analysis of cognitive meaning, implies a strict criterion of reducibility of theoretical terms to the terms of the observation language. In an ideal theory, it would be possible to reduce the content of all second-order theoretical concepts to a set of 'primitive terms', utilizing the procedures of formal logic. The primitive terms of theoretical sociology as a whole refer to observations of the behaviour of actors in interaction.[48]

Zetterberg answers affirmatively the age-old question: are there sociological laws parallel to those discovered in the natural sciences? There are many such laws or theoretical propositions that have been turned up by social science; e.g: 'persons tend to issue prescriptions that maintain the rank they enjoy in the social structure'; or, 'the more favourable evaluations rank-and-file members receive in a group, the more their ideas converge with those of other group members'.[49] Two factors influence the specification of such laws in the sociological literature: the conditions of their application are often only vaguely indicated, and it is not made clear what procedures are necessary to confirm or 'verify' them. Everyday life abounds with generalizations that people make of their own conduct or of the activities of others; the task of

sociology is to test these so as to turn them from lay hypotheses
into confirmed findings and laws, discarding those shown to be
invalid.

I think sociology should make a more serious effort to incorporate
in its theories the best thoughts (theoretical hypotheses) of the human
conditions found in Homer, Dante, Shakespeare, Cervantes, Twain and
other great writers, who now provide the lion's share of any educated
layman's conception of the human drama. In the end, however, the
outcome of the theoretical enterprise should be 'high informative content, well backed by experience', that is, laws.[50]

Zetterberg's discussion touches only marginally on functionalism, and does not elucidate the bearing of what he has to say
for the significance of functional explanation in sociology. Nagel has
treated the question at some length; but here I shall consider the
account provided by Hempel, which is concerned to connect
deductive-nomological to functional explanation.[51] According to
Hempel, functional analysis is a form of teleological explanation,
the latter referring not to the causes of an event, but to the ends
to which it is directed. Teleological explanation, however, has
traditionally been impervious to empirical testing: Hempel quotes
the example of entelechy or vital force as a metaphysical
principle which, in biology, has been involved in unacceptable
teleological theories. The problem is to strip functional analysis
away from any association with such non-testable vitalistic
principles.

In biology, Hempel says, functional analysis is concerned with
the explanation of a recurrent activity (e.g. the beating of the
heart) in terms of its contribution to a state (e.g. the circulation
of the blood through the body) of the organism required for the
maintenance of life. In the social sciences, the objects of analysis
are similarly patterned and repetitive modes of social conduct
examined in relation to states of the larger social system. But
what is the explanatory element in functional explanation? It is
not to be found in the type of nomology characteristic of either
deductive-nomological or inductive-statistical explanation. There
is a close similarity in logical form nevertheless. When, in giving
physical explanations, we say that an ice cube melts because it
was put into warm water, we are able to justify this as an explanation of the melting by reference to general laws of which the
specific case is an instance. In a similar way, the 'because' of

functional explanation implies a principle such that, within specified conditions, a system will either invariably or with a high degree of probability meet the functional exigencies needed for its survival in the face of forces threatening to change it. That is to say, the general propositions involved in functional analysis refer to the self-regulation of biological or social systems; thus understood, they yield predictions which can be objectively tested.[52] This depends upon defining concepts like 'system need' operationally.

It will no doubt be one of the most important tasks of functional analysis in psychology and the social sciences to ascertain to what extent such phenomena of self-regulation can be found, and can be represented by corresponding laws. Whatever specific laws might be discovered by research along these lines, the kind of explanation and prediction made possible by them does not differ in its logical character from that of the physical sciences.[53]

The three examples I have chosen here are arbitrary, in so far as they could have been replaced by many others expressing similar views – although each has been influential in its own right. I do not want to claim, of course, that the general standpoint they represent has ever become an unrivalled one, but it has undoubtedly been quite recently the dominant approach in English-speaking sociology. This is not just because the main tradition has insisted that the social sciences should model their aspirations on the sciences of nature: rather, many authors in the former field have accepted, explicitly or implicitly, that 'science' can be identified with the positivistic philosophy of science. Functionalism has played an important part in this, as the conceptual vehicle of the continuity between natural and social science: the division between the physical and the life sciences appears as great, if not larger, than between biology and sociology.

The post-positivistic philosophy of science

In the philosophy of science, as contrasted to the methodological self-understanding of the social sciences, the 'orthodox model' has long since become subject to broad-ranging attack, led by such authors as Toulmin, Feyerabend, Hesse, Kuhn and others. While these writers disagree about the conclusions that should be drawn from their critical analyses of positivistic philosophy, it is clear that they have successfully displaced the orthodox model: it is an orthodoxy no longer. The work of Karl Popper, however, is both prior to theirs and in some part one of its sources; a tracing of the critical views which Popper has expressed of logical positivism, as well as the evident themes which connect his writings to those of the Vienna Circle, necessarily precedes any commentary on the 'newer philosophy of science' of the past two decades.

The relation between Popper's views and those of the leading members of the Vienna Circle, particularly Carnap, has been a controversial one from the beginning. Popper was not himself a member of the Circle, but had a close intellectual contact with it. His first and still his major work, *Logik der Forschung*, was discussed within the group, and regarded as basically in accord with the perspective of logical positivism. Popper, on the other hand, emphasized that the work was radically critical of the philosophy of logical positivism, and since its first publication has continued to stress the differences between his position and any kind of empiricism or positivistic philosophy.[54] The points at issue are not easy to disentangle. In assessing the differences between Popper's ideas and those of logical positivism, even in its more liberalized versions, one should mention the following of Popper's views as the most distinctive sources of contrast: his complete rejection of induction, and his concomitant rejection of 'sensory certainty', whether manifest as phenomenalism or physicalism; his substitution of falsification for verification, with the corresponding stress upon boldness and ingenuity in the framing of scientific hypotheses; his defence of tradition which, in conjunction with the operation of the critical spirit, is integral to science; and his replacement of the logical-positivist ambition of putting an end to metaphysics by revealing it as nonsense, with the aim of securing criteria of demarcation between science and pseudo-science. These differences are certainly considerable, and underlie Popper's continual insistence that not only is he not a 'positivist', but that he is one of its foremost critics in the philosophy of science. However there are also some major overall similarities between Popper's writings and those of the logical positivists that are clearly apparent. Popper shares the conviction that scientific knowledge, imperfect though it may be, is the most certain and reliable knowledge to which human beings can aspire; his endeavour to establish clear criteria of demarcation between science and pseudo-science shares much of the same impetus as the concern of the logical positivists to free science from mystifying, empty word-play; and, like the logical positivists, his characterization of science is a procedural one: science is separated from other forms of tradition in so far as its theories and findings are capable of being exposed to empirical testing and therefore to potential falsification.

Popper's first formulation of the principle of falsification as the key to the demarcation between science and non-science was arrived at, according to his own testimony, as a result of reflection upon the gulf between certain types of social theory – especially Marxism and psychoanalysis – and the physical sciences. The former, Popper came to the conclusion, have more in common with primitive myths rather than with science; they are more like astrology than astronomy.[55] The reason for this, according to Popper, lies less in their lack of precision, as compared to physics, than in what to their adherents is their most attractive characteristic: the range of their explanatory power. As total systems of thought, they gain their support from a quasi-religious experience of conversion or revelation and, once converted, the believer is able to explain any event in terms of them. Since they can explain anything or everything, there is no source or type of empirical evidence that could be pointed to as a basis of showing the ideas involved to be mistaken. This stands in marked contrast to relativity theory in physics, which generated specific predictions about the movement of material entities, and delivered itself as a hostage to the outcome of the testing of those predictions; such an element of risk is absent from theories such as Marxism and psychoanalysis, which protect themselves against counterfactual evidence. The distinctive characteristic of science, therefore, is that instead of merely seeking confirmation or verification of a theory, the scientist attempts to refute it. Confirmation, or what Popper has subsequently come to call 'corroborating evidence', of a theory results from its successful withstanding of empirical assaults which have the aim of falsifying it. 'One can sum up all this by saying that *the criterion of the scientific status of a theory is its falsifiability, or refutability, or testability.*'[56]

Popper's emphasis upon falsification stands in the closest possible relation to the critique of inductive logic with which he began his *Logik der Forschung*. A major tension had always existed at the heart of empiricist philosophies of science. Science was supposed to yield certain knowledge; on the other hand, the logical form of the induction of laws from observations precludes certainty. However many tests we may make confirming a theoretical proposition, there always remains the possibility that the next test would disconfirm it were it to be made: hence the validity of scientific laws can never be conclusively verified. Popper's response to this classical problem of empiricism is to deny the premise on which it rests: that is to say, he denies that science proceeds through induction at all, and accepts as inevitable that no abstract proposition in science can ever be finally verified. There is, as Popper puts it, an asymmetry between verification and falsification. No matter how many white swans we may observe, this does not justify the conclusion 'all swans are white'; but while such a universal statement cannot be ever derived from singular statements reporting observations, it can be contradicted or shown to be wrong by singular statements.[57] Thus although Popper's philosophy of science is sceptical in the sense that it accepts that no scientific law, even that which scientists may feel is completely securely founded, can be conclusively proved, it insists that scientific advance is possible through the empirical refutation of hypotheses. The object of science is still conceived of in a traditional manner as the securing of abstract generalizations that are true in so far as they correspond to facts; but we can never be logically certain that we have attained truth, although we can approach closer and closer to such certainty by the elimination of false theories.

Just as scientific theories are not tested inductively, neither are they arrived at inductively: the manner in which a theory is discovered or invented has nothing to do with its scientific status, which depends solely upon its being able to specify falsifying conditions and being able to withstand empirical testing of those conditions. There is no 'logic of discovery', since new ideas may be conceived as a flash of intuition, or as the result of religious reflection, or in many other contexts. Nor is there any 'observation' which is prior to 'theory' in the manner integral to the notion of inductive logic, and fundamental to logical positivism in the form of protocol statements. All observations are 'theory-impregnated', and are interpretations of facts. There can be no foundation of certain or incorrigible knowledge upon which science builds, as logical positivism, and positivistic philosophy more generally, assumes. Scientific knowledge is built on shifting sand, and what is important is not where we begin but how far we are able to subject our conjectures to empirical test, and hence to rational criticism. This also supplies the guiding thread in Popper's social philosophy. An 'open society' is one in which no single system of ideas is able to monopolize the social order: where freedom is ensured by the critical confrontation of diverse ideas and policies, whose outcomes can thus be rationally assessed.

Popper has consistently attempted to separate his thought from the preoccupation with language characteristic of so much contemporary philosophy, holding that the latter obscures the true nature of the scientific enterprise, which is above all concerned with the relation between hypotheses and the world of real objects and events. Terminology, Popper says, does not matter, save in so far as clarity and unambiguousness of expression are demanded for the rigorous testing of scientific theories. The same ideas can be expressed in different words; all that matters is that they should be clearly expressed, and formulated in such a way that the circumstances in which they can be declared to be falsified are known. Popper's philosophy possesses the boldness of formulation that he requires of science itself: the appeal of his substitution of falsification for verification derives in large part from the simple and incisive way in which it disposes at a stroke of the traditional dilemmas of induction. But the simplicity of the notion is belied by difficulties which it conceals, consideration of which forces us to confront more directly issues of language which Popper tends to dismiss as being at most of only marginal importance.

In the first place, the notion of falsification sits uneasily in Popper's writings with his commitment to a correspondence theory of truth. The aim of science, according to Popper, is more accurately described as concerned with 'verisimilitude' rather than truth.[58] But the idea of verisimilitude is only defensible if we assume that there are a finite number of possible conjectures or theories about nature, such that by progressively refuting them we get nearer and nearer to the truth. There seems no warrant for such an assumption, all the less so given Popper's injunction that it is incumbent on the scientist to look for 'unlikely' hypotheses since these are the easiest to test. Second, the very idea of falsification, which looks so concise and clear presented as a logical solution to difficulties of induction, when applied to the analysis of actual scientific activities of testing and the comparison of theories, becomes quite murky. Popper, of course, acknowledges that the logic of falsification is in some part separable from its implementation in scientific procedures. The universal statement 'all swans are white' is in principle contradicted by the discovery of a black swan, but in practice matters are not so simple because we have to decide, for one thing, what is to count as a black swan, i.e. as a falsifying observation. It would be possible, for example, for someone accepting the universal statement 'all swans are white' to discount any case of a black swan that might be found as not being a swan at all, and hence place it outside the scope of the law. Popper's response to such a tactic is to declare it unscientific, as alien to the spirit in which science should be carried on. But this is not very convincing, and one could claim that here Popper is hoist with his own petard, because such an argument seems to do just what it criticizes: namely, to propose that any instance which does not accord with the thesis should be disregarded as 'unscientific procedure'. One of the consequences of Kuhn's work is to affirm that this will not do, and the same holds for that of Feyerabend and Lakatos – in spite of the fact that the latter author regards Popper as the main originator of what he calls 'sophisticated falsificationism'.

Kuhn's most important study, *The Structure of Scientific Revolutions*, has become very well known indeed, and there is no need to do more than refer in the most cursory manner here to its main themes. Kuhn's views may differ considerably in certain respects from those of Popper, but they also connect up closely with them, because both authors recognize the significance of the history of science for the philosophy of science (and vice versa). This has not been true, by and large, of the logical positivists, who have concentrated primarily upon producing abstract, formal analyses without giving any detailed attention to the historical study of the development of science. Hence, as Kuhn points out, they have tended to operate with accounts of scientific discoveries as finished achievements, as they are recorded in textbooks: but these no more satisfactorily describe the substance of what actually happens in science than tourist brochures do the culture into which they initiate the traveller.[59]

Kuhn's work was partly stimulated by his awareness of a contrast between the natural and social sciences, not of the kind traditionally stressed in the *Geisteswissenschaften*, but concerning the lack of agreement among social scientists over the basic character of their intellectual endeavours. The social sciences, in short, lack 'paradigms'. Thus they do not show the characteristic pattern of development of the natural sciences, which is one of periods of relatively stable 'normal science', involving puzzle-solving activity within the confines of a shared paradigm, inter-spersed with periods of revolutionary change as a result of which a new paradigm comes to supersede the old. Revolutions are written out of textbooks of science, or rather never written in: a textbook expresses a paradigm as the consolidated achievements of a particular science to date. Periods of revolutionary change in science are none the less a consequence of the activities of nor-mal science, for it is through the puzzle-solving activities of normal science that contradictions or anomalies emerge within the exist-ing framework of knowledge. A revolution in science is a change in world-view, a gestalt-switch: the conceptual transformation thus effected infuses 'observation' itself.

Is sensory experience fixed and neutral? The epistemological view-point that has most often guided Western philosophy for three centuries dictates an immediate and unequivocal, Yes! In the absence of a developed alternative, I find it impossible to relinquish entirely that viewpoint. Yet it no longer functions effectively, and the attempts to make it do so through the introduction of a neutral language of observations now seem to me hopeless.[60]

The Structure of Scientific Revolutions has provoked a great deal of discussion, to which Popper, among many others, has con-tributed. In the course of this debate, Kuhn has attempted to clear up ambiguities in the original work, and to elaborate upon it in various ways. I shall concentrate only upon mentioning issues relevant to the subsequent sections of this study. The most useful way to identify these is to indicate some of the differences of emphasis in Kuhn's work as compared to that of Popper. Three such differences are the following: 1) For Kuhn, 'normal science' is integral to scientific progress, since the suspension of criticism involved in the common acceptance of a paradigm makes possible a concentration of effort upon clearly defined problems. Constant critical assessment of the most basic elements of a 'disciplinary matrix' would prevent such a concentration of effort: this is just what occurs in pre-paradigmatic disciplines, such as the social sciences, in which the inability to agree over basic premises of the substance and method of inquiry blocks the development of know-ledge in the form achieved in many areas of natural science. The sort of 'permanent revolution' in science envisaged by Popper neither describes the actual conduct of science, nor is a desirable framework for it; normal science is not merely deformed science.

This view also separates Kuhn from Feyerabend's 'scientific anarchism': a proliferation of basic theories is only to be striven for in times of revolutionary crisis. 3) Kuhn's writings demonstrate the hazards in transferring the idea of falsification to the actual practice of science. He says he takes the notion of 'the asymmetry of falsification and confirmation very seriously indeed';[61] but 'testing' has to be related to the conjunctions of normal and revolutionary science. Scientists working within a paradigm often either ignore or treat as consistent with their accepted theories findings that are subsequently – following the dissolution of the paradigm – recognized as incompatible with, or as refuting, those theories. 3) Meaning-variance or the 'incommensurability' of paradigms appears as a fundamental problem in Kuhn's work in a way in which it does not in that of Popper; partly as a consequence of this, Kuhn finds Popper's account of verisimilitude unacceptable. Kuhn has consistently denied that he is a relativist, and it is quite obvious that he could not be one: for if the succession of paradigms is not regarded as 'progressive', in some sense, the differentiation between pre-paradigmatic and post-paradigmatic sciences effectively loses its significance: on the logical level, successive paradigms would only be 'laterally' distributed, each equivalent to any other – the same situation that is claimed to exist in the social sciences. On the other hand, Kuhn has found some considerable difficulty in spelling out how scientific progress occurs through revolution, and what the consequences of the resolution of this problem are for a theory of truth.[62]

The critique of positivism in Frankfurt philosophy

Since Hume, positivistic philosophers have generally adopted the stance that the sensory experience which provides the basis of scientific knowledge cannot be extended to encompass moral judgements or ethical values. Disputes concerning morality cannot be settled by appeal to intersubjectively available observations as debates over factual issues can. In the social sciences, this has long been the common assumption of most otherwise divergent schools of thought, including various forms of revisionist Marxism (such as that led by Eduard Bernstein). Perhaps the most well-known and influential exposition of the standpoint in sociology is that of Max Weber, who perhaps more than any other major writer pursued the implications of the 'fact–value dichotomy' to its furthest limits, and was prepared to accept these implications in full. For Weber, who drew his views on this issue from neo-Kantianism rather than from British empiricism, the findings of natural or social science stand in a purely instrumental connection to moral values. Science can show us which of a given choice of means is the most effective way of achieving a certain end, and what other consequences of the achievement of that end are likely to be; but it cannot give us the slightest degree of help in deciding to opt for that end itself (save in so far as that end might be in some part a means to other ends).[63] One consequence of this is that there can be no rational arbitration between the sets of 'ultimate values' upon which the major world civilizations rest, and which Weber set out to analyse in his studies of the 'world-religions'; such a clash of values is settled in the area of power-struggles.[64]

The imposition of strict limits upon moral reason in positivistic philosophies is something which two generations of Frankfurt philosophers, from Horkheimer, Adorno and Marcuse to Habermas, have been concerned to criticize. The critique of positivism in this respect has been one of the most central preoccupations of what has come to be called 'critical theory'. If there is a single dominating element in critical theory, it is the defence of Reason (*Vernunft*) understood in the sense of Hegel and classical German philosophy: as the critical faculty which reconciles knowledge with the transformation of the world so as to further human fulfilment and freedom.[65] Frankfurt philosophy attempts to follow Marx, and thereby to refurbish modern Marxism itself, by appealing to Hegel's transcendence of Kantian dualisms: not only that of pure and practical Reason, but that of the apperception of phenomena and the unknowable 'things in themselves'. Such dualisms are regarded as both expression and source of a passive, contemplative attitude to knowledge: an attitude which reduces the practical import of knowledge to 'technology' or 'technique' robbed of the unifying potentialities of historical Reason. Whereas in Hegel, as Horkheimer puts it, Reason is seen to be inherent in reality, in Hume and in Kant, as well as in Cartesian philosophy it becomes a 'subjective faculty of the mind'.[66] The individual subject is the sole possessor of reason, and the latter concept is taken to mean merely the calculative relating of means to ends.

The origins of the 'Frankfurt School' were contemporaneous with those of the Vienna Circle, and the members of the former

c

group sharpened their critical assessment of the influence of empiricism in the past by means of onslaughts upon its most prominent representatives in the present. In one such discussion, written in the late 1930s, Horkheimer connects up logical positivism to the tradition of Hume and Locke, but argues that the critical character which the writings of these authors possessed has been sacrificed by the modern logical positivists.[67] The sceptical empiricism of Hume was directed subversively against the prevailing dogmas in order to forge a new beginning, in which rationalism would prevail over the forces of unenlightened mythology. In this sense, the Enlightenment had a moral impetus which in actuality cut across the belief of Hume that facts could be separated from values. This is largely absent from logical positivism, which seeks only to complete and to sanction the domination of science as the contemplative reduction of experience to a logically coherent order of laws. This might be thought unfair to Neurath in particular and untrue to the Marxist leanings of various members of the Vienna Circle. But for Horkheimer such a consideration would be largely beside the point, because Marxism has not stood apart from the positivistic nature of much modern philosophy. On the contrary, the relapse of Marxism into positivistic philosophy is the origin of the twin characteristics of Marxism in the twentieth century: its quietism when in opposition (as in Germany) and its transformation into bureaucratic domination when in power (as in the Soviet Union).

The Frankfurt philosophers have attempted to diagnose the beginnings of 'positivistic Marxism' in the writings of Marx himself. What for Althusser and his followers is an 'epistemological break' separating the speculative, idealistic Marx from the first formation of scientific Marxism, for the critical theorists marks the phase of the incipient degeneration of Marxism into positivistic philosophy. The Frankfurt authors have differed among themselves about their evaluations of the nature and origins of positivistic Marxism, but their analyses – including that of Habermas in the 'younger generation' – have major overall points of agreement. The critical inspiration of Marxism derives from the dialectic of subject and object, and is lost where 'materialism' means the denial of the active intervention of the subject in history, or the reduction of culture and cultural ideals to epiphenomena of physical events. Monistic materialism, which regards all change as the interplay of natural occurrences, converges

directly with non-Marxist positivistic philosophy. Several of the
critical theorists have had doubts about the use of the notion of
labour in Marx's writings: in so far as this refers merely to the
material transformation of nature, and the critique of contemporary society is tied to this, socialism comes to be conceived of
merely as a technically more efficient version of capitalism. According to Habermas, in 'turning Hegel back on his feet', Marx com-
pressed two elements of Hegel's philosophy into one: man's
reflexive awareness as the maker of history, and the self-
constitution of humanity through labour. When the former is
reduced to the latter, the integral tie between history and freedom
is dissolved.[68]

In critical theory, 'positivism' has a much broader and more
diffuse meaning than it does for most other writers, wider even
than what I have distinguished as 'positivistic philosophy'. This
use of the term has to be understood against the background of
the attempts of the Frankfurt philosophers to effect an ambitious
critique of the tendency of development of Western culture since
the Enlightenment, and indeed in certain basic respects since
Classical times. The progenitors of the Enlightenment set out to
effect the disenchantment of the world, to replace myth by solidly
founded knowledge, and by the application of that knowledge in
technology. In so doing they prepared the way for the domination
of modern culture by technical rationality: the undermining of
Reason against which Hegel struggled and which, with the disintegration of the Hegelian system, became largely lost to
philosophy. In the name of freedom from the domination of myth,
the Enlightenment created a new form of domination, hidden
from view by its own philosophy: domination by instrumental
rationality.

Subject and object are both rendered ineffectual. The abstract self,
which justifies record-making and systematization, has nothing set over
against it but the abstract material which possesses no other quality
than to be a substrate of such possession. The equation of spirit and
world arises eventually, but only with a mutual restriction of both
sides. The reduction of thought to a mathematical apparatus conceals
the sanction of the world as its own yardstick. What appears to be the
triumph of subjective rationality, the subjection of all reality to
formalism, is paid for by the obedient subjection of reason to what is
directly given. What is abandoned is the whole claim and approach of
knowledge: to comprehend the given as such; not merely to determine

the abstract spatio-temporal relations of the facts which allow them just to be grasped, but on the contrary to conceive them as the superficies, as mediated conceptual moments which come to fulfilment only in the development of their social, historical, and human significance.[69]

Critical theory is a defence of just those traditions of philosophy which the logical positivists wished to show consist largely of empty metaphysics. Consequently, it is not surprising that the two schools have kept at arm's distance from one another, and their mutual influence has been slight indeed. However, in recent times, with the increasing strains to which the positivistic philosophy of science has been subject, the influence of the philosophy of the later Wittgenstein and Austin's 'ordinary-language philosophy' in Britain and the United States, and of hermeneutic phenomenology on the Continent, the situation in philosophy (as in social theory) has become much more fluid. Among the younger Frankfurt philosophers, Habermas has been particularly influential in connecting critical theory to each of the types of philosophy mentioned above, as well as to pragmatism – while sustaining most of its established themes. Habermas, together with Adorno, played the central part in the controversy over Popper's views that has come to be called (following the usage of critical theory rather than that of Popper) the 'positivism debate' in German sociology. The debate is an odd one, in so far as none of the participants regard themselves as defending positivistic philosophy, much less describe themselves as positivists; given the standpoint of critical theory, however, in which the term 'positivism' is applied very broadly to traditions of thought that would not ordinarily be thus designated, it is not difficult to appreciate that the contested meaning of the term is at the heart of the matters at issue, not merely a linguistic curiosity of the controversy. The initial origin of the dispute was Popper's presentation of 'twenty-seven theses' on the logic of the social sciences at the meeting of the German Sociological Association at Tübingen in 1961; this was followed by a paper by Adorno. Popper and Adorno did not attack each other's contributions directly, however, and their confrontation only ramified into a wide-ranging debate through the subsequent interventions of Habermas, Albert and others.[70]

In his paper, Popper reiterates his well-known view that the aim of the social sciences is the explanation of conduct through the 'situational logic' of action: that is to say, through the rational reconstruction of the circumstances (goals and knowledge) under which individuals act, and of the consequences of their behaviour. This is an 'interpretative sociology', but not one, according to Popper, that retains any residue of the subjective, empathic qualities with which it has characteristically been associated. It is a 'purely objective method'.[71] As such, it differs in content but not in logical form from the methods of the natural sciences, which Popper elucidates in terms made familiar by the general corpus of his writings. He rejects what he calls 'naturalism' in the social sciences on the same basis as he rejects 'positivism' in natural science: naturalism supposes that sociology begins by collecting observations and measurements, induces generalizations from these which then become incorporated within theories. This derives from a mistaken (positivistic) philosophy of natural science; the 'objectivity' of science lies in its critical method of trial and error. Popper thus affirms his support of 'critical rationalism', meaning by this his advocacy of falsification as the most integral procedure of science.

INDUCTION

Habermas's critique of Popper concentrates mainly upon the limits of Popper's critical rationalism which, according to the former author, still contains a strong residue of positivistic philosophy. Popper's theory of science is an analytical, as opposed to a dialectical, one. Habermas suggests that the 'objectivity' of natural science cannot be transferred directly to the social sciences, since the latter are concerned with a pre-interpreted universe of occurrences: that is to say, with a social world in which the categories of experience are already formed by and in the 'meaningful conduct' of human subjects. Hermeneutic understanding, involving the sustaining of communication between the social scientist and those whose conduct he studies, is an essential element of procedure in the social sciences, and cannot be encompassed by simple appeal to the 'observation' of events in nature, even if transposed as 'situational logic'. To conceive of the aim of sociology as that of discovering laws has the practical implication of making of it a social technology.

In contrast, dialectical theory of society must indicate the gaping discrepancy between practical questions and the accomplishment of technical tasks – not to mention the realization of a meaning which, far beyond the domination of nature achieved by manipulation of a reified relation, no matter how skilful that may be – would relate to the structure of a social life-context as a whole and would, in fact, demand its emancipation.[72]

To accomplish this, a dialectical or critical theory must transcend the boundaries of critical rationalism as expressed by Popper.

The separation between fact and value, or cognition and evaluation, made in positivistic philosophies, Habermas says, condemns practical questions to irrationality, or to the 'closed world' of myth which is supposedly the object of positivism to dispel. Unlike most philosophers, Popper openly acknowledges this by declaring that his adherence to rationalism is an article of faith. This makes the adoption of rationalism an arbitrary initial decision. Some followers of Popper, notably Bartley, have accepted that there cannot be a deductive foundation for rationalism, but have tried to ground critical rationalism by reference to itself: that is to say, by holding that the commitment to critical method as formulated by Popper can itself in principle be criticized.[73] But this will hardly do: Bartley is unable to specify the conditions under which the commitment to rationality would have rationally to be abandoned; this is because what is understood as 'criticism' here is too narrow, and is not grounded in the historical conditions of human social life and communication. Habermas points to the connection between Popper's adherence to a correspondence theory of truth and the thesis of the dualism of fact and value. Popper shields himself against some of the problems which the correspondence theory raises, when combined with his acceptance of the theory-impregnated character of observation statements, by stressing the difference between knowing what truth means and having a criterion for deciding the truth or falsity of a statement. According to the notion of falsification, we cannot have such a criterion or standard of truth; all we can achieve is the progressive elimination of false views. What this involves, however, Habermas says, is the surreptitious incorporation of standards of evaluation that are uncritically taken over from everyday life: the hermeneutic understanding of ordinary language and intersubjective experience is taken for granted. Critical discussion, as formulated by Habermas, involves three uses of language: the description of a state of affairs; the postulating of rules of procedure; and the critical justification of the former two.[74] Criticism thus cannot be terminated within the sphere of science itself, but must concern itself with the standards or values which structure science as one mode of activity among others. So far as the historical context of modern science is concerned, positivistic acceptance of the dualism of fact and value leads to a failure to appreciate that technical rationality supports a system of domination as its legitimating ideology.

Neither Albert, defending Popper, nor Popper himself in his commentary on the debate, accept that their views do place the sort of bounds upon critical rationalism that Habermas claims. According to Albert, the empirical sciences are able to deal with the type of experience Habermas allots to hermeneutics, and can represent these as 'facts' like any others. This is, for Albert, potentially a more profoundly critical standpoint than that of Habermas, since it is a more sceptical one, which finds its critical impetus in the premise that science often shows that assumptions made within the ordinary day-to-day world are erroneous. Popper's theory of science as myth that is self-critical is the only way of avoiding the twin dilemmas of an infinite regress on the one hand, and the supplying of 'foundations' through sheer dogma on the other.[75] Popper's critical rationalism, he repeats, is quite distinct from positivism in all major respects; the critical theorists use the term in such a lax way that they are able to blanket out these differences, and hence obliquely charge Popper with some of the very same weaknesses that he has in fact shown to be characteristic of positivistic philosophy. In his comments, Popper concurs:

> The fact is that throughout my life I have combated positivist epistemology, under the name of 'positivism'. I do not deny, of course, the possibility of stretching the term 'positivist' until it covers anybody who takes any interest in natural science, so that it can be applied even to opponents of positivism, such as myself. I only contend that such a procedure is neither honest nor apt to clarify matters.[76]

Comments on the philosophy of natural science

It would obviously be completely out of the question to attempt in this essay a comprehensive discussion of many of the issues raised by the matters referred to in the previous sections: Hence I shall confine my comments to a few problems in two major categories: the philosophy of natural science, and the relation between the natural and social sciences.

So far as the first of these is concerned, there are two issues raised by the post-positivistic philosophy of science that loom particularly large. One is the status of falsification, as elaborated by Popper and his disciples (particularly Lakatos), and more generally that of deductivist accounts of scientific knowledge, including within this the 'deductive-nomological model'; the other is the problem of the 'incommensurability' of paradigms such as derives from the writings of Kuhn.

Popper's 'solution to the problem of induction', which he has relentlessly advocated from his earlier works, gains much of its attractiveness from its simplicity: the idea that it takes only a single disconfirming instance to falsify a universal statement. But the logic of falsification, he has to admit, is discrepant from the practice. Lakatos's studies, although nominally directed at supporting main elements of the Popperian standpoint, show how wide the discrepancy is. Lakatos distinguishes three kinds of falsificationism: dogmatic falsificationism, and naive and sophisticated 'methodological falsificationism'. The first is the weakest, treating the logical form of falsification as equivalent to its practice: as if a simple observed event, or unequivocally defined finite set of events, provide the means of refuting scientific theories. This is an empiricist version of falsificationism, in contrast to methodological falsificationism, which accepts the theory-impregnated character of observations. All testing of theories depends upon acceptance of a theoretical framework which, in any given context, represents unproblematic background knowledge.[77] Naive methodological falsificationism, however, still maintains the view that theories can be refuted, and therefore should be abandoned, in the light of 'observations' thus conceived. This will not do because a defender of a theory can always, if he is prepared to be ingenuous enough, 'rescue' it from any number of apparently contravening instances. Sophisticated methodological falsificationism recognizes this, and states that there is no falsification where the discarded theory is not replaced by a superior one, where superiority is indexed by the following factors: the second theory has surplus empirical content over the first, predicting facts excluded by or improbable in the light of the theory it replaces; the second theory explains all that was explained successfully by the first; and some of the surplus content of the second theory is corroborated (in Popper's sense of that term). If these criteria are met, in any given circumstance of the abandonment of a theory by another, we may speak of a 'progressive problem-shift'. If they are not met, the problem-shift is a 'degenerating' one; it does not in effect constitute the falsification of the pre-existing theory by the one which supplants it.

Lakatos's sophisticated methodological falsificationism is self-confessedly an attempt to reconcile a version of Popper's philosophy of science with some of the major difficulties created for the latter by the works of Kuhn and others. As such, as Kuhn points out, it actually expresses a standpoint quite close to that of his own.[78] One of the consequences of Lakatos's emendation of Popper is to downplay the decisionism that brooks large in Popper's own writings (which Habermas emphasizes), and to provide standards for the critical comparison of theories; Lakatos argues that such standards, or 'rules of acceptance and falsification' are in fact not provided, or at least are not made explicit, by Kuhn. But the question then arises whether Lakatos, having originally rejected justificationism in favour of fallibilism, has not in the end arrived at a justificationist position, which can better be defended and expanded by discarding falsificationism altogether. For Lakatos admits:

'Falsification' in the sense of naive falsificationism (corroborated counter-evidence) is not a *sufficient* condition for eliminating a specific theory: in spite of hundreds of known anomalies we do not regard it as falsified (that is, eliminated) until we have a better one. Nor is 'falsification' in the naive sense *necessary* for falsification in the sophisticated sense: a progressive problem-shift does not have to be interspersed with 'refutations'. Science can grow without any 'refutations' leading the way.[79]

As Lakatos uses it, 'falsification' a) only applies to the 'degenerating phase of research programmes' (in other cases anomalies are largely ignored, or accommodated to the existing theory), and b) only is effective when a better theory supersedes the existing one. It is clear that here refutation no longer forms the main substance of falsification. Lakatos has to all intents and purposes accepted the two major flaws in falsificationism, where that term is used in a sense that still retains any connection with Popper's critique of inductive logic. These two objections to falsificationism are the following. First, in deciding among theories, scientists do not do what Popper's account suggests: that is to say, look for the most bizarre, 'unlikely' theory on the grounds that it is the most easily falsifiable. Nor could there be any defence of the thesis that they should do so. Popper's usage here seems to trade on two different senses of what is 'unlikely'. A theory may be 'unlikely' in so far as it is highly innovative; or it may be 'unlikely' in the sense that it appears very improbable in the light of what is currently regarded as the relevant empirical evidence. Scientists would be wasting their time if they deliberately sought out as often as they could the latter type of unlikely hypotheses. The fact that they do not, however, indicates that they operate with an implicit notion of inductive inference.[80] Second, as I have mentioned earlier, Popper's attempt to provide a plausible analysis of scientific progress in terms of 'verisimilitude' is unsuccessful, since there is no reason to suppose, within Popper's epistemology, that there is a finite number of potential theories available to interpret any specific range of occurrences.

In rejecting falsificationism, we also at the same time reject the Popperian criterion of the demarcation between science and non-science, and the rigid dislocation between the psychology of discovery and the logic of testing. But how can we do so without reverting to the ideas that Popper set out to criticize: those involved in positivistic philosophies of science? In attempting to provide the beginnings of an answer to this question, it is helpful to reconsider the problems that came to light with early formulations of the Verification Principle, and subsequently with the liberalized version of logical positivism. The early formulations were based upon the thesis, which stands in direct line of descent from Hume and Mach, that the meaning of scientific concepts can always be in principle reduced to empirical observations. The later differentiation between observation and theoretical statements abandoned this standpoint, replacing it with the notion of correspondence rules linking observations and theories; the liberalized model retains the same image of science as a hierarchy of statements built upon a secure foundation of observations. Some of the difficulties created by the distinction between observational and theoretical terms can, as Shapere has pointed out, be linked to this context in which the distinction was elaborated.[81] One such difficulty is that of the ontological status of 'theoretical entities'. What was no problem in the earlier phase of logical positivism emerges as a major obscurity in its liberalized version. A phenomenalist or physicalist standpoint connects observation terms unproblematically to entities that exist; but it is not clear in what sense a theoretical entity such as an 'electron' exists, or is some sort of handy fiction. The 'surplus content' of a theoretical term, i.e. that which cannot be directly expressed in the observation language, is supposed to be created by the place of the term in the deductive hierarchy of statements. This seems to lead to the uncomfortable and unsatisfactory conclusion that, as there is a continuum from the observable to the unobservable, so there is from objects that exist to ones which do not exist.[82] A second, related, difficulty concerns the character of the deductive relations presumed to hold between the levels in the hierarchy of observational and theoretical statements as interpreted axiomatic systems. The 'correspondence rules' that intervene between observation and theory are conceived of in a manner parallel to the interpretation of formal systems of mathematical logic, as rules of logical derivation. But logical connections of this sort are obviously different from the connections that may pertain between entities, such as causal relations; and hence we are again led to conclude that theoretical terms are linked to observational ones in such a way that the former do not refer directly to the properties of existent things.

The outline of an alternative scheme, involving a revised model of inductive inference, is suggested by the writings of Quine, and has been elaborated in some detail by Hesse.[83] This draws upon Duhem's notion that scientific knowledge should be represented as a network of statements, while not accepting some of the aspects of Duhem's conventionalism.[84] Within such a network, what is 'observable' and what is 'theoretical' can only be distinguished in a pragmatic and relative way. The connecting statements in the network are laws, but laws are treated as pertaining to finite domains; hence one of the classical dilemmas of inductivism, that one cannot move from particular statements to universal ones, is superseded, for all inductive inference involves movement from particulars to analogous particulars. Such a view of scientific laws, Hesse argues, does not imply that universal laws are statistical generalizations, or that statistical generalizations are to be regarded as preferable to universal laws in finite domains.[85] Nor does it imply an instrumentalist account of science, but rather a realist one in which the analogical character of theoretical innovation is made central. 'Scientific language', as Hesse puts it, 'is therefore seen as a dynamic system which constantly grows by metaphorical extension of natural language, and which also changes with changing theory and with reinterpretation of some of the concepts of the natural language itself.'[86]

This view of scientific theory does away with the idea of correspondence rules. The network involves observational predicates, which are the 'knots' that attach it to the object-world, but these are not a fixed and invariable foundation; where the knots are depends upon the state of development of the theory and the form

of its language, and they may be altered in the course of its transformation, especially where this is of the 'revolutionary' character
described by Kuhn. Scientific theory does not involve two
languages, a language of observation and a language of theoretical
terms; rather, it involves two overlapping and intersecting uses of
the same language. Nor is there an absolute differentiation
between formal languages of science and natural languages, since
the former proceed by metaphorical extension of the latter, and
of experiences originally organized by the latter in the 'natural
attitude'. In everyday life – and in learning scientific theories –
we manage to get to understand observational terms and use them
in their relevant contexts, but only by at the same time coming
to grasp more abstract terms to which their meanings are connected. If the mode in which this is accomplished conforms to the
process suggested by Quine, then all descriptive predicates, however 'theoretical', are learned in conjunction with definite
stimulus-situations, or through sentences that contain such predicates (or the two combined). No such predicates, however, are
learned by empirical association alone; they do not form an
'independent' class of observational terms such as is presupposed
in positivistic philosophy. What counts as an observational term
cannot be specified without presupposing a framework of accepted
laws, which constitute the integrative elements of the network,
but which in principle and in practice can be radically changed.
It is not possible to know, at any given point of time, which laws
and predicates may have to be revised or discarded in the light of
research findings.

The network model of science provides a way of recognizing
the poetics of theoretical innovation while at the same time offering a mode of distinguishing sense and reference in regard of
'paradigms'. Writings, such as those of Kuhn, which show the
importance of discontinuities in the development of science, push
to the forefront two sorts of problems, each potentially posing
dilemmas of relativism: one concerns how it is possible to make
the transition from one paradigm to another, if they are distinct
and different 'universes of meaning'; the other concerns how it is
possible to sustain a notion of truth, given that the succession of
paradigms involves transforming what are recognized as 'facts'
within divergent systems of theory. The first, the so-called problem of 'meaning-variance', is in some part an outcome of
exaggerating the internal unity of paradigms, or 'frames of mean-

ing' more generally.[87] If paradigms are treated as closed systems of concepts, whose meanings are determined only by their mutual relation within the system, it becomes difficult to see how transference from one paradigm to another is achieved. The mediation of paradigms or frames of meaning should, however, be more aptly regarded as normal in human experience rather than extraordinary; becoming a scientist, for example, involves distancing oneself from common-sense views of the world as part of the process of mastering scientific theories. The capacity to shift between what Schutz calls 'multiple realities', involving the control of allegory and metaphor, is a routine feature of everyday human activity, although placed in relief in so far as it is consciously organized as a process of learning new frames of meaning, or one of becoming able to move from one paradigm to another within the context of scientific activity. In this view the mediation of radically discrepant paradigms, such as is involved in scientific 'revolutions', is not qualitatively different from meaning-transformations required in moving between quite closely related theories; the role of learning by analogy and metaphor is central to both.

The relativistic implications of Kuhn's writing in respect of truth have been a core issue in the debate surrounding his work from the first publication of *The Structure of Scientific Revolutions* up to the present time (although Kuhn himself has consistently rejected relativism in this sense). Such implications also emerge in the writings of some recent philosophers not concerned specifically with the philosophy of science, e.g. in the works of Gadamer in hermeneutics, and those of Winch in 'post-Wittgensteinian philosophy', and are one focal point in the respective controversies to which these have given rise.[88] The source of the strain towards relativism is easy to trace: it derives from the idealist leanings of these authors. If 'paradigms' ('traditions', 'language-games') are treated as constitutive of an object-world, rather than as modes of representing or relating to an object-world, there are as many 'realities' as there are meaning frames. Kuhn has made it clear that he does not accept such a view, without however elaborating an account of what notion of truth should replace the versions of the correspondence theory of truth (including that of Popper) which he rejects.[89]

Hesse has suggested that the network model of science involves breaking with the time-honoured dichotomy between correspon-

78   *Studies in Social and Political Theory*

dence and coherence theories of truth, borrowing elements from
each while discarding some of their traditional features; and that
this position is most appropriately connected to a realist ontology.
Acceptance of the theory-impregnated character of observations
has seemed to some to foreclose altogether the possibility of doing
what scientists usually claim to be doing, that is comparing
different theories in the light of the evidence, since what counts
as 'evidence' is influenced by the theories themselves: the
phenomena can always be saved by the interpretation and reinterpretation of observations. But in this view there lurks a strong
residue of positivist philosophy: a purely instrumental account of
science is the last refuge of the disillusioned positivist. As against
such a standpoint we can pose two integral elements of scientific
procedure. One is an insistence upon the significance of sanctioned
standards of criticism which help to separate science – although
not to demarcate it cleanly – from religious cosmologies. Acknowledgement of the importance of science as self-critique has no
necessary connection with a falsificationist epistemology. Indeed
separating the one from the other helps to add force to Habermas's analysis of the shortcomings of Popperianism, by making it
clear that the 'critical tradition' of science presupposes normative
standards that cannot be validated as such in terms of the procedures of scientific testing, because they are the legitimating framework within which those procedures are organized. The second
point is that the mediation of divergent theories, or paradigms,
involves the conjunction of referential parameters which, given
the normative orientation of science always provide an 'empirical
intersection' subject to disputation in respect of truth claims. This
follows directly from the network model of science. The mediation
of paradigms is a hermeneutic task, in the sense that it involves
the capability of moving between frames of meaning; but such
a capability cannot be acquired purely on the level of intension,
since the terms comprising the network are tied in in a complex
(and variable) way to extensional predicates.

Since the correspondence theory of truth has been traditionally
bound up with positivistic philosophies, it has usually been presumed by critics of such philosophies that rejection of them neces-
sitates discarding it also. There are several features of established
correspondence theories of truth, however, which are the substantial part of the residue of positivistic philosophy, and which can
be separated out without disavowing the correspondence notion

altogether.[90] One is the assumption that a correspondence theory presupposes at least some statements which are founded upon indisputable observations: which are not open to revision. This can be traced in large part to the thesis that the meaning of terms employed in a theoretical language can either be expressed directly as empirical observations, or must rest upon a foundation of such observations. The view of language which this involves is an impoverished one, and muddies over the distinction between the relation of concepts within a theoretical network, and the relation between statements involving those concepts and the object-world. The former relation can be illuminated, in respect of truth-values, by the incorporation of coherence criteria or 'coherence conditions' as these are suggested by the network model. Such coherence criteria cannot be taken for granted here, as in the positivistic scheme, where the connection between concepts is implicitly explained through the operation of correspondence rules. The criteria can be specified as a set of conditions providing for the interrelatedness of concepts within the networks. The interrelatedness of the components of the network only concerns the object-world with regard to its production as a system of classification: as such it pertains to the network as an organizing medium whereby truth as a relation between statements and the object-world is made possible, but does not provide the substance of that relation itself.

Two further assumptions deriving from the association of correspondence theory with positivistic philosophies are that advocacy of a correspondence theory presupposes the explication of 'correspondence' in some more basic philosophical terms; and that such advocacy necessarily involves providing an account of the existence of the object-world itself. The first gets to the nub of the objections that are traditionally raised against correspondence theory, which concern the difficulty of defining what 'correspondence' *is*.[91] The presumption that such objections have to be answered by specifying the nature of correspondence in terms of some other type of relation, however, is bound up with the positivistic view of the character of observation statements, since observation is taken as a more 'primitive' relation than correspondence, i.e. as one to which the latter can be in some way reduced. If we break with such a view of observation statements, we can also reject this mode of treating the correspondence relation; 'correspondence' then becomes the more primitive term, and as such is regarded as a necessary element of the extensional character of a knowledge claim.[92]

The assumption that a correspondence theory has to provide a justification of the independent existence of the object-world is similarly connected with the central concerns of positivistic philosophies, because these are directed towards tying the conditions of knowledge to sensory experience, the latter being taken (in phenomenalism) to actually constitute the object-world. Rejection of positivistic philosophy frees us from the obligation to ground a correspondence version of truth in such a justification, or at least indicates that an account of the concept of truth does not logically entail it. To propose that the network model of science may be conjoined to a realist epistemology is therefore not to claim that the latter is necessarily the only view which could potentially be reconciled with a reworked theory of truth of the sort suggested here. Moreover this in turn would involve a detailed reworking of pre-existing formulations of 'realism'.

The natural and the social sciences

The foregoing discussion of the philosophy of natural science does not provide, in and of itself, an adequate scheme for a treatment of the connections and divergencies between the natural and the social sciences. It rather indicates some elements of an approach to epistemological problems that span whatever differentiations may exist between them. But the formulation of a post-positivistic philosophy of natural science undoubtedly has direct implications for social-scientific method, which has usually been analysed against a background of positivistic philosophy, explicitly stated or implicitly assumed. This is not only true of that tradition of thought I began by discussing, which links Comte, Durkheim and modern functionalism; it also applies to the 'counter-tradition' associated with the notion of the *Geisteswissenschaften*.

The contrast between *erklären* (explaining) and *verstehen* (understanding) as portrayed by Droysen and Dilthey, is at the heart of the tradition of the *Geisteswissenschaften*. In establishing his version of this contrast, Dilthey opposed his views to those of authors, such as Comte and J. S. Mill, who emphasized the continuity of the scientific study of nature and society, stressing instead that the subjective, meaningful character of human conduct has no counterpart in nature. The natural sciences develop causal explanations of 'outer' events; the human sciences, on the other hand, are concerned with the 'inner' understanding of 'meaningful conduct'. But Dilthey also accepted important elements of the ideas of Comte and Mill, accentuating the need to make the human sciences as precise and empirical as the sciences of nature. The differences between the natural and the social sciences concern not so much the logical form of their investigations and their results, as the content of their objects of investigation and the procedures whereby they may be studied.

Some of the main tensions in Dilthey's writings (and in those of Max Weber) stem from his attempt to combine elements of positivistic philosophy with the idealistic conception of 'life-philosophy' taken from the earlier development of the *Geisteswissenschaften* tradition. The 'understanding' of human action or cultural products is held to be, following Schleiermacher, a process of the re-experiencing or re-enactment of others' inner experiences. But at the same time, this process is not one of mere intuition: it is one which must be made the basis of a scientific history, and which consequently forms the centrepiece of the method of the human sciences. Dilthey's term *Erlebnis* ('experience'), as Gadamer has pointed out, expresses the strain between the positivistic and idealistic strands in his works.[93] Unlike the verb form *erleben*, the word *Erlebnis* only became common in historical works in the 1870s, largely because of Dilthey's use of it. The word is more restricted than the other German term that may also be translated as 'experience', *Erfahrung*, and in Dilthey's writings is introduced as the specific focus of the process of interpretative understanding; in understanding the meaning of what another person does, we grasp the content of that person's 'experience' of the world. *Erlebnis* constitutes the fundamental content of consciousness, which Dilthey sometimes refers to as 'immediate lived experience'; it is prior to any act of reflection. The term thus ties together the influence of empiricism (only that which can be directly experienced is real) and the influence of life-philosophy (the meaningful character of human life is given in the inner experience of consciousness).

The critical response to the *Geisteswissenschaften* tradition on the part of the logical positivists, or those close to logical positivism, has been a consistent one. *Verstehen* cannot supply the sort of evidence necessary to scientific research, since it depends upon some sort of empathic identification with others. The observation language of social science must refer to overt behaviour, not to hypothetical states of consciousness. No matter how much one might try to provide a concrete specification of *Erlebnis*, the latter remains inaccessible to the intersubjectively agreed observations upon which all the sciences must depend. The value of *verstehen*, if it has any at all, is as a mode of suggesting hypotheses; but such hypotheses have to be tested against observations of behaviour.[94] In this respect, the views of the logical positivists converge closely with behaviourism in the social sciences.

There are three ways in which this critique of *verstehen* can be assessed: one is in terms of assessing what 'understanding' is; another is in terms of assessing what 'observable behaviour' should be taken to mean; a third is in terms of evaluating the significance of 'subjective' elements in conduct. In Dilthey's works, particularly in his earlier writings, *verstehen* is represented as a procedure, or *the* procedure, whereby the human sciences gain access to their subject-matter; and as founded upon some sort of empathic process of 're-enactment'. The notion that *verstehen* is primarily a mode of procuring data is also taken for granted in positivistic critiques. Thus Abel says that *verstehen* is an 'operation' that produces 'evidence', and goes on to claim that such an intuitional mode of procedure simply begs the question of whether the process of 'understanding' that takes place is a valid one.[95] Such an objection has definite force if the notion of *verstehen* is represented as specific research procedure, and as involving some kind of empathic process; Dilthey indeed did not successfully manage to reconcile subjectivity and objectivity in the manner in which he sought to do, within a framework strongly influenced by empiricism. But the dismissal of *verstehen* as a mere propaedeutic writes off major elements of the *Geisteswissenschaften* tradition; the preoccupation with the 'meaningful' character of human conduct and culture that characterizes that tradition is abandoned in positivistic philosophy, which attempts to reduce this to the content of 'empirical observation'. Hence it is important to recognize that recent contributions from within the tradition, as revitalized by hermeneutic phenomenology, have reworked the notion of *verstehen* in such a way as to detach it from its dependence upon the idea of the 're-enactment' or 're-living' of the experiences of others. Thus for Gadamer *verstehen* is to be treated, not as a special procedure of investigation appropriate to the study of social conduct, but as the ontological condition of intersubjectivity as such; and not as founded upon an empathic grasp of the experiences of others, but upon the mastery of language as the medium of the meaningful organization of human social life.[96]

To associate the notion of *verstehen* with language as the medium of intersubjectivity offers direct points of connection with the post-positivistic philosophy of science. Recognition of the significance of frames of meaning, and of their mediation, appears both in Gadamer and in Kuhn, although in the writings of the former this is incorporated into a broad exposition of hermeneutics. In so far as all 'understanding' occurs through the appropriation of frames of meaning, it is no longer regarded as a procedure that distinguishes the social from the natural sciences, but as common to both. The question of the relation between the social and natural sciences can then be seen in a new light. Natural science involves the development of frames of meaning, organized as networks, and discontinuities in the progression of scientific theories pose hermeneutic problems similar to those relating to the mediation of meaning frames in other spheres of activity. But the social sciences are concerned with a pre-interpreted world, in which meaning-frames are integral to their 'subject-matter', i.e. the intersubjectivity of practical social life. Social science thus involves a 'double hermeneutic', linking its theories, as frames of meaning, with those which are already a constituent part of social life.[97] The ramifications of this, of course, are complex and difficult to trace out, involving identifying the relations between lay beliefs and ordinary-language concepts on the one hand, and the concepts and theories of the social sciences on the other.

Let us move to the problem of what the notion of 'observable behaviour' should be taken to refer to. It should be clear that what has already been said about the reformulation of the concept of *verstehen* connects with this, in so far as it helps to indicate the residual difficulties in the claim of positivistically-minded critics that *verstehen* is no more than a preliminary source of hypotheses that then have to be matched against behaviour. Abel explains this as follows. At the onset of a spell of freezing weather, a man sees his neighbour go out to his woodshed, chop some logs, carry them into the home and light them in his fireplace. He understands what his neighbour is doing as 'lighting a fire to warm himself because he feels chilly'. But he cannot know, it further investigation, that this is correct; the neighbour for example, have lit the fire as a signal of some sort to one else. Hence *verstehen* only provides a plausible hypothesis as to what happened.[98] This conclusion, however, begs one type of question by assimilating it to others. It presupposes that the observer already understands the ordinary language terms 'freezing weather', 'neighbour', 'woodshed', etc. Because such understanding is taken for granted, the question of how it is accomplished is not distinguished from the issues of how behaviour may be characterized, and in what sense, if any, 'subjective' elements are relevant to the explanation of human conduct in the social sciences.

The affiliation of positivistic philosophy with behaviourism stems from a common mistrust of features of conduct that are not 'observable', where the latter term means 'directly apprehended by the senses'. Rejection of phenomenalism or physicalism frees us from some of the restraints of this view, which has never managed to come to terms with the difference between 'behaviour' and 'agency', i.e. between involuntary reactions and acts that are 'made to happen' by the individual. The notion of agency or action has been much discussed in the recent philosophical literature, in some substantial part as a result of the emphases of Wittgenstein's *Philosophical Investigations*. Some philosophers, particularly those strongly influenced by Wittgenstein, have argued that human conduct can be described on two discrete levels, one being that of 'movements', employing something like the language of behaviourism, the other being that of 'actions'. To speak of 'an arm moving up' is to describe a movement; to speak of 'raising one's arm' is to redescribe the movement as an action. But this is misleading, if it assumes that these are two alternative modes of description that are equally applicable to any specific form of human conduct. They are more appropriately seen as rival, rather than complementary, types of predicate: to refer to action as if it were merely (reactive) behaviour is to *misdescribe* it. In the distinction between 'movement' and 'action' there is still a residue of the view that only 'overt behaviour' can be directly observed. But there is no warrant for this, if the positivistic view be relinquished; we observe 'actions' as directly as we do 'behaviour'.[99]

This still leaves unresolved the status of 'subjective elements' in action. Abel's example makes it clear that he is referring to the purposes for which an act may be undertaken: the actor in question lights the fire in order to keep himself from feeling chilly. He employs a behaviouristic terminology in expressing this, and holds that the event of lighting the fire can only be adequately explained when it is made part of a type of deductive-nomological scheme. The explanation takes the following form: low temperature reduces body temperature; heat is produced by making a fire; the 'stimulus' (freezing weather) is connected to the 'response' (lighting the fire) via the generalization, 'those feeling cold will seek warmth'. This, as it were, formalizes the assimilation of reactive behaviour and action. The scheme recognizes no difference between cases in which what Abel calls the 'feeling-states' of an individual are connected by some kind of mechanical effect, and those which are within the scope of his agency. Hence the treatment of purposive components of conduct is thin and barren: purpose or intention appears only as a 'feeling-state' tying stimulus to response. There is no place for a conception of the actor as a reasoning agent, capable of using knowledge in a calculated fashion so as to achieve intended outcomes.

This is one of the major points at which the line of thought running from Comte and Durkheim to modern functionalism, and modern positivistic philosophy as stemming from logical positivism, coincide: in the absence of a theory of action. Each involves a deterministic form of social philosophy, although the logical positivists have regarded as suspect the proclivity of the former for 'holistic' concepts such as *conscience collective, représentation collective*, etc.[100] The writings of Talcott Parsons have played a major part in connecting Durkheim's works to modern functionalism. Parsons has specifically sought to break with some of the main emphases of positivistic philosophy; he has also formulated an 'action frame of reference', originally established in order to incorporate an important element of 'voluntarism' into social theory.[101] But the voluntaristic features of Parsons's scheme turn out to depend mainly upon the Durkheimian theorem that the collective values which facilitate social solidarity are also 'internalized' as motivational components of personality. The attempt to provide a treatment of voluntarism in the context of a theory of institutions becomes reduced to a stress that social analysis needs to embody a theory of motivation, rather than providing a framework that relates motives to the rational monitoring of action.

A developed theory of action must deal with the relations between motives, reasons and purposes, but must also attempt to offer, as functional theorists have always tried to do, an account of institutional organization and change. For if it is the case that functionalism, even in its most sophisticated form in Parsons's writings, has not been able to produce an adequate theory of action, it is also true that those schools of thought which have been most preoccupied with the philosophy of action, including particularly post-Wittgensteinian philosophy and existential phenomenology, have skirted problems of institutional orders and their transformation. I have suggested elsewhere, following Schutz, that the terms 'motive', 'reason' and 'purpose' are misleading as employed in ordinary terminology, because they presuppose a conceptual 'cutting-into' or segmentation of the uninterrupted flow of action; such a cutting-into the on-going course of action is normally made only when an actor is queried about why he acted as he did, when he reflexively categorizes a segment of his action, or when an observer does.[102] Thus it is more appropriate to regard the above three terms as processual ones: the subjective orientation of action can then be regarded as directed purposively in conjunction with on-going processes of the motivation and rationalization of action. The latter implies that the socially competent actor routinely monitors his action by 'keeping in touch' theoretically with the content of what he does; or, expressed in an alternative way, that when asked for an explanation of a specified 'segment' of his conduct, he is able to provide one. The problem of connecting the subjective orientation of action to institutional structures has always appeared an enormously difficult one, but this is at least in some part because 'structure' has usually been conceived of in a fundamental way as a *constraint* upon action. Durkheim explicitly makes this the defining property of social structure separating 'social facts' from 'psychological facts'; if others have been less direct, they have accepted much the same notion.[103] But the structural properties of institutions are not just constraints upon action, they are enabling: a central issue facing social theory in this regard is that of developing a reformulation of the key concepts of 'structure' and 'system' in such a way as to acknowledge the enabling as well as the constraining aspect of institutional forms. In such a conception, the reflexive rationalization of action must be seen as operating through the mobilization of structural properties, and at the same time thereby contributing to their reproduction.[104]

Recognition of the central importance of such an approach to a theory of action involves repudiating the positivistic tendency to regard reflexivity as merely a 'nuisance', and also has direct consequences for the question of the status of laws in the social sciences. Nagel's discussion of self-influencing predictions, referred to previously, is typical in respect of the first of these issues, in so far as reflexivity is treated only from the point of view of prediction, and in so far as it is assumed that its influence is a 'problem' for the social sciences. Even within these terms of reference, however, 'self-fulfilling' and 'self-negating' prophecies do not have, as he claims, direct analogies in the natural sciences. The point is the manner in which such things happen, not the fact of their happening, in society and in nature. That is to say, in the sphere of the former, as contrasted to the latter, self-influencing predictions occur because the predictions made come to be taken over and reacted to as part of the behaviour of reasoning agents: as an element of the 'knowledge' they employ in the reflexive rationalization of their conduct.

Human beings are reasoning agents who apply knowledge of their contexts of action reflexively in their production of action, or interaction. The 'predictability' of social life does not merely 'happen', but is 'made to happen' as an outcome of the consciously applied skills of social actors. But the scope of the reflexive rationalization of action of concrete individuals is bounded, in several ways; each indicates specific matters of concern for social science. One concerns the formalization of the knowledge that is applied in action. In producing a grammatical English utterance, for example, a speaker demonstrates and draws upon knowledge of syntactical and other rules involved in speaking English; but he is not likely to be able to give a formal account of what those rules are, although he does 'know' them, i.e. know how to use them. However the application of such 'knowledge' is made within a parameter of influences that are not part of the on-going rationalization of his action. Such influences include repressions and unconscious elements of personality; but also external conditions, including the conduct of other actors. A third boundary of the reflexive rationalization of conduct is found in the unintended consequences of action. This connects closely to the second, in so far as the production and reproduction of institutional structures appears as the unintended outcome of the conduct of a multiplicity of actors.

A crucial point to recognize is that the boundaries between these three types of unacknowledged conditions of action are fluid, as is the scope of the rationalization of action in relation to them. We then have a basis for an analysis of the question of the status of 'laws' in the social sciences. Zetterberg suggests that there is no shortage of generalizations in social science: the object of the latter should be to make their formulation more precise, and to verify them in the light of empirical research. His discussion follows the characteristic lines of positivistic sociology, in holding that such laws will derive from the progressive accumulation of research, and should form a deductive hierarchy. Adoption of the network model of natural science involves rejecting the latter. We can represent theories in social science, as in natural science, as networks involving laws or abstract generalizations. But in the second of these the network is not in interaction with the object-world it seeks to explain, whereas in the former it is. Generalizations in the social sciences are always in principle unstable in relation to their 'subject-matter' – i.e. social conduct and its institutional forms – in so far as their acceptance alters the relation between the rationalization of action and its unacknowledged grounds. This is distinct from the 'technical' possibilities of intervention in nature offered by laws in the natural sciences. Knowledge of laws in natural science allows men to alter the empirical incidence of the circumstances under which they apply: or, if this be desired, to extend their range. But while knowledge of the laws allows for material transformation in such ways, this does not alter the causal connections involved in or underlying them. In the social sciences, on the other hand, the causal connections that are specified or implied in generalizations depend upon particular alignments of the rationalization of action and its unacknowledged conditions, and hence are in principle mutable in the light of knowledge of those generalizations.

The degree to which this happens, and its consequences, are of course limited by practical circumstances. But however this may be, the implication is unavoidable that the relation of social science and its subject-matter cannot be handled within a differentiation between 'pure' and 'applied' science. In a longer study, discussion of this would mean taking up in a direct way the character of social science as critique, and offering an analysis of the thesis of the dualism of fact and value. For just as the idea of a transcendental language of observation turns out to be mistaken, so also is the idea of 'ultimate values', upon which the notion of the fact/value dichotomy depends: what constitutes a factual statement, and what constitutes a judgement of value, is contextually variable.

Max Weber on facts and values

The metaphysical principle of the logical separation of 'facts' and 'values' has always been closely associated with positivistic philosophies. In the social sciences, however, its strongest and most influential advocate has been Max Weber, who derived it from Kant rather than from Hume. In Weber's writings, the implications of the fact/value dichotomy (or his version of it)[105] are rigorously traced out in respect of a series of problems; I shall treat here only those concerning the logical status of the differentiation of facts and values, and the relation of values within 'calculi' or 'hierarchies' of values.

Weber's insistence upon the logical gulf between facts and values was as oriented to the rejection of two sorts of competing ethical views: theories of natural right, and Marxist theories of the rational progress of history. According to the first, in Weber's words, 'what was normatively right was identical . . . with the immutably existent', while according to the second the 'normatively right' is to be discovered in 'the inevitably emergent'. Each involves an illegitimate extension of the significance of empirical knowledge, for 'it can never be the task of an empirical science to provide binding norms and ideals from which directives for immediate practical activity can be derived'; or alternatively expressed, 'An empirical science cannot tell anyone what he *should* do – but rather what he *can* do – and under certain circumstances – what he wishes to do.'[106] This does not mean to say that empirical knowledge is irrelevant to the pursuit of values.

The relevance of the one to the other, Weber holds, can be explicated in terms of the categories of means and ends. We want things either in themselves, or as means to other objectives that are desired. Empirical knowledge, or the findings of the natural or social sciences, can serve to adjudge the appropriateness of a particular means to a given end. This provides a basis for possible 'indirect' criticism of the end as, for example, 'impracticable' in the specific set of historical circumstances, although it is logically precluded from determining whether or not the end itself should be chosen. Empirical findings can also allow us to specify the consequences which the attainment of an end might bring into being. This too has a practical bearing upon action since we can thereby indicate the likely costs, in respect of the person's other ends, that the achievement of the end in question will incur. Finally, through a process of analysis rather than empirical investigation, we can help a person to clarify the ends he holds by making clear the hierarchy in which they stand. Any claim of ends terminates in an 'ultimate value', or set of 'ultimate values', to which the actor's more specific ends are actually in some part means.

We can summarize this position by saying that, for Weber, empirical knowledge can be placed in the service of practical ends only in an instrumental fashion. The logical disjunction between facts and values, however, does not rule out the disputation of standards of value, which of course Weber accepts as a chronic phenomenon in social life. His point is not in some way to disqualify such debate, but to claim that, in so far as it rests upon conflicting ultimate values, it cannot be resolved by dint of appeal to empirical procedures. We have to 'recognize that general views of life and the universe can never be the products of increasing empirical knowledge, and that the highest ideals, which move us most forcefully, are always formed only in the struggle with other ideals which are just as sacred to others as ours are to us'.[107] Undoubtedly in Weber's writings this theme of the irreconcilable conflict of the 'warring gods', the conflict between the 'demons' that inspire men's practical activities, is directly connected with his stress upon the primacy of power, and power-struggles, in social development. The mutual hostility of the 'warring gods', of divergent systems of cultural values, cannot be resolved by demonstration of the rational superiority of one over the other, but only by the power of a group to impose its will upon those of different persuasions.[108] This is an historical rather than a logically necessary feature of Weber's view, however: for one *could* hold that foremost among one's ultimate values should rank the principle of respect for the validity of contrasting systems of ultimate values to one's own.

In recent philosophical writings, in the English-speaking world at least, criticism of the fact/value dichotomy has been led by authors influenced by the philosophy of language of Wittgenstein and Austin, such as Anscombe, Foot, Searle and others.[109] Searle's work has provoked the most controversy, since he tries to show in some detail how an 'ought' can be derived from an 'is'. According to Searle, the descriptive statement, 'A uttered the words, "I hereby promise to pay you, B, ten pounds" ', in a set of specifiable conditions, leads to the evaluative statement, 'A ought to pay B ten pounds'.[110] The conditions involved are those making the utterance of the first statement the performative of promising (rather than warning, entreating, joking, etc.). Searle's thesis has been attacked on various different grounds.[111] Two of the more important are: that the initial statement conceals an unacknowledged value premise; and that the description of a promise as a binding obligation can be eliminated by rendering it in *oratio obliqua*, in the form, 'people in society C treat utterances of type D as "promises" '.

The first sort of objection has a certain intuitive plausibility about it, since it may seem that all Searle manages to show is that there are linguistic connections between 'promises' and 'obligations': the real moral commitment, it might be supposed, is separate and additional to this. To argue in this way, however, is to miss Searle's basic point, which is concerned with the intimacy of the relation between language and the organization of social life:

I am here challenging a certain model of describing linguistic facts. According to that model, once you have described the facts in any situation, the question of any 'evaluations' is still left absolutely open. What I am here arguing is that, in the case of certain institutional facts, the evaluations involving obligations, commitments, and responsibilities are no longer left completely open because the statement of the institutional facts involves these notions.[112]

Society and language do not exist as object and description of object; language is the medium both of the expression and the accomplishment of normative commitments and transactions. Any literal use of concepts involved in those commitments and transactions implicates the speaker in the social web in which language and conduct are conjoined.

This leads through to the second kind of objection: the notion that we can avoid embodying evaluative connotations in descriptions of social institutions through the 'distancing' effect of *oratio obliqua*. But this presumes that the introduction of the indirect voice makes no difference to the description that is being offered. Such is not the case, as can be shown by reference to a concept that looms large in Weber's writings: that of legitimacy.[113] 'Legitimate', in ordinary usage, means something like 'being in accordance with law or right', or 'serving as justification for'. But Weber does not define legitimacy in this way, since he tries to provide a conceptualization that is neutral in respect of whatever is the content of any specific claims to legitimacy; to do otherwise would be to fail to effect the necessary severance of description and evaluation. Weber defines 'legitimacy' as 'belief in the validity of an order', stressing that 'validity' is anything defined as valid by the members of a given group.[114] If this is an 'empirical' or 'descriptive' concept of legitimacy, then we can infer that an 'evaluative' one would be something like 'justification of the validity of an order'. But 'legitimacy' in fact is closer in meaning to the second rather than to the first. Weber's definition, nominally an attempt to strip the ordinary concept of 'legitimate' of its evaluative content, is really a substantial redefinition. And it is one which, as even a casual glance at Weber's writings on authority shows, he applies only inconsistently, more often than not using the term in the usual manner.[115] It would indeed be difficult and quite unsatisfactory in terms of the sorts of analyses he seeks to develop, were he able to stick carefully to his own version of 'legitimacy'. For, as Schaar has noted, to speak of legitimacy in the usual sense implies the existence of standards external to he who claims it, whereby his claim can be scrutinized or assessed; but this is inconsistent with Weber's redefinition, which reduces the content of the concept to the (necessarily irrational) beliefs of the actors involved.[116]

Let us at this point return to Searle's discussion of promising. A further objection which might be made against Searle is that his position is inherently a conservative one, which forecloses the possibility of critique: that is to say, that it excludes the possibility of anyone holding the view that one should not honour promises. Searle's reply to this is as follows. We must distinguish what is internal to the social practice of promising, and what is not. What is internal to the practice is that promising obligates, and this is hence involved in any description of it. But there is no logical barrier to someone morally rejecting the practice as a whole. There are two different meanings, Searle says, to the phrase 'commit oneself to [accept] the institution of promising'. One is to undertake to use 'promise' in its literal sense; it is quite a different thing to commit oneself to accept the institution where the meaning is 'endorse the institution as good'. This second type of commitment, Searle says, is 'subjective', or 'really a matter of opinion'.[117] But this is not convincing. Here we encounter, in moral philosophy, similar limitations to accounts of meaning-frames inspired by or indebted to Wittgenstein: the strongly defined tendency to take a form of life (in this case the 'institution' of promising) as a given, and to 'read off' meanings from within it, coupled to a disregard for the mediation of forms of life and for their historical development.[118] Searle's discussion is unsatisfactory on two grounds. First, the internal/external distinction upon which his analysis of the evaluative status of the practice of promising depends is not at all as clear-cut as he implies. The obligation or commitment of making a promise does not stand as a part of an isolated 'institution', but is interdependent with other beliefs and practices which influence the operation of 'bonds', 'undertakings', 'contracts', 'liabilities', etc. If there is no precise dividing-line between what is internal and what is external to promising, then Searle's distinction between two *types* of commitment in talking about promising breaks down. But it is also inadequate in the manner in which the contrast between commitments is formulated, suggesting that 'endorsing the institution externally' is 'subjective' or 'a matter of opinion' in a way in which the other type is not. This merely re-introduces the fact/value dichotomy at one step removed.

In order to attempt to meet these difficulties, it will be useful to move on to consider the second element of Weber's views mentioned above: that concerning hierarchies of values, and the existence of so-called 'ultimate values'. First of all it is important to notice a major conceptual confusion Weber makes in developing the position that the relevance of empirical knowledge to the pursuit of values can be expressed as a relation of means and ends. Weber here uses 'ends' as equivalent to 'values' ('value-ideas', 'axioms'). But ends or desires ('aims', 'objectives') are not the same as 'values', in a crucially important respect. Desires are characteristics of the individual personality; moral values or value-standards, on the other hand, are components of an institutional order. There is hardly need to point out that the conflict which can arise between personal desires and moral obligations is a classic concern of philosophy. More important is the fact that desires do not have to be rationalized, whereas value-standards do. In the course of social life, an actor may be called upon to explain why he desires what he desires, but (unless what he desires contravenes some definite value-standard) he can defend a desire merely by saying that he wants to do *x* because he likes doing *x*. This is not the case with value-standards, which are rationally defended (or attacked) in respect of the judgements that are made through and in terms of them: here just 'liking doing *x*' is experienced as a retreat from rational evaluation.[119] In the sphere of both ethical and aesthetic judgements, we differentiate mere personal preference from informed evaluation. The relation between empirical knowledge and values cannot be expressed as one in which the former relates only to 'means' (and the consequences of the achievement of ideals); such knowledge is definitely involved in the rationalization of evaluative statements.

This conclusion can be further supported by an analysis of what Weber calls 'ultimate values'. On examination, these turn out to be as elusive as observation statements in the positivistic philosophy of science. What defines a value as an ultimate value? Weber speaks of ultimate values as involved in both the value hierarchies of individual actors, and those of overall cultures. But we have already seen that the first only makes sense when portrayed as 'ultimate ends' or 'overriding ambitions'; value-standards are not elements of a personal hierarchy in this way. When, however, Weber refers to the 'ultimate values' of cultures, he tends to identify his 'warring gods' with empirically differing cultures. But this does not show that such cultures differ in terms of the *logical* incompatibility of their value-standards: different values are not necessarily different 'ultimate values'. How is a value shown to be an 'ultimate value'? According to Weber's view, if it is not a means to any other values – if it is not dependent upon other values. But what could such a value possibly look like? Let us suppose that 'freedom' is a candidate for an 'ultimate value'. Now the notion of 'freedom', however it be defined, is connected by a multiplicity of ties to other concepts in a language, from which it derives both evaluative and descriptive content, and upon which it is dependent. This suggests it is as misleading to represent the values, or the value-standards, of a society as a hierarchy with an easily ascertainable 'ultimate' baseline as it is to represent scientific theories as hierarchies resting upon an 'indubitable foundation' of theoretically neutral observation statements. A network conception is as appropriate in the case of the former as in that of the latter, and similarly has to be considered from an historical perspective. According to this conception, value-judgements are no more 'arbitrary' than scientific theories, and are always in principle subject to empirical appraisal, although underdetermined by it just as scientific theories are underdetermined by facts. Evaluative appraisal always involves factual elements, so that difference of moral opinion is never merely a clash of discrepant 'ultimate values'. A person may question any particular aspect, or the totality, of the practice of promising, but both involve the (potential) provision of rationalization that is in principle 'justifiable'. It is an elementary qualification to point out that an unprincipled rejection of the need or the possibility of rationalization is irrelevant here. A person *can* of course reject any knowledge-claim, by simply refusing to accept a claim of reasoning while not offering counter-arguments of his own.

2 Functionalism: *après la lutte*

The debate over the merits and shortcomings of functionalism, which overshadowed most theoretical discussions in sociology and anthropology in the 1950s and 1960s, today appears spent. The battlefield is largely empty, even if from time to time isolated bolts continue to be launched. The dust having settled, perhaps this is an apt time to take stock of the residue of the controversy. Although one might argue that the diversity of critical attacks to which functionalism, in its various guises, was subjected increasingly forced its advocates on to the defensive, it would be difficult to claim that the controversy has lost its vigour because one side has retired defeated. Rather, new types of theoretical approach have emerged into prominence, and have caused the focus of debate to move elsewhere. That this should have happened is surely for the most part a blessing: the functionalism controversy was never an enthralling one at best, and – if I may abandon the martial metaphor in favour of another – occasionally plumbed the depths of dull formalism. But it would be a mistake to suppose that all the issues raised can be quietly forgotten. For whatever the limitations of functionalism (and I shall conclude in this discussion that they are decisive and irremediable), it always placed in the forefront problems of institutional organization, and was firmly opposed to subjectivism in social theory. I believe this emphasis still to be necessary, indeed all the more urgent in view of the upsurge of subjectivism and relativism that has accompanied the waning influence of functionalist notions in the social sciences. My aim is not to rescue functionalism from its critics, nor to re-examine the course of the debate as a whole; it is, by identifying certain of the inherent flaws in functionalist thought, to develop the rudiments of a theoretical scheme that can replace it.

The origins of functionalism, in its modern form, are bound up with the advances made within biology in the nineteenth century. If classical mechanics remained the ideal form of a matured science, biology, and more specifically evolutionary theory, became the more immediate inspiration among leading schools of social thought. Comte's works, although antedating Darwin, provided a cogent rationale for the proximity of the relation between biology and 'sociology', and his formulation of 'social statics' was a major influence upon the subsequent spread of functionalist notions, as worked out first by Herbert Spencer, and later by Durkheim. The idea of social evolution, of course, played a basic part in the writings of all of these authors, as did biological analogies borrowed directly to explicate the 'anatomy and physiology' of social life.[3]

Durkheim's works have been without doubt the most important single influence upon the development of functionalism in the present century, in spite of the fact that the only significant explicit discussion of 'functional explanation' offered by him occupies no more than a few short pages in *The Rules of Sociological Method*. The incorporation of these ideas within what emerged as a distinctive, although only loosely knit, school of 'structural-functionalism' in sociology, however, only came about through the dislocation of 'function' from 'evolution'. In Durkheim, the notion of social evolution had already become attenuated. Mechanical and organic solidarity were still treated against a broad evolutionary background, but took the form more of an abstract typological contrast than a connected flow of evolutionary change. The transfer of the concept of function to anthropology, through the agency of Radcliffe-Brown and Malinowski, was directly connected to the repudiation of evolutionary theories. In breaking with the nineteenth-century preoccupation with evolution, these authors reacted specifically against the tradition of speculative attempts to reconstruct the origins of social institutions such as religion, marriage, etc. But they also reacted against 'scissors and paste' ethnology of the sort which, in attempting to chart the stages in the evolution of society, assembled together examples from numerous different societies without regard to the social context in which they were embedded. 'Functionalism' (a name that Malinowski willingly applied to his theoretical views, but which Radcliffe-Brown disliked) had much to do with the origins of modern field-work in anthropology, the emphasis being placed upon studying institutions in relation to social totalities.

Functionalism re-entered sociology when it crossed the

D

Atlantic. Through his teaching while at Chicago, Radcliffe-Brown contributed directly to its influence. But this was, of course, strongly reinforced by the works of Talcott Parsons. Although Parsons studied briefly under Malinowski while in Britain, the themes he developed, and has continued to elaborate through the rest of his career, were closer to Radcliffe-Brown's views. The concept of 'structure', in the work of both authors, was conjoined to that of 'function'. Rather than Malinowski's 'instrumental functionalism', it was structural-functionalism which became, for some three decades the pre-eminent, if never an unrivalled, stream of social theory within American sociology.[4] Structural-functionalism has provided an articulation of functionalist notions that is more coherent and detailed than anything achieved previously; and the majority of its adherents have put forward the claim, in some version or other, that it is *the* theoretical basis identifying the distinctive tasks of social-scientific explanation. Most authors linked to functionalism in this modern form have been to greater or lesser degree influenced by Parsons. But it has become notorious that 'functionalism' is understood in a variety of ways by different authors, both sympathetic and critical. Since Parsons's writings certainly embrace many themes not immediately relevant to a discussion of functionalism, I shall not attempt to confront them directly here. Instead, I shall direct my attention solely to three major contributions from other authors: first, two relatively early sources, R. K. Merton's 'codification' of the tasks of functional explanation, and the subsequent critical emendation of this offered by Ernest Nagel.[5] Although first published in 1949, and thus antedating the main body of the functionalist controversy, for which it was an essential point of reference, Merton's essay was later revised and expanded. More important, it anticipates and in some degree attempts to meet criticisms of functionalism that later became focal to the debate: such as that functionalist schemes allow no mode of approaching problems of conflict, power and so on. Moreover, Merton's work was also of major importance in the reincorporation of functionalism within sociology, the thrust of his argument being that the ideas of Radcliffe-Brown, Malinowski and other anthropological authors provide a theoretical frame for sociology, but only if substantially amended so as to be able to encompass problems that are peculiarly acute in, even if not specific to, the more developed societies.

To these, I shall add an examination of a third, more recent, piece of work: that of Stinchcombe.[6] This is not a contribution to the functionalism debate as such, but it does confront, in a detailed, sophisticated way, several of the same issues, and stands in direct line of descent from Merton.

Merton: functionalism systematized

The themes of Merton's account are, of course, very well known indeed and I shall only briefly recapitulate those elements that are relevant to the arguments I shall develop in the latter part of the paper.

Merton begins by noting the very thing that became the despair of later participants in the functionalism controversy: the 'plenty and variety of functional analysis' (p. 10). But he advises against disillusion; this diversity makes a codification both possible and necessary. A systematization of functional analysis has to connect theory and method: but it must also prove itself in the handling of empirical materials. The latter is given some considerable attention by Merton, who attempts to provide extensive illustration of the fruits of the functionalist orientation – thus differing notably from the more rarified nature of many subsequent commentaries. The main features of Merton's discussion can be characterized as follows. To begin with, certain deficiencies in the pre-existing literature have to be clarified or remedied:

1) The term 'function' has to be precisely defined. It has various different lay uses, e.g., as equivalent to 'public gathering', as well as a technical sense in mathematics. Moreover, just as great a variety of lay terms are often used as synonymous with it: 'purpose' and 'consequence' among others. We must separate out notions that refer to 'subjective states' of actors from those that refer to the outcomes of action. 'Social function', Merton says, 'refers to *observable objective consequences,* and not to *subjective dispositions* (aims, motives, purposes)' (p. 14). What a person intends to achieve may or may not coincide with the outcome of his action.

2) Several of the typical emphases of functionalism in anthropology have to be revised, or rejected altogether. The thesis that society always has a 'functional unity', or implicit harmony, which Merton associates with Radcliffe-Brown, has to be abandoned. Or at least, it cannot be taken as an axiom: the de͏͏

of integration of a society has to be treated as empirically variable. Similarly with the 'postulate of universal functionalism', expressed by Malinowski: the idea that every standardized social practice and cultural item has a function, by virtue of its persistence. Malinowski's assertion of the 'indispensability' of functional needs is also questioned. To claim that, for example, 'religion has certain indispensable functions in every society' hides a confusion: is it the institution of religion, as such, which is necessary to society, or is it the functions it is held to fulfil? To say that the existence of society involves certain functional prerequisites is not the same as to say that certain particular institutions are indispensable, for the same functions may be performed by different institutions.

3) Merton is at some pains to reject the charge that functionalism is inherently 'conservative', a view which, according to him, can no longer be sustained once the emphases noted in the previous paragraph are dispensed with. In documenting this, Merton seeks to show that a revised functionalist scheme, far from being intrinsically conservative, an assimilation of the existent and the inevitable, is fully compatible with the 'dialectical materialism' of Marx and Engels – a demonstration that numerous other authors after Merton have also found it necessary to attempt.[7]

Among the elements regarded by Merton as involved in such a revision, these are the most important:

4) Functions are defined as 'those observed consequences [of standardized practices or items] which make for the adaptation or adjustment of a given system' (p. 43). Function is contrasted to dysfunction, which refers to phenomena that act against the 'adaptation or adjustment' of the system.

5) Functional analysis involves the assessment of a 'net balance of an aggregate of consequences': a particular social practice may, for instance, be functional in some respects, or on certain levels, for the system of which it is a part, and dysfunctional in others.

6) Manifest functions, being 'those objective consequences contributing to the adjustment or adaptation of the system which are intended and recognized by participants in the system' (p. 43) have to be separated from latent functions, which are not intended and recognized.

7) Analysis of the functional requirements or prerequisites of social systems has to be complemented by recognition that there

is a range of variation of functional alternatives. The possibilities of change that exist in any given case, however, are limited by 'structural constraints' deriving from 'the interdependence of the elements of a social structure' (p. 44).

Nagel: a critical emendation

Although Merton's essay has been much discussed, few can have given it as thorough a review as that offered by Nagel, writing as a sympathetic critic concerned to relate Merton's views to concurrent developments in biological science.[8] Nagel begins by drawing attention to a traditional point (noted, for example, by Comte, who regarded biology and sociology as 'synthetic' disciplines, in which there is a 'priority of entity over element', in contrast to the 'analytic' sciences of chemistry, physics, etc.): that functional notions are rare in sciences other than biology. The difference seems to depend upon the fact that biology studies entities that are self-regulating in respect of changes in their surroundings. Functional analysis applies to such entities, regarded as systems, but not to systems which lack self-regulating capabilities.

A main thread of Nagel's argument consists in an attempt to trace through ambiguities which Merton's account, although itself directed to a clarification of previous literature, in Nagel's view leaves unresolved. These concern, to begin with, the significance of 'subjective dispositions' in Merton's discussion. It is not clear, Nagel claims, why – in distinguishing a class of 'manifest functions' – Merton singles out actors' purposes and motives for special attention. Why shouldn't we regard subjective orientations as merely a systemic variable like any other? If 'subjective aim-in-view' is not introduced as such a variable, Merton's distinction of manifest and latent functions is not necessary, since it does not distinguish a type of function; if it is such a variable, on the other hand, the distinction is one between substantive 'items', in Merton's sense, not between types of function. Hempel apparently concludes that it is more useful to consider subjective states as functional variables: one can then trace out the functional consequences of an 'intended and recognized' outcome as potentially different from circumstances where the outcome is not known to those involved. Merton's discussion of functional consequences, Hempel holds, is itself ambiguous. The 'function' of an item could refer simply to a characteristic of a system which it serves to maintain; or to the totality of effects which it produces that contribute to the 'adaptation or adjustment' of the system. But this makes it difficult, perhaps impossible, to employ Merton's notion of a 'net balance of functional consequences', since there is no 'final' or 'decisive' baseline along which this can be judged as a 'net balance'. Functions and dysfunctions are relational, in respect of definite traits of the system which the analyst is interested in explaining.

Nagel concludes by trying to show that Merton's formulations of 'functional alternatives' and 'structural constraints' need elaboration. Merton fails to follow through an implication of his own distinctions here. A 'functional alternative' might refer to an alternative item which fulfils the same function as another – the only sense which Merton considers – or it might refer to an alternative *function*, which (perhaps in conjunction with others) meets certain system 'needs'. The difference is consequential for functional analyses of potential social change: 'structural constraint', if connected only to the first sense, is obviously likely to be more narrowly conceived, and 'conservative', than if connected also to the second.

These points comprise what I take to be the critical import of Nagel's discussion. It is perhaps as well to add, for any reader who is unfamiliar with the essay itself, that Nagel accepts much of Merton's analysis, and is concerned primarily to translate it into a series of formalized propositions.

Stinchcombe: functionalism and theory construction

Stinchcombe's assessment of the logic of functional analysis is of more recent provenance (1968) than those so far referred to. It occurs in the context of an 'eclectic' discussion of method, with functionalism being represented as one strategy of explanation among others: this is the only part of Stinchcombe's work that I shall refer to here.

Functional explanation, for Stinchcombe, is a type of causal explanation within 'multi-component' theoretical schemes. 'By a functional explanation', he says, 'we mean one in which the *consequences* of some behaviour or social arrangement are essential elements of the *causes* of that behaviour' (p. 80). Three causally related links are involved: a 'structure or a structure activity';

a 'homeostatic variable'; and 'tensions' disturbing the relation of the first two. An illustration is offered from evolutionary biology, concerning the activity of the liver in sustaining blood sugar at constant levels. There are wide variations, because of differences in food eaten, etc., in sugar content of blood entering the liver from the digestive system. Hence those animals or types of animals which develop effective livers tend to survive at the expense of those which do not. 'Tension' is a necessary element in this, according to Stinchcombe, since if digestive activity were constant, there would be no selective survival tendency of animals with 'functional livers' to survive. In this example, the storage of sugar represents the structure activity, the blood-sugar level the homeostatic variable, and variations in digestive demands the tension between the first two.

Functional analyses, Stinchcombe suggests, are appropriate in circumstances of equifinality. In closed systems, final states can in principle be explained in terms of their initial conditions. In biological or social systems, on the other hand, a uniform consequence can result from the recurrence of different types of activity. Thus social organizations normally 'try to pursue their goals in the face of uncertainty and variability of the environment', but they do this in different ways: by, for example, attempting to be flexible in response to external changes, by trying directly to control markets, by predictive planning, and so on. 'Such an equifinal pattern suggests a functional explanation of organizational behaviour in terms of uncertainty reduction' (p. 81).

Stinchcombe also takes up the themes of the 'conservative' nature of functionalism, and its relation to Marxism. Like Merton, he argues that the 'conservative cast of functional theory is not logically necessary', although it is 'an inherent rhetorical opportunity in the theory' (p. 91). Such opportunity derives from the possibility of looking upon homeostatic variables as morally desirable, and their upsetting as necessarily unfortunate. Functional analysis can be placed in the service of radicalism by showing which particular structures operate to perpetuate phenomena that are deemed morally undesirable, or which operate to the advantage of sectional groups; 'as Marx realized, some consequences are more consequential than others' (p. 99).

The appeal of functionalism

Before passing to a critical appraisal of these versions of functional analysis, I wish to briefly consider the question: what has drawn so many to functionalist notions or approaches in the social sciences?

As far as the development of functionalism in the nineteenth century is concerned, it is clear, as I have previously mentioned, that functionalist notions gained popularity under the sway of evolutionary biology. If the modern period of functionalism dates from a break with evolutionism, there have been very few functionalists who have abandoned the view that functional analysis in the social sciences shares major logical uniformities with its counterpart in biology. In the three accounts summarized above, for example, Merton draws upon the writings of Cannon, the physiologist, while seeking 'not to backslide into accepting the largely irrelevant analogies and homologies which have so long fascinated the devotees of organismic sociology' (p. 40). Hempel's discussion is explicitly an attempt to clarify Merton's analysis in the light of principles established in macrobiology. Stinchcombe makes use of the writings of the nineteenth-century physiologist, Claude Bernard, whose works in fact had an important influence upon those of Cannon.

There are perhaps three main factors which have stimulated the endeavour to connect up the social sciences and biology. First, simply the wish to demonstrate that there is a logical unity between the social and natural sciences, at least in so far as the latter deal with complex, 'open' systems rather than with closed systems or aggregate populations of elements. It is perhaps worth noting that the initiative has not come only from the sociological side of the fence. Cannon's writings, for example, contain attempts to extend his theories to the explanation of social institutions, using organic analogies very reminiscent of 'organicism' in nineteenth-century social theory. Second, obviously, the belief that it is fruitful, indeed necessary, to regard forms of social organization as integrated unities of interdependent parts. 'Interdependence' is of course variously conceived, but usually centres upon a notion of reciprocal effect: a modification which affects one part will tend to have repercussions on other parts, finally returning to influence the initial source of modification itself. In so far as this sustains equilibrium, homeostatic principles observed in physiology apply also to social systems. Third, the belief that social systems manifest a 'hidden teleology', operating through unintended consequences of social action. Merton's differentiation of manifest and latent functions makes explicit an integral feature of functionalist theory in the social sciences: that social institutions demonstrate a teleology which cannot be necessarily inferred from the purposes of the actors involved in them. In sociological functionalism, this *always* depends ultimately upon the thesis, or the assumption, that there are 'social needs' which have to be met for society to have a continuing existence. The teleological element in this is normally presumed to be similar to that operating in biological adaptation: 'needs' are defined in terms of the facilitation of 'survival value'.

There is a fourth factor, of a different type: that of ideological persuasion, a matter never far from the centre of the functionalism debate. It is not my aim in this paper to give detailed attention to this, although I shall want to revert briefly to it at a later stage. But one should point out that the conventional claim that functional notions are only contingently associated with 'conservatism' in politics is hardly borne out by their history in social thought. 'Conservatism', as I have suggested elsewhere,[9] is not really an appropriate word to use in this connection; but from Comte to Spencer to Durkheim to Parsons the terminology of functionalism has appeared in conjunction with a rejection of radical politics in favour of the necessary reconciliation of progress with order. Such an observation of course, as Merton remarks, does not show that functionalism is logically tied to such views.

What I propose to do in the sections which follow is provide a *decodification* of functional analysis, an examination of certain fundamental weaknesses in functionalism in the concern, not to reject its emphases in favour of subjectivism, but to encompass them within a different theoretical scheme. To approach this task, concentrating principally on the three accounts I have singled out for special attention, I shall group the shortcomings of functionalism under the following headings: functionalism and intentional or purposive action, the explanatory content of functionalism, and the concepts of 'system' and 'structure'.

Functionalism and intentional action

First decoding: *functionalism is a teleological theory which, however, allows for only a limited and deficient explication of purposive human action.* Every major school of social theory incorporates an explicit or implicit treatment of intentional action. That often characteristic of functionalist schemes treats purposes as the 'internalization' of social values: a view that shows a direct line of continuity from Comte through Durkheim to its fullest elaboration in Parsons. I have criticized this elsewhere, and shall not confront it directly here.[10] Nor would it be strictly relevant to do so, since the problems I wish to analyse can be illuminated clearly enough through the more partial treatments of purposive action that occur in the three versions of functionalism outlined above.

Nagel criticizes Merton's distinction between manifest and latent functions, which is essentially an attempt to separate out 'subjective' intent and 'objective' consequences, on the basis that 'it is not evident why it ["subjective disposition"] should be listed under a special category in what is ostensibly a *general* paradigm of functional analysis' (p. 82). Stinchcombe apparently agrees with this because, while he does not refer to Nagel, he specifically regards 'motivation' as prototypical, although not exhaustive, of functional analysis. To say that someone 'wants' something, according to Stinchcombe, is to say that 'the consequences of behaviour are its principal cause' – for him the basic feature of functional explanation. Wanting, he claims, is equifinal by definition, although of course the reverse does not hold.

Now the difficulty of regarding 'subjective states' of wanting as a special instance of functions in general is precisely that which Merton established the differentiation of manifest and latent functions in order to avoid: that is, to distinguish the teleology of intentional action from the hidden teleology of its consequences. Stinchcombe is surely wrong to treat wanting as a case of a general class of situations in which 'conduct is caused by its consequences'. For in intending and wanting it is not the achieved *circumstance* which is the cause of the behaviour, but the desire for its realization. A person may want something, but not initiate any course of action to obtain it: and *per contra* a want may be realized by a concurrence of events that is quite independent of the conduct of the actor. More important, however, for functional analysis is the fact that a course of action undertaken with certain intentions, or with a particular motivation, may have outcomes quite different from those anticipated by the person undertaking it. The thesis that action has 'unintended and unrecognized consequences', as Merton makes clear, is a necessary element of any sort of even modestly sophisticated scheme of functional analysis in the social sciences, as contrasted with functional analysis in physiology.

Nonetheless, Merton's distinction between manifest and latent functions itself does not withstand close scrutiny. For Merton uses the terms 'unintended' consequences, on the one hand, and 'unrecognized' or 'unanticipated' consequences, on the other, as synonymous.[11] But they are not synonymous. The difference is one of great consequence for a theory of social action, but it is one which is glossed over in most schools of social theory that tend towards determinism.[12] A useful example to take to illustrate the issue is Durkheim's formulation of the concept of suicide, and the part which it plays in his attempted explanation of the phenomenon. Durkheim defines suicide, famously, as 'all cases of death resulting directly or indirectly from a positive or negative act of the victim himself, which he knows will produce this result'.[13] What Durkheim does here is quite consciously – perhaps one should say intentionally – obliterate the difference between doing something knowing a particular outcome will come about, and doing something intending that a particular outcome will come about.[14] Not to acknowledge a distinction between these inevitably tends to define as irrelevant to the causal explanation of action the intentions, reasons, motives, etc. with which people act. One may undertake a particular course of conduct knowing that a particular outcome may result, but either be indifferent to that outcome x because one is really after something else, y; or because one is prepared to seek to achieve x in spite of knowing that y, an undesirable outcome, may result. On the one hand, the accomplishment of self-destruction is what the actor wants and intends to achieve through his act; on the other, it is what he is prepared to accept, or risk, in order to accomplish some other end in view.[15]

While Merton may accept that there is a difference between 'intending' and 'anticipating' that a consequence of action will occur, he makes nothing of it, since he brackets the terms together and uses them interchangeably. It is perhaps the fact that he does use *both* terms in this way, however, which makes the distinction between manifest and latent functions appear to be more novel in the pre-existing functionalist literature than in fact is the case. The differentiation between purpose and function, after all, had already been made strongly by Durkheim, in *The Rules of Sociological Method* as well as more substantively in his other works. But 'manifest function' means more than this, implying that not only *a*) the person knows that the consequence he intends to bring about will come about, but also *b*) he knows in what way that consequence is functional (or dysfunctional in the case of 'manifest dysfunctions') for a given social system. One should notice that, while bracketing 'intending' and 'anticipating' together so far as *a*) is concerned, Merton's discussion is ambiguous in relation to *b*). The same differentiations, however, apply. Does one have to undertake an action intending (and knowing) that the particular *function* should be a consequence, for a 'manifest function' to exist? The whole matter becomes further complicated if one attempts to connect it to Merton's concept of a 'net balance of functional consequences'. An actor may intend (and know about) only some of a ramified series of functional and dysfunctional consequences of what he does, thus possibly mingling all four potential combinations of the manifest/latent/functional/dysfunctional distinctions. Finally, yet one more ambiguity, and an important one. Merton does not specify *who* has to intend and know what the function of an item is for it to be a manifest function. Manifest functions, he merely says, are those intended and recognized 'by participants in the system' (p. 43) to which they relate. But which participants? One may say: those whose conduct produces the functional consequences in question. Perhaps this is what Merton means. But the circumstances may easily exist in which some participants in a social system know what the functional consequences of the behaviour of *others* are, and where those others themselves are ignorant of such consequences. The significance of such a situation is not hard to see: it is likely to contribute to, and express, the power of those who are in the know over those who are not.

All this shows that what initially appears as a neat, inclusive distinction, between manifest and latent functions, papers over various basic problems concerning the nature of intentional action and its implications for social theory. I shall take up some of these problems subsequently. What I have said so far, however, only bears on the manifest/latent distinction, not on the concept of 'function' itself, to which I shall now turn.

The explanatory content of functionalism

Second decoding: *functionalism is a social theory in which the teleology of the capital term, 'function', is either redundant or falsely applied.* The question: is functional analysis causal analysis? is one that has frequently cropped up in the functionalism debate. The issue is connected to the traditional division drawn between 'statics' and 'dynamics', to use the terms Comte adopted from physical theory or, in the terminology of Radcliffe-Brown, 'synchronic' versus 'diachronic' studies. Durkheim has not been alone in regarding such a differentiation as coterminous with that between function and cause. It is, of course, precisely the teleological flavour of the notion of function that is involved here: for how can a consequence of behaviour also be its cause? It might seem, therefore, that we have to reserve causal explanation, as Durkheim did, for historical accounts of the origins of things, where effects follow causes in linear sequence, treating functional explanation as distinct.[16]

Such a view *prima facie* can be supported by the sort of physiological examples favoured by functionalists. That is to say, it might be held that the functions of an organ in the body can be examined without much, or perhaps without any, reference to the causes which brought that organ into being. But this is a specious idea. A statement such as 'the function of the brain is to co-ordinate the nervous system' can in principle be transposed into causal statements about the typical effects of a definite range of events in the brain upon a range of events in the rest of the nervous system.[17] The three versions of functionalism I have looked at above all seem to agree that 'function' can be rendered as 'functional effect' or 'functional consequence'. What is the difference, then, according to them, between functional explanation and causal explanation?

Stinchcombe provides the most explicit answer to this. Functional explanation is a particular *type* of causal explanation; and he has no hesitation about saying that it is an 'inverted' one in which the consequences of action are 'elements of its causes'. What this really turns out to refer to is the operation of a homeostatic process, explicated in terms of equifinality. Now Stinchcombe says that 'it is not true that equifinal causal structures indicate wanting' (p. 82). This is consonant with his analysis because, for him, just as functional explanation is a subtype of causal explanation in general, so wanting is a subtype of functional explanation in general. This implies, although Stinchcombe does not say so, that 'wants', or the properties of actors, can be distinguished from 'system needs'. For homeostasis, if it is to be made the exemplar of functional analysis, has to be conjoined to a notion of system. A homeostatic process is essentially one of adjustment in which, through the operation of what Stinchcombe calls a 'causal loop', change in one element causes change in another, causing in turn a readjusting change in the first element. But such a phenomenon cannot be called 'functional' unless it is related in some way to the survival or continuity of a more inclusive system within which it exists. Otherwise the term 'function' itself is again redundant. A homeostatic process is merely a set of causes and effects unless it can be said to be operating with some 'end in view' or to fulfil some need.

I want to claim two things: that the notion of system need, even in biology, always presupposes the existence of 'wants' or 'interests'; and that, in the social sciences this has the result that the idea of system need – on which, as I have tried to show, the use of the concept of function depends – is characteristically an illegitimate or falsely applied one. Functional analysis in the setting of biology or physiology normally takes the form of showing that a given homeostatic mechanism in the body involves adjustments that contribute to the life of the organism as a being. This takes for granted, I think, that the organism 'wants' or 'has an interest' in its continuing survival, and is why it sounds odd to apply the term 'function' to purely mechanical systems even though they may involve homeostatic processes. We may speak of the function of the mainspring of a watch, or of the carburettor in an engine, but these are man-made systems, where the element of need or interest exists as a latent human one. Social systems, unlike organisms, do not have any need or interest in their own survival, and the notion of 'need' is falsely applied if it is not acknowledged that system needs presuppose actors' wants. Many functionalists, of course, have recognized that system needs depend upon wants and some, like Malinowski, have made this the centrepoint of their analyses. But if there are no independent system needs, as we have seen, the notion of function is superfluous, for the only teleology that has to be involved is that of human actors themselves, together with the recognition that their acts have consequences other than those they intend, and that these consequences can involve homeostatic processes.

This leaves aside, however, a further way in which 'survival' constantly enters into functionalist theories, on the basis of analogies with evolutionary biology. It is not fortuitous that while the origins of modern structural-functionalism coincide with the abandonment of nineteenth-century evolutionary anthropology, some of its foremost exponents have recently returned to evolutionary models. I shall argue in the next section that functionalist interpretations of social change are closely bound to evolutionary conceptions. At this point I shall consider evolution only from the point of view of the possible significance of 'survival functions'. It is frequently proposed that, although it is inadvisable to claim that social systems have 'needs' as such, we can nevertheless assume that every society which has enjoyed a continuity of existence over time *must* have met certain exigencies. A correlate viewpoint holds that the introduction of particular social forms or institutions in certain societies, that are lacking in others, gives them 'adaptive advantages' and thus promotes their survival at the expense of those others.

This latter viewpoint might initially appear to be quite different from that emphasizing 'functional prerequisites', but it can be demonstrated that it is not. Upon examination, what are claimed as functional prerequisites turn out to fall into two types. First, there are those that are actually tautologous: that are logically implied in the conception of 'human society'. Two functional prerequisites distinguished by Aberle *et al.,* for example, are those of 'shared cognitive orientations' and 'role differentiation and role assignment'. In every society, 'members must share a body of cognitive orientations' which, among other things, 'make stable, *meaningful,* and predictable the social situations in which they are engaged'; and in every society, there must be different roles that are regularly performed, 'otherwise everyone would be doing everything or nothing – a state of indeterminacy which is the antithesis of a society'.[18] But the authors have already defined 'society' in such a way as to make these conceptually necessary elements of it. A society is defined as a 'self-sufficient system of action', where 'action' is implicitly conceived of in the Parsonian sense as 'meaningful' conduct oriented by shared expectations, and 'system' as stably connected activities – exactly the characteristics later treated as if they were empirically independent. Second, there are factors which enhance the 'adaptive capacity' of societies: e.g. the development of modes of 'provision for adequate relationship to' the material environment, or 'the prescription of means for attaining the socially formulated goals of a society and its subsystems'.[19] Such elements still seem to hover perilously near to being logically involved in the authors' concept of 'society', but if we accept that they are separable, then they are no longer 'prerequisites', but 'adaptive advantages' which some societies are liable to develop more effectively than others. Take as an illustration the first of these. If this means nothing other than the provision for material production sufficient to keep the members of society alive, and to allow them to reproduce their numbers, it relapses into the former type of logical implications of the notion of society: for the authors have previously held that a society involves 'a self-sufficient system of action which is capable of existing longer than the life-space of an individual, the group being recruited at least in part by the sexual reproduction of the members'.[20] If it means more than this, on the other hand, it must involve reference to such characteristics as, for instance, the capacity of a society which has developed a particular technology to *dominate* its environment. But this will give it an 'adaptive advantage' over others.

The concepts of 'system' and 'structure'

Third decoding: *functionalism, or more specifically structural-functionalism, mistakenly assimilates the notions of system and structure.* Both the terms 'system' and 'structure' appear chronically in the literature of structural-functionalism. Neither, of course, is specific to it: 'system' is used in various branches of contemporary social and biological theory, as in so-called 'General Systems Theory'; 'structure' appears almost everywhere, but has also been used to designate a particular tradition of thought, 'structuralism'. Now if there is anything distinctive about the latter, it is that 'structure' is employed in an 'explanatory' way, in the sense that underlying or deep structures are held to explain surface appearances.[21] This is not the sense of structure that is the characteristic usage in structural-functionalism, where the term usually refers to a discernible pattern in surface particulars: i.e. in social relations in general, or the organization of institutions within a global society. In structural-functionalism, it is 'function' rather than 'structure' that is called upon to play an explanatory role in directing our attention beyond surface appearances.

As structure is used in a diffuse way to refer to 'discernible pattern', it is not surprising that in the functionalist literature it is often used as more or less equivalent to 'system'. If a pattern represents an enduring arrangement of 'parts', then one only needs to inject 'functioning' into it for the 'structure' to become a system. Perusal of Merton's text, for example, shows that he often uses structure and system as interchangeable terms. Moreover, while he devotes a considerable segment of his discussion to trying to correct indiscriminate uses of function, he does not provide a comparable analysis of structure, the meaning of which is largely taken for granted in what he has to say. Much the same is true of Stinchcombe's discussion. The term structure appears throughout his book, but is not subjected to special analysis as function is; in the sections dealing with functional explanation, 'structure' is treated as synonymous with 'behaviour', 'pattern of behaviour', and 'structure activity'. Although structural-functionalist writers tend to assimilate structure and system in their actual usage, there is a distinction between the two which is frequently recognized by them in a formal way. It is essentially one that corresponds to that between anatomy and physiology in the study of an organism. If 'structure' refers to anatomical pattern, 'function' to how that pattern operates, then 'system' refers to the former two taken conjointly. Merton perhaps implicitly accepts something of this sort. In the course of his attack on the 'postulate of functional unity', for example, he quotes (p. 16) from Radcliffe-Brown who says that a social system is 'the total social structure of a society together with the totality of social usages, in which that structure appears and on which it depends for its continued existence'.[22] Merton does not, however, comment upon this explicitly.

Now the use of structure as 'anatomy' can perhaps be defended in biology, where, say, the skeleton, or organs such as heart and liver, are in a way 'visible' independently of their 'functioning'. Even here it may be difficult to suppose that one could describe what they are independently of what they do, and there is a sense in which they are continually 'in process': that is to say, continually changing, being built up, eroded away, etc. The distinction does not in fact apply at all in social life where 'patterns' only exist in so far as they are constantly *produced and reproduced* in human action. There is no place for the two terms structure and system as these are ordinarily applied in 'structural-functionalism': this is why, even where authors set out to employ such a distinction, they tend to collapse the one into the other. There can be 'structures' that 'function' in particular ways, but then there is no need or place for an independent concept of system; there can be 'systems' that 'function' in definite ways, but then the notion of structure is superfluous. For 'structure' means, in the usage of structural-functionalism, something akin to 'stable, patterned arrangement'. When this refers to social life, it cannot but refer to regularities that are reproduced in human action or interaction; that is, structure and function necessarily presuppose each other. 'Functioning structure' – organized, patterned elements in interaction – means nothing different from 'system', since the notion of interdependence of parts is clearly already there in the idea of stably reproduced patterns, as interconnected elements. Structure and function cannot here be treated as 'independently observable' phenomena, that can then be taken together as 'system'. What makes some sense when one considers a dead body, which is observed independently of its 'functioning', or an unwound watch, which can be observed when it is not working, makes no sense at all when applied to human society, which only exists *in* its 'functioning'. (To forestall misunderstanding, it should perhaps be said that nothing of importance hinges on the meaning of 'observe' here: one could easily substitute 'conceive of'.)

I shall claim that we need to salvage the concepts of both structure and system, although not that of function itself; but that each of these terms has to be understood differently from their characteristic use in structural-functionalism. The notion of system which usually appears in structural-functionalist writings is inadequate not only because it is not clearly distinguishable from structure, but because of the particular way in which 'interdependence of parts' is typically conceived. Both Merton and Stinchcombe treat the latter as satisfactorily explicated on the basis of a homeostatic model borrowed from biology: Stinchcombe in particular makes the homeostatic process or causal loop integral to his definition of function. The use of the term system, and the not infrequent appearance of terms such as 'feedback' in functionalist writings make it seem that functionalism and systems theory are more or less the same: as if functionalism is simply an early anticipation of systems theory. But homeostasis, as various commentators have noted, is not the same as feedback proper.[23] The former involves only the blind adjustment of system parts such that a part in which modification is initiated is 'readjusted' as an outcome of the process that it sets in motion. This is a more primitive process than is involved in feedback, which relates to the existence of self-regulating systems governed by cybernetic controls. Nagel is the only one of the three authors discussed previously to specifically link his analysis to the idea of self-regulation, but he once more in fact only concerns himself with homeostasis or 'compensating mechanisms' (p. 78).

Let us assume that Stinchcombe's formulation of homeostatic process as the operation of causal loops is adequate. Homeostasis then can be distinguished from self-regulation in systems, the latter involving the selective filtering of 'information' that is applied to control 'lower-level' mechanical processes. Homeostatic processes of the mutual adjustment of causally connected elements may or may not be cybernetically regulated in this sense. I want to claim that this distinction is an important one, which can be profitably applied in social analysis, and that is largely neglected in the functionalist literature (although not by Parsons, whose standpoint in this respect I shall come to immediately). But this certainly does not mean that one can accept what some have called General Systems Theory, as it stands, as appropriate for the social sciences. Von Bertalanffy counterposes the 'mechanistic' views characteristic of nineteenth-century physical science with the twentieth-century perspective of systems theory. The former represented things as the 'aimless play' of atomic elements, without direction or *telos.* General Systems Theory, however, reintroduces teleology into natural science, and thereby closes the distance between nature and society.[24] But purposiveness, in human affairs, cannot be grasped in terms of a version of teleology which merely involves cybernetic control through the feedback of information. This is a point of quite fundamental importance, which will have to be further amplified subsequently when I return to questions posed earlier about intentions or purposes. For the moment I shall be content to make the assertion that purposiveness in human action involves not just self-regulation, but self-consciousness or reflexivity.[25] 'Purpose' in relation to human affairs is related in an integral way to the possessing of reasons for action, or to the rationalization of action in processes of self-reflection. In this respect it is quite different from whatever teleology is involved in self-regulating processes in nature.

A specific version of cybernetic information control has quite recently been introduced into the social sciences by Parsons. Here it is assumed that hierarchies of control can be discerned in social systems, in which the controlling elements are values, with social, economic relations, etc.[26] being regarded as the 'lower level' processes subject to such governance. This has an obvious affiliation with Parsons's well-known emphasis on the significance of 'shared values' in social cohesion, and is essentially a reworked version of the theory of social integration developed earlier in his writings. It is therefore subject to all the objections which a diversity of critics have made of that theory. But, however that may be, 'values' cannot anyway serve as 'information regulators' in the sense which is demanded in systems theory: as control centres which process information so as to regulate feedback.

To summarize at this point: we can distinguish in the abstract three types of circumstances that may prevail in social systems relevant to the 'interdependence of parts', which are progressively more inclusive. These are, shortly expressed, regulation, self-regulation, and reflexive self-regulation. The first, as a homeostatic process, involves a loop of causally interrelated elements; the second, a homeostatic process that is coordinated through a control apparatus; the third, the deliberate accomplishment of such coordination by actors in the pursuit of rationalized ends. An example of the first might be the 'vicious cycle' of circumstances whereby poverty, poor educational achievement, and unemployment are interconnected, such that any attempt to modify, say, educational attainment tends to be defeated by the causal loop that interconnects the three states of affairs. In so far as, for instance, the state is an institution through which the relations between all three are processed and stabilized, as is suggested in Marxist theory, there is a situation that approximates to the second type. The third circumstance only comes into being when men purposively control the processes involved in cognizance of the conditions under which they occur, thus subordinating the

teleology of feedback to their own *telos.* Such might be the d
ference between the state in nineteenth-century capitalism, ai
the 'planning state' of modern times.

Let me now turn to the concept of structure. What I have said
so far carries the implication that while one may, if one likes,
continue to talk of social 'patterns', this should be taken to refer
to the stable reproduction of systems of social interaction. If the
notion of structure should not be used in this sense, where it is
superfluous, how can it be otherwise conceptualized? A ready
answer might seem to lie in the concept as employed in 'structuralism'. Although the latter term has been used in a diffuse
variety of ways, 'structure' here refers to something like an underlying message or code explaining the surface appearance of myths,
linguistic expressions, etc. The specific difficulty with this version
of the concept of structure is that it dispenses with the active
subject altogether. Although I have argued that functionalism is
unable to develop a satisfactory treatment of intentional action, it
certainly does not ignore it: Merton's distinction between manifest
and latent functions is directed precisely to such an end. No
correlate analysis appears in the structuralist literature in which,
if human subjects appear at all, it is typically only in such a guise
as the nebulous shapes of Althusser's 'bearers' (*Träger*) of a mode
of production. Many structuralists have made a virtue of necessity.
Thus Lévi-Strauss, commenting on Ricoeur's characterization of
his work as 'Kantianism with an absent subject', willingly accepted
the designation.[27]

I shall offer no particular defence of the claim that any such
approach to social theory is at best partial, and that action – and
reflexivity – has to be regarded as central to any comprehensive
attempt to provide a theoretical explanation of human social life.
At the same time, it is of the first importance to avoid the relapse
into subjectivism that would attend an abandonment of the concept of structure. How can we reconcile a notion of structure with
the necessary centrality of the active subject? The answer, I think,
lies in the introduction of a series of concepts that are not found
either in functionalism or in structuralism, together with a reformulation of 'structure' itself.[28] These other concepts are those of
the *production and reproduction of society; structuration;* and the
duality of structure. Once we finally drop, once and for all, misleading analogies with the visually easily represented 'anatomical
structure' of organisms, we are able to realize the full import of

the fact that social systems only exist in so far as they are continually created and recreated in every encounter, as the active accomplishment of subjects. Where this has been acknowledged theoretically in existing schools of social theory, it has only been at the expense of the recognition of a structural dimension – as in 'symbolic interactionism'. Let us at this juncture reconceptualize 'structure' as referring to *generative rules and resources* that are both applied in and constituted out of action. Under the heading 'generative rules' I group two analytically separate types of rules: semantic and moral. Semantic rules include those of syntax or grammar but also, equally importantly, the totality of largely implicit, taken-for-granted rules that structure everyday discourse and mutual understandings of action as 'meaningful'. Moral rules include any sort of rule (or formalized legal statute) generating evaluation of acts as 'right' or 'wrong'. By 'resources' I mean whatever possessions (material or otherwise) actors are able to bring to bear to facilitate the achievement of their purposes in the course of social interaction: that therefore serve as a medium for the use of *power*. Rules and resources must be regarded as both the media whereby social life is produced and reproduced as ongoing activity, yet at the same as produced and reproduced by such activity: this is the crucial sense of the 'duality of structure'. Structure is the generative source of social interaction but is reconstituted only in such interaction: in the same way as a spoken sentence is both generated by syntactical rules and yet by virtue of this serves to participate in the reproduction of those rules.

The senses in which I am using the terms 'structure' and 'system' demand a concept of *structuration*: this can be used effectively to connect the two. To examine the structuration of a social system is to examine the modes whereby that system, through the application of generative rules and resources, is produced and reproduced in social interaction. Social systems, which are systems of social interaction, are not structures, although they necessarily *have* structures. There is no structure, in human social life, apart from the continuity of processes of structuration – unlike in the case of organisms where, in a certain way I have noted earlier, 'structure' can be considered independent of 'function'.

In this concluding part of this section, I want to revert to a brief consideration of functionalist accounts of social change.

Critics of functionalism have not infrequently asserted that it cannot supply a theory of conflict, or of social change. This is easily shown to be mistaken. If the 'postulate of functional unity' is rejected, as it is by Merton, and a central place is accorded to the concept of dysfunction as well as that of function, the result is a quite sophisticated approach to sources of social strain that may be important in stimulating change. But all I have earlier said of the concept of function also applies to that of dysfunction: if the first is redundant, so is the second. I shall shortly suggest a terminology for analysing sources of strain that can conceptually handle the sort of problems to which Merton applies the function/ dysfunction opposition, so rather than consider that in further detail here I shall turn to what seems to me to be the proto-typical functionalist account of change: the theory of social evolution. Merton's account belongs to the period when notions of social evolution, as a consequence of the emphases of Radcliffe-Brown and Malinowski, were temporarily under a cloud. Their later re-emergence, in the hands of Parsons, Eisenstadt and others attests to their integral connection with functionalism generally.

The nature of the connection is not difficult to tease out, although obviously the versions of evolutionary theory adopted by such authors have differed considerably. There are perhaps two levels at which the implicit or explicit dependence on biological models has had clear consequences in functionalist theory in the social sciences. The first involves an analogy with the growth of the individual organism, rather than with evolution of species as a whole. In most complex organisms, such as the human body, growth involves progressive differentiation rather than intermittent, radical transformation. Hence *one* consequence has been that models of social change as involving the differentiation of system parts in progressive and continuous fashion have often been popular among functionalist authors, and the image of such progressive differentiation towards increasing complexity is *one* meaning that the term 'evolution' has had in the social sciences. However the view of social change as progressive differentiation can readily go along with a broader treatment of evolution as involving discontinuities, on the basis of a parallel with the emergence of new species in biological evolution. Change equals differentiation except when interrupted by major phases of transformation which involve the appearance of new 'social species-types'. Now there are many objections which can be made against the use of evolutionary models in the social sciences, even where these do not involve assumptions of unilateral development. One is the difficulty of defining species-types: animal species have definite and easily identifiable characteristics, for the most part, and there are usually very large numbers of members of a species. In the case of human societies, distinctions between 'types' are much more difficult to draw with any precision; and no type has more than a limited number of known members. But I shall not be especially concerned with this kind of objection, which may or may not be conclusive if pursued in detail. Instead I want to concentrate upon the dependence of evolutionary models on the notion of 'adaptation' to an externally given 'environment', and the consequences of this for the type of theory of social change that tends to emerge. The idea of adaptation to environments is central to most models of evolution in the social sciences because, as with biological evolution, it is held that the survival, and thus overall development, of different forms of human society can be explained in terms of differential adaptive capacity to external exigencies. Just as problems arise in designating 'social species-types', there are difficulties here in giving any sort of precision to the key terms 'adaptation' and 'environment', since the latter does not always mean, in functionalist theories of evolution, 'physical environment'. Ignoring these also, I want rather to point to three ways in which, even if such difficulties can be satisfactorily resolved, evolutionary theory in the social sciences which involves the notion of adaptation is deficient. (In saying this I am leaving open the possibility that there may be evolutionary models that can be generated from non-functionalist schools of social thought, such as Marxism, which have a different basis.)

The three problems at issue are the following: *a*) 'Adaptative success' in the struggle for survival is treated as the explanatory element in the theory of social change: the sources of stimulus to change thus tend to be regarded as exogenous. An evolutionary standpoint of this sort is hard to reconcile with, say, Merton's scheme of functions versus dysfunctions in a 'net balance of functional consequences', that is, with internally generated change that originates in clashes between classes or interest groups.[29] *b*) Evolution in the animal world operates blindly, as the outcome of 'successful' mutation. Such a model transferred to human society cannot cope with the distinctive characteristic of the latter: purposeful intervention in the course of social development in the attempt to consciously control or direct it. *c)* A connected point: the relation of human society to its material environment is ill-conceived as one of mere adaptation. Animals, as Marx pointed out long ago, simply 'adapt' to the environment, accepting its exigencies; where animals produce, they do so mechanically, and their production does not constitute a significant intervention in nature. But human beings actively transform nature, and subordinate it to their own ends.

A recodification of basic concepts for social analysis

Having decodified 'functional explanation', let me recodify a series of basic concepts which, I want to claim, supersede functionalism without abandoning to the four winds the sorts of theoretical tasks which Kingsley Davis once claimed are so integral to sociology that it and functionalism are one and the same.[30] I shall first set out a general scheme, and then detail some of its implications.

Functionalism, and the broad-ranging traditions of social thought influenced by it, originated in a view of human social activity which has become so integral to 'sociology' – the very term coined by Comte himself – that one can see a definite plausibility in Davis's claim that the two are identical. This is a view which seeks to discover the causes of human action in features of social organization, and consequently persistently dismisses agents' intentions and reasons – in short, what I call the rationalization of action – as irrelevant to the explanation of what they do. In Comte, what is nominally a project directed to the attainment of human freedom, in the escape from the mystifying bonds of religion, eventuates in the discovery of a new form of bondage: to the 'higher reason' of society itself. Thus Comte's 'sociology' rediscovered religion having initially proclaimed the arrival of human emancipation from its fetters. If the theological penumbra of functionalism, still clearly discernible in Durkheim, has been progressively stripped away in modern structural-functionalism, the residue of Comte's theme of 'progress with order' remains. In so far as it does remain, the thesis that functionalism is ideologically neutral, that it can be applied equally to 'conservative' or to 'radical' ends, is belied. Merton's account, it is clear enough, is one of the most liberal versions of functionalism.

(*Structural-*)*functionalist theory*	*Theory of structuration*
Basic concepts:	Basic concepts:
A. system	A. system
B. structure	B. structure
C. function/dysfunction	C. structuration
D. manifest/latent functions	D. production and reproduction of society
Explication	*Explication*
A. System = interdependence of action, conceived of as homeostatic causal loops	A. System = interdependence of action, conceived of as (i) homeostatic causal loops; (ii) self-regulation through feedback; (iii) reflexive self-regulation
B. Structure = stable pattern of action	B. Structure = generative rules and resources
C. Function = contribution of system 'part' in promoting integration of system Dysfunction = contribution of system 'part' in promoting disintegration of system	C. Structuration = generation of systems of interaction through 'duality of structure'
D. Manifest function = intended (anticipated) contribution of action to system integration Latent function = unintended (unanticipated) contribution of action to system integration Distinction also in principle applicable to dysfunction	D. Production and reproduction of society = accomplishment of interaction under bounded conditions of the rationalization of action
	Additional concepts:
	E. Social integration/system integration
	F. Social conflict/system contradiction

His version of the 'structural constraints' on the possibili
deliberately engineered social change is quite easily sep
from functionalism as such – and in any case he does not
generic specification of what they are.

In place of the central concept of the social (functional) determination of action, the theory of structuration begins from the
concepts of the production and reproduction of society. That is to
say, social interaction is regarded as everywhere and in all circumstances a contingent accomplishment of actors: and as a skilled
production which is sustained under conditions of the reflexive
rationalization of action. The purposive component of human
action has no counterpart in nature, since the teleology of human
conduct is carried on within the context of a reflexive awareness
of reasons that is intimately and integrally interwoven with 'moral
responsibility' for activity. I have already pointed out that those
schools of social theory which have recognized such distinctive
characteristics of human conduct, such as 'symbolic interactionism', have shirked analysis of structures – perhaps because
the latter appear, in their connotation in functionalism, as basically 'constraining' influences on behaviour. Another way to put
this is to say that symbolic interactionists have concerned themselves with the production of society, as a skilled accomplishment
of actors, but not with its reproduction. The theory of structuration treats the reproduction of systems of interaction in terms of
the duality of structure, whereby the structural generation of
interaction is also the medium of its reproduction. This breaks
completely with the abstract dichotomy of 'statics 'and 'dynamics',
or 'functional' versus 'historical' explanation, typical of functionalism. Change is regarded as inherent in every circumstance
of the reproduction of a system of interaction, because every act
of reproduction is *ipso facto* an act of production, in which society
is created afresh in a novel set of circumstances. It also makes
power an axial feature of all social interaction, since reproduction
always involves the use of (generalized) resources which actors
bring to any social encounter.[31]

While the notion of function is redundant to the theory of
structuration, that of 'social integration' can still be regarded as a
basic one – together with the further one of 'system integration'.
If the former concerns integration within systems of interaction,
the latter concerns the integration *of,* or 'between', systems of
interaction. The notion of integration needs to be given some

attention. Integration should not be treated as, as such, equivalent to 'cohesion', the latter referring to the degree of 'systemness' of parts, as expressed in terms of any or all of the three levels of interdependence. Integration is most appropriately used to refer to the degree to which each part of a social system has direct ties or interchanges with every other part. The integration of social systems is always crucially connected to the distribution of power within them. This is easily clarified, at least on a conceptual plane. 'Ties' or 'interchanges' in the above sentence should not be regarded as mutually equivalent: that is to say, such ties normally involve imbalanced exchanges in terms of resources that are applied in interaction.[32]

The separation of 'social integration' from 'system integration' was introduced by Lockwood in the context of a critique of Parsonian functionalism.[33] Although not strictly implied by the logical issues I have discussed so far, the distinction is an important one, because it bears directly upon difficulties that have long been associated with functionalism, although in this case more with the versions of Durkheim and Parsons than with that of Merton. The difficulties in substantial part stem from the tendency of such authors to focus upon the integration of the 'individual' in 'society' as the overriding problem for functional analysis, regarding 'society' as any and every form of social interaction from the single encounter up to the global social order. This has three consequences: *a*) for these writers social integration, that is the conjunction of the behaviour of individual actors within reproduced systems of interaction, depends primarily upon the moral coordination of their acts. Since this is applied as a theorem to 'society' generally, it follows that the integration of the global order (system integration) itself depends upon a *consensus universel* – a notoriously suspect view that Merton certainly distances himself from. *b*) As the emphasis is placed above all upon the integration of the 'individual' in 'society', via processes of moral socialization, there is great difficulty in dealing conceptually with sectional group interests and conflicts. The only theoretical avenue for explaining conflict is in terms of lack of moral regulation of individuals by the community as a whole: in other words, the theory of anomie. *c*) Since the only 'interests' that tend to play any significant part in this type of perspective are those of either the 'individual' or 'society' (the latter being conceptualized as functional needs), little conceptual place is found either for *divergent* interpretations of 'normative elements' founded on clashes of group interests (such as class interests), or for adherence to moral obligations founded upon 'pragmatic acceptance' rather than 'internalized moral conviction'.

A distinction between social and system integration helps to overcome such shortcomings, because we can hold that modes of social integration are in definite ways different from those of system integration. The theory of structuration suggests a treatment of social integration that contrasts rather profoundly with that characteristic of the 'normative functionalism' of Durkheim, Parsons and others. Such authors concentrate upon 'internalization', meaning basically the 'internalization of values', in explaining the reproduction of forms of interaction through purposive conduct: the values that provide the cohering moral consensus also figure as internalized, motivating elements in the personalities of the actors. The theory of structuration differs from this standpoint in two main ways: *a)* The explanatory schema of 'internalization' is a deterministic one in which, for all Parsons's stress upon a 'voluntaristic' conception of action, interaction does not appear as negotiated and contingent. For this we substitute the view that interaction is a skilled accomplishment, reflexively negotiated against the backdrop of the rationalization of conduct. *b)* In contrast to the thesis of 'internalization', which tends to operate with a gross notion of 'motivation' as the 'subjective component' of action, a differentiation is made between *motives, reasons* and *intentions or purposes* in action. Motives refer to wants (conscious or otherwise) involved in the impulsion of conduct. To suppose that this is all there is to the 'subjectivity' of action, however, is to ignore the reflexive monitoring of conduct that distinguishes specifically human behaviour from that of the animals. By the rationalization of action I mean the capability of all ('competent') human actors to control their activity through a chronic awareness of its conditions and consequences, thereby connecting wants to intentions, to what they actively seek to attain in interaction with others.

In social integration, the 'parts' are purposive actors. In system integration, the 'parts' are collectivities, or systems of social systems. The sense of 'part' is not easy to explicate in either of these cases, although I shall not deal here in any detail with the issues involved, which have been much discussed in the literature on 'methodological individualism' and its critique.[34] What I have to say here, however, and in what follows immediately, presupposes a definite stance on these issues. Those who have advocated methodological individualism, in one version or another, have frequently regarded functionalism as one of their major targets of critical attack. In so far as they object to notions such as 'system need', I regard their criticisms as entirely justified. In so far as they object to the use of notions such as 'collectivity' or equivalents altogether, or regard them as shorthand descriptions of individual action, their position is untenable. What I have designated as the structural components of social action are not properties of individuals,[35] but of collectivities or social systems. This can be illuminated by reference to speech acts and language. Speech acts are always the situated products of particular actors, and presuppose, for example, knowledge of (ability to use) syntactical rules whereby those acts are generated; but those rules, as such, are properties of the language community. To avoid the reification potential in such phrases as 'properties of the collectivity', however, it is essential to stress that such properties exist only in and through their reproduction in concrete acts.

It should be clear from what I have said previously that the distinction between social and system integration does not depend upon supposing that the first involves 'subjective' elements (purposes, etc.), while the second relates to the 'objective' consequences of action. We must reject the idea that social integration concerns 'social processes seen . . . from the point of view of actors', while system integration treats social processes 'from the "outside" so to speak, from the point of view of the social system as a functioning whole'.[36] This is not the case, however, with the second conceptual distinction I propose to suggest: that between social conflict and system contradiction. In discussing social conflict, one has to be careful to recognize the difference between 'conflict of interests' or 'division of interest', and active conflict or struggle. In referring to 'conflict' here, I mean the latter of these. Conflict may involve the confrontation of either individuals or collectivities but, as I specify it here, necessarily entails conscious struggle, in which such confrontation enters into the rationalization of conduct of at least one – normally both or all – of the parties concerned. It is not important for the generalized analysis I am offering here to indicate anything about the sources of social conflict, save to point out that conflict is not, as power is (the application of resources in purposive action), integral to every social relation. While all cases of conflict involve the use of power, the reverse does not hold.

Now we know that conflict in this sense is not the same as what Merton means by 'dysfunction', even though he gives the latter concept prominence in order to break with the 'postulate of functional unity' and to show that a functionalist schema can cope with the analysis of tensions and strains in society. 'Dysfunction' is not equivalent to 'conflict', of course, because the former is tied to the same explanatory exigency as that of function: system needs, or the adaptive success of the system. The idea of dysfunction is also treated by Merton as a basis for dealing conceptually with the complexity of the advanced societies: the object of functional analysis is to trace out a 'net balance of functional consequences' that stem from a given social item. This view initially seems an attractive one, especially when set against the 'normative functionalism' of Durkheim and Parsons. But on closer examination, its weaknesses are apparent. The difficulty of applying the notion of a 'net aggregate of functional outcomes' is already pointed out by Hempel, and it is definitely a logical deficiency. But if this is abandoned, further problems ensue. Although it seems a straightforward pairing of concepts, the function/dysfunction relation is in fact asymmetrical in terms of the logic of functional explanation. Without the notion of system need, the homeostatic casual loop involved in 'function' does provide (one type of) explanation of why a social practice persists. But, stripped of any connection with 'system need' or 'functional prerequisite', the notion of dysfunction explains nothing at all. That is to say, it does then become equivalent to conflict – or covers that as well as what I shall now characterize as system contradiction.

By 'system contradiction' I mean a disjunction between two or more 'principles of organization' or 'structural principles' which govern the connections between social systems within a larger collectivity. Two such structural principles might be, for example, those of the bonded allocation of labour characteristic of feudalism, and the free mobility of labour stimulated by emergent capitalist markets, the two coexisting within post-feudal society in Europe. Stated thus shortly, system contradiction sounds identical to 'functional incompatibility' within the language of functionalism. To make clear its distinctiveness from the latter, it is essential to point out that the existence of a structural principle *always* presupposes an explicitly or implicitly acknowledged dis-

ibution of interests on the level of social integration. Once we
ave dropped any notion of system need, it is evident that there
can be no talk of system contradiction without the presumption
(on the part of the theorist) of identifiable division of interest
(which in turn presupposes mutually exclusive wants) between
actors or categories of actors. It is this and only this which makes
structural principles such as those mentioned above *contradictory*:
the example presumes that certain actors (entrepreneurs) have
interests in promoting the free mobility of labour, while others
(feudal landowners) do not. The important point is that the
existence of system contradiction does not inevitably imply the
occurrence of social conflict, as I have specified the latter notion;
the connection is a contingent one.

This is an apposite point at which to return to the problem of
purposive action, since in that great traditional rival to functionalist theory, Marxism, comprehension of the system contradictions
of capitalism, and their translation into active struggle, is regarded
as the very crux of contemporary historical potentialities of transformation. Reflexivity and the rationalization of action are thus
in this respect central to Marxism, at least in its less mechanistic
forms. But, with few exceptions,[37] those sympathetic to or
influenced by Marxism have not attempted to pursue these into
the theory of action as such. While functionalism, in its various
versions, always involves reference to intentional action, which is
contrasted to the hidden teleology of function, it has not produced
an account of the *transformational capacity* of self-reflection
within human affairs. The theory of structuration, however, is predicated upon just such an account, which in conclusion can be
represented briefly as follows. The production and reproduction of
society is everywhere and always a skilled creation of situated
actors, grounded in the reflexive rationalization of action. But the
rationalization of action is bounded. There are three basic
respects in which we can explicate the aphorism that, 'while men
make history', they do not do so universally 'under conditions of
their own choosing': in respect of unacknowledged factors of
motivation (repressed/unconscious wants); in respect of the
structural conditions of action; and in respect of unintended consequences of action. The latter two are those which concern us
here. For the structural conditions of action are constraining
elements in human conduct only in so far as they are themselves
unintended consequences, rather than the intended instrument of

the realization of ends. This is why it is important to separate out the 'recognized' or 'anticipated' consequences of action from their 'intended' consequences. For human freedom consists, not in merely knowing the consequences of action, but in applying that knowledge in the context of the reflexive rationalization of conduct.

Notes on the theory of structuration

Everything that has a fixed form, such as the product, etc., appears as merely a moment, a vanishing moment in . . . [the] movement . . . [of society]. The direct production process itself appears only as a moment. The conditions and objectifications of the process are themselves equally moments of it, and its only subjects are the individuals, but individuals in mutual relationships, which they equally reproduce and produce anew . . . in which they renew themselves even as they renew the world of wealth they create.

MARX, *Grundrisse*

Linguists commonly recognize three sorts of activities in which the speaker of a language engages: he is able to produce 'acceptable' sentences, to 'understand' sentences, and make judgements about 'potentially acceptable' sentences.[38] This is a useful classification when applied to the activities of a social actor more generally: the study of speech and language provides us with important insights into the conduct of social life, not because the latter is like a language or can be represented as an 'information system', 'sign system', etc., but because language is such a central feature of social life that it exemplifies certain characteristics of all social activity. The three types of linguistic activity mentioned above are what a person 'knows' when he knows how to speak a particular language. Similarly, what an actor 'knows' when he knows how to sustain social encounters with others within a specific community is how to produce 'acceptable' modes of action, to 'understand' both what he himself says and does and what others say and do, and to make judgements about 'potentially acceptable' forms of activity. 'Acceptability' here has to be taken to

E

involve two elements (which are not always empirically discrete):
the identification or typification of 'meaningful acts', and the
normative evaluation of such acts. The capability of judging
potentially acceptable activities within the context of interaction
with others is basic to the reflexive monitoring of conduct, and is
characteristically applied as part of the rationalization of action;
but it is also crucial to social research itself, as a means of acquiring the mutual knowledge[39] necessary to generate 'adequate'
characterizations of social conduct.

The production of interaction can in this way be treated as an
active, contingent accomplishment of social actors, grounded in
the reflexive rationalization of action, and located contextually.
A crucial move in social theory, however, concerns the conceptual
transition between production and reproduction. Most leading
schools of social theory divide between those which opt for a
voluntaristic approach (often connected to subjectivism), and
those which adopt some version of social determinism. Neither is
able satisfactorily to reconcile a theory of action with an acknowledgement of the fundamental importance of institutional analysis
in the explanation of human social conduct. Both voluntaristic
and deterministic schools of social theory actually tend to culminate in a similar viewpoint in this respect: one which identifies
'structure' with 'constraint' and thereby opposes 'structure' to
'action'. Placing the notion of what I have called the duality of
structure as central conceptually, connects social production and
social reproduction by rejecting these oppositions. Structure enters
into the explanation of action in a dual way: as the medium of its
production and at the same time as its outcome in the reproduction of social forms. Thus the study of social reproduction cannot
be conceived as the aggregation of numerous 'productive acts',
which tends to be the conclusion that voluntaristic forms of social
theory lead to; nor, on the other hand, can the production of
action, as a rationalized accomplishment, be treated as merely
'structurally determined'. Marx has some apt comments on the
first of these positions, discussing the conditions involved in the
reproduction of capital. Such conditions, he says, can only be
grasped if we concern ourselves with 'the ensemble of social production'. We must consider, 'not the single capitalist, and the
single labourer, but the capitalist class and the labouring class,
not isolated acts of production, but capitalist production in its
full continuous renewal, and on its social scale'.[40] As Balibar

points out, Marx here characterizes the isolated act of production 'twice negatively': 'as something which is not repeated and as something done by an individual'.[41] However, Balibar, following Althusser, treats this as a basis for proclaiming a particularly direct form of structural determinism, in which actors appear merely as the 'bearers of a mode of production'.

Clarification of the implications of the above paragraph demands two things: a formal consideration of how the term 'structure' is to be applied, and an amplification of the content of a theory of structuration. If 'structure' is to be used not to refer to 'patterns of social relationships', but rather to refer to rules and resources, we obviously then have to specify how the latter terms are to be used – and how they connect to the notion of 'system'. What are rules, and what are resources, in this terminology? I shall subsequently distinguish two types (which in actual social life may only represent two aspects) of 'rules', but for the moment I shall confine my attention to general remarks. A preliminary approach to explicating a notion of 'rule' that will be appropriate here can be derived from Wittgenstein's analysis of 'knowing a rule'.[42] A player in a game knows a particular rule of the game, when he knows 'how to play according to that rule', when he knows 'how to go on'.[43] The rules involved in a social activity are not like those of most games in one crucial respect: that they are more frequently the subject of disputation over their central character or legitimacy; but this is not relevant at this stage of the discussion. To know a rule is to know, then, what one is supposed to do, and others are supposed to do, in all situations to which that rule applies, or potentially applies. A person may grasp a rule through observing regularity in what people do; but a rule as such is not a generalization of what people do. A rule can be formally stated as an abstract precept of the form, 'when in situation $a, b, c \ldots$, activity $n, m, u \ldots$ is appropriate or called for'. To apply a rule is to generate a form of ('meaningful') activity. This does not imply, however, that 'meaningful' action can be simply equated with 'rule-following' conduct, as Winch holds.[44] One reason for this is that 'what happens' in any given situation of the application of rules to generate social interaction depends on the resources that those who are party to that interaction are able to mobilize in the encounter. 'What happens' here has to include not just the 'outcome' of interaction, in respect of motivations that participants bring to it, but in principle may concern the very nature of that interaction itself. For if knowledge (mutual knowledge) of rules is the condition of the production of interaction, it is not in and of itself a condition of how those rules are 'interpreted' or are made to 'count'. These latter depend upon the relative influence that those who participate in the interaction bring to bear upon its course. The resources thus mobilized may be of many different kinds; all that needs to be said at this juncture is that a 'resource' is any kind of advantage or capability which actors may draw upon to affect the character or the outcome of a process of interaction.

It may still sound odd to claim that the notion of 'structure' can be most usefully applied in social analysis to refer to generative rules and resources. But it is not a particularly idiosyncratic usage, for the following reasons. First, it should be emphasized that social rules are not to be treated as properties of specific actors, but only of collectivities. It may indeed be true, if Wittgenstein's arguments about the impossibility of a private language are correct, that the very notion of a rule as an 'individual property' is logically contradictory.[45] Second, application of the concept of 'structure' in the sense I wish to suggest, can only be carried through in conjunction with that of 'system', and more specifically with that of 'systems of social interaction'. Rules and resources are not distributed in a random form in society, but are coordinated with one another, in and through the coordination of the systems of interaction in whose production and reproduction they are implicated. Third, this usage does not imply that structure is inert. Rules and resources are the media of the accomplishment of social interaction, and as such are constantly embroiled in the flux of social life.

Let us try to lend some substance to these formal considerations. A representation of the duality of structure in social interaction can be given as follows:

INTERACTION	communication	power	morality
(MODALITY)	interpretative scheme	facility	norm
STRUCTURE	signification	domination	legitimation

All processes of the structuration (production and reproduction) of systems of social interaction involve three elements: the communication of meaning, the exercise of power, and the evaluative judgement of conduct. The three terms on the lowest line refer to analytically distinguishable aspects of structure. Structure as signification involves semantic rules; as domination, unequally distributed resources; and as legitimation, moral or evaluative rules. Rules and resources are properties of communities or collectivities rather than of actors. Hence I use the terms 'interpretative scheme', 'facility' and 'norm' to refer to the knowledge and capabilities which actors are able to call upon in the production of interaction.[46]

The application of semantic rules as interpretative schemes in actual contexts of interaction normally draws heavily upon tacit knowledge. The fact that such knowledge has been 'taken for granted' by social researchers, just as it is by lay actors in their day-to-day life, undoubtedly has hindered this being made available as a phenomenon for study.[47] Moreover, since semantic rules are often in a way 'familiar', because they are tacitly employed by members of a community, their formal elucidation as precepts may appear trivial or banal. Under the heading of 'semantic rules' I include all types of rules that are drawn upon as interpretative schemes to make sense of what actors say and do, and of the cultural objects they produce. Some important aspects of the application of interpretative schemes (typifications) in everyday life have been well analysed by Schutz.[48] But the tacitly known rules involved in 'meaningful' interaction also overlap with those involved in the encoding of information in symbolism and in myth, which are presumably transformational in character.[49] Under the heading of 'moral rules' I classify all types of rules that are drawn upon as norms in the evaluation of conduct. Winch has argued that an indication of whether behaviour is 'rule-following' is given by whether or not it makes sense to ask of that behaviour, 'Is there a right and a wrong way of doing it?'[50] I want to say, however, that there are two senses in which one may distinguish 'right' (acceptable) and 'wrong' (unacceptable) ways of doing things, corresponding to the differentiation of semantic and moral rules. One is that an act may be appropriately described or identified; the other is that it may be evaluatively the 'right' or 'wrong' way to behave in a particular set of circumstances. It is obviously important to recognize that interpretative schemes and norms interlace in actual conditions of social life. For how an act is evaluated depends upon how it is characterized, both in terms of what an actor 'did' and what he 'intended to do'.

The latter comment connects directly with the significance of the use of power in social interaction. I shall make no attempt to classify substantive forms of power relation here: the facilities that may be brought to a situation of interaction range from command of verbal skills to the application of means of physical violence. The capabilities that an actor has to influence the events involved in a sequence of interaction depends upon the resources he is able to mobilize. 'Resources' I treat as properties of structures; actors 'possess' resources in a parallel sense to that in which they 'know' rules. This is clear enough in the case, for instance, of the mobilization of authority rights in the context of interaction, where such rights 'belong' to the individual actor only in the sense that he can – in principle – demand and obtain certain responses from others. Authority is a structured resource that can be potentially drawn upon by actors to influence the conduct of others. But the same holds true of many (not all) capabilities that are seemingly wholly 'individualized'. Thus command of verbal or dialectical skill as a facility uses as a resource knowledge of (acceptable) language structures. In its aspect as resources, power may be defined as 'transformative capacity'.[51]

While social systems only exist in so far as they are continually produced and reproduced via the duality of structure, the conditions influencing such processes of structuration can be analysed as 'impersonal' connections. But generalizations which establish such connections are inherently unstable in respect of the shifting compass of the rationalization of action. The conceptions of structure, and structural causation, involved here cross-cut the traditional lines of the debate over the status of methodological individualism. Social systems only exist as transactions between actors; but their structural features cannot be explicated except as properties of communities or collectivities. The debate has not led to much in the way of any definite outcome in some degree because its participants have followed conventional assumptions in not recognizing a distinction between system and structure.

3 Habermas's critique of hermeneutics

Habermas's writings are still only poorly understood in the English-speaking world. This is in part because they are often treated as merely a latter-day offshoot of the so-called 'Frankfurt School', whereas in fact there are major differences between the work of Habermas and that of the 'older generation' of Frankfurt philosophers. Another reason is to be found in the opposition of certain Marxist authors who have dogmatically rejected the strongly marked revisionism integral to the whole of Habermas's endeavours, rather than attempting to give them the detailed consideration which they deserve. There is, however, a third factor involved also. Habermas's writings draw extensively, albeit critically, upon streams of thought which Anglo-Saxon philosophy has for the most part held at arm's length: in particular, Hegelianism and the tradition of the *Geisteswissenschaften*.[1] Here I shall use Habermas's critical connection with the latter as a mode of entrée into his work and its own critique.

Gadamer and hermeneutics

The tradition of the *Geisteswissenschaften* or 'hermeneutic tradition' has always been more or less closely tied to idealism in philosophy, although not specifically to Hegel's 'objective idealism', which it antedates. If there is a central unifying notion involved, it is of course that of *verstehen*. *Geisteswissenschaften* was a term coined by the German translator of J. S. Mill to render the latter's 'moral sciences'. Dilthey, whose earlier work culminates the first phase of development of the hermeneutic tradition, and whose later writings presage the more recent version of hermeneutics as formulated by Gadamer, was by no means wholly opposed to Mill's views. While insisting upon the differentiation of *verstehen* (understanding) and *erklären* (explanation) as established by Droysen, Dilthey was as sympathetic as Droysen to the need to bring into being a precise science of history. An emphasis upon the necessary subjectivity of human action was to be complemented by an acknowledgement of the demand that the study of human conduct meet similar standards of 'objective' assessment as those paramount in the natural sciences. For the early Dilthey, *verstehen* was conceptualized as involving *Erlebnis*, the 're-living' or 're-enactment' of the conduct by the historical analyst. The difficulties of achieving a satisfactory reconciliation of this, as depending upon an imaginative grasp of the subjective experience of others, with an objective foundation of the human sciences comparable to that achieved in natural science, are evident enough. Dilthey's struggle with them led him to move away from his early position. Max Weber, who from the beginning rejected the idea of the causal exclusiveness of natural science as favoured by Dilthey, also tried to distance his version of the logic of *verstehen* from the notion of re-living. That he was unsuccessful however is indicated by definite paradoxes to which his views give rise.[2]

The more recent revival of the hermeneutic tradition, as led by Gadamer, has been heavily influenced by the rise of phenomenology, although not in the form advocated by Husserl. It seems useful to distinguish three broad stages in the development of phenomenology.[3] The first was that established by Husserl's own programme of transcendental phenomenology, the search for the basis of 'knowledge free from presuppositions'. In the second phase, several of Husserl's most prominent followers, including Scheler, Sartre and Schutz, implicitly or explicitly abandoned such a quest in favour of an existential phenomenology, prefigured in Husserl's *Crisis of the European Sciences*, in which the emphasis is placed upon the primacy of the self in the lived-in world. The third phase is that of hermeneutic phenomenology, developed particularly in Heidegger's later writings and by Ricoeur, where the leading theme is the linguistic character of human 'being in the world'. In Gadamer's hands, hermeneutic phenomenology is used to formulate a radical rethinking of the idea of *verstehen* and of the character of the *Geisteswissenschaften*.

Whereas for earlier authors *verstehen* was treated primarily as a method which an historian or social scientist uses to gain a systematic access to his 'subject-matter', Gadamer regards it as the condition and mode of human intersubjectivity as such. Language, not 're-living', is the medium of understanding, which is specifically not a 'psychological' matter. For Gadamer, as for

Heidegger, 'language speaks its own being'. The proper locus for an historically oriented hermeneutics is not in the behaviour of individuals but in the reading of texts. Texts manifest the autonomy of language; they can be understood as meaningful products without any particular knowledge of their authors, for language is not the intentional creation of language-speakers but is the public medium of social being. *Verstehen* can be represented as the mediation of traditions through dialogue, where 'tradition' is the frame of meaning constituted by a language community – a 'form of life'. There is no escaping the historicity of traditions: hence it is futile to seek a foundation in knowledge free from presuppositions. 'Knowledge' is generated by, and is only possible within, traditions. The reading of a text that originates in a past tradition involves a creative mediation of traditions, a process that can never be 'completed' because of the very historicity of human understanding. Hence there cannot be an 'objective' foundation for hermeneutics in the manner in which that term is conceived of in positivistic philosophies. The abandoning of 'method' in hermeneutics however, according to Gadamer, does not entail the abandoning of 'truth': the latter is guaranteed by the authenticity of the tradition from within which understanding is accomplished. It is exactly here that hermeneutics finds its task; hermeneutics is the universal principle of philosophy.[4]

Habermas on the 'claim to universality' of hermeneutics

Gadamer's claim as to the universality of hermeneutics, and its critique by K.-O. Apel and by Habermas, bear interesting similarities to the critical reception of the writings of Peter Winch by Gellner and others in Anglo-Saxon philosophy. Although Winch's views have not been worked out in anything like as elaborate a way as those of Gadamer, they can be construed as making a parallel case for the 'universality of hermeneutics' in the explication of human action. Understanding human conduct is not a causal endeavour, and consists in uncovering its intelligibility by relating it to the rules that constitute a form of life. The mediation of forms of life or language-games then emerges as a focal point of interest, although Winch's discussions of this are confined to problems of understanding alien cultures rather than oriented towards history.[5]

Gellner's various polemical discussions of Winch's writings point out some of the difficulties, and more especially the limitations, of a formulation of method in the social sciences which sees the latter as concerned with nothing more than the self-understanding of human beings in society. Such a standpoint apparently precludes any possibility of examining the causal origins of social institutions, the divergent modes in which symbolic meanings are 'interpreted' in the light of conflicting group interests, and the existence of forms of false consciousness or ideology.[6] But Gellner's attitude towards Winch's work is very largely negative: an outcome, it seems, of his earlier swingeing condemnation of Wittgensteinian philosophy generally.[7] Although his approach to Gadamer's hermeneutics is directed along generally similar lines, Habermas's critique of the latter is informed by the view that Gadamer's work, and hermeneutic issues more broadly, are of fundamental relevance to the social sciences. In his earlier work, particularly in *Zur Logik der Sozialwissenschaften* (1967), Habermas stresses the point that the generalizing sciences and hermeneutics have for a long while gone their separate ways; the problem is to show what logical relations connect them on the level of epistemology.[8]

In order to grasp the force of Habermas's discussion of hermeneutic phenomenology, it is first of all necessary to consider his theory of the grounding of human knowledge in interests. Habermas's *Knowledge and Human Interests* continues, but greatly amplifies, as well as makes more concrete, the critique of positivism that has always been a leading theme of Frankfurt philosophy. Where positivism has triumphed, as it has for the most part in the dominant streams of thought over the past two centuries in the philosophy of both the social and the natural sciences, knowledge becomes portrayed as independent of interests and consequently of the reflexive historical awareness of the knower. 'Since Kant', according to Habermas,

science has no longer been seriously comprehended by philosophy. Science can only be comprehended epistemologically, which means as *one* category of possible knowledge . . . For the philosophy of science that has emerged since the mid-nineteenth century as the heir of the theory of knowledge is methodology pursued with a scientistic self-understanding of the sciences. 'Scientism' means science's belief in itself: that is, the conviction that we can no longer understand science as *one* form of possible knowledge, but must rather identify knowledge with science.[9]

Scientific knowledge, thus portrayed, actually conforms to only one type of knowledge-constitutive interest, that in the prediction and control of occurrences, or 'technically exploitable' knowledge. It is only one logical form which the disclosure of reality can take, and is directly connected with what Habermas calls 'instrumental action', 'purposive-rational action' or simply 'labour'.[10] Labour is one of three basic elements of the human self-formative process distinguished by Habermas, the others being interaction and authority (or power).

Interest in technically exploitable knowledge, according to Habermas, is not specific to the natural sciences, although perhaps exemplified most clearly by them. An orientation to prediction and control implies generalizing explanation: that is to say, explanation which is grounded in terms of causal laws. Such an orientation characterizes both the natural and social sciences. In instrumental action, reality is constituted from within a specifically bounded realm of experience, organized conceptually in mono-logical technical metalanguages that can in principle be expressed formally. To call such conceptual systems 'monological' is to claim that their form is governed by identifiable rules of inference, which are in turn corrigible in the light of the results of measurement operations. Objectivity of knowledge is guaranteed, or at least sought after, through the interpretation of observations, procedures of measurement, and inferential rules.

Interaction, on the other hand, is founded in ordinary language communication, which is the organizing mode of intersubjectivity. The norms governing everyday communication are rooted in the practical demands of sustaining community existence. Language here, Habermas agrees with Gadamer (and with Wittgenstein), is not merely a system of descriptions, but the medium whereby an intersubjectively formed social life is carried on: language is a medium of 'doing' things through communication with others. As such, to speak a language 'correctly' means being able to use it in the contexts of day-to-day life in accordance with the norms of the language community. Whereas meanings in instrumental action are created artificially and connected only to the purposive-rational employment of 'means', observers who confront inter-action must recognize that they confront a world which is pre-interpreted by those whom they wish to study. Interaction is dialogical rather than monological, and one cannot be concerned with it without being able in principle to enter the dialogue. This is the locus of hermeneutics, which conforms to the knowledge-constitutive interest in understanding. Hermeneutic problems relate to the intertwining of language and experience in different forms of life, which ordinary language both expresses and mediates.

These two types of knowledge-constitutive interest generate two sorts of discipline. The 'empirical-analytic sciences' are founded in concerns with prediction and control, derivable from knowledge that is nomological in form. In them, 'Theories comprise hypothetico-deductive connections of propositions, which permit the deduction of lawlike hypotheses with empirical content'.[11] The 'historical-hermeneutic sciences' are concerned with the understanding of traditions and their artistic and literary products. To these, however, must be added a third: critical theory. Critical theory finds its task in the furtherance of an interest in emancipation, in the achievement of rational autonomy of action freed from domination. For Habermas, this is crucially bound up with the historicity of self-understanding as limited by unacknowledged causal conditions of interaction. Such unacknowledged conditions of interaction include the ideological framing of asymmetrical relations of dependence within systems of power. The object of critical theory is to render the nomological bounds of interaction reflexively accessible to its participants so as to offer the possibility of their transformation. It is concerned to ensure

that information about lawlike connections sets off a process of reflection in the consciousness of those whom the laws are about. Thus the level of unreflected consciousness, which is one of the initial conditions of such laws, can be transformed. Of course, to this end a critically mediated knowledge of laws cannot through reflection alone render a law itself operative, but it can render it inapplicable.[12]

We can represent all this schematically as follows:

Ontological elements of self-formative process	Knowledge-constitutive interest	Type of study
labour (instrumental action)	prediction and control	empirical-analytic sciences
interaction	understanding	historical-hermeneutic sciences
authority (power)	emancipation	critical theory

Habermas takes reflexivity to be fundamental to the interest in emancipation just because it is in the course of self-reflection that the subject is able to grasp, and transform, the conditions under which he acts through embodying his knowledge of these conditions within the rationalization of his action. He has tried to explicate this further as expressing circumstances of *distorted communication*: first of all in the context of a psychoanalytic model of critical theory, and subsequently in regard of his notion of communicative competence (which is distinct from that employed by others, e.g. Hymes).

Habermas on distorted communication

The formulation of critical theory which Habermas develops is based upon an abstract analysis of shortcomings in Marx as well as upon an elaboration of ideas derived from Freud. Habermas distinguishes two strands in Marx's account of the human self-formative process. One is the thesis that 'man makes himself' through productive activity: that human beings separate themselves from the animals in so far as they produce in creative interplay with their environment. The other is that human social development can be regarded as a reflexive project in which classes actively promote the self-transformation of society. Marx failed to work out a satisfactory meta-theory which would relate these two elements, however, in so far as he conceived of science only on the level of instrumental action. Hence he was not able to develop the special significance of the critique of ideology, reducing the Hegelian emphasis upon the primacy of self-reflection to the 'materialist' theme of labour as the medium of social transformation.[13]

This collapse of labour and interaction in Marx can be prised open again through treating psychoanalysis as the exemplar of 'self-reflection as science'. Freud's understanding of his own creation was itself limited, manifesting a strongly positivistic strain just as Marx's writings did in a previous generation. But if appropriately reformulated philosophically, psychoanalysis nonetheless offers a comprehensive framework for the theoretical and practical tasks of the critique of ideology. Psychoanalysis is organized through dialogue between analyst and analysand, and on one level operates as a hermeneutic investigation. Habermas points out that in fashioning his theory of dream interpretation, Freud was in some part influenced by an analogy with philology, comparing such interpretation to the translation of foreign texts. Habermas relates Freud's account of unconscious imagery, and its recovery by the analyst, to Dilthey's treatment of the object of hermeneutics as exploring horizons of meaning that lie behind subjective consciousness. Freud's is a 'depth hermeneutics'.[14] According to psychoanalytic theory, the 'text' of interaction as ordinary linguistic communication is distorted by repressions. In analysing the nature of repressions, the clinician tends to move to a nomological level, using a mechanical terminology rather than an interpretative one phrased in terms of meanings. On this level, psychoanalytic procedure is concerned to identify as causal mechanisms the underlying deformations which restrict the analysand's consciously accessible self-understanding. Because Freud wished to present psychoanalysis as a natural science in the orthodox sense which that term held in his time, he treated this as something which it should be the object of psychoanalytic theory to universalize: when fully developed, psychoanalysis should become just another branch of medical science. From the point of view of Habermas's meta-theoretical account of psychoanalytic procedure however, it is only one moment in the emancipatory project of therapy. The aim of therapy is to extend the rational autonomy of the analysand by recovering those unconscious sources that impel the individual's behaviour without the mediation of his reflexive consciousness. Self-understanding, autonomy of action (*Mündigkeit*), and linguistic expression, are here all tied to one another. For it is the 'translating' of unacknowledged causal conditions of action deriving from repressions into accessible self-understanding, which makes it possible for the individual to achieve rational control over influences upon his conduct which previously dominated him. But this possibility itself can only be realized through language, which is the medium of reflexivity and at the same time a public mode of communication with others. Thus dialogue between analyst and analysand both furthers the progress of emancipation, and simultaneously expresses it, since it permits an expansion of mutual understanding between the two parties. The requirement that anyone who practises psychoanalysis must first undergo analysis himself must be seen in a different light to an ordinary professional qualification: he has himself to be freed from influences that would distort the analytic dialogue from his side rather than from that of the patient.

The theme of the grounding of the critique of ideology and power in recognition of the conditions of distorted communication is further pursued in the abstract theory of 'communicative competence'. The concept is introduced as parallel to Chomsky's idea of 'linguistic competence' as separated from linguistic performance, the latter referring to what a speaker actually says, the former to an ideal-typical representation of his capabilities (or what Habermas calls 'language reconstruction'). Chomsky is concerned with the monological skills of language-speakers, Habermas with the conditions underlying the sustaining of dialogue. The communication of meaning in interaction demands far more than linguistic competence in Chomsky's sense; it involves mastery of features of the context in which interaction occurs. Any situation of dialogue, Habermas claims, implicitly acknowledges three elements of interaction, which if analytically combined to form a model of complete mutual understanding in an ideal speech situation, offer a baseline against which distortions in communication can be specified. Such an ideal speech situation involves the following. First, the attainment of consensus solely through rational discussion. Second, complete mutual understanding on the part of the participants in the interaction. Third, mutual recognition of the authentic right of the other to take part in the dialogue as an autonomous and equal partner. In so far as, in empirical circumstances of communication, these implied features are contravened, through, for instance, the power of one participant to impose his views on another as a basis for securing 'consensus', that communication rests upon distortions which it is the business of the critique of ideology to bring to light.

These ideas have recently been expanded and clarified in relation to a conception of what Habermas calls 'universal pragmatics', in which he draws extensively from Austin and Searle on speech acts.[15] 'Truth' here is no longer connected diffusely to the conditions of dialogue between traditions, as in Gadamer, but becomes one among several 'validity claims' that can be redeemed in discourse. Truth relates to validity claims made in respect of constative speech acts, and thus to the propositional content of statements. This is a 'consensus theory of truth', but the phrase, as Habermas admits, is a bit misleading: truth does not consist in consensus, but concerns the process of argumentation in discourse whereby validity claims of a constative form are redeemed. 'The condition of the truth of assertions is the potential agreement of all others. . . . Truth involves the promise of reaching a rational consensus.'[16] Rationality is not, however, in principle confined to statements, but concerns other classes of speech act also. There are four such classes, in which the redemption of validity claims concerns respectively *Verständlichkeit* (intelligibility), *Wahrheit* (truth), *Richtigkeit* (adequacy or correctness) and *Wahrhaftigkeit* (veracity or 'truthfulness'). We have to be concerned not just with assertions, as properties of abstract discourse, but also with the rationality of norms, as elements of practical action; and each in turn has to be connected to the intelligibility and veracity of the interchanges involved in processes of communication. When the intelligibility of an utterance is problematic, we ask questions of a sort such as: 'What does that mean?', 'How is that to be understood?'. The answers to such questions supply interpretations of meaning (*Deutungen*). Where the truth of the propositional content of an utterance is concerned, we ask questions of the form: 'Are the facts of the matter as they are claimed to be?'. We respond to such inquiries by assertions and explanations (*Erklärungen*). When it is the fairness of the normative grounding of a speech act that is problematic, we ask questions of the type, 'Why did you do that?' or 'Were you right to do that?'. The answers to such questions are justifications (*Rechtfertigungen*). Finally, where in a process of communication we question the veracity of an utterance, relating to the intentions of the speaker in saying what he said, we ask questions such as: 'Is he deceiving me?', 'Is he trying to cheat me?'. However, we characteristically address this latter type of question to a third person, although this type of interrogative is also used to 'bring the untrustworthy person to account'.[17]

This classification supplies the basis of a universal pragmatics. The latter, Habermas says, 'has the task of identifying and reconstructing universal conditions of possible understanding'.[18] Universal pragmatics differs from what Habermas calls the 'empirical pragmatics' of Austin and Searle; whereas the latter is concerned mainly with the descriptive classification of speech acts in particular types of context, the former attempts to reconstruct the rule systems which allow actors to communicate in any type of context. The four classes of speech acts relate to four object domains: those of speech itself, external nature, society, and 'internal nature'. Consensual interaction can be carried on only to the extent that a speaker credibly sustains validity claims in each domain: truth in respect of the propositional content of what is said; legitimacy in respect of the norms justifying the speaker's right to say what he does; veracity in respect of his intentions; and intelligibility of meaning. Since understanding or intelligibility is in a sense 'factually redeemed' whenever a process of communication occurs, Habermas treats this as an overarching category: the other three are elements *within* communication. (This threefold division again seems to reflect those represented schematically earlier.)[19] Among these three, validity claims relating to veracity have to be separated from those concerning the other two, in that they are resolved in actual conduct: genuineness of intention has to be demonstrated in how one actually behaves. Validity claims concerning truth and fairness are open to redemption through discourse: these constitute what Habermas calls respectively 'theoretical-empirical' and 'practical' discourse. We can distinguish the following levels of argumentation in these two arenas of discourse:

	Theoretical-empirical discourse	Practical discourse
conclusions (C)	statements	precepts/evaluations
controversial validity claim demanded from opponent	truth	correctness/propriety
	explanations	justifications
data (D)	causes (in respect of events) motives (in respect of behaviour)	grounds
warrant (W)	empirical uniformities, hypothetical laws, etc.	behavioural/ evaluative norms or principles
backing (B)	observations, results of surveys, factual accounts, etc.	interpretations of needs (values), inferences, secondary implications, etc.

Thus, adopting an example given by Toulmin, Habermas illustrates the form of theoretical-empirical discourse as follows. The statement, 'Harry is a British subject' (C) can be explained by the identification of a cause: 'Harry was born in Bermuda' (D). This explanation is reached through the deductive application of a generalization: 'A man born in Bermuda will generally be a British subject' (W). The plausibility of such a generalization can be indicated in terms of legal provisions of national status (B). Argumentation in practical discourse can be analysed according to a parallel scheme, as indicated in the column on the right-hand side. These systems of discourse allow us to order explanation and justification respectively in relation to specific ranges of phenomena. Assertions and normative evaluations can only be grounded as elements of such conceptual hierarchies. The grounding of arguments thus 'has nothing to do with the relation between individual sentences and reality, but above all with the coherence between sentences within systems of speech'.[20] In this connection, Habermas makes much of what he calls the 'double structure' of speech acts. The illocutionary force and propositional content of speech acts may vary independently of one another. The same propositional content, as Austin originally pointed out, can be expressed in different forms of speech act (assertions, commands, etc.). This 'uncoupling' of illocutionary force and propositional content is the condition of the differentiation of mutual understanding (inter-subjectivity) in interaction from sensory experience or the apprehension of an object-world. The double structure of speech ties in with a basic feature of language: its inherent reflexivity. In so far as speakers master the double structure of language, they have to conjoin the substance of what is communicated, to metacommunication about its illocutionary or practical application.[21]

If a process of argumentation is to eventuate in conclusions rationally arrived at, the discourse must be of such a form as to allow for continual revision or review. Here Habermas returns to the themes of *Knowledge and Human Interests*, claiming that each type of discourse must make possible a 'step-by-step radicalization' of the self-reflection of the knowing subject.[22] This can be represented as shown opposite.

The first step in the 'radicalization' of theoretical discourse is the initial incorporation of a statement or assertion, as an act, into a process of argumentation; the second is its theoretical clarification; the third is a transition from or modification of the language system initially adopted; the final, and 'deepest', level of argumentation is reached with reflection on the nature of theoretical knowledge as such (as an example of which Habermas instances the controversy between Kuhn, Popper and others in the philosophy of science).[23] The form of practical discourse is similar, in respect of the self-reflection of the subject. Commands or prohibitions enter discourse when they become, or are made, problematic; the second level consists in their theoretical justification; a

Steps in radicalization	Theoretical discourse	Practical discourse
acts	statements	commands/ prohibitions
grounding	theoretical explanations	theoretical justifications
substantive language-criticism	metatheoretical transformation of language and conceptual systems	meta-ethical/ metapolitical
self-reflection	critique of knowledge	formation of rational political will

deeper level still is the consideration of alternative normative conceptions or evaluations; the most profound level of argumentation concerns reflection on the nature of political will.

A consensus reached through a process of argumentation, Habermas concludes, is only a sufficient criterion for the redeeming of a validity claim if it is possible to move freely between the different levels of discourse: the condition of this is precisely the existence of an ideal speech situation as previously described. Habermas continues to hold that psychoanalytic dialogue is directly relevant to the clarification of the circumstances preventing the realization of an ideal speech situation. Psychoanalytic dialogue accomplishes both less and more than usual discourse. Less in the sense that the patient is initially very far from being a full participant in the course of the dialogue, which is guided by the analyst. A successful therapeutic 'discourse' has as its first consequence that which is claimed from the beginning in more conventional discourse: symmetry of chances of participation. Therapeutic dialogue is more than ordinary discourse, however, in the sense that it culminates not just in the redemption of claims to truth or correctness, but also of a claim to veracity – which as Habermas has said before, cannot normally be discursively redeemed. 'In accepting the proposals and the "worked-through" interpretations of the analyst as valid and confirmed, the patient at the same time sees through his own self-deception.'[24]

Hermeneutic understanding and nomological explanation

In offering some remarks upon Habermas's attempt to create a meta-theory for a critical social science, I shall confine my attention primarily to the ideas just sketched in above. That is to say, I shall not give any consideration to his various discussions of the development of the legitimate order of bourgeois society, or of the crises to which that order is now exposed.[25] This should not be taken to mean that such analyses bear no relation to Habermas's meta-theory; on the contrary, they are obviously closely tied to one another as integral to his version of critical theory. Further, I shall make no effort to refer in any detail to the now quite considerable critical literature, mostly in German, which Habermas's writings have stimulated. Habermas's works are not always set out with as much clarity as one would wish, and I shall concentrate upon making a series of comments upon what, if my formulation of Habermas's main concerns is accurate, appear to be difficulties which they raise: regardless of whether or not these are the same as those identified by other critics.

When *Knowledge and Human Interests* first appeared in English, some critics accused Habermas of adopting a misleading differentiation between the natural and social sciences, based on the idea that whereas the former are 'nomological' in their explanatory form, the latter are 'interpretative'. But this rests upon a misapprehension of Habermas's views. An interest in prediction and control is not specific to natural science, and is not offered as a criterion for approaching traditional debates about divergencies between the natural and social sciences. The point is to identify two logically discrepant forms that claims to knowledge can assume; and to substantiate the notion that the relation between the two is of an historical character, such that unacknowledged causal conditions of action can be transformed when these are made accessible to reflexive self-consciousness. Gadamer's 'claim to universality' of hermeneutics has been matched, Habermas argues, with a comparable claim to universality emanating from positivism: that all happenings, whether in the social or in the natural worlds, are determined by the operation of causal laws. Neither of these competing claims recognizes the different type of knowledge-constitutive interest on which it itself rests; such recognition undermines each claim, without entirely repudiating either. This is a persuasive viewpoint and, I believe, basically a correct one. None the less, I do not think that Habermas's characterization of it is wholly acceptable. This can be shown by reference to his treatment of each of the key concepts involved: the nomological and the hermeneutic. If Habermas does not claim that the nomological form of explanation he identifies is peculiar to the natural sciences, he still tends to argue (as Horkheimer was prone to do) as if it is adequate to express the logic of method which they embody – albeit one which supplies only a partial and slanted self-understanding of the place of science within human culture as a whole. But this gives too much to positivism, or more accurately to the 'orthodox' hypothetico-deductive view of what science is all about.[26] The writings of authors such as Toulmin, Hesse, Kuhn, etc. have subjected this view to a major frontal assault, and have left it largely in ruins – albeit without having managed to replace it with an equally comprehensive alternative. Now in one important sense, this literature accords well with Habermas's emphases. Science, he says, presupposes the intersubjectivity of ordinary-language communication, which can never be completely transposed into monological formal languages. This was shown by Peirce, and again by the later Husserl. Such intersubjectivity constitutes what Apel calls the *'a priori* of communication'. But it is a clear implication of writings such as those of Kuhn, which claim that scientific development involves a discontinuous series of paradigms, that hermeneutic problems are as basic to science as to more sedimented 'traditions'. Science is certainly as much about 'interpretation' as 'nomological explanation': the former certainly cannot be disposed of as a transcendental *a priori* – as Gadamer has noted in commenting on Kuhn. 'Explanation' in science is most appropriately characterized as the clarification of queries, rather than deduction from causal laws, which is only one sub-type of explanatory procedure. In scientific analysis 'why-questions' are normally answered by rendering a phenomenon intelligible or meaningful within the context of a paradigm or theory.[27] Recognition of the hermeneutic character of scientific theories and their mediations shows that science is oriented in a fundamental way to 'understanding' – which is precisely why it is a rival to other types of religious or magical cosmology against the backdrop of which interaction, prior to the development of Western industrial culture, has been carried on. In sum, Habermas's view still retains much of the old *verstehen/erklären* opposition, although in reworked form and supplemented by an 'interest in emancipation'.

Kuhn's discussion is confined to the internal history of science, while Gadamer's hermeneutic philosophy ranges much more broadly, but there are clear similarities between 'paradigms' and 'traditions', and the concerns of each author with their mediation. There is a basic sense in which Gadamer is legitimately able to claim the universality of hermeneutics – and is puzzled by Habermas's rejection of the claim. This is precisely the sense in which all 'knowledge', whether in science, literature, or art, is achieved within and by means of frames of meaning rooted in natural-language communities. If the 'circular' character of knowledge as always located in history be accepted, as Habermas does accept it, an epistemology of the form set out by Gadamer can be defended as necessary to each of the three forms of knowledge-constitutive interest identified by Habermas.[28] Habermas's position at this point seems to contain an unresolved difficulty of a major kind, immediately related to his residual acceptance of a deductive-nomological version of scientific explanation. This concerns his view of the role of nomological analysis, rather than that of critical theory as such, which is what his attention is most concentrated upon. The 'empirical-analytical sciences' take as their object the study of reality according to the knowledge-constitutive interest of prediction and control, organizing 'findings' in terms of hypoethetico-deductive systems of causal laws. But what are the criteria in terms of which such claims to knowledge are to be substantiated? For the 'orthodox view' has an answer which Habermas has apparently (although as it later turns out, not finally) rejected: correspondence to sensorily apprehended reality, grounded in the descriptions of a theory-neutral observation language. Can we say that, for Habermas, science can aspire to objectivity in so far as scientific theories allow of increased capacities of prediction and control? Surely not. For a knowledge-constitutive interest in prediction and control is actually not logically tied to a nomological form of explanatory scheme in the way in which Habermas apparently assumes it to be. I have already made the point that an interest in meaningful 'understanding' is more integral to science than Habermas allows. This is the reverse side of the coin: the point that 'prediction and control', as expressing a constitutive interest or logical form of knowledge, are by no means limited to the sphere of the nomo-logical. On the contrary, they are of primary significance in inter-action itself, and are manifestly crucial to the constitution of that form of knowledge (which I have elsewhere called generically 'mutual knowledge') whereby the understanding of others is achieved.[29] In this sense, the 'predictability' of interaction, and the control operated over its course, is a contingent accomplishment of parties to interaction. I shall revert to this below because it bears in a direct way upon Habermas's formulation of the notion of labour.

There are various loose ends to what I have said so far which will need to be tied up later. One implication, however, is that Habermas's classification of disciplines into the 'empirical-analytical' and the 'historical-hermeneutic' is unsatisfactory. Hermeneutic problems cannot be at the same time confined to one class of disciplines, and yet also span them all. If those fields of study (as Habermas agrees) which concern human action involve what I call a 'double hermeneutic', the hermeneutic media-tion of meaning-frames (paradigms) must be regarded as posing central problems for any epistemology of natural science that seeks to go beyond the discredited formulae offered by logical empiricism.

Labour and interaction

Habermas derives his distinction of 'labour' and 'interaction' in some part from his critical assessment of Marx's transposition of self-reflection into the thesis of the self-constitution of humanity through production. Marx thereby reduces to one concept, that of 'productive labour', two features of human social development that have to be analytically separated from one another. But while this permits him to develop an incisive polemic against Marx's relapse into positivism, the mode in which he develops the dis-tinction in his own theoretical scheme is less than completely satisfactory.

To differentiate labour and interaction, at least in the way Habermas does, treating the former as equivalent to strategic or instrumental action, seems to allow no conceptual mode of treat-ing interaction as itself a 'productive enterprise'. This applies whether or not labour is regarded as generic to all activity or as a type of activity (social labour): for in neither sense can the 'labour' that is put into the sustaining of meaningful interaction be treated simply as 'purposive-rational action'. Here it is necessary to stress, as against Habermas, the conceptual significance of Marx's observations on social life as *Praxis*, although first of all these have to be clarified since they oscillate between an encompassing and a more limited conception of terms such as 'production' and 'productive labour'. In his early writings in particular, Marx uses such terms with very broad application, as elements of an ontology (one, of course, that owes much to Hegel). The distinctive characteristic of human species-being, the special quality that differentiates human beings from the animals, is that human behaviour is not tied to the merely 'adaptive' character of instincts. Habermas's critique of Marx at this point concentrates upon showing that the idea of the 'self-constitution' of human history through labour finds no place for reflexive awareness of the conditions of action as the 'human' mode of self-transformation. But he then goes on to connect labour with instrumental action, and interaction with communication or dialogue. I consider that, in his writings, this has two consequences. First, it becomes difficult to make conceptually central divergent interests – in the usual sense of the term – that are rooted in interaction, since the latter is conceived of basically as the symbolic communication of meaning. Second, it becomes difficult to treat interaction as *itself* always the product of 'labour', in a broad sense of that term, since labour is conceptually tied in an abstract way to an ideal-typical formulation of purposive-rational action. The ramifications of these, I shall argue subsequently, run deep through the whole of Habermas's elaboration of the project of critical theory. What is supposedly at the very heart of Habermas's analysis – domination – tends to disappear from view. Or, expressed more precisely, the domination of some groups of men over others as founded in asymmetry of material interest slips away; it is replaced by the idea of domination as equivalent to distorted communication. Power enters into interaction only as filtered through the ideological slanting of the conditions of communication, not as fundamental to the relations between actors whereby interaction is constituted as an ongoing activity.

In some part this can be traced back to the premises of Habermas's critique of Gadamer in *Zur Logik der Sozialwissenschaften*. In the conclusion of the book, Habermas acknowledges the force of the hermeneutic claim that language is the essential medium of intersubjectivity, but emphasizes that none the less it will not suffice to concern ourselves only with the connecting of disparate 'traditions'. Language is not just the medium of inter-subjectivity, but 'is *also* a medium of domination and social power'; in so far as it expresses power relations 'speech is *also* ideological'.[30] But this cedes too much and too little to hermeneutics. Too much because, accepting the universality of language as the medium of being, it complements the mediation of traditions with an emphasis on power only at the cost of trans-muting power into ideologically deformed communication; too little because it thereby fails to acknowledge the sense in which hermeneutics, in so far as it is concerned with all 'meaningful comprehension', must be as basic to a critique of ideology as to any other human enterprise. Habermas appears to recognize this in his more recent writings (without drawing out its full con-sequences), since he separates *Verständlichkeit* or intelligibility from the three types of validity claims, as the necessary basis of all dialogue.

Instead of equating labour with instrumental action, and separating these analytically from interaction (both linked to 'quasi-transcendental' cognitive interests), I think it important to place in the forefront the concepts of the production and repro-duction of interaction, as contingent accomplishments of human actors. If, as I have outlined elsewhere, processes of production and reproduction are treated as involving the reflexive application of rules and resources in the service of the realization of interests (wants), power emerges, together with symbolic meanings and normative sanctions, as integral to interaction rather than analy-tically separate from it.[31] The phrase 'production and reproduction of society' has to be understood as equivalent to the encompassing sense of 'labour' distinguished above: as integral to any and every case of interaction, regarded as a skilled accomplishment. This frees the terms 'labour' or 'work' for the narrower, and more orthodox, sense of a distinctive social type of activity that may be contrasted to 'play', etc. Reflexivity or self-reflection remains as central to this conceptual scheme as it does in that of Habermas, and is treated as fundamental to the production and reproduction of interaction as rationalized human conduct. But it is stripped of the Hegelian overtones that remain strongly defined in the ambiguous formulation of the subject as the 'self' in 'self-reflection', the latter term being used by Habermas to characterize both the reflexive awareness of 'society' as a whole and that of definite subjects.

Reflexivity, autonomy and critical theory

The concepts Habermas develops in his theory of an ideal speech situation share a certain difficulty of application with those comprising the trilogy of work, interaction and communication. That is to say, they are offered as idealized notions which clarify certain logical relations; but Habermas also seems to want to use them in the service of concrete social analysis. It is not clear, for example, how it is possible to apply the theory of communicative competence to the study of actual circumstances of communication, since it is an idealized form which, oriented to the demands of grounding critical theory, abstracts from the contextual character of interaction.[32] But the contextual location of ordinary-language communication, as Habermas himself emphasizes, is in no way just incidental to interaction. The reflexive use of context, including within that latter term temporally extended 'glossing' and conversational 'formulation' as specified by Garfinkel, is quite basic to the sustaining of intersubjectivity in interaction. However, I shall not be concerned to develop this type of objection any more fully, but in discussing the theory of communicative competence shall concentrate, as in the foregoing section, upon more substantive problems – ones which derive from what I have already isolated as difficulties in Habermas's meta-theoretical scheme. These, as I have tried to make clear, stem from the conceptualization of labour as instrumental rationality, and that of interaction as communicative action or dialogue. In this section, I shall trace through some of their implications for the third element in Habermas's tripartite division, and the one which absorbs him pre-eminently: critical theory, as involving the isolation of conditions of distorted communication.

Let us briefly recapitulate Habermas's exposition of knowledge-constitutive interests. There are three categories of knowledge in terms of which reality can be apprehended, founded in three existential conditions of social life: labour, interaction and authority or power. 'Accordingly the interests constitutive of knowledge are linked to the functions of an ego that adapts itself to its external conditions through learning processes, is initiated into the communication system of a social life-world by means of self-formative processes, and constructs an identity in the conflict between instinctual aims and social constraints.'[33] There is no way of cancelling out interest, in the manner presumed by positivistic and some versions of hermeneutic philosophies. Knowledge is always ultimately practical – or, in Habermas's expression, carries within it a germinal idea of the 'good life'. The practical impact of positivistic philosophy is to facilitate the substitution of technical control, or technology *tout court,* for morally enlightened action, guided by the thesis that all problems of social transformation can be reduced to technical decisions. A hermeneutics which (unlike that of Gadamer) severs knowledge from interest merely reinforces this succumbing to technicism, for it separates off our knowledge of the past from the demands of the present, and 'locks up history in a museum'. The dislocation of past from present in this way provides exactly the sort of rationale required by the belief that contemporary social life can be guided by purely technical, non-historical imperatives.

In each case, what happens is that the ideal of 'pure theory' has displaced recognition of the grounding of knowledge in interest: such recognition can only be achieved precisely through the medium of the third interest, that in emancipation. Here we reach the crux of Habermas's thesis, that of the necessary connection between reflexivity and critical theory. 'In self-reflection', as Habermas puts it, 'knowledge for the sake of knowledge attains congruence with the interest in autonomy and responsibility.'[34] This is connected with the theory of communicative competence in two principal ways. One is via the thesis that every situation of communication expresses implicitly the intention of achieving perfect and unconstrained consensus – that the 'validity' of statements expressed in dialogue thus anticipates the 'good life' of an emancipated society. The other is through the thesis that the conditions of distorted communication, as ideology, can be explicated through nomological analysis as the unacknowledged ground of interaction and thus, being grasped reflexively by the subject, returned to his control. I shall discuss the latter in this section, leaving the former to the following section in relation to a critique of the 'psychoanalytic model'.

The proximate source of Habermas's exposition of 'self-reflection' as an historical principle is in Hegel. In Hegel's philosophy self-reflection appears as both an ontology and epistemology: perhaps it would not be inaccurate to say that Hegel abandons the traditional differentiation between the two characteristic both of Kantian philosophy and Hume's empiricism. Self-reflection in Hegel is the coming-to-itself of the Spirit. Now of course Habermas breaks with this on the level of ontology, while insisting that reflexivity has to be accorded an independent significance besides the self-transformation of human society through labour. Reflexivity becomes, in fact, as I have just indicated, the very medium of the actualization of the knowledge-constitutive interest in emancipation. For in self-reflection the impetus to the acquisition of knowledge becomes one with those of autonomy of action and mutual understanding. The argument is initially compelling, but is shown to be weak at its centre when subjected to close scrutiny. For Habermas's indebtedness to Hegel conceals problems every bit as basic as that which he identifies in Marx's 'transposition' of that same thinker. In Habermas's scheme ontology and epistemology are separated in the attempt to break free from Hegel's idealism. Self-reflection, and the recovery of the alienated self, are no longer regarded as elements of the constitution of reality itself, but are instead treated as at the origin of the transformative capacity of critical theory. However, this leaves as only weakly elaborated, and apparently contingent, the relation between reflexive awareness of the conditions of action and the capability of actually transforming those conditions.[35] These remarks apply with particular force to the themes of *Knowledge and Human Interests*.[36] Habermas's more recent work, especially as documented in *Legitimation Crisis* and *Zur Rekonstruktion des Historischen Materialismus*, seems clearly an attempt to confront these problems. In the context of a reworked theory of evolution, the development of self-reflection is examined historically in terms of the expansion and transformation of the conditions of 'social learning processes'. How successful this approach is likely to prove, however, as well as how far it in fact marks a definite departure from some of the central arguments of *Knowledge and Human Interests*, remains to be seen.

The question of *who* becomes reflexively aware of the conditions of their action – and the conditions under which they become so aware – is obviously crucial to the possible transformative effects of that awareness. While it is acceptable to argue that such reflexivity offers a (potential) medium for expanding actors' autonomy of action, that very autonomy can be used as a means of ensuring the restriction of that of others. Habermas avoids such problems in *Knowledge and Human Interests* by moving unconcernedly between using self-reflection to refer to a total human project, in a quasi-Hegelian way, and using it to refer to the reflexivity of particular subjects.[37] It might be countered that the objection I have made here is an unfair one, since the whole object of critical theory, as the latter is formulated by Habermas, is to make manifest the underlying asymmetries in circumstances where the autonomy of some is bought at the expense of the autonomy of others. In fact, Habermas's theory of ideological domination as distorted communication shows with particular clarity the significance of the differentiation I have made in the previous paragraph.

This can be helpfully illuminated by connecting it to another point made earlier: that 'power' appears in Habermas's theory only as the ideological deformation of circumstances of communication. A reflexive grasp of the conditions of action, it is held, is the mode in which distorted communication is corrected on the level of interaction. This tends to assimilate ways in which the conduct of men is held in thrall through being dominated by unacknowledged causal conditions, and ways in which their autonomy is subject to domination by other men. The means of achieving freedom from domination are not the same in the two cases. The first conforms the more closely to Habermas's analysis of reflexivity as the means of the transformation of action in the direction of expanded autonomy. This is the sense of what I have called the transformative capacity of human action. From this regard, reflexive awareness of previously unacknowledged causal grounds of action does indeed normally yield an increased autonomy of action on the part of human subjects. This is so in so far as such awareness becomes incorporated into a reconstruction of the rationalization of action. Such a theorem does not hold where power equals the domination of some over others, where that domination is normally likely to be used not only to obfuscate the asymmetry of their interaction, but to actively resist any attempts to upset that asymmetry by those in a position of subordination.[38]

In a new preface to the fourth German edition of *Theory and Practice,* Habermas has admitted certain shortcomings in his original formulations of reflexivity in the context of critical theory. 'Self-reflection', he now says, is not the same as 'reasoned justification', the latter being a necessary adjunct to the former if the reflexive moment is to achieve practical impetus. The theoretical knowledge necessary to grasp conditions of action is something which has to occur independently of and in addition to self-reflection as such. Such 'theoretical discourse' is not supplied in psychoanalytic dialogue, where the reflexive autonomy attained by the patient in the course of successful analysis does not provide him with much in the way of an abstract theoretical reconstruction of his newly expanded self-understanding.[39] But this is only a limited acknowledgement of the contingencies in the relation between reflexivity and action, and does not really seem to meet the objections I have registered previously. Habermas is evidently not inclined to introduce major modifications in the psychoanalytic model of critical theory, and it is appropriate at this juncture to turn to that model directly.

The psychoanalytic model

Habermas's reworking of a traditional theme in Frankfurt philosophy – the complementarity of Marx and Freud – has already attracted a great deal of criticism. In order to assess how far any or all of it is justified, we have first of all to try to get clear what Habermas's position is. Habermas's use of Freud differs substantially from that of the earlier generation of Frankfurt philosophers, although the continuities can also be distinguished without difficulty. Habermas seems less interested in the content of psychoanalytic theory than in its form as critical dialogue (in the substance of his most recent writings, he borrows more from Piaget than from Freud). One could not justifiably say that his adoption of psychoanalysis is purely formal, regarding the latter as nothing more than an exemplar of the relations between the nomological, the hermeneutic and the critical. It is not easy however to tell from Habermas's discussions of Freud how far he accepts the total corpus of Freudian theory, appropriately reconstrued as a reflexively founded therapeutic endeavour. For Habermas's own model of psychoanalysis as critical theory is definitely, and quite deliberately, offered on an idealized level. He has no concern to examine concrete clinical materials, because the psychoanalytic model is offered as a meta-theoretical framework for the rectifying of distorted communication. For this reason he is able to some extent to avoid rejoinders to his arguments which look to the actual practice of psychoanalysis. One might point out, for example, that there is profound disagreement between analytic schools as to proper modes of therapy, as to how far the therapist should participate directly in the dialogue, and what form his participation should take. Or, from another aspect, we might remark that psychoanalytic therapy could easily be represented as an authoritarian situation, monopolized and covertly manipulated by the therapist. We do not have to go so far as to regard psychoanalysis as a mode of brainwashing[40] to recognize that the pretensions of analytic theory to uncover what is there in the patient, rather than what is forcefully implanted by the analyst himself, can scarcely be accepted without more evidence than that given by clinical material as such. Habermas does not consider such issues of substance, but it is difficult to see that he could dismiss them as irrelevant to his case, in so far as his appeal to psychoanalysis does depend upon acceptance of at least some of the concrete details of Freud's theory and his version of therapy.

Because Habermas's views on such matters seem elusive, it is probably more relevant to concentrate upon the formal level of the meta-theory of psychoanalysis as a model for ideology-criticism. Two major objections have been registered against this in the course of the interchanges between Habermas, Gadamer and others.[41] These are the connected assertions that psychoanalysis is a dialogue between individuals, whereas a critical theory of society has to concern itself with relations between groups; and that the therapeutic dialogue is one that is sustained voluntarily by both analyst and analysand, while group dependencies in society exist in a framework of coercion. Habermas's response to these is to admit the force of the points, without conceding that they undermine his position in any significant sense. Where others refuse to enter into dialogue, the type of confirmation of critical theory that is possible in the psychoanalytic encounter cannot be obtained: enlightenment is confined to those who share a common situation in conflict with others. We can distinguish, Habermas goes on to add, three components in the relation of theory and practice, as these are mediated by the critique of ideology: the specification of modes of critical analysis of a given set of social circumstances; the appropriation of these reflexively by those to whose circumstances they refer; and the articulation of definite practical strategies of action. The differences between these three have been obscured in Marxism, since in parties attached to European labour movements they have been entangled together as an overall historical project. There is no way of validating strategies on the level of theory, because they have to be worked out in relation to particular conjunctures of circumstances.[42]

What this attempted defence really does is to make clear some of the problems that seem inherent in Habermas's theoretical scheme. It in fact barely addresses itself to the objections made by critics to the psychoanalytic model, and simply adds to the differentiation between theoretical discourse and enlightened self-reflection a third element: that of strategy or tactics. Habermas severs off strategy from enlightened self-reflection itself. But it is not clear what this implies. Quite clearly the severance cannot be complete, or strategy would become an irrational matter. There must be some way in which 'appropriate' strategy is suggested by theory, even if we acknowledge (as Habermas stresses in criticizing Lukács) that its validation does not rest upon its successful application in any specific time and place. The distance which Habermas's analyses maintain from political involvement he tries at this point to turn into a virtue. But it really makes manifest the distance of his theoretical system from political practice.

Let us take up the criticisms of the psychoanalytic model made by Gadamer and others, but develop them also in the context of arguments set out previously. The first point is to do with the circumstance that psychoanalysis is a dialogue between individual persons, not a relation between groups. This can be developed in various ways, but I shall only take up one, which seems to me to be the most important. It is that psychoanalysis is basically a conversation between two persons in which the only 'practical' grounding of the interchange is that of the reconstruction of the self-understanding of the patient. The psychoanalytic encounter, as it were, places an *epoché* upon the interests (in the usual sense) and involvements of everyday life, and reconstitutes them on a symbolic level as components, or deformations, of dialogue. Such a framework is thus peculiarly apposite to Habermas's conceptualization of interaction as 'communicative action' or symbolic interchange, which also abstracts from the 'material' context of practical day-to-day conduct. I have already stated my objections to this, and have tried to trace through its implications in regard of the complementary notion of labour. It is evident that, expressed in this way, the first critical rejoinder to Habermas's psychoanalytic model ties in closely to the second. For if group relations inevitably occur in a practical context of material interests, such interests also underlie the modes of ideological domination whereby asymmetries of power are legitimized; these are not, in any simple sense at least, entered into 'voluntarily' by the subordinate groups. Now Habermas's response to this, as described above, is to declare that enlightened self-reflection and strategy operate at different levels. (In his more recent writings, and in the debate with Luhmann, he has given more and more prominence to the abstract category of 'strategic action', distinguished from 'instrumental action' as such.) I have already suggested that the contingent character of practical strategies of action is implied in Habermas's meta-theoretical position itself. We can now see more clearly why such a view is inherently unsatisfactory: because it provides no general mode of connection between social transformation and power. In other words, *power itself tends to become another contingency in the relation between enlightened reflexivity and practice.*

Truth and discourse

In conclusion, we might revert to the starting-point of this discussion in Gadamer's hermeneutics. For Gadamer, 'truth' resides in the mutuality of traditions, and hence cannot claim any sort of transcendental foundation. Habermas rejects the limitations which Gadamer's 'claim to universality' of hermeneutics seems to place upon the possibilities of critical theory. But there is more than a trace of Gadamer's version of truth in Habermas's attempt to construct a consensus theory of truth in conjunction with the theory of communicative competence. 'Truth' refers to the conditions of argumentation whereby consensus is achieved in theoretical discourse: every concrete communication between actors contains the promise of the realization of agreement through autonomous and freely conducted dialogue. Gadamer's formulation of truth in reciprocity of dialogue is thus inadequate because it leaves as unexamined distortions in the framework whereby communication is carried on.

Habermas follows Ramsey and Strawson (although without accepting the redundancy thesis of truth) in distinguishing between objects of experience and facts: the event of Caesar's death is thus separated from the fact 'that Caesar died'. Events or

F

happenings are the objects of experience or action; facts are asserted in propositions. Facts presuppose the existence of objects, but when we say 'so-and-so is a fact' we do not mean the existence of the relevant objects or events but the truth of the contents of the proposition. To state something as a fact is thus to make the claim that its propositional content could be discursively justified. Discourse brackets action, permitting only the argumentative examination of truth claims, in contrast to communicative action as such, in which truth claims are always implicit.

Truth *qua* justification of the truth claim inherent in a proposition does not reveal itself, like the objectivity of experience, in feed-back controlled action but only in a process of successful reasoning by which the truth claim is first rendered problematic and then redeemed . . . Facts . . . are not happenings. That is why the truth of propositions is not corroborated by processes happening in the world but by a consensus achieved through argumentative reasoning.[43]

The nature of objectivity of experience has to be explicated through a theory of object-constitution, while the theory of truth has to be developed as a logical articulation of the conditions of discourse.

But the thesis that truth concerns the process of argumentation whereby consensus is established in theoretical discourse leaves unexplicated a basic element in Habermas's analysis of the differentiation of critical theory from hermeneutics. For while it is perhaps consistent with Gadamer's position to restrict 'truth' to the achievement of dialogue between traditions, such a view does not conform to the requirements of a theory of distorted communication of the sort which Habermas tries to establish, since he is required to penetrate below the dialogic process itself as understood by those participating in it. Presumably Habermas wishes to claim that a disclosing of the distortions in the framework of dialogue finds its truth in showing that such dialogue diverges from the components of the idealized speech situation. But what then is the status of the nomological components of inquiry, or those elements which compose the 'scientific discourse' that one is supposedly able to validate prior to and independent of the process of self-reflection? These cannot be simply validated by the (successful) achievement of enlightened self-reflection, if we are also to be able to acknowledge that the connection between them is not a logical, but an historically contingent, one. Here precisely the question at issue is that of the relation between the 'objectivity of experience', the constitution of an object-world, and the redemption of truth claims, a matter that Habermas, having stressed the distinction between the two, passes over. The first demand here, although not the only one, is for an elaborated theory of reference.

Habermas's theory of truth as yet seems only partially developed, but so far as it goes at the moment he has not succeeded in generating a satisfactory defence against the charge – familiar enough in the context of any approach like his own – that he provides no means for distinguishing modes of substantiating truth claims from the nature of truth as such.[44] His response to this sort of objection is to emphasize that the consensus theory of truth universalizes the redemption of validity claims, rather than relating truth to specific modes in which statements may be supported. But this seems unlikely to meet the needs of what the analysis is designed to accomplish. Even if we accept that what 'truth' means is discursive justification of a particular type of validity claim, this would not in and of itself resolve the question of how theoretical–empirical discourse is to be validated independent of its potential incorporation within enlightened self-reflection.[45] However, the view as it stands is difficult to sustain in any case. It is one thing to hold that the notion of truth necessarily implies discursive justification, or its possibility; it is quite another to hold that this can provide an adequate mode of expressing its meaning.

*

In the concluding sections of this discussion, I have concentrated upon critical commentary. It hardly needs saying that this is not in order to dispute the importance of Habermas's writings. On the contrary, Habermas must rank as one of the most pre-eminent of contemporary social philosophers, who has done more than any other to bridge the chasm between Continental and Anglo-Saxon philosophies. But Habermas's works must be judged on a level commensurate with the ambitiousness of the projects which they embody. Habermas's critique of hermeneutics, and the approach to critical theory which has in some part emerged from it, appear to embody certain rather basic shortcomings. I have identified these as: a failure to break radically enough with the residue of the *erklären/verstehen* opposition, with consequent difficulties for Habermas's treatment of the interconnections of the nomological and hermeneutic; the unsatisfactory character of Habermas's fundamental distinction between labour and interaction, which has the effect that the latter becomes treated as equivalent to symbolic or communicative action; the persistence of a strongly marked Hegelian strain in the posited relations between 'self-reflection' and autonomy, especially in Habermas's earlier works, such that the transformative capacity of human action is not adequately connected to rational understanding of conditions of action; the associated reliance upon a psychoanalytic model of ideology-critique which does not effectively illuminate the conjunction of differentials of power and asymmetries of material interests between groups in society; and the dearth of a theory of reference which would tie in Habermas's more recent discussions of truth as the redemption of validity claims in theoretical discourse to the themes of his preceding treatment of self-reflection.

It seems that Habermas's current preoccupations with universal pragmatics, the development of cognition and ego-identity in the child, and with a scheme of evolutionary change,[46] move away from, as well as attempt to elaborate, some of the emphases of his first works. In lieu of a direct statement from Habermas himself, it is difficult to assess how far he may have abandoned or substantially modified his earlier views. Certainly there is a strong line of continuity in his works from his initial analysis of changes in the nature of public life (*Strukturwandel der Öffentlichkeit*, 1962) up to the present time, and it is difficult to resist the conclusion that several of the problems I have indicated remain deeply embedded in Habermas's most recent writings.

4 Hermeneutics, ethnomethodology and problems of interpretative analysis

In this paper, I shall connect up some of the themes found in the writings of Garfinkel and others influenced by him with some relatively recent developments in European social philosophy. By submitting both to a 'constructive critique' I shall hope to elucidate their importance for contemporary social theory.

The developments in European social thought to which I wish to call attention involve a revitalization of the notion of *verstehen* in the context of the latter-day evolution of the *Geisteswissenschaften*. In Germany, this centres above all upon the work of Hans-Georg Gadamer, which in turn draws extensively upon Heidegger's 'hermeneutic phenomenology'. But Gadamer's writings demonstrate clear connections and overlaps with the work of such authors as Winch in Britain and Ricoeur in France.[1] In this brief paper, I shall not attempt to single out the distinctive views of such authors, but only to characterize certain notions arising from them – ones that contrast rather radically with those embodied in Max Weber's version of 'interpretative sociology', which more than any other has served to introduce the concept of *verstehen* into English-speaking sociology. More qualifications are in order with respect to 'ethnomethodology' – already a term, of course, that embraces a number of mutually dissident views. What I have to say is not directed at Garfinkel's programme of practical studies of 'everyday accomplishments', which seems to me at once deeply interesting and poorly elucidated philosophically. All I want to do is to take hold of a few ideas expressed in the writings of Garfinkel and others which parallel those emanating from the very much more abstract traditions of European social philosophy.[2]

I shall argue that a grasp of these themes, and an appreciation of their significance, signals a major break with the erstwhile dominant schools in sociology (and with at least certain versions of Marxism), according to whom the social sciences can be narrowly modelled upon natural science. An important emphasis of these schools is that sociology is (or can hope to be) *revelatory* in respect of the confusions or misapprehensions of 'common sense'. That is to say, just as the natural sciences seem to have stood in opposition to common-sense views of the physical world, to have penetrated the mystifications of ordinary lay thought, so sociology can strip away the musty errors of everyday beliefs about society. The claimed 'findings' of social research, like the findings of natural science, are frequently resisted or disclaimed by laymen on the basis of what 'common sense shows'. As far as natural science is concerned, such 'resistance' normally takes the form of the refusal to abandon a 'common-sense' belief in the face of findings that contravene it: e.g. the clinging to the belief that the earth is flat rather than spherical. Something like this certainly may occur in respect of the claims generated by sociology; but another – almost diametrically opposed – response is common. This is not that social science reports conclusions that laymen cannot accept because they go against trusted beliefs, but rather that it merely *repeats the familiar* – that it 'tells us what we already know', albeit perhaps wrapped up in a technical language. Sociologists are prone to dismiss this sort of rejoinder to their work rather cursorily, holding that it is the business of social research to check up upon the convictions of 'common sense', which may be right or wrong. But to regard lay beliefs as in principle corrigible in this sense is to treat them as if they were merely adjuncts to human action, rather than integral to it. Lay beliefs are not merely *descriptions* of the social world, but are the very basis of the *constitution* of that world, as the organized product of human acts. Recognition of this point, I shall seek to demonstrate, makes us aware that sociology stands in more complex relation to its 'subject-matter' – human social conduct – than natural science does. The natural world is transformed by human activity, but it is not constituted as an object-world by human beings. The social world, on the other hand, is constituted and reproduced through and in human action; the concepts of 'common sense', and the everyday language in which they are expressed are drawn upon by lay actors to 'make social life happen'.

Let me distinguish five themes that can be discerned in at least some of the writings of those involved with, or close to, 'ethnomethodology'. These by no means exhaust the interest of such writings, but I consider them to be particularly important. First, the theme of the significance of the notion of human *action* or *agency* in sociological theory. Most of the leading schools of sociology, with the partial exception of symbolic interactionism, lack a concept of action. Now this initially seems an odd thing to say, because perhaps the leading figure in English-speaking sociology, Talcott Parsons, has explicitly based his scheme of sociological theory upon an 'action frame of reference', and in his first major work, *The Structure of Social Action*, attempted to incorporate 'voluntarism' as a core component of it. It is sometimes argued that, whereas Parsons began his intellectual career as a 'voluntarist', his theories become more and more deterministic. I think it more accurate to claim that Parsons did not successfully embody such a perspective within his system of theory in the first place. What Parsons did was to treat voluntarism as equivalent to the internalization of values in personality, thereby attempting to relate motivation to the *consensus universel* upon which social solidarity is held to depend. But this has the consequence that the creative element in human action becomes translated into a causal outcome of 'need-dispositions', and the adoption of voluntarism merely a plea for complementing sociology with psychology. Here the actor does indeed appear as a 'cultural dope', rather than as a knowing agent at least in some part the master of his own fate. As against the determinism inherent in the sort of approach favoured by Parsons, it is fruitful to place in the forefront the thesis that society is a skilled accomplishment of actors; this is true even of the most trivial social encounter.

Second, the theme of reflexivity. The notion of action, as the writings of philosophers have made clear, is integrally bound up with the capacity of human agents for self-reflection, for the rational 'monitoring' of their own conduct. In most orthodox forms of sociology (including Parsonian functionalism), but not in ethnomethodology, reflexivity is treated as a 'nuisance' whose effects are to be minimized as far as possible, and which is only recognized in various marginal forms, as 'bandwagon effect', 'self-fulfilling prophecies', etc. Moreover, these tend to compress together two aspects of reflexivity: that of the social observer in relation to the theories he formulates, and that of the actors whose behaviour he seeks to analyse or explain. There is an irony here that ties together these two aspects of reflexivity, or rather the neglect of them, in positivistically inclined forms of social ght. For what is denied, or obscured, on the level of theory – nely, that human agents act for reasons and are, in some sense, sponsible' for their actions – is implicitly assumed on the level of sociological discourse: that is to say, it is accepted that one has to provide 'reasoned grounds' for the adoption of a particular theory in the face of the critical evaluations offered by others in the sociological community.

Symbolic interactionism is perhaps the only leading school of thought in English-speaking sociology that comes near to assigning a central place to agency and reflexivity. G. H. Mead's social philosophy hinges upon the relation of 'I' and 'we' in social interaction and the development of personality. But even in Mead's own writings, the 'I' appears as a more shadowy element than the socially determined self, which is elaborately discussed. In the works of most of Mead's followers, the social self displaces the 'I' altogether, thus foreclosing the option that Mead took out on the possibility of incorporating reflexivity into the theory of action.[3] Where this happens, symbolic interactionism is readily assimilated within the mainstream of sociological thought, as a sort of 'sociological social psychology' concentrated upon face-to-face interaction.

Third, the theme of language. Now language, in the form of the symbol, is obviously stressed within symbolic interactionism, as the term itself indicates. But this is distinct from the standpoint of ethnomethodology, in which language is conceived, not simply as a set of symbols or signs, as a mode of representing things, but as a 'medium of practical activity', a mode of doing things. Language, to use Wittgensteinian terminology, operates within definite 'forms of life', and is routinely used by lay actors as the medium of organizing their day-to-day social conduct. The meanings of utterances thus have to be understood in relation to the whole variety of uses to which language is put by social actors – not just those of 'describing', but also those of 'arguing', 'persuading', 'joking', 'evaluating', etc., etc. I have alluded briefly to the significance of this above. One of its consequences is that ordinary language cannot be ignored by sociological investigators in favour of a wholly separate technical metalanguage which 'clears up' the 'fuzziness' or the 'ambiguity' of everyday speech. Ordinary language is the medium whereby social life is organized *as* meaningful by its constituent actors: to study a form of life involves grasping lay modes of talk which express that form of life. Ordinary language is not therefore just a topic that can be made available for analysis, but is a resource that every sociological or anthropological observer must use to gain access to his 'researchable subject-matter'.

Fourth, the theme of the temporal and contextual locating of action. I think it would be plausible to say that it is only in respect of societal evolution that orthodox sociological theory has attempted to build temporality into its analyses. In ethnomethodology, on the other hand, the locating of interaction in time becomes of central interest. In the conduct of a conversation, for example, it is pointed out that participants typically use the conversation reflexively to characterize 'what has been said', and also anticipate its future course to characterize 'what is being said'. The context-dependence or indexical character of meanings in interaction, of course, involves other elements besides that of time. Garfinkel is undoubtedly correct in emphasizing the indexical character of ordinary language communication – and also in seeing this as a basic source of 'difficulty' for orthodox views of the nature of sociological metalanguages.

Fifth, and finally, the theme of tacit or 'taken for granted understandings'. In the active constitution of interaction as a skilled performance, the 'silences' are as important as the words that are uttered, and indeed make up the necessary background of mutual knowledge in terms of which utterances 'make sense' or, rather, sense is made of them. Tacit understandings are drawn upon by actors as ordinary, but unexplicated, conditions of social interaction. The emphasis upon this in ethnomethodology is one of the direct points of connection between it and the forms of European social philosophy I shall turn to in the next section, reflecting Garfinkel's indebtedness to Schutz, thereby linking the former's work to the great traditions of phenomenology such as exemplified, for example, in Husserl's *Crisis of European Sciences.*

In so far as ethnomethodology shares certain common origins, in 'existentialist phenomenology', with the developments in European social thought I shall now go on to mention, it is not particularly surprising that we should be able to discern similarities between them. If these are not immediately apparent it is because the styles of writing in which they are couched are so different, ethnomethodology being mainly oriented to generating an empirical research programme, the other being expressed in the style of abstract philosophy. In approaching the traditions of thought that have breathed new life into the notion of *verstehen*, it is important to appreciate the contrast which they offer to the earlier phases of development of the *Geisteswissenschaften*, as represented by Dilthey and (in spite of many reservations) Max Weber.[4] In the 'older tradition', *verstehen* was regarded above all as a *method*, to be applied to the human sciences, in contrast to the sorts of methods of external observation employed in the natural sciences. For Dilthey, especially in his earlier writings, the process of understanding was conceived to depend upon the re-experiencing or re-enactment of the thoughts and feelings of those whose conduct was to be understood. That is to say, in some sense or another — which Dilthey increasingly found difficult to specify — in understanding the action of others one mentally 'puts oneself in the other's shoes'. Weber adopted much the same stance, although suspicious of notions such as 're-experiencing' and 'empathy', and rejecting the idea that there is a logical gulf between the methods of the social and natural sciences. Weber's version of interpretative sociology meshed closely with his commitment to what has subsequently come to be called methodological individualism: the thesis that statements that refer to collectivities can always in principle be expressed as the behaviour of concrete individuals.

Both Dilthey and Weber wished to claim that their particular understandings of 'understanding' could be reconciled with the achievement of objective sciences of history (Dilthey) or sociology (Weber). Their views have been sharply attacked by critics writing from a positivistic standpoint, on the basis that *verstehen* cannot yield the sort of evidence that would seem to be necessary to 'objective science'.[5] According to such critics, the process of interpretation can be useful as a source of hypotheses about conduct, but cannot be used to test hypotheses thus derived. It is difficult to resist the force of such criticism within the context of Weber's endeavour to make the idea of *verstehen* compatible with criteria of evidence that are supposed to have the same logical form as those characteristic of natural sciences. Moreover, there are a series of other difficulties with Weber's views, of which I shall mention here only two. One is to do with 'empathy', the other with Weber's formulation of 'social action'. Weber wished to distance himself from the view that empathic identification plays a major part in understanding the meaning of actions; but that he was unable to do so is illustrated by certain puzzles to which his position gives rise. Thus he supposed that mysticism is 'on the margins of meaningful action', since the behaviour of mystics can only be understood by those who are 'religiously musical'. Let us suppose that some, and only some, social scientists are 'religiously musical': how could they ever communicate their understanding to those who are not? To admit that they could not compromises Weber's views upon the possibility of achieving an intersubjectively agreed set of criteria in terms of which an objective 'observation language' can be established in the social sciences. As against Weber's view, I would want to claim that to call conduct 'mystical' is already in a certain sense to have 'understood it meaningfully': and that 'understanding' is tied to the capacity to describe actions linguistically: to typify them in Schutz's term. There are a series of problems relating to what Schutz calls, rather unhappily, 'objective meaning', that Weber's analysis, concerned only with 'subjective meaning', fails to come to terms with. Weber's preoccupation with subjective meaning was closely bound up with his methodological individualism, since 'meaning' only comes into being through the subjective consciousness of actors. It is against this backdrop that Weber distinguished between meaningful action and social action, the latter being the main interest of interpretative sociology, defined as action which is oriented towards others and thereby influenced in its course. In Weber's famous example, if two cyclists who do not see each other coming bump into one another, this is not a case of social action, since the behaviour of the one did not figure in the subjective orientation of the other. If having collided, they start quarrelling about who was responsible for the accident, this then becomes social action. But this formulation, which specifies what is social only in terms of the subjective standpoint of actors, does not seem at all satisfactory: it is neither easy to apply, nor does it encompass the range of elements that I would wish to claim are 'social'. It is not easy to apply to actual conduct because there are many cases of behaviour in which the other, to whom the action may be said to be oriented, is not present on the scene. What are we to make, for instance, of a man shaving prior to going out for the evening? Is he orienting his action towards another particular person he anticipates meeting later on? The answer is that he may or may not have another's possible responses clearly in mind while he carries on the activity; and this is in fact not particularly relevant to the social character of what he is doing, which is likely to reside more in conventions or norms of 'cleanliness', etc. Similarly, I want to say that the action of a cyclist pedalling along the road is already social, regardless of whether others are in sight or not, in so far as what the cyclist does is oriented towards, and 'interpretable' in terms of, the social rules governing traffic behaviour.

In the more recent series of writings to which I have referred previously, *verstehen* is treated, not as a method of investigation peculiar to the social sciences, but as an ontological condition of life in society as such; it is regarded, not as depending upon a psychological process of 're-enactment' or something similar, but as primarily a linguistic matter of grasping the content of familiar and unfamiliar forms of life; to understand others, it is held, is in an important sense to enter into *dialogue* with them; such understanding cannot be 'objective' in any simple sense, since all knowledge moves in a circle, and there can be no knowledge 'free from presuppositions'; and, finally, *verstehen* is linked to norms of meaning in such a way as to break free from methodological individualism.

There can be no question of pursuing these very complex ideas in any sort of detail within the scope of a short paper, and all I shall try to do is to spell out a few of their implications in such a way as to help clarify what they share with the points of interest in ethnomethodology that I have distinguished earlier.

To argue that *verstehen* should be regarded as an ontological condition of human society, rather than as a special method of the sociologist or historian, is to hold that it is the means whereby social life is constituted by lay actors. That is to say 'understanding' the meaning of the actions and communications of others, as a skilled accomplishment, is an integral element of the routine capabilities of competent social actors. Hermeneutics is not simply the privileged reserve of the professional social investigator, but is practised by everyone; mastery of such practice is the only avenue whereby professional social scientists, like lay actors themselves, are able to generate the descriptions of social life they use in their analyses. One of the consequences of this, of course, is to reduce the distance between what sociologists do in their researches, and what lay actors do in their day-to-day activities. To revert to the terminology of ethnomethodology, not only is it the case that every social theorist is a member of a society, and draws upon the skills associated with such membership as a resource in his investigations: it is equally important that every member of society is a 'practical social theorist'. The predictability of the social world does not just happen, it is 'made to happen' by lay actors.

The centrality of language as the organizing medium of the 'lived in world' is stressed alike in the hermeneutic phenomenology of Heidegger, Gadamer and Ricoeur, and in the writings of those following the later Wittgenstein in English-speaking sociology. Garfinkel has of course drawn directly upon Wittgenstein's writings. It is particularly interesting to see, however, that Continental philosophers have begun to emphasize the relevance of Wittgenstein's writings to their own concerns. For while Wittgenstein gave no special technical meaning to *verstehen*, his later philosophy certainly moves towards recommending that the understanding of actions and communications can only be approached within the practical involvements of definite 'language-games'. Gadamer emphasizes that man 'lives in and through language', and that to understand a language is to understand the mode of life which that language expresses. In focusing upon the importance of dialogue *between* different forms of life, however, Gadamer goes beyond Wittgenstein. The characteristic problem that Wittgenstein's philosophy seems to lead to is: how does one ever get out of one language-game into another? For language-games appear as closed universes of meaning. In Gadamer, on the other hand, the mediation of language-games through dialogue is placed as a beginning-point rather than as a conclusion; the emphasis is upon what is involved in grasping the meaning of long-distant historical texts, understanding alien forms of life, etc. It is perhaps not too fanciful to suppose that the prominence of dialogue in Gadamer's philosophy finds something of a parallel, on a much more modest scale, with the prominence of conversation in Garfinkel's work.

The 'circle' in which all knowledge moves is a preoccupation of many different modern philosophies. If one breaks – as in the philosophy of science Popper, Kuhn and others have broken – with the idea of a 'first philosophy', founded upon a bedrock of certainty, one becomes committed to the notion that it is the business of epistemology to make the circle of knowledge a fruitful rather than a vicious one. That is, for example, what Popper tries to do for science by means of his philosophy of conjecture and refutation; and what, from what is in most respects a very different standpoint, the modern phenomenological philosophers seek to do via the notion of the 'hermeneutic circle'. One does not find, in Garfinkel's writings, or in those of others immediately influenced by him, a sophisticated discussion of such matters of epistemology. Such a concern would appear to be foreign to the style of work characteristic of ethnomethodology. None the less, the theme of 'indexicality' is certainly directly relevant to the sorts of issues raised by philosophies that stress the inherent circularity of knowledge – although again on a more minor scale. Some of the similarities are quite easy to see. One of the notions associated with the 'hermeneutic circle' is that in, say, understanding a text, the reader grasps each part through an initial appreciation of the whole; there is thus a constant process of moving from part to whole and back again, whereby an enriched understanding of the whole illuminates each part and vice versa. A similar idea appears in Garfinkel's discussion of indexicality in conversations, where it is pointed out that a conversation is constantly drawn upon by participants both as a mode of characterizing itself and so as to 'gloss' the meaning of each particular contribution to that conversation. Garfinkel (cf. also Cicourel on 'indefinite triangulation') seems to present a version of the idea that the circularity of knowledge can be fruitfully explored, but does not feel any need to elucidate this on any kind of abstract level; in fact, this idea seems to go along with a defined strain of naturalism in Garfinkel's writings, as expressed for example in the claim that it is the task of ethnomethodology to describe indexical expressions 'free of any thought of remedy'. Such unresolved perplexities seem to underlie the very different directions which the work of those originally influenced in some part by Garfinkel has taken: on the one hand, in the writings of Sacks and Schegloff, towards a naturalistic form of 'conversational analysis'; on the other, in the writings of Blum and McHugh, towards a concern with the abstract ramifications of the 'hermeneutic circle'.[6]

The newer version of *verstehen* depends upon the thesis that understanding the meaning of either actions or communications involves the application of 'publicly accessible' linguistic categories connected to tacitly known norms or rules. In tracing out some of the connections between this and ethnomethodology, we return to the origins that each party shares in the development of phenomenology after Husserl, in Schutz and in Heidegger. It is highly important to appreciate the degree to which this development, as culminating in hermeneutic phenomenology and linking up to the largely independent evolution of post-Wittgensteinian philosophy, makes a movement away from the original impetus to phenomenology. 'Hermeneutic phenomenology' in the hands of Heidegger and Gadamer breaks with the subjectivism characteristic of the earlier phase of development of phenomenology. (Schutz never managed to complete this break.) From this perspective, as from that of the later Wittgenstein, language is essentially a social or public phenomenon grounded in forms of life: the self-understanding of the individual can only occur in terms of 'publicly available' concepts. A person can only refer to his private sensations in the same framework of language as he refers to those of others. This is very different from the philosophical schema within which Weber worked, and cuts across the assumptions of methodological individualism, since the locus of the creation of meaning is taken to be the standards or rules of the collectivity rather than the subjective consciousness of the individual actor, the latter in fact presupposing the former. Garfinkel's writings certainly assume the same stance as this, and it is thus quite misleading to represent ethnomethodology, as many critics have been prone to do, as a form of subjectivism.

Several of the ideas mentioned in the foregoing sections are of basic significance to the social sciences; but they cannot be accepted as they stand, within the traditions of thought that have given rise to them: it is as vital to recognize the shortcomings of these traditions as it is to appreciate the signal value of their contributions. The limitations of certain versions of ethnomethodology bear definite similarities to those apparent in the *verstehen* tradition. In identifying some such shortcomings, however, in the interests of brevity, I shall refer directly only to ethnomethodology.

First, in Garfinkel's writings (and most of those who have made use of them at all extensively in seeking to do the sort of 'remedying of constructive analysis' with which Garfinkel himself disclaims concern), 'accountability' is severed from the pursuance of practical motives or interests. 'Everyday practical activities' refers to much more than the sustaining of an intelligible world. The achievement of an 'ordered' social world has to refer not only to its meaningful or intelligible character, but to the meshings – and conflicts – of interests that actors bring to 'accounting processes' and which they endeavour to pursue as part and parcel of those processes. This is one reason, I think, why the reports of conversations that figure in ethnomethodological writings have a peculiarly empty character: conversations are not described in relation to the goals or motives of speakers, and appear as disembodied verbal interchange. Terms such as 'practical accomplishment', etc., that brook large in ethnomethodological discourse are in this sense not used appropriately. 'Doing bureaucracy', 'doing science', and so on, involve more than merely making such phenomena 'accountable'.

Second, to recognize the force of this comment is to imply that every relation of meaning is also a relation of power – a matter of what makes some 'accounts' *count*. In the most transient forms of everyday conversation there are elements of power, that may exist in a direct sense as differential resources that participants bring to the interaction, such as the possession of superior verbal skills, but may also reflect much more generalized imbalances of power (e.g. class relations) structured into the society as a totality. The creation of an accountable world cannot be explicated apart from such imbalances of resources that actors bring to encounters.

Third, acknowledgement of the central importance of the notion of human agency to sociological theory has to be complemented with something akin to orthodox 'structural' analysis in sociology. I would express this by saying that ethnomethodological studies are concerned with the production of society, as a skilled accomplishment of lay actors, but much less with its *reproduction* as a series of structures. However, the problem of the social reproduction of structures is also dealt with quite inadequately in orthodox functionalist theory, where it appears in the guise of the 'internalization of values'. To reconcile the notions of agency and structure it is necessary to refer to what I call the duality of structure, an idea quite readily explicated in terms of the relation between speech acts and the existence of a language. When a speaker utters a sentence, he draws upon a structure of syntactical rules in producing the speech act. The rules in this sense generate what the speaker says. But the act of speaking grammatically also *reproduces* the rules which generate the utterance, and which only 'exist' in this way.[7]

Fourth, the term 'common sense' has to be elucidated more carefully than is characteristic of common-sense thought itself. The 'incorrigibility' of common sense as a necessary resource for social analysis should not blind us to its status as a topic. To 'understand' a form of life is to be able in principle (not necessarily, of course, in practice) to participate in it as a 'competent member'. From this angle, common sense – that is to say, the forms of mutual knowledge shared by the members of a common culture – is a resource that sociologists and anthropologists have to make use of. As a resource such mutual knowledge is not corrigible for the social scientist. The mistake of many of those influenced by ethnomethodological writings is to suppose that there is not another sense of common sense, represented as beliefs that are in principle open to scrutiny in the light of the findings of social science. If common sense is itself set up as a 'topic', the beliefs that are involved, whether about society itself or about nature, are in principle open to rational examination. To study, say, the practice of sorcery in an unfamiliar culture, an anthropologist has to master the categories of meaning whereby sorcery is organized as an activity in that culture. But it does not follow from this that he has to accept as valid the belief that sickness can be induced in a victim by means of magical ritual.

At this point we can return to the problem, introduced in the early part of the paper, of the conditions under which sociology can aspire to be revelatory with regard to common sense. In one respect, this becomes easy to deal with. What we can hope to do in social analysis is to offer explanations of the unacknowledged grounds of action whereby society is produced and reproduced by its constituent actors as a skilled accomplishment. But the matter cannot be left there, since I have so far not mentioned a key respect in which one of the themes of ethnomethodology conjoins to those of the newer *verstehen* tradition: that of reflexivity. The notion of 'self-reflection' enters ethnomethodology only in respect of the 'members' whose 'ethnomethods' are subjected to study. The reflexivity of the ethnomethodological observer, on the other hand, is rarely mentioned at all. This in some part serves to conceal the unresolved character of the two strains in Garfinkel's writings noted earlier: a recognition of the hermeneutic circle on the one hand, and a tendency towards naturalism on the other. For if it is the case that we should treat lay actors as knowledgeable agents, who reflexively monitor their own behaviour, surely the same has to be said of the self-reference of the ethnomethodologist? That is to say, the providing of ethnomethodological accounts of lay actions is itself a reflexively monitored skilled accomplishment. At this point, the circle threatens to become a vicious one: for any ethnomethodological account must display the same characteristics as it claims to discern in the accounts of lay actors; it could in turn be subjected to ethnomethodological analysis, and so could *that* account and so on. Garfinkel obviously accepts this fact of 'infinite potential elaboration', and indeed in one way wants to point it up as a feature of all 'accounting procedures'. But it is hardly satisfactory to leave matters there. We have to attempt to explicate the relation between observers' and lay actors' accounts of their connected forms of 'practical activity'.

The importance of the European schools of social philosophy referred to previously is that they do seek to confront reflexivity on these two levels – that of the observing social scientist and that of lay actors. In this respect some of the critics of 'hermeneutic phenomenology' have more interesting things to say than those who have remained within its confines. Apel, Habermas and Lorenzer have developed important analyses of some of the relevant issues.[8] It is a principal emphasis of their writings that there is a shifting relation between elements that actors reflexively apply as reasons for their acts, and features of those acts that operate independently of their awareness. The greater the range of knowledge that is made available to actors, such that previously unacknowledged grounds of action become available to the reflexive monitoring of their conduct, the greater the scope of the rational autonomy of action. The social scientist can contribute to extending the compass of such knowledge; it follows, for such authors therefore, that *his* reflexivity should be tied to an awareness of the potentialities of social theory as *critical* theory.

Max Weber on interpretative sociology

Weber's critique of intuitionism, in his essays on Roscher and Knies, was based upon an appraisal of the significance and scope of rationality in human conduct. It is erroneous, Weber argues, to suppose that because human action is 'subjective' it is also 'unpredictable'; on the contrary, as lay members of society we depend upon the general predictability of the actions of others, just as they do of our own actions; conversely the accurate prediction of physical happenings is normally only possible under artificially manipulated conditions. Human conduct tends to be predictable, to either the lay or the social scientific observer, to the degree to which it is 'rational' in terms of the selection of means to attain specific ends. This, for Weber, disposes of the argument of some of his contemporaries that the freedom of will enjoyed by human beings separates their action from the behaviour of objects in the natural world. According to Weber, the 'freer' the action of the person, that is to say, the less his conduct is influenced by emotional impulses over which he has no conscious control, the more easily it can be analysed according to a means–ends scheme of rationality.[9] This also leads Weber to reject the idea, advocated by some of the authors subject to his critical attack – and an idea which has lately resurfaced in a new guise in the writings of some modern philosophers – that intentional action cannot be subjected to causal analysis as natural events can. Thus, in Weber's view, what he calls 'motive-explanation' is definitely causal explanation, but it is causal explanation that can only be attained via a prior grasp of the 'subjective meanings' that men attach to their actions. The task of sociology, therefore ('in the sense in which this highly ambiguous word is used here', as Weber remarks in a characteristic phrase) is to concern itself 'with the interpretative understanding of social action and thereby with a causal explanation of its course and consequences'.[10]

Weber's definition of 'social action', in contrast to the formulation of 'social fact' in Durkheim, is expressed in terms of the subjective orientation of the agent: action is social, he says, if the actor takes account of the behaviour of others in orienting his own conduct. But while this appears neat and precise, it turns out to be quite unsatisfactory. Who are the 'others' in this formulation? Do they have to be immediately present? It is evident enough that according to the definition, as Weber says, the instance of two cyclists who collide because neither sees the other approaching is not a case of social action – that is, not until they start arguing over who was responsible for the accident. But what of the individual who, as a beginner, directs his actions when cycling along by consciously remembering the instructions of the person who told him how to steer straight? What of the instance quoted in the previous paper: a man shaving? The significance of the latter example is easy to see, because here the action is oriented to *a convention or norm*. But this then creates difficulties with Weber's original definition, however, since an orientation to a legal or moral standard or convention does not necessarily involve any conscious component of the sort that is integral to Weber's formulation. By driving on the left-hand side of the road, I am certainly acting according to a definite set of social conventions, whether any other car is in sight or not. There is something awry in Weber's view.

Let us at this point move to the core of Weber's analysis, his outline of 'interpretative sociology' as such. Weber first of all distinguishes behaviour (*Verhalten*) from action (*Handeln*); each of these, according to him, can be explained by an observer, but the explanation of the first cannot be framed in terms of the subjective intent of the actor, since it is either reactive or habitual in character, whereas the explanation of the latter, which is 'meaningful' to the actor, *has to* be framed in these terms, and is hence the province of interpretative sociology (or is so, in so far as it is 'social' action – but I have already noted that there are difficulties with this). The rudiments of Weber's position are as follows. The process of interpreting the meaning of social action, as employed by social observers, should be undertaken with the aim of meeting the same standards of precision and verifiability as are sought in natural science. The empathic 'reliving' of an experience is important for understanding, particularly of conduct that has a strongly affective or mystical content, but it is rational action which can be understood and described with the greatest degree of certainty in the correctness of the interpretation. The fact that no one can capture the experience of another fully is not important, for 'one need not have been Caesar in order to understand Caesar'. There are two sorts of understanding: that which is achieved directly (*aktuelles Verstehen*), and 'explanatory understanding'. Thus we understand in an immediate way 'the meaning of the proposition 2 × 2 = 4 when we hear or read it', 'an outbreak of anger as manifested by facial expression, exclamations or irrational movements', 'the action of a woodcutter or of somebody who reached for the knob to shut a door'. But when we understand the motive which a person attaches to an action, we explain what impels him to write down the expression 2 × 2 = 4, what makes him give vent to an outburst of anger, etc. What we do here is to place the action 'within a broader social context of meaning': we are able to explain why a man writes '2 × 2 = 4' 'if we know that he is engaged in balancing a ledger or in making a scientific demonstration'. What Weber called the 'causal adequacy' of such an explanation entails that 'according to established generalizations from experience, there is a probability that it [the action] will always actually occur in the same way'.[11]

This exposition of understanding and explaining action raises several major difficulties, however. The best way to show this is to consider some of the examples Weber gives in separating 'direct' from 'explanatory' understanding. Direct understanding is where we immediately grasp the meaning of an action, without reference to the wider context in which it is carried out. But this is not really possible, or at least it covers various discriminations that Weber did not make. Take the example of the man chopping wood. There are various answers to the question 'What is he doing?' as there are to the question 'Why is he doing it?' From the 'subjective' standpoint of the person it would seem possible, at least, to say that what he is doing is 'having fun' or 'amusing himself', and that this is therefore the 'meaning' of the action. But he could equally well be said to be 'bringing a cutting implement down sharply on a wooden object', 'cutting wood', 'chopping logs', 'preparing firewood' – and to choose one expression rather than another might perhaps be a matter of some significance, since the 'meaning' of the act is 'understood', that is to say, identified, differently in the different descriptions. Weber does not seem to perceive this as a source of difficulty, nor does he appear to see that it could be plausibly argued that such 'understandings' are not formulated in terms of the subjective experience of the actor, but are publicly accessible descriptions, in which it may seem possible for the observer's judgement to override that of the person who acts. The fact that no single description is immediately noticeable as the 'correct' one indicates that the idea of 'direct understanding' that Weber expounds is wrong. In understanding an 'outburst of anger', the action of a woodcutter or someone reaching for the knob to shut the door, what the observer does is precisely what Weber characterizes as 'explanatory understanding', that is, he 'places the act in an intelligible and more inclusive context of meaning'. This becomes easier to see if we pick examples from an alien context: in a society in which anger is expressed in a manner unfamiliar to us, say by clapping the hands, we 'understand' what is happening only when we are able to identify this *as* an expression of anger.

What Weber effectively does in distinguishing direct and explanatory understanding is to transform the division between *verstehen* and *erklären* into two sequential aspects of social scientific method. The former becomes the premise of the latter. We have to understand the meaning of what an actor is doing before we can explain why he is doing it: hence we have to be concerned with both the 'adequacy on the level of meaning' and 'causal adequacy' – in his critique of Stammler's philosophy of law, Weber tries to show in some detail the unfortunate consequences of ignoring such a distinction. He is quite right to insist upon it, and also to point out that upon it depends the possibility of a social science which does more than merely describe actors' own understanding of their acts. But because he still proceeds from a notion of subjective meaning, the theoretical terms in which he couches the differentiation are inadequate.

5 Marx, Weber and the development of capitalism

There are few intellectual relationships in the literature of sociology which present as great an interpretative problem as that posed by the assessment of the connections between the writings of Karl Marx and those of Max Weber. It has been the view of many that Weber's writings – particularly *The Protestant Ethic and the Spirit of Capitalism* – provide a 'refutation' of Marx's materialism; others have taken a completely opposite view, considering that much of Weber's sociology 'fits without difficulty into the Marxian scheme'.[1]

One main problem which has helped to obscure the nature of the relationship between the views of the two thinkers is that it is only relatively recently – since something like a decade after Weber's death – that it has become possible to evaluate Marx's writings in the light of works which, while of fundamental importance to the assessment of Marx's thought, were not published until almost a century after they were first written.[2] These previously unpublished works have made two things clear. First, that Marx's conception of 'historical materialism'[3] is considerably more subtle, and much less dogmatic, than would appear from certain of his oft-quoted statements in such sources as the Preface to *A Contribution to the Critique of Political Economy*.[4] Second, that Engels's contributions to Marxism[5] have to be carefully distinguished from the underlying threads of Marx's own thought.[6] In order, therefore, to assess the main points of similarity and divergence between Marx and Weber, it is necessary to reconsider the nature of historical materialism in general, and Marx's conception of the genesis and trend of movement of capitalism in particular. While one must, of course, respect Weber's own statements on the subject of his relationship to Marx, these are not always a sufficient index.

The confusion in subsequent literature over the nature of Weber's critique of Marx stems also from a failure to distinguish

a number of different, although interrelated, themes in Weber's
writings. Weber's insistence upon the absolute logical separation
between factual knowledge and value-directed action should not
be allowed to obscure his equally emphatic stress upon the
relevance of historical and sociological analysis to practical participation in politics.[7] Some of Weber's most important sociological
ideas are, indeed, more clearly revealed in his directly political
writings than in his academic publications.[8] Weber wrote, therefore, not simply as an intellectual critic of Marx, but also in
response to the writings and political involvements of the prominent Marxist politicians and authors of his day. Three partially
separable aspects of Weber's views may thus be isolated: *a*) his
attitude towards 'Marxism' in the shape of the main Marxist
political agency in Germany, the Social Democratic Party; *b*) his
views upon the academic contributions of Marxist authors to
history and sociology; *c*) his views upon what he considered to
be Marx's own original ideas. These three aspects of Weber's
thought may in turn be distinguished from the analytic problem
of how far Weber's understanding of Marx's theory of historical
materialism was in fact valid.

In analysing these four dimensions of the relationship between
Marx and Weber I shall concentrate mainly on that issue which
was of primary importance to both: the interpretation of the
development of modern capitalism in Europe. The sequence of
changes which took place in the social and political structure of
Germany from the middle up until the concluding years of the
nineteenth century constitutes an essential background to the
whole of the paper: Weber's attitudes towards Marx and Marxism
cannot be adequately understood and analysed outside of this
context. Weber's work was not written merely as a rejoinder to a
wraith-like 'ghost of Marx', but also formed part of a debate
involving a force – Marxism – which played a major political and
intellectual role in Imperial Germany. The paper thus falls into
three parts: the historical background of the development of
German society over the latter half of the nineteenth century;
Weber's attitudes towards, and views upon, Marx and Marxism;
the analytic problem which faces an observer today who attempts
to assess the logical and empirical similarities and divergences
between the writings of Marx and Weber. These three parts are,
however, linked together by a single underlying theme. This is
that the series of changes described in the first category – the

social and political development of Germany in the second part of the nineteenth century – help to elucidate key features in both the evolution of Marxism in that country[9] and also in Weber's response to it as a political influence and an academic doctrine.

The historical background

At the turn of the nineteenth century, Germany consisted of thirty-nine competing principalities. The two leading German states, Prussia and Austria, were both major powers: their very rivalry was one factor hindering German unification. The hopes of German nationalism were, however, also obstructed by the ethnic composition of Austria and Prussia themselves. Austria, after 1815, had more non-Germans in her population than Germans; Prussia incorporated large numbers of Poles within her territories to the East. The nationalist doctrine could foreseeably entail, for Prussia, the return of these lands to a Polish state. Thus the Austrian government was flatly opposed to any movement towards an integral German state; and, in spite of a strong current of nationalism, the case with Prussia was not very different.

But of greater importance than these factors in retarding the political unification of Germany were more basic characteristics of the social and economic structure of the country. Germany was, compared to the most advanced capitalist country, Britain, still almost in the middle ages, both in terms of the level of her economic development, and in terms of the low degree of political liberalization within the various German states. In Prussia, the landed aristocracy, the Junkers, whose power sprang from their ownership of the large ex-Slavic estates to the east of the Elbe, maintained a dominant position within the economy and government. The emergent German bourgeoisie, then, had virtually no access to the reins of government in the early part of the nineteenth century.

But Germany could hardly remain completely isolated from the sweeping currents of political change which had been set in motion in France by the events of 1789. Marx's early works were written in the anticipation of a German revolution. Indeed, it might be said that Marx's awareness of the very backwardness of Germany in its social and economic structure was at the root of his original conception of the role of the proletariat in history. In

France, Marx wrote in 1844, 'partial emancipation is the basis of complete emancipation'; but in Germany, so much less developed, a 'progressive emancipation' was impossible: the only possibility of advancement was through a radical revolution. In Germany, 'complete emancipation is the *conditio sine qua non* of any partial emancipation'. This can be accomplished, Marx wrote, only by the formation of the proletariat, 'a class which has *radical chains* . . . a class which is the dissolution of all classes, a sphere of society which has a universal character because its sufferings are universal. . . .'[10] The proletariat at this time barely existed in Germany; a fact which, if Marx was not fully aware of it in 1844, he certainly recognized by 1847. By the latter date Marx was clear in his mind that the imminent revolution in Germany would be a bourgeois one;[11] but the peculiar characteristics of the social structure of Germany, so it still seemed to Marx, might make it possible for a bourgeois revolution to be followed closely by a proletarian one.[12] Marx was, however, conscious of the weakness of the German bourgeoisie, and noted that, even before having made any direct claim to power, the bourgeoisie were prone to waste whatever strength they possessed in premature and unnecessary conflicts with the nascent working-class.[13] The failure of the 1848 revolutions in Germany bore witness to this fact, and dispelled Marx's optimism about an immediate 'leap into the future' in Germany – or indeed in Britain or France.

The 1848 uprisings were nevertheless a salutary experience for the ruling circles in the German states, and especially in Prussia. Following this date, a number of social and political reforms were instituted which moved the country away from the traditional semi-feudal autocracy. The failure of 1848 to produce any more radical reforms, however, served as something of a death-knell to the hopes, not merely of the small groups of socialists, but also of the liberals. The maintenance of Junker economic power, of their dominance of the officer corps in the army and in the civil-service bureaucracy, led the German liberals perforce to acceptance of a series of compromise measures introducing nothing more than a semblance of parliamentary democracy.[14] The events of 1848 mark a line of direct linkage between Marx and Weber. For Marx, the result was physical exile in England, and an intellectual recognition of the importance of showing in detail the 'laws of movement' of capitalism as an economic system. Within Germany, the failures of 1848 paved the way for the ineptness of liberalism which, as compared to the bold successes of Bismarck's hegemony, formed such an important background to the whole of Weber's thinking in his political sociology. Perhaps most important of all, the persistence of the traditional social and economic structure in Germany after 1848 drastically affected the role of the labour movement, placing it in quite a different position to that of either Britain or France.[15]

There is no space here to discuss in any detail the complicated issue of Marx's relationship to Lassalle and to the movement which Lassalle founded.[16] Certain aspects of this relationship are, however, pertinent. There was from the beginning of the Social Democratic movement a built-in ambivalence towards Marx's doctrines which formed a permanent source of schism within the party. While on the one hand Lassalle was deeply indebted in his theoretical views to Marx's theory of capitalism, in his practical leadership of the new movement he constantly acted in a way opposed to Marx's own views on specific issues, and advocated policies contrary to the very theory which he professed to accept. Thus, in contrast to Marx, who held that the German working-class should throw in its weight with the bourgeoisie, in order to secure the bourgeois revolution which would subsequently provide the conditions for the assumption of power by the proletariat, Lassalle led the working-class movement away from any sort of collaboration with the liberals. In doing so, Lassalle fostered the sort of separation between theory and practice which was heinous to Marx, and he also thereby sowed the first seeds of the debate between 'evolution' versus 'revolution' which later was really the *caput mortuum* of the Social Democratic Party as an agent of radical social change.

Lassalle died the same year that Weber was born. By this time the future of Germany had already been set. The detachment of the labour movement from the liberals, in conjunction with other factors, set the scene for Bismarck's unification of Germany in which, as Bismarck said, 'Germany did not look to Prussia's liberalism, but to her power'. In 1875, when Marx's leading advocates in Germany – Liebknecht and Bebel – accepted union with the Lassallean wing of the labour movement, Germany was in both political and economic terms a very different nation from that which Marx originally wrote about in the 1840s. Political integration had been achieved, not through the rise of a revolutionary bourgeoisie, but as a result, largely, of a policy of

Realpolitik founded essentially upon the bold use of *political* power 'from the top', and occurring within a social system which retained, in large degree, its traditional structure.

The difficult phases of initial political integration and the 'take-off' into industrialization, were accomplished in quite a different fashion in Germany from the typical process of development in Britain – and, in *Capital*, Marx accepted the latter country as providing the basic framework for his theory of capitalist development. In Germany, political centralization and rapid economic advancement took place without the formation of a fully liberalized bourgeois society. Thus neither the Marxists of the Social Democratic Party – even before Marx's death in 1883 – nor the German liberals, possessed an adequate historical model within which they could comprehend the peculiarities of their own position within the German social structure. The Social Democrats clung tenaciously to a revolutionary catechism which became increasingly irrelevant to the real social and economic structure of an industrialized German state. Eventually, therefore, the inherent tension within the Social Democratic Party between Marxian views of the revolutionary transcendence of capitalism and the Lassallean emphasis upon the appropriation of the capitalist state *from within* through the achievement of a fully universal franchise, became forced out into the open. Bernstein's *Evolutionary Socialism* (1899),[17] although itself based partly upon a British model, provided a coherent theoretical interpretation of the social forces which were driving the Social Democratic Party towards acceptance of the putative acquisition of power from within the existing order. *Evolutionary Socialism* made manifest the realization that the relationship between the political and economic development of capitalism could not be adequately comprehended in terms of the main theses of *Capital*: the progressive formation of a two-class society, the 'pauperization' of the vast majority, and the imminent collapse of capitalism in a 'final' catastrophic crisis. These latter conceptions survived as Social Democratic orthodoxy in the face of Bernstein's challenge; but they assumed an increasingly deterministic form. What were for Marx tendential properties of capitalism thus became regarded by his followers as mechanically given inevitabilities. This perspective allowed the preservation of revolutionary phraseology without demanding a concomitant revolutionary activism; if capitalism was necessarily doomed, all that needed to be done, so it appeared, was to wait in the wings until the final disintegration of the capitalist economy occurred.

Weber's attitude towards Marx and Marxism

The German liberals faced comparable dilemmas. Liberalism also had its roots in an earlier period, and in forms of society considerably different from that of Imperial Germany. While maintaining an adherence to the liberal values of individual freedom and political participation, the liberals were heavily compromised by their enforced adaptation – and subordination – to the dominant autocratic order. Weber's own political writings and involvements constantly manifest his consciousness of this.

Weber's appreciation of the significance of political power, particularly as wielded by Bismarck in successfully promoting the rapid internal consolidation and economic development of Germany (and, more specifically, his use of the bureaucracy to do so), is one key dimension of Weber's approach to politics, and of his sociology more generally.[18] Weber's commitment to nationalism, and his lifelong emphasis upon the primacy of the German state, also have to be understood in these terms.[19] This determination to recognize the realities of the use of political power, however, was counterpointed in Weber's writing by an equally resolute adherence to the values of classical European liberalism. The pathos of Weber's thought, whereby he found himself compelled to recognize an increasing divergence between the main lines of development in modern societies, and the values which he himself recognized as representing the distinctive ethos of Western culture, was an expression – albeit in a highly subtle and ratiocinated form – of the peculiar dilemmas of German liberalism as a whole.

a) *Weber's attitude towards the Social Democratic Party.* Weber's famous inaugural address at Freiburg in 1895 outlined his interpretation of the hopes of German liberalism in the face of Romantic conservatism on the one side, and the Marxist party on the other.[20] Weber specifically dissociated himself from the 'mystical' advocacy of the German state,[21] but he also expressed the conviction that the working-class was politically incapable of leading the nation. While expressing agreement with some elements which constituted part of the programme of the Social Democrats, including that the working-class should enjoy full rights of political representation, Weber argued that the working-class 'is politically immature'. According to him much of the revolutionary fervour of the leaders of the working-class movement was quite divergent from the real trend of development of the Social Democratic Party – which, as he perceived at an early date, would move towards accommodation to the prevailing German state rather than providing a realistic revolutionary alternative to it. As Weber expressed it, the German state would conquer the Social Democratic Party, and not vice versa.[22]

Weber was scornful of the continuing claims of the Junkers to power, although he was forced to recognize that, in practice, their influence in the officer corps and, to a lesser degree, in the government bureaucracy was still considerable. The Junkers were, nevertheless, in Weber's eyes, obviously a declining class. The main source of hope, therefore, for a German state which would maintain its national integrity, but which would reach a level of political democracy compatible with an industrialized society, was through the strengthening of the liberal bourgeoisie as a group capable of providing national leadership. This meant, Weber increasingly came to emphasize, developing a governmental system which would vest real political power in parliament. The result of Bismarck's domination, he believed, had left Germany without effective political leadership which could take control of the bureaucratic machine of government, and threatened Germany with 'uncontrolled bureaucratic domination'.[23] His attitude towards the possibility of socialism in Germany was by and large simply a logical extension of this position. Should a socialist government, and a planned economy,[24] be set up, the result would be an even greater bureaucratic repression. Not only would there be no counterweight to the spread of bureaucracy in the political sphere, but this would inevitably be true of the economic sphere also. 'This would be socialism,' Weber wrote, 'in about the same manner in which the ancient Egyptian "New Kingdom" was socialist.'[25]

Weber's views on the Social Democratic Party remained fairly consistent over the course of his life; his evaluation of his own political position with regard to the policies of the Party did, however, change, together with the changing nature of the German social and political structure. Thus, towards the end of his life, having witnessed the occurrence of what he had previously foreseen – the increasing integration of the Social Democratic Party into the existing parliamentary order – he declared in 1918 that he was so close to the Social Democratic Party as to find it difficult to separate himself from it.[26] But his consistent view of 'Marxism' in the shape of the Social Democratic Party in Germany, was that its professed objectives – the revolutionary overthrow of the State, and the institution of a classless society – were entirely divergent from the real role which it was destined to play in German politics.

b) Weber's views on the academic contributions of Marxist authors. Weber's position with respect to the theoretical notions which the main spokesmen for and 'interpreters' of Marxism expounded cannot simply be deduced from his relationship to the Social Democratic Party, since the latter was determined in some degree by his appreciation of the political realities of the German situation. Weber recognized that certain of the leading Marxist theoreticians of his time had made distinct and even brilliant contributions to history, economics and jurisprudence; and he maintained close academic contact with some scholars who were heavily influenced by Marx.[27] It is important to recognize that the bulk of Weber's writing on capitalism and religion was written within the context of the appearance of a spate of scholarly works which claimed Marxian ancestry, but many of which either employed what Weber regarded as a vulgarization of Marx's ideas, or which departed considerably from what he considered to be the main tenets of Marx's historical materialism.[28]

Although Weber once spoke of *The Protestant Ethic and the Spirit of Capitalism* as offering 'an empirical refutation of historical materialism', the essay had, in fact, a complicated genealogy. Weber was interested in religion as a social phenomenon from his early youth.[29] While his studies of law and economic history diverted him for some period from following this interest in his academic writings, the *Protestant Ethic* is clearly an expression of concerns which had always been in the forefront of Weber's mind.[30] He undoubtedly wrote the essay in some part as a conscious polemic against the 'one-sided' conception of religion as portrayed by historical materialism. But 'historical materialism' here referred partly to the writings of Kautsky and others.[31] Moreover, it was probably Weber's association with Sombart which provided the most direct source of stimulus to his attempt to analyse the role of ascetic Protestantism in the rise of capitalism.[32]

Weber was sympathetic to the ideas of some of the prominent Marxist 'revisionists', although he regarded them as still being caught up, whatever their departures from Marx, within a metaphysical theory of history which was simply a handicap to their accurate perception of socio-economic reality. In general, he accepted, in common with Bernstein and others, that modern capitalism is not marked by a progressive differentiation between an increasingly wealthy minority and a 'pauperized' mass; that the white-collar middle class do not develop a consciousness of class identity with the manual working class; and that there is no sign of an imminent cataclysmic break-up of capitalism.[33] It can hardly be said, however, that Weber derived these views from any of the Marxist 'revisionists': Weber was clear in his own mind that the capitalist mode of production was not leading towards an open and irresistible class struggle between labour and capital. His own references to stratification in modern society show that he recognized the existence of multiple divisions of interest and of status which tend to obscure the Marxist class divisions. Thus he pointed out, for example, that the manual working-class, far from having become a homogeneous unskilled group, is cut across by differences of skill-level which create divisions of class interest within the working class as a whole.[34]

Weber's relationship to the leading Marxist thinkers of his time was, therefore, a complex one; necessarily so, in virtue of the variety of differing positions assumed by those who claimed to be following Marx.

   c) *Weber's views on Marx.* Weber, of course, considered that Marx had made fundamental contributions to historical and sociological analysis. But, to Weber, Marx's theories could not be regarded as anything more than sources of insight, or at most as ideal-typical concepts, which could be applied to illuminate particular, specific sequences of historical development. The radical neo-Kantian position which Weber adopted from Rickert and Windelband[35] effectively excluded any other possibility: in Weber's conception, Marx's attribution of overall 'direction' to the movement of history was as illegitimate as the Hegelian philosophy of history which helped to give it birth.[36] While Weber admitted, with strong reservations, the use of 'developmental stages' as a 'heuristic means' which could facilitate the explanatory interpretation of historical materials, he rejected totally the construction of 'deterministic schemes' based upon any sort of general theory of historical development.[37]

The necessary corollary of this was the rejection of Marx's materialism as a key to the explanation of historical change. The thesis that economic factors in any sense 'finally' explain the course of history, Weber asserted, as a scientific theorem is 'utterly finished'.[38] He recognized that Marx's writings varied in the degree of sophistication with which the materialist conception of history was presented – the *Communist Manifesto*, for example, set out Marx's views 'with the crude elements of genius of the early form'.[39] But even in its more thorough formulation in *Capital*, he pointed out, Marx nowhere defined precisely how the 'economic' is delimited from other spheres of society. Weber's distinction between 'economic', 'economically relevant' and 'economically conditioned' phenomena was aimed at clarifying this problem. Economic action he defined as action which seeks by peaceful means to acquire control of desired utilities.[40] There are, however, many forms of human action – such as religious practices – which, while they are not 'economic' according to this definition, have relevance to economic phenomena in that they influence the needs or propensities which individuals have to acquire or make use of utilities. These are economically relevant forms of action. Phenomena which are economically relevant can in turn be separated from those which are economically conditioned : these are actions, which although again not 'economic' according to Weber's definition, are causally influenced by economic factors. As he pointed out: 'After what has been said, it is self-evident that: firstly, the boundary lines of "economic" phenomena are vague and not easily defined; secondly, the "economic" aspect of a phenomenon is by no means *only* "economically conditioned" or *only* "economically relevant" . . .'[41] Calvinism was in these terms both economically conditioned and economically relevant with regard to the early formation of rational capitalism in Western Europe.

He also pointed to another source of conceptual ambiguity in Marx's 'economic' interpretation of history: that Marx failed to distinguish in a clearly formulated way between the 'economic' and the 'technological'. Where Marx slipped into a more or less direct technological determinism, Weber claimed, his argument is inadequate. Marx's famous assertion that 'the hand-mill gives us feudalism, the steam-mill, capitalism'[42] was, according to Weber, 'a technological proposition, not an economic one, and it can be

G

clearly proven that it is simply a false assertion. For the era of the hand-mill, which lasted up to the threshold of the modern period, showed the most varied kinds of cultural "superstructures" in all places.'[43] A given form of technology may be associated with varying types of social organization, and vice versa; this can be seen in the very fact that socialism, as Marx expected it to develop – although being a different social and economic system from capitalism – would involve essentially the same technological base as capitalism.

The positive influence of Marx's writings over Weber is most evident in Weber's insistence that values and ideas, while most definitely not being merely 'derivations' of material interests, nevertheless must always be analysed in relation to such interests. Weber, of course, recognized the importance of class conflicts in history, while denying that their prevalence or significance is anything like as great as that postulated by Marx. For Weber, conflicts between status groups of various kinds, and between political associations – including nation-states – are at least equally important in the historical development of the major civilizations. The conception of sectional 'interest', therefore, cannot be limited to economic interests, but must be extended to other spheres of social life; political parties, for example, have interests which derive from their situation as aspirants to or as wielders of power, and which do not necessarily in any direct sense rest upon shared economic interests.[44]

There has been some considerable debate over the degree to which Weber's methodological works,[45] written relatively early on in his career, accord with the substantive content of his later writings, particularly *Economy and Society*.[46] What is certain, however, is that Weber never abandoned his basic stand upon the complete logical separation of fact and value, nor his correlate assumption of the irreducibility of competing values. It was this epistemological position, Weber recognized, which separated him most decisively from Marx. Marx's work involved an 'ethic of ultimate ends', and therefore committed he who accepted it to a 'total' conception of history. For Weber, science cannot answer the question: ' "Which of the warring gods should we serve"?'[47]

Weber and Marx: the analytic problem

Weber's critique of Marx was sophisticated, and was not simply an abstract analysis of the 'logic' of Marx's theories, but embodied the very substance of Weber's studies of history and society. This very fact, however, means that Weber's own explicit evaluations of Marx's views cannot be regarded as the sole source of evidence on the matter. That Weber's own remarks on *The Protestant Ethic*, for instance, are not completely unambiguous is indicated by the confusion over the objectives of the work in the large literature which has surrounded the subject since the first publication of Weber's essay.[48] Obviously, moreover, the evaluation of the differences between Marx and Weber must depend upon an accurate evaluation of the characteristic views of the former. In order to make clear the substance of Marx's basic theoretical position, it is necessary to touch briefly upon some themes in Marx's writings which, thanks to the enormous body of secondary works written on Marx since the Second World War, have by now become very familiar.

Much of the post-war literature on Marx has centred upon the writings of the 'young Marx': that is, prior to the completion of *The German Ideology* (1846). The debate over the relevance of these early writings to Marx's mature works will certainly continue; but it cannot be doubted that, firstly, there are, at the very least, certain definite threads of continuity which run through the whole of Marx's work, and that, secondly, some of the early writings allow us to clarify what these continuities are.[49] Marx did not ever write a systematic exposition of his 'materialism'. But certain of his early writings make it absolutely clear that his conception of his materialistic approach to history is quite different from what he called 'perceptual materialism'.[50] Marx, in common with the other 'Young Hegelians', began his intellectual development from the standpoint of the critique of religion, derived from a radicalization of Hegel, and based largely upon the thought of David Strauss and Feuerbach. Feuerbach's philosophy was founded upon a reversal of the major premise of Hegel's system. In place of Hegel's idealism, Feuerbach substituted his own version of materialism, stating bluntly that the starting-point of the study of man must be 'real man' living in the 'real material world'.[51] Feuerbach's writing remained mainly confined to the examination of religion: by 'standing Hegel on his feet',[52] he

tried to show that the divine is an illusory product of the real.
God is an idealized projection of man himself; God is the mythical
projection of man's most cherished values, man alienated from his
own (potential) self-perfection.

The consequence of Feuerbach's position is that religion is a
symbolic 'representation' of human aspirations, and that to elimi-
nate human self-alienation all that needs to be done is for religion
to be de-mystified, and placed on a rational level. Marx rapidly
perceived what appeared to him as fundamental defects in this
view. Feuerbach's errors were, first, to speak of 'man' in the
abstract, and thus to fail to perceive that men only exist within
the context of particular societies which change their structure in
the course of historical development; and, second, to treat ideas
or 'consciousness' as simply the 'consequence' of human activities
in the 'material' world. In Marx's words: 'The chief defect of all
previous materialism (including Feuerbach's) is that the object,
actuality, sensuousness, is conceived only in the form of the
object of perception, but not as *sensuous human activity, practice*,
not subjectively'.[53]

Marx referred to his materialism only as 'the guiding thread'
in his studies: ideologies are 'rooted in the material conditions of
life', but this does not entail that there is a universal or unilateral
relationship between the 'real foundation' of society (the relations
of production) and 'legal and political superstructures'.[54] On the
contrary, the specific conclusion which Marx reached in criticizing
Feuerbach was that ideas are social products, which cannot be
explained by the philosopher who stands outside of history, but
only by the analysis of particular forms of society.[55] We must
reject, Marx insisted, any kind of 'recipe or scheme . . . for neatly
trimming the epochs of history', and must 'set about the observation and arrangement – the real depiction – of our historical
material. . . .'[56]

Where Marx did generalize about the relationship between
ideology and material 'substructure', this was in terms of the
specification that the class system is the main mediating link
between the two. The class structure of society exerts a determinate effect upon which ideas *assume prominence* in that society.
This is the sense of Marx's proposition that the ruling ideas in any
epoch are the ideas of the ruling class.[57] It should be pointed out
that, even in Feuerbach's theory, religion is something more than
merely a complete reflection of material reality: it also provides

values and ideals towards which men should strive. God is man as
he ought to be, and therefore the image of the deity holds out the
hope of what man could *become*. Marx took over this notion from
Feuerbach, but mated it with the dialectical conception that it is
the reciprocal interaction of such religious ideas with the social
actions of 'earthly men' which must be examined. This reciprocity
can be understood in terms of analysing the historical development of societies; we cannot understand the relationship between
ideology and society if we 'abstract from the historical process'.[58]
There is no question, then, but that Marx recognized both that
ideologies may have a partially 'internal' autonomous development, and that the degree to which this is so depends upon factors
particular to specific societies, which in every case have to be
studied in empirical detail. This is both consistent with his general
conception of materialism, and is evidenced in his more detailed
          s.[59] Marx's position, in other words, is not incompatible with
          ition of the unique characteristics and influence of ascetic
          tantism in Europe.

          this is, by now, quite well known; what has not been so
          lly appreciated is that even in matters of detail, Marx's dis-
          of the course of historical development in Europe is in
          ways strikingly close to Weber's analysis: this is a fact
          las only become fully apparent with the publication of the
          ites (*Grundrisse*) which Marx wrote for *Capital* in 1857-8,
          cknowledged the importance of the early forms of capi-
          /hich developed in Rome, and his explanation of why these
          'dead-end' is quite similar to that subsequently set out by
          p Marx pointed out that certain of the conditions – includ-
          existence of a nascent capitalist class – which played an
          part in the development of capitalism in Western Europe
          er period, were already present in Rome. Among the
          ie isolated as significant in inhibiting the emergence of
f   capitalism in Rome is that there was strong ideological
pressure against the accumulation of wealth for its own sake:
'Wealth does not appear as the aim of production . . . The inquiry
is always about what kind of property creates the best citizens.
Wealth as an end in itself appears only among a few trading
peoples . . .'[61] Wealth was valued, not intrinsically, but for the
'private enjoyment' it could bring; moreover, labour in general
was regarded with contempt, and as not worthy of free men.
    Marx recognized that there existed numerous prior forms of

capitalism before the emergence of bourgeois society in post-medieval Europe. Thus mercantile capital has often existed – as in Rome – in societies in which the dominant mode of production is not capitalist. Mercantile operations have usually been carried on by marginal groups, such as the Jews. Mercantile capital has existed 'in the most diverse forms of society, at the most diverse stages of the development of the productive forces'.[62] There are cases of societies, other than Rome, where certain segments of the social structure have been quite highly evolved, but where the lack of development of other sectors has limited the ultimate level of economic advancement. Marx quoted the instance of ancient Peru, which in certain respects had a developed economy, but which was kept to a low level of development by the geographical isolation of the society, and by the lack of a monetary system.[63]

Marx's views on the emergence and significance of Christianity in the development of the European societies have to be inferred from various oblique statements in his critiques of Hegel and the 'Young Hegelians'. As a close student of Hegel, Marx was obviously aware of the overriding importance which historians and philosophers attributed to Christianity in the West. Marx did not question the validity of this. What he did attack was the idealistic standpoint within which the influence of Christianity was analysed. Thus he objected to Stirner's treatment of the rise of early Christianity in that it is conducted wholly upon the level of ideas.[64] Christianity arose, Marx stated, as a religion of wandering, uprooted vagrants, and the causes of its expansion have to be related to the internal decay of the Roman Empire: 'the Hellenic and Roman world perished, spiritually in Christianity and materially in the migration of the peoples.'[65] The Christian ethical outlook formed a vital new moral current, contrasting with the moral decadence of Rome. Christianity substituted for Roman pantheism the conception of a single universal God, whose authority is founded upon uniquely Christian notions of sin and salvation. In the later evolution of Christianity in Europe, the Reformation provided a similar moral regeneration in relation to an internally disintegrating feudal society. 'Luther . . . overcame bondage out of devotion by replacing it by bondage out of conviction. He shattered faith in authority because he restored the authority of faith . . . He freed man from outer religiosity because he made religiosity the inner man.'[66]

To suppose that Marx was unaware of the 'ascetic' and 'rational' character of modern European capitalism is to miss some of the most basic premises upon which his analysis and critique of bourgeois society is founded. The 'rationalizing' character of capitalism is manifest most directly, for Marx, in the utter dominance of money in human social relationships, and in the pursuit of money as an end in itself. Money is the epitome of human self-alienation under capitalism, since it reduces all human qualities to quantitative values of exchange.[67] Capitalism thus has a 'universalizing' character, which breaks down the particularities of traditional cultures: 'capital develops irresistibly beyond national barriers and prejudices . . . it destroys the self-satisfaction confined within narrow limits and based upon a traditional mode of life and reproduction.'[68] Capitalism is 'ascetic' in that the actions of capitalists are based upon self-renunciation and the continual re-investment of profits. This is manifest, Marx pointed out, in the theory of political economy: 'Political economy, the science of wealth, is, therefore, at the same time, the science of renunciation, of privation and saving . . . Its true ideal is the ascetic usurious miser and the ascetic but productive slave.'[69] The pursuit of wealth for its own sake is a phenomenon which is, as a general moral ethos, found only within modern capitalism. Marx was as specific on this matter as Weber: 'The passion for wealth as such is a distinctive development; that is to say, it is something other than the instinctive thirst for particular goods such as clothes, arms, jewellery, women, wine . . . The taste for possessions can exist without money; the thirst for self-enrichment is the product of a definite social development, it is not natural, but historical.'[70]

The point to be stressed, however, is that in broad terms Marx's conception of, and empirical treatment of, the role of ideology in society is quite compatible with the more detailed studies undertaken by Weber of the sociology of religion. Marx did not study religion in any detail because, in breaking with the 'Young Hegelians' and with Feuerbach, and in perceiving the need to begin to analyse sociologically the relationships between economy, politics and ideology, Marx effectively overcame – in terms of his own objectives – the need to subject religion to detailed analysis. The 'Young Hegelians', as Marx made clear in *The Holy Family*, continued to devote most of their efforts to the critique of religion, and thus always remained imprisoned within a world-view which was, even if only negatively, a religious one.[71]

To emphasize the general theoretical congruity of much of what Marx and Weber wrote on the history and origins of capitalism is *obviously not* to argue that their views are wholly identical, either in relation to particular problems or in respect of more general issues of social and political theory. It is evident that Marx, while disavowing 'the *passe-partout* of a general historical–philosophical theory whose main quality is that of being super-historical',[72] sought to impose a pattern on historical development which Weber treated as quite impermissible. The concept of charisma, and the basic role which it plays in Weber's sociology, expresses Weber's conviction that human history is not (as Marx believed it to be) rational. The attribution of a discoverable rationality to history is an essential element in the whole of Marx's thought, and is the main tie by which he always remained bound to Hegel. But charisma is specifically irrational; thus the revolutionary dynamic in history, which for Weber is constituted by the periodic emergence of charismatic movements, cannot be connected to any overall rational pattern in the historical development of man. Moreover, by stressing the importance of class, and thus of economic interests, in social development, Marx tended to assimilate economic and political power much more than Weber.[73] This is very definitely a difference of fundamental significance between the two authors. Nevertheless, the divergence here must not be over-exaggerated.[74] Marx anticipated Weber, for example, in recognizing a parallel between the organization of professional armies and the separation of the labourer from his product under modern capitalism. Thus Marx noted: 'In Rome there existed in the army a mass already quite distinct from the people, disciplined to labour . . . it sold to the State the whole of its labour-time for wages . . . as the worker does with the capitalist.'[75]

Conclusion

My objective in this paper has been to separate out several basic strands in the relationship between the writings of Marx and Weber. I have tried to make it clear that the tendency to assimilate these together as forming a blanket 'critique of Marx' has led many commentators to oversimplify Weber's assessment of 'historical materialism'. It has become something of a truism to say that the 'founders' of modern sociology – Weber, Pareto, and

Mosca in particular – developed their theories, at least in part, as 'refutations' of Marx. Each of these authors has at some time been called 'the bourgeois Marx'. This label, however, is inapt in the sense that it implies that their work represents nothing more than a bourgeois response to Marxism. It was this, but it was also much more. Thus Weber's relationship to Marx and to Marxist thought cannot be assessed along a single dimension of 'confirmation' or 'refutation'; Weber's historical studies both destroy some of the cruder Marxist interpretations of historical development, and at the same time, as I have tried to show in this article, *partly* vindicate Marx against his own professed disciples.

Weber wrote at a period when the character of the leading Western European countries generally, and that of Germany more specifically, had changed considerably from the time at which Marx formed his main views. All of the economically advanced societies of the West, by the turn of the twentieth century, had reached a high degree of economic maturity without experiencing the revolutionary re-organization which Marx expected. In Weber's time Marx's thought was carried, in Germany, by the Social Democratic Party. 'Historical materialism' came to be largely identified, in the eyes of Weber and other liberal critics of Marxism, as well as by Marxists themselves, with the systematic exposition of Engels in *Anti-Dühring* and later, *The Dialectics of Nature*.[76] While some commentators have exaggerated the difference between the thought of Marx and Engels,[77] the implications of the position which Engels took in these works are quite definitely at variance with the conception central to most of Marx's writing. By transferring the dialectic to nature, Engels obscured the most essential element of Marx's work, which was 'the dialectical relationship of subject and object in the historical process'.[78] In doing so, Engels helped to stimulate the notion that ideas simply 'reflect' material reality.[79] The political quietism of the Social Democratic Party – which Weber accurately perceived behind its revolutionary phraseology – was bound up with the general adoption of such an outlook, which made possible the preservation of a revolutionary posture in a set of social circumstances which had diverged substantially from the pattern of development anticipated by Marx. The wheel thus in a way came almost full circle. At the risk of oversimplifying what is actually a complicated question, it could be said that Weber's critique of Marxism, as regards the role of ideas in history, in fact came

202 Studies in Social and Political Theory

close to restating, in vast detail, certain elements of the original Marxian conception.

This went hand in hand, ironically, with a rejection of certain key aspects of Marx's analysis of contemporary capitalism, and of the latter's hopes for a future form of radically new society. Marx, writing a generation before Weber, believed that capitalism could, and would, be transcended by a new form of society. Weber wrote with the hindsight of having witnessed the formation of industrial capitalism in Germany in quite different circumstances from Britain or France. Weber's appreciation of this fact was one element in his thought allowing him, while drawing heavily from Marx, to escape from the strait-jacket which the followers of Marx in the Social Democratic Party sought to impose upon history in the name of historical materialism.

But it might be held that, in his analysis of the imminent trend of development of capitalism, Weber himself fell prey to a sort of materialistic determinism of his own. Weber perceived a primary irrationality within capitalism: the 'formal' rationality of bureaucracy, while it makes possible the technical implementation of large-scale administrative tasks, is 'substantively' irrational in that it contravenes some of the most distinctive values of Western civilization. But he foresaw no way of breaking through this irrationality: the future holds out only the likelihood of the increasing submergence of human autonomy and individuality within an ever-expanding bureaucratization of modern life.[80] For Marx, on the other hand, the essential irrationality of capitalism – the contradiction between the alienative impoverishment of the individual and the immense potential opportunities for self-fulfilment offered by modern industry – creates the very conditions for the movement to a form of society in which this irrationality will be overcome. Undoubtedly there are problems of major significance for modern social philosophy which stem from the question of how far the alienative characteristic which Marx attributed to capitalism as a specific form of class society, in fact derive from a bureaucratic rationality which is a necessary concomitant of industrial society, whether it be 'capitalist' or 'socialist'. Does the future promise only the progressive expansion of an order in which, as Weber wrote, 'the technical and economic conditions of machine production . . . determine the lives of all the individuals who are born into this mechanism . . . with irresistible force'?[81] Or is there a realistic possibility that, as Marcuse has expressed it, 'not "pure", formal, technical reason but the reason of domination erects the "shell of bondage", and that the consummation of technical reason can well become the instrument for the *liberation* of man'?[82]

Marx and Weber: problems of class structure

Over recent years, there has grown up a tradition of scholarship, particularly among American authors, which treats the writings of Max Weber on issues of class structure, class conflict and capitalism as 'extensions' or 'elaborations' of Marx's views on these matters. Perhaps the origin of this standpoint is to be found in Gerth and Mills's introduction to what was, and probably remains, the most widely used selection of translations from the spectrum of Weber's works. 'Much of Weber's work', they say, is 'informed by a skilful application of Marx's historical method'; and they continue: 'Part of Weber's own work may be thus seen as an attempt to "round out" Marx's economic materialism by a political and military materialism.'[88] The intellectual relation between Marx and Weber is a matter of some complexity since, as has just been indicated, Weber's proximate polemical targets were often the leading Marxists of his time, whose versions of Marxism were mainly of a 'mechanical' kind. But there are clear conceptual continuities between Marx and Weber in the latter's use of the terms 'class', 'class conflict' and 'capitalism',[84] and it is important to recognize that such terminological similarities readily may serve to gloss over what are perhaps the most deep-lying divergencies between the two thinkers.

Weber's specific use of 'class' connects both with his characterization of 'capitalism' as a type of socio-economic organization, and more generally as the modern Western form of society and culture, on the one hand, and with the emphases of his methodological writings on the other; all of these decisively separate his views from those of Marx. It is commonly accepted that Weber's

famous threefold differentation of class, status and party is in
some part directed polemically against what Weber saw as Marx's
tendency to reduce too much of history to the history of class
struggles. 'Status groups' (*Stände*) play a major role in history,
and are not based directly upon economic relations as classes are;
and in recognizing the third mode of organization linked to the
promotion of interests, the formation of parties in the modern
polity, Weber gives conceptual recognition to his theme that
politics is not merely, or even perhaps primarily, an expression of
class divisions. But it is not these factors alone that set Weber's
analysis off from that of Marx: the more basic differences centre
upon the notions of 'class' and 'class conflict' themselves.

Weber, like Marx, accepts that ' "property" and "lack of property" are . . . the basic categories of all class situations';[85] and
his typology of 'ownership' and 'acquisition classes' is based upon
such a categorization. But most of the weight in Weber's discussion is placed upon the advantages that can be mobilized in
market relations by the possession of particular types of property –
combined with the stress that the kinds of services that can be
offered on the market also provide for the differential mobilization
of market advantages among the propertyless. For Weber, 'class'
is thus distinctively associated with the growth of *markets*, and
'class interests' refer to the distribution of interests in the competitive encounters of labour and commodity markets. Thus Weber
says, for example, that the creditor–debtor relation only becomes
the basis of class situations where a 'credit market' comes into
existence: 'therewith, "class struggles" begin.'[86] 'Class situation'
equals 'market situation'. For Marx, the connection between class
and property, or more accurately private property, is quite different, and is bound in a most basic way to the characterization
of global types of society. His very definition of capitalism or
bourgeois society is in terms of the class relation between capital
and wage-labour, expressed as relations of production: this is both
the most integral feature of capitalism and of course the medium
of its transformation. Weber recognizes that the preconditions of
modern capitalism (as distinct from the various prior types of
capitalistic activity that have existed) include not just the accumulation of capital itself, but the development of formally 'free'
wage-labour, severed from control of its means of production.[87]
But while the capital/wage-labour relation is necessary to the
formation of modern economic enterprise, it is not its most basic

defining feature. The most essential characteristic of modern capitalism is the 'rational', routinized organization of economic activity within organizations having a stable and disciplined division of labour.

This characterization of capitalism is undoubtedly connected with themes in Weber's methodological writings, and more particularly with his emphasis upon the subjective interpretation of meaning. The subject-matter of history and of sociology is essentially 'meaningful social action' and its objective consequences. The decisive impetus to the emergence of modern capitalistic activity was given by the unintended consequences of conduct oriented to the Puritan ethos. The 'spirit of modern capitalism' is an ideal-typical formulation of the meaningful content of a definite form of economic activity. Weber's methodological position, which ties understanding the meaning of conduct to a version of what has subsequently come to be called 'methodological individualism', precluded him from systematically integrating a treatment of modern capitalistic activity, regarded as meaningful conduct, with the overall institutional character of capitalist society and its dynamics. Weber's discussions of modern capitalism as a generic form of economy and society thus tend to cluster into those concerned with capitalistic action and its 'spirit' on the one hand, and those offering an abstract classification of types of economic organization on the other. The same tendency appears in his analyses of class. There are two general, although brief, discussions of class in *Economy and Society*. One, now familiar as 'Class, status and party', discusses the modes of action that may be associated with economic interests; the other outlines the formal typology of ownership and acquisition classes. But it is not easy to discern how the first discussion is supposed to relate to the typology abstractly detailed in the latter. Weber does mention what he calls 'social class', as differentiated from 'class situation' (i.e. market position), but provides only a cursory and uninformative description of what the term is supposed to refer to.[88]

Weber's concept of class or 'class situation' cannot be accepted as a basis for a theory of class structure, for three reasons, each connected with what has been said above. First, the identification of class situation with market situation, and the general thesis that class divisions and class conflicts are phenomena of market relations, have to be rejected. Class relations, we should insist, as

Marx did, are phenomena founded in production. Second, Weber's characterization of modern capitalism as involving above all the 'rational' organization of resources geared to the accumulation of profit is unsatisfactory, if only for the reason that it is not connected to a systematic treatment of the tensions created by the class system integral to capitalist society as a global order. Third, Weber's methodological standpoint, as reflected in his discussion of class, does not provide an adequate medium for connecting 'types of action' on the one hand, with 'supra-individual' institutions on the other.

To disavow the Weberian viewpoint in these terms is not, however, to write off Weber's contributions as worthless. For in emphasizing the importance of market advantages, and the collective interests associated with them, Weber's notion of class helps illuminate areas that are not clearly elucidated in Marx. Class relations, for Marx, are relations of production involved in the extraction of surplus value: but the phrase 'relations of production' covers several types of socio-economic relationships that Marx tends to run diffusely into one another.[89] We may distinguish the following such relationships: 1) those presumed in the operation of the 'task division of labour' in a given technique of production, e.g. between workers engaged in assembly-line production (paratechnical relations); 2) those more broadly involved in the organization of the enterprise, including especially the authority or power relations that pertain within it; 3) those involved in the linkages between productive organizations within commodity and labour markets; and 4) those brought into being through the connections between production and distribution, or the 'consumption' of goods. Weber's discussion of class concentrates upon 3) and indicates the importance, within the societies in which the economy is insulated from direct and overall political control, of the mobilization of advantages stemming from divergent 'market capacities' in class formation. But by identifying class situation and market situation, severing off 1) and 2) to a generalized theory of the rational organization of modern economic life, and 4) to the province of 'status groups', Weber moved away in a basic fashion from the Marxian standpoint.

I have suggested elsewhere how a reconstructed theory of classes and class conflict, which still insists that class divisions are founded in the system of production, and accepts the transformational potential of class conflict, can acknowledge the significance of market relations.[90] The essentials of this position are as follows. 'Class' is a phenomenon of the totality, in the sense in which, in a capitalist society, it expresses a system of exploitative domination cohered in terms of a definite alignment of economy and polity, sanctioned by the state. While this takes different forms in the period of 'classical capitalism' as contrasted with 'neo-' or 'corporate capitalism', it involves in each case the existence of a protective insulation that separates economic from political life – that neutralizes conflicts in industry by declaring them 'non-political'. Private property is the crucial support to this differentiation, guaranteeing definite rights to the mobilization of economic resources, and ensuring the dominance of the 'commodity form'. But in and of itself this is not enough to explicate or analyse class relations as definite structural forms: the generic concept 'class society' covers a variety of different types of class structuration. The structuration of classes as definite social forms, I have suggested, can be examined as in terms of the several aspects of the relations of production distinguished previously. Differential market capacity within the labour market, from this perspective, especially in so far as it is connected with 'closure' in mobility chances both inter- and intra-generationally, is basic to class structuration. But the consequences of the differentiation of market capacities can be either concentrated or fragmented by the influence of the more 'proximate' sources of structuration: the division of labour, and authority system, within economic organizations, and 'distributive groupings' (especially community or neighbourhood segregation). These influences upon class structuration should not be regarded as aggregate factors, but as systematically connected with one another.

6   Four myths in the history of social thought

In this paper I wish to discuss, and to question, four prevalent interpretations of the history of social thought – interpretations which, while they have often been applied very broadly, have derived particularly from the exegesis of the writings of Emile Durkheim. These interpretations, I want to argue, while they are very widely accepted, are either false or highly misleading. As popular myths centring upon the works of one of the most influential contributors to the formation of modern sociology, they have exerted a major effect upon assessments and evaluations of the past development of the subject: and they have thereby helped to obscure the real nature of important aspects of that development.

They are the following: 1) The myth of the *problem of order*. According to this interpretation, the thought of certain authors whose work has been of outstanding importance to modern sociology – but above all that of Durkheim – can be understood as an attempt to resolve an abstract 'problem of order' which has deep roots in Western social philosophy. 2) The myth of the *conservative origins of sociology*. This thesis holds that the most significant intellectual parameters underlying modern sociology – and here again the writings of Durkheim are singled out for special emphasis – derive from various forms of conservative ideology which came into being as a reaction against the changes produced by the 'two great revolutions' of the late eighteenth century in Europe: the French Revolution of 1789 and the Industrial Revolution. 3) What might be called the myth of the *great divide*: the conception that a decisive break occurred in the development of social thought with the writings of the generation of authors (stretching roughly from 1860 to 1920) to which Durkheim belonged. According to this view, whereas the leading thinkers in the earlier part of the nineteenth century devoted themselves to creating grandiose, speculative theories of a 'prescientific' character, those of the subsequent generation abandoned these in favour of a more modest, scientific approach, rejecting philosophies of history. 4) The fourth myth has actually arisen from attempts to criticize the first one mentioned above – that of the problem of order. The problem of order, it is held, has occupied only one tradition of social thought; there is a counter-trend which takes as its starting-point an endeavour to examine problems of conflict and change in society. According to this view – which, I wish to say, shares most of the assumptions of that which it nominally sets out to criticize – the history of social thought since the turn of the nineteenth century can be usefully understood as involving a persisting debate between what has been called 'consensus', 'integration' or 'order' theory on the one hand (of which Durkheim is regarded as a leading exponent), and what has been termed 'conflict' or 'coercion' theory on the other (represented above all by Marx).

Like all myths, these four interpretations of the development of social thought contain elements of truth, and genuinely illuminate aspects of Durkheim's work in particular, and of the formation of modern sociology in general. But if each possesses a certain validity, each also constitutes a distortion. What has to be done is to disentangle that which is valid from the misconceptions with which it is cloaked. Again like all myths, these interpretations of the development of social thought are the result of the collective elaboration of many subsequent secondary writers; in the analysis which follows, however, I shall confine myself to discussion of some of the more prominent expositions of these viewpoints.

The problem of order

The myth of the problem of order has received its most forceful and authoritative formulation in the works of Talcott Parsons. It forms a major theme of what has probably been the most influential study of the development of social theory produced in the last thirty years, *The Structure of Social Action* – a study which has also helped to spread the myth of the great divide.[1] In the book, Parsons traces the origins of concern with the problem of order in Western social thought back to Hobbes's *Leviathan*. The 'Hobbesian problem of order', as Parsons presents it, is essentially very simple in character. According to Hobbes, the desires of individuals (in a state of nature) tend to be mutually incompatible. Hence men are involved in a war of all against all – or they would be, if it were not that they cede their natural liberty to a sovereign power in return for security against the potential assaults of others. Hobbes's solution to the problem of order was unsatisfactory, however, because it did not explain *why* men accept the sovereign authority, assuming it to be a matter of individual contract. None the less, Parsons argues, the essential components of Hobbes's solution remained largely unquestioned so long as utilitarianism retained a dominant position in social theory. Only near the end of the nineteenth century, when utilitarianism came under fire, did social thinkers manage to approach a satisfactory resolution of the Hobbesian problem – and Durkheim took the lead in this.[2]

It is not possible to discuss, within a relatively small compass, all of the issues raised by Parsons's analysis. But it might be pointed out that it is dubious, first of all, how far Parsons's treatment of the problem of order, even in Hobbes, is acceptable. As Parsons formulates it, the 'Hobbesian problem' turns upon a contrast between 'man in nature' and 'man in society'. But although this has been traditionally ascribed to Hobbes, recent scholarship indicates that this statically conceived antinomy is foreign to Hobbes's own thinking, which is much more historically oriented.[3] However this may be, the significant question is how far the Hobbesian problem of order, in Parsons's exposition of it, helps to yield an accurate understanding of the main thrust of Durkheim's sociological interests.

In fact, Parsons's exposition of Durkheim's sociological concerns is highly misleading, as I have sought to show in some detail elsewhere,[4] in various ways:

a)   It is untrue to the intellectual influences which Durkheim sought to combat. The problem of order, Parsons makes clear, depends upon postulates implicit in utilitarian theory, whereby society is assumed to be the outcome of contractual relationships. He therefore takes the critique of utilitarianism to be virtually the only polemical foil of any importance in Durkheim's writings. But, although it is less overt, of equal consequence in Durkheim's thought is his critical evaluation of idealism, in two forms: first, 'holistic' idealism; and, second, Kantian philosophy.[5]

b)   This leads to a misrepresentation of the key themes of Durkheim's first and most basic work, *The Division of Labour in Society*. According to Parsons, there is a fundamental ambiguity in the work: while Durkheim shows that the Hobbesian resolution of the problem of order is inadequate, because there must be a 'non-contractual element in contract', he does not show what the relationship is between this 'non-contractual element' and the growth of organic solidarity. The replacement of mechanical by organic solidarity would seem to presuppose the eradication of the *conscience collective*; but this cannot be so if there still must be general consensual values which govern the formation of contracts.[6] The 'ambiguity' identified by Parsons disappears, if it is understood that *The Division of Labour* also involves a critique of the idealist view that 'order' in society always presupposes the existence of strongly defined and precise moral codes of the sort characteristic of traditional societies. What Durkheim shows is that the emergence of organic solidarity entails the development of a different *form* of moral structure ('moral individualism') to that characteristic of mechanical solidarity.

c) Since Parsons treats *The Division of Labour* as representative of an early, and transitory, phase in Durkheim's thought, his discussion tends to sever this work from Durkheim's later writings. Thus *The Elementary Forms of the Religious Life* is regarded simply as a subsequent, and more sophisticated, attempt to solve the problem of order. If, however, the evolutionary scheme set out in *The Division of Labour* is regarded, not as a rather inadequate resolution of the problem of order, but as a framework within which the whole of Durkheim's subsequent writings have to be placed, then again quite a different picture emerges to that portrayed by Parsons. The guiding theme of Durkheim's sociology then becomes that of establishing the continuities and the *contrasts* between 'traditional' and 'modern' society. The theory developed in *The Elementary Forms* shows that even the apparently secular ideals embodied in moral individualism have a 'sacred' character: the decline of (theistic) religion does not entail the disappearance of the sacred, even though its content changes radically.[7]

d) The institutional component of Durkheim's analysis becomes almost entirely lost to view. Much of Durkheim's writing concentrates upon the authority structure of the modern state, contrasting this with the characteristics of the less developed forms of society. What disappears from Parsons's discussion is Durkheim's consistent stress upon the fact that the moral revitalization of contemporary society, necessary to reduce anomie, can only take place given the occurrence of important institutional change. The 'anomic division of labour' can be alleviated only if the 'forced division of labour' is abolished: this demands that the class structure become systematically reorganized.[8]

e) While Parsons himself does not discuss the political background to Durkheim's writings, his account of the latter's work has served to reinforce a not uncommon misinterpretation of the political grounding of Durkheim's sociology. According to this view, the parallel theme to the problem of order in Durkheim's sociological writings is his political commitment to re-establishing 'order' in French society in the wake of the disasters which attended the fall of the Second Republic. But if this is taken to mean, as is sometimes implied, a desire to reconstruct the society in the form which it took prior to 1871, it is quite a misconceived representation of Durkheim's political views. In common with other Republican intellectuals with whom he was closely affiliated (such as Jaurès), Durkheim saw the demise of the Second Republic as offering the possibility – and, indeed, showing the necessity – of implementing quite basic social and political changes in France: changes which had been heralded, but not concretely achieved, in the Revolution of 1789. These transformations he saw as the condition of attaining unity within the Third Republic.[9]

'Order', of course, is a term with various possible connotations (see below, pp. 230–1); but the perspective comprised in the 'Hobbesian problem of order' was one, in fact, which Durkheim rejected at the very outset of his intellectual career.[10] Far from supplying the guiding theme of Durkheim's sociology, it was not, in the terms in which Parsons formulates it, a problem for Durkheim at all.

The conservative origins of sociology

It is apparent that the thesis that Durkheim's writings constitute a prolonged investigation of the problem of order has close connections to that which stresses his indebtedness to 'conservative' ideology.[11] This thesis has been stated with greater and lesser degrees of subtlety. It is hardly necessary to discuss at any length the opinion that Durkheim was a conservative in his political views. Durkheim made very few forays into the sphere of practical politics, and the specific characteristics of his attitudes towards the concrete political issues of his day are impossible to evaluate. But it is quite certain that the tendency of some commentators to connect Durkheim to right-wing nationalistic movements of his time is wholly incorrect.[12] Durkheim's political affiliations were always with liberal Republicanism, and his participation in the Dreyfus affair on the side of Dreyfus's defenders gave unambiguous evidence of where his sympathies lay.[13]

Most of those who emphasize Durkheim's heavy reliance upon ideological conservatism, however, have recognized his liberalism in politics.[14] The argument is that, Durkheim's political liberalism notwithstanding, on the intellectual level he adopted the key conceptual theorems which formed part of the 'revolt' against the legacy of the eighteenth-century rationalist philosophers – as manifest in the writings of such authors as de Maistre, Bonald and Chateaubriand:

> The conservatives at the beginning of the nineteenth century form an Anti-Enlightenment. There is not a work, not a major idea indeed, in the conservative renaissance that does not seek to refute ideas of the *philosophes*. Some, such as Chateaubriand, delighted in seeming occasionally to espouse one of the Enlighteners as the means of mounting attacks on another – usually on Voltaire, whose brilliant attacks on Christianity were vitriol for the deeply Christian conservatives. Even in Burke there are kind words occasionally where these will serve to promote a sense of inconsistency and division within the Enlightenment. But hatred of the Enlightenment and especially of Rousseau is fundamental in philosophical conservatism . . . And, at the end of the century, in the writings of the non-religious and politically liberal Durkheim we find ideas of French conservatism converted into some of the essential theories of his systematic sociology: the collective conscience, the functional character of institutions and ideas, intermediate associations, as well as his whole attack on individualism.[15]

In assessing this view, it is useful to separate two propositions which it embraces: the first concerns the intellectual *origins* of Durkheim's thought, and the second relates to the theories embodied in Durkheim's sociology itself. For a man may lean heavily upon an intellectual source, but put the ideas comprised within it to a very different use to those which were current previously. It does not follow that because a thinker uses notions taken from conservative social philosophy that his own theories will assume a conservative character. I shall argue, however, that it is mistaken to regard Durkheim as a conservative in either of these senses.

In his discussion of the significance of conservatism upon the development of modern social thought, Nisbet distinguishes three main 'ideological currents' in the nineteenth century. Besides conservatism there were, vying for supremacy, the powerful influences of 'radicalism' and 'liberalism'. Each of these also helped to shape the emergent sociological perspectives of major thinkers in the nineteenth century: e.g. Marx ('radicalism') or John Stuart Mill and Spencer ('liberalism'). Even a cursory examination, however, shows that none of these currents of thought was nearly as clear-cut or distinct as Nisbet tends to imply. In the first place, 'conservatism' and the other labels which Nisbet affixes to the ideological framework of social thought are extremely broad in scope, and he lumps within them authors whose ideas were really quite widely divergent. Second, and perhaps more important in this regard, it is difficult to find any significant figure in nineteeenth-century social thought whose ideas did not involve some sort of – more or less successful – synthesis of all three ideological currents. Marx is a case in point. It can hardly be denied that Marx was strongly influenced, and not just in a negative fashion, by 'conservatism', in the shape of Hegel's philosophy. But, of course, he sought to integrate this with ideas taken from each of the other two 'currents' – from political economy and 'radical' French social philosophy, while rejecting *all* of these as adequate representations of the social processes he sought to analyse. This is the relevance of the distinction mentioned above: what a thinker makes of received ideas is not simply contained in those ideas themselves – however much he may find it difficult to escape from the confines of inherited concepts and theories.

Durkheim's writings, while not as all-embracing in their intellectual indebtedness as those of Marx, embody ideas originating in various prior traditions. Nisbet distinguishes only two intellectual sources of Durkheim's work: one methodological and the other substantive:

positivism (in its large sense – that of a methodology founded on the vigorous application of scientific values to the study of human nature and society) and conservatism . . . It was Durkheim's feat to translate into the hard methodology of science ideas and values that had made their first appearance in the polemics of Bonald, Maistre, Haller and others opposed to reason and rationalism, as well as to revolution and reform.[16]

But the principal sources of Durkheim's work are not so simply classified. To begin with, Durkheim's debt to eighteenth-century rationalism was not limited, as Nisbet states, to a methodological spirit. In no small degree, Durkheim's writings, especially upon state and politics, were shaped by a confrontation with Rousseau's social philosophy – and this was not simply a negative influence. The work of Saint-Simon and Comte, however, was evidently much more important in helping to form the general outlines of Durkheim's thought. It is certainly the case that Comte drew upon the ideas of the conservative Catholic apologists. This is especially true of the ideas expressed in the *Positive Polity*. But it was Comte's *Positive Philosophy* which particularly influenced Durkheim; and, in working out his substantive ideas concerning the trend of development of modern society, Durkheim leaned more heavily upon Saint-Simon than upon Comte's version of the emergent hierocratic society as envisaged in the *Positive Polity*. Evaluation of the significance of Saint-Simon as a precursor of Durkheim's sociology is, of course, of some significance, since the writings of Saint-Simon represent a common source both of Comtean positivism and Marxian socialism. As will be indicated below, Durkheim was by no means blind to the 'radical' aspects of Saint-Simon's interpretation of industrial society, and he incorporated parts of it into his own theory.

Durkheim's thought also has to be connected to more proximate sources if the intellectual background to his works is to be fully understood. Two sets of influences are particularly relevant here. One is to be found in the writings of the older generation of 'academic socialists' in Germany. Early in his career, during the course of a period of study in Germany, Durkheim became acquainted with the writings of authors such as Schmoller, Wagner and Schäffle, and he discussed their contributions in several lengthy articles.[17] While the precise extent of Durkheim's indebtedness to these thinkers is a matter of some debate,[18] it is undoubtedly the case that certain of their ideas helped to filter his use of the legacy of French positivism. The 'science of morality' of which Durkheim set out to lay the foundation in *The Division of Labour* took its point of departure from certain of the ideas of the German reformist socialists. The second set of influences, rather more concealed, but of very profound importance in Durkheim's writings, derives from Kant and the French neo-Kantians, such as Renouvier. Indeed, if there is any single 'problem' underlying Durkheim's writings, rather than the

'Hobbesian problem of order' it is the 'Kantian problem' of the moral imperative. Kantian formulations constantly appear in Durkheim's works, even though they are not always explicitly acknowledged as such by him; and from the outset of his intellectual career he sought to effect a fruitful critique of these ideas by placing them within a social context, making particular use of Renouvier's conceptions.[19]

If, therefore, conservatism, as defined by Nisbet and others, was an influence in Durkheim's intellectual heritage, this influence was much less unequivocal and direct than has been asserted. But how far is it true that the theoretical edifice which Durkheim fashioned from these various sources has an inherently conservative cast? It has been argued that Durkheim's sociology constitutes an all-out offensive against individualism: hence his stress upon the primacy of society over the individual and upon the need for authority.[20] The error here lies in a failure to distinguish two senses of the term individualism. Durkheim was not unremittingly hostile to all forms of individualism. He set out to criticize the 'individualism' which was entailed in the works of the English utilitarians, but he accepted, and undertook to study in a systematic fashion, that form of 'individualism' which he believed to be the necessary foundation of the organization of modern society. He sought to show precisely that the latter cannot be adequately understood given the ontological postulates of the former.[21] The distinction between the two senses of individualism was explicitly recognized by Durkheim himself (although in his earlier writings he was not yet aware of its full implications). Individualism in the first sense, Durkheim identifies with 'the utilitarian egoism of Spencer and the economists': this must be rejected as comprising any sort of valid starting-point for sociology. But individualism in the second sense is an altogether different matter; this is 'that of Kant and Rousseau, that of the idealists, that which the Declaration of the Rights of Man sought, more or less successfully, to give expression to'. This is *moral individualism*, something which, as he put it, has 'penetrated our institutions and customs, and which pervades our whole life'.[22] Individualism, in this sense, is a creation *of* society, an outcome of a long-term process of social development.

Many of the tensions and ambiguities in Durkheim's work, as well as much of what was distinctively original in his contributions, stem from his attempt to detach methodological from sociological individualism.[23] Durkheim's array of conservative concepts, such as are supposedly involved in his use of 'society' (read: 'moral community'), *'conscience collective'*, 'authority' and 'discipline' can only be adequately understood in these terms. Those who stress the conservative nature of Durkheim's thought, in common with those who emphasize the significance of the problem of order, have neglected the importance of the historical dimension in Durkheim's sociology.[24] Consequently, Durkheim's functionalism is presented *in abstracto*; it appears as if these concepts are applied to reinforce a bluntly authoritarian theory of social control.[25]

Thus it seems that Durkheim holds to a position very akin to that of Freud, according to which there is (as in the 'Hobbesian problem') an inherent antinomy between the individual and society, which necessarily entails that the existence of 'society' is tied to the repression of individual faculties and propensities.[26] In fact, Durkheim's view is quite different to this. In traditional societies men are subject to what Durkheim frequently refers to as the 'tyranny of the group'. Not only is there little toleration of deviation from the moral codes embodied in the *conscience collective*, but there is only a low development of individual capabilities and faculties. The increasing complexity of society brings about both an extension of human freedoms and a growth in the richness of the individual personality. In such a situation, the forms of moral authority characteristic of traditional types of society become obsolete. Contrary to the conservative social thinkers, Durkheim consistently argued that there can be no reversion to the sort of moral discipline which pertained in previous times. 'The old gods are dead', and there can be no question of reviving them.

He certainly did not manage to resolve in a successful way all of the issues raised by his adoption of this standpoint.[27] But the relevant aspects of his position are clear enough. In criticizing utilitarianism, he opted for the Kantian view that morality can never be reduced to the wants of the individual actor. Hence there is no form of moral phenomenon which does not have a 'constraining' aspect to it. But the important point is that constraint or obligation are not simply to be identified with repression. For moral conduct, according to Durkheim, never merely involves constraint alone: it also always has a positive valence. This is the basis of his attempted synthesis of utilitarianism and of Kant's moral philosophy: no moral conduct is founded either upon desirability alone, or upon duty alone, but upon a fusion of the two. In these terms, Durkheim sought to transcend the old philosophical dichotomies. While 'authority' and 'discipline' are components of all forms of social organization, it is mistaken, in Durkheim's view, to oppose them to 'freedom'. This is the very substance of Durkheim's sociological discussion of the development of individualism: moral individualism retains a constraining character, but acceptance of this form of moral authority is the very condition of escape from the 'slavish submission' characteristic of traditional types of society. 'Freedom' and 'authority', Durkheim asserts, have often been treated as if they were opposed: 'But this opposition is spurious. In fact these two terms imply, rather than exclude, each other. Freedom is the daughter of authority properly understood.'[28]

The great divide

The myth of the great divide has been elaborated in two quite contradictory forms. The predominant version in Western academic sociology is that which I have mentioned previously in this paper, which dismisses social thought prior to the last twenty-five years of the nineteenth century as pre-scientific in character.[29] The contrast here is usually between 'philosophical' theories and 'scientific' or 'empirically founded' sociology. The other version of the myth of the great divide puts things in the reverse perspective, although the nature of the supposed contrast at issue is different. This is the view set out by some Marxists. The thesis here is that while Marx's writings established a scientific basis for social theory, the writings of the 1860-1920 generation of social thinkers represent little more than an ideological defence of bourgeois capitalism in the face of the threat of revolutionary socialism.

This latter version, which is only found in the cruder variants of Marxism, is hardly worth discussing in any detail. It is inconsistent with Marx's own standpoint: if bourgeois political economy was 'ideological', it nevertheless contained basic elements of validity. In order to understand the framework of Durkheim's sociology, it is undoubtedly important to examine the sociopolitical context in which he wrote – and it is certainly the case that there is a close relation between his political and sociological views, as I have tried to demonstrate above. But while this helps us to unravel the sources of some of his errors, it does not, in itself, show them to be such.

The other thesis is more complicated, and, so it might seem, more defensible. Durkheim is often regarded, especially by American sociologists, as the founder of empirical sociology – as the first writer to apply systematic empirical method to the examination of definite sociological issues. Suicide is taken as the model here. A typical statement is: 'Sociological study of suicide began in a systematic fashion with the publication of Emile Durkheim's *Le Suicide* in 1897. Durkheim's was the first theoretical and empirical exploration of the persistent variations of suicide in relation to sociological variables.'[30] This view is manifestly false, however, and is written in ignorance of the prior history of empirical research in the nineteenth century. The systematic use of official statistics to examine, in a supposedly objective fashion, the distribution of 'moral phenomena', began much earlier in the century, under the tutelage of the 'moral statisticians' such as Quetelet.[31] It is not generally realized today, in fact, how far back the tradition of quantitative research into social phenomena can be traced.[32] Durkheim drew upon a wealth of previous studies which had connected the distribution of suicide to social factors, and there was little that was particularly original either in the statistical method which he employed or in the empirical generalizations which he made use of in his study. (Thus, for example, the correlation between suicide rates and religious denomination was well demonstrated in previous research.) The originality of Durkheim's work lay much less in the methods which he used in *Suicide* than in the theory which he advanced; and the latter was worked out in the considerably broader context of the problems which occupied him in *The Division of Labour* and his other writings.

But it is clearly not enough to deal with the matter in these terms. The real question is how far Durkheim succeeded in separating 'sociology' from 'speculative philosophy'. Such was certainly the perspective within which he viewed his own work. Recognizing that Comte, in attempting to establish an autonomous science of sociology, conceived of himself as a 'positive scientist' of human conduct, Durkheim nevertheless denied the validity of the appellation. Comte was never able to free himself from the trappings of speculative philosophy. This is manifest, according to Durkheim, in the 'law of the three stages', which is imposed upon history rather than being derived from the empirical study of social development. The same is true of Spencer: Spencer 'did sociology as a philosopher', because 'he set out, not to study social facts in and for themselves, but to show how the evolutionary hypothesis may be verified in the social world'.[33]

Durkheim's own stress upon the partial character of scientific work, the laborious manner in which scientific advances are made, and upon the need to define in a precise way the subject-matter of sociology, all were conceived with the object of completing the break with philosophy which writers such as Comte and Spencer had advocated, but had failed to achieve. However, Durkheim's abstract statements on the issue can no more be simply admitted at their face value than can those of the authors whom he took to task. While it may be accepted that *Suicide* and perhaps even Durkheim's work on religion, conform to the prescription that, in order to establish itself upon a 'scientific' basis, sociology must concern itself with restricted, clearly delimited problems, it is difficult to see how such a claim can be made for the theory developed in *The Division of Labour*. If it is not a 'philosophy of history', it is none the less of a sweeping and all-embracing character which is by no means completely alien to the sort of schemes which previous nineteenth-century thinkers had produced. Moreover, Durkheim himself remarked that he found himself unable to escape from philosophical problems and constantly found himself reverting to them: 'Having begun from philosophy, I tend to return to it; or rather I have been quite naturally brought back to it by the nature of the questions which I met with on my route.'[34] To be sure, he tried to demonstrate that age-old philosophical questions could be seen in a new light by the application of a sociological perspective; but this was no more than had been claimed by various of his precursors, including Marx and Comte.

Durkheim also shared another concern with most prior social thinkers in the nineteenth century: the attempt to use 'scientific' observations to reach evaluative prescriptions. He frequently emphasized, of course, that sociology is a worthwhile endeavour only if it ultimately yields some practical application. But, far more than that, he tried to establish exactly how theory could be linked to practice – in his conception of the 'normal' and the 'pathological'.[35] Few aspects of Durkheim's work have been more universally rejected than this one; yet none is more central to his thought. The role of the sociologist is to be like that of the clinician: to diagnose and to propose remedies for sicknesses of the body social. This is particularly important, Durkheim made clear, in situations of transition or 'crisis' in society, where new social forms are appearing, and others are becoming obsolete. In such circumstances, only sociological investigation can diagnose, in the flux of competing values and standards what is of the past, and to be discarded, and what is the emergent pattern of the future. It is this task – that of identifying the roots of the 'modern crisis' – which Durkheim set himself in his sociology, and this takes up again the problems which Saint-Simon and Comte had set themselves a half century earlier.[36]

Integration and coercion theory

The best-known exposition of integration and coercion theory is that originally offered by Dahrendorf. According to him, two conceptions of society have stood, since the beginnings of Western social philosophy, in opposition to one another. Each constitutes an answer to the problem of order, and each 'has grown in intensity' with the development of modern social thought:

> One of these, the *integration theory of society*, conceives of social structure in terms of a functionally integrated system held in equilibrium by certain patterned and recurrent processes. The other one, the *coercion theory of society*, views social structure as a form of organization held together by force and constraint and reaching continuously beyond itself in the sense of producing within itself the forces that maintain it in an unending process of change.[37]

The principal source of coercion theory in modern social thought, according to Dahrendorf, is to be found in the writings of Marx. In contrasting integration and coercion theory, he compares the works of Marx directly with those of Parsons, but many other writers have looked back to Durkheim as the main modern founder of integration theory. The differences which separate the views of Marx and Durkheim, it is held, rest upon divergent conceptions of the natural state of man. According to Horton and others, these are focused through the concepts of alienation and anomie respectively.[38] Durkheim's model of man in a state of nature, it is held, owes most to Hobbes; Marx derived his from that portrayed by Rousseau. Whereas in the latter model the evils in the contemporary human condition are conceived to derive from the repressive effects of society – from which men must be liberated – in the former view these evils are seen as originating from the very opposite state of affairs: a lack of social regulation. The Marxian model inevitably concentrates upon coercion and power, at least as regards the character of existing societies, and since it looks to future transformations, emphasizes change rather than order; the Durkheimian model concentrates upon consensus, and is essentially static in character.

It is worth distinguishing two partially separable issues here: the question of the supposed divergencies between the underlying perspectives which inform the work of Mark and Durkheim; and the question of the role of coercion versus consensus in the more concrete analyses of the two thinkers.

The first of these is fairly easily disposed of. What seems now to have become the conventional comparison of the conceptions of alienation and anomie in the writings of Marx and Durkheim is simply not true to the respective standpoints of either writer. The errors here certainly lie as much in the interpretation of Marx's thought as in that of Durkheim. Marx did *not* proceed in terms of an abstract contrast between 'man in nature' (non-alienated, free) and 'man in society' (alienated, unfree) in utilizing the conception of alienation.[39] Man does not become 'human', in Marx's terms, by escaping from society: as he perceived very early on in his career, this view is quite untenable, since most human faculties are developed through society. Both the eighteenth-century philosophers and the utilitarians began from the conception of the 'isolated individual': but man is first and foremost a social being, and the very notion of the isolated individual is one which is created as part of the ideology of a specific form of society (and is itself an expression of alienated consciousness).[40] Primitive man is not in a condition of self-alienation, but in a condition of alienation from nature; as man's mastery of nature grows, his alienation from nature becomes transcended – but this is only accomplished by means of man's alienation from himself. Expressed in less general terms: the technological progress created by capitalism has allowed man to conquer nature, but this very process has ramified and maximized man's self-alienation. The point is that the two elements in the equation are both social in character: alienation does not refer to a process whereby man's natural needs are denied by his membership of society, but one where socially generated capacities are denied by specific social forms.

The same is true of Durkheim's usage of the concept of anomie. It is, or should be, quite obvious that the same two sides of the equation enter in here also: that is to say, that the condition of anomie also involves a dislocation between two sets of socially generated phenomena (needs and the possibilities of their realization). Like Marx, Durkheim stresses that most human faculties and needs are shaped by society. Man in a state of nature would not be anomic, since, like an animal, his needs would be primarily organic, and hence adjusted to relatively fixed levels of satiation. 'All instinct is bounded because it responds to purely organic needs and because these organic needs are rigorously defined.'[41] Socialized man, however, is in quite a different position. Since his needs are socially created, it follows, according to Durkheim, that their *limits* must also be set by society. The problem of anomie does not simply rest upon the social restraint of (given) needs, but upon the social penetration of both needs *and* means of satiation.

It is not necessary to argue that either Marx or Durkheim managed to clarify all of the difficulties raised by their respective viewpoints,[42] in order to emphasize what an oversimplification it is to hold that, while the concept of alienation presupposes that man is in some sense naturally 'good', but is degraded by his membership of society, the concept of anomie presumes that man is naturally refractory to social organization, and must therefore be subject to restraint. The divergences between the concepts of alienation and anomie, in other words, depend less upon contrasts in underlying 'conceptions of man' than upon differences in the respective analyses which Marx and Durkheim set out of the development of society from primitive to more complex forms. The question is, however, how far these differences are accurately expressed in the opposition between integration and coercion theory. From the sort of exposition given by Dahrendorf and others,[43] various factors may be derived as separating Durkheim's integration theory from Marx's coercion theory: e.g., the first emphasizes 'consensus', the second 'power'; the first neglects the importance of 'conflict' in society, the second accentuates it.

Now the Comtean term 'consensus' is one which Marx did not use, nor would ever have contemplated using. Durkheim makes use of it fairly often – although he much more frequently employs the phrases *'conscience collective'* or *'conscience com-*

mune'. But it is important not to be misled by terminological differences here. The place of the concept 'ideology' in Marx's theory is not, as it was in its original usage, a completely pejorative one. It is certainly true that 'ideology' refers to what Engels called 'false' consciousness, and that this is a conception which is completely absent from the notion of consensus. But while ideology is ontologically false it is not *sociologically* false.[44] That is to say, moral ideas, as expressed, for example, in religious idea-systems, are of basic significance in stabilizing existing social systems, and in legitimating the class relationships which prevail within them. Marx's very hostility to religion, and his life-long attempt to effect a critique of political economy as a major element in the ideology of bourgeois society, only make sense if this is recognized.[45]

It is a familiar theme that, whereas Marx saw society as an unstable system of groups (classes) in conflict, Durkheim conceived of it as a unified whole – as an entity 'greater than the sum of its parts';[46] and that consequently he provided no analysis of the sources of social conflict. The misleading factor in this is the use of the blanket term 'society'. In order to adjudge upon the validity of the contrast, the only proper comparison is between Marx's and Durkheim's respective analyses of specific *forms* of society, and especially of that type of society which Marx called 'bourgeois society' or 'capitalism'. For if conflict, or class conflict, plays an essential part in Marx's analysis of extant societies, he did, after all, envisage the emergence of a type of society in which such conflict would disappear. Expressed in terms of this more tangible comparison, the contrast between integration and coercion theory again is evidently quite inadequate as a mode of identifying the differences between the two thinkers. The differences lie, not in the fact that one recognized the fact of class conflict in nineteenth-century Europe, while the other ignored it, but in their respective diagnoses of the origins of – and hence the remedies for – that conflict. Like Marx, Durkheim anticipated the emergence of a 'classless' society: but this was to be Saint-Simon's 'one-class' society, preserving a high degree of economic differentiation, rather than the Marxian form.

Marx regarded class conflict as the main motive-force in history, a theorem which Durkheim explicitly denied;[47] and it can be argued, of course, that there is in Marx some sort of overall framework of a 'theory' of social change (in class societies) which is lacking in Durkheim's writings, apart from the fragment on the causes of the expansion of the division of labour in the book of that title. But this is not at all the same thing as to say that Durkheim was unconcerned with social change. What Dahrendorf says of integration theory, that it 'conceives of social structure in terms of a functionally integrated system held in equilibrium by certain patterned and recurrent processes', is sufficiently plastic to be as applicable to Marx's model of capitalism as to Durkheim's model of industrial society. Of course, the former is not a static, but an inherently mobile and temporary, equilibrium between the classes. But the same may be said of Durkheim's analysis of the 'transitional phase' between feudalism and industrialism. Moreover, Durkheim, like Marx, stressed that society is, in Dahrendorf's words, 'in an unending process of change', and that it is the task of the sociologist to chart the lines of development of society.[48]

Myth and reality

The four interpretations of the history of social thought whose shortcomings I have tried to indicate in the foregoing sections of this paper do not, taken together, constitute a single and unitary conception of the development of modern sociology. Those who have accepted the myth of the conservative origins of sociology have not necessarily accepted the myth of the great divide;[49] those who have promulgated the myth of the problem of order have not always accepted the dichotomy between integration and coercion theory.[50] Nevertheless, as applied to the interpretation of Durkheim's writings, there are some evident and close connections between all of these views.

The notion of the problem of order as Durkheim's overriding concern, and that of the conservative bent of his sociology, have naturally fostered the opinion that there is a clear discrepancy between Durkheim's political views and interests on the one hand, and the general character of his sociological writings on the other. This is explicitly stated by Nisbet: 'He (Durkheim) was a liberal by political choice and action, but his sociology constitutes a massive attack upon the philosophical foundations of liberalism . . . the substance of his thought is composed almost exclusively of perspectives and insights that have an umbilical relation to . . . early nineteenth-century conservatism . . .'[51] If, as is suggested

H

in this paper, however, this interpretation is rejected, then the discrepancy evaporates; Durkheim's political liberalism finds its direct counterpart in his attempt, in his more general sociological analysis, to identify the characteristic authority structure of the modern nation-state.

I have said that each of the four myths discussed in this paper possesses elements of validity. At this point it is possible to attempt to unravel these from the tangle of confusions with which they have become overlain.

In order to accomplish this, it is most useful to begin with the question of 'conservatism'. The element of truth which links the sociology of Durkheim's generation to a conservative reaction to the 'two great Revolutions' can be more adequately understood only if this sociology is related to the social and political development of the major countries of Western Europe in the nineteenth century. This is a commonplace enough observation, but it is nevertheless a perspective which has been conspicuously absent from those accounts which have sought to show the indebtedness of sociology to conservatism.[52] The 'conservatism' of Bonald and his contemporaries in France was above all a response to the apparent consequences of the events of 1789. As has been rightly written of Bonald, 'contemptuous of the urban communities and manufacture, which he does not discuss, it is apparent that he wished to close his eyes to contemporary economic realities . . . Bonald did not write an economic treatise: he struggled against the Revolution.'[53] Throughout the nineteenth century, in France, social thought continued to be dominated, in one way or another, by the legacy of the 1789 Revolution. Now the occurrence of the Revolution, of course, created shock-waves of anxiety and fear among the ruling groups in both Britain and Germany, and inevitably provided an essential backdrop to the most elaborate theoretical system produced in the latter country: the philosophy of Hegel.[54] But while fear of revolution continued to haunt the dominant strata in these two countries for decades, other trends of development separated them quite decisively from the French experience. In Britain, an accelerating rate of industrial development was accompanied by a unique process of the mutual accommodation and interpenetration of the landed aristocracy and the rising commercial and industrial élite. The result was a society unmatched elsewhere by the relatively even tenor of its development, and which produced neither a large-scale revolutionary socialist movement nor its counterpart, an aggressive irrationalist conservatism. In certain respects, Britain was strikingly 'conservative' in actuality; but this conservatism, especially marked in the political sphere, proved to be compatible with major and progressive changes in the social infrastructure. In his famous lectures on *Law and Public Opinion in England*, Dicey showed how this phenomenon could be indexed by the changing nature of the legal system:

> France is the land of revolution, England is renowned for conservatism, but a glance at the legal history of each country suggests the existence of some error in the popular contrast between French mutability and English unchangeableness. In spite of revolutions at Paris, the fundamental provisions of the Code Napoléon have stood to a great extent unaltered since its publication in 1804, and before 1900 the Code had become invested with a sort of legal sanctity which secured it against sudden and sweeping change. In 1804 George the Third was on the throne, and English opinion was then set dead against every legal or political change, yet there is now hardly a part of the English statute-book which between 1804 and the present day has not been changed in form or in substance . . .[55]

Thus both the internal content of 'conservatism', and the interconnections between conservative ideology and social theory, differed in quite a fundamental way between the three leading European societies. In Britain, utilitarianism, although of course undergoing significant modifications from Bentham to Spencer,[56] remained the dominant form of social theory throughout most of the nineteenth century. While it was eventually challenged by T. H. Green and the Oxford philosophers,[57] their critique remained embroiled in idealist metaphysics. In neither of the other countries did utilitarianism ever enjoy anything like the same pre-eminence (even in its guise as political economy). It has been a common tendency of British and American writers, when discussing Continental social thought of the nineteenth century, to exaggerate the significance of utilitarian individualism.[58] In France, it was from the beginning overshadowed by the writings of the eighteenth-century philosophers; in Germany, the strongly historical bent in philosophy and economics effectively limited its penetration. The development of German society in the nineteenth century was above all conditioned by three sets of factors: the failure to effect a 'bourgeois revolution' in 1848, and the consequently persisting domination of an autocratic land-owning élite

228 Studies in Social and Political Theory

until well into the twentieth century; the fact that the unification of Germany was accomplished under the hegemony of Prussia, whose power was founded upon the position of this élite; and the occurrence of a late, but very rapid, period of industrial development whose effects were concentrated in the period immediately following the unification of the country. These factors created various streams of social thought, some largely peculiar to Germany, involving odd fusions of 'conservative' and 'progressive' philosophies, as is found in the works of such authors as Oldenberg, Wagner and Schäffle.[59] 'Conservatism' here, however, means primarily a nostalgic and romantic attachment to the (idealized) pre-industrial village community.[60]

The history of France in the nineteenth century, as Dicey's remark aptly indicates, was one of a superficial political volatility which masked a deeply engrained set of social and economic divisions which either survived or were themselves engendered by the 1789 Revolution. The most revolutionary nation in Europe turned out to be anything but revolutionary in terms of actually creating the bourgeois society which was proclaimed in its slogans. 'Conservatism' in France was always linked to Catholicism and to the claims of embattled but militantly tenacious landowners, rentiers – and independent peasantry. While for the German thinkers of Max Weber's generation the overwhelming problem was that of the antecedents and consequences of 'capitalism' (analysed here primarily in terms of the destruction of traditional values by the spread of the 'rationalization' of culture), in France the debate was centred upon the problem of 'individualism' in the face of the claims of Catholic hierocracy. Durkheim's theory of the state was conceived as an attempt to resolve the 'legacy of the Revolution': the distance between the ideals of freedom and equality of opportunity heralded in 1789, and the reality of continuing stagnation in the social infrastructure. In France, since the turn of the nineteenth century, Durkheim remarked, 'Change follows on change with unparalleled speed. . . . At the same time, these surface changes mark an habitual stagnation . . . all these surface changes that go on in various directions cancel each other out. . . .'[61] This phenomenon is to be explained in terms of the lack of differentiation between state and society. In these circumstances, the state is not independent enough to take firm action in initiating and realizing policies; it is simply swayed by the changeable moods of the mass. What must be established,

Durkheim concluded, was a form of the state strong enough to resist the volatile whims of the mass (which, if allowed to hold sway, simply secure the rule of an underlying 'relentless traditionalism'), but which does not lose touch with the will of the majority and thereby create a coercive autocracy.[62]

This is effectively a theory of the Republican state such as Durkheim saw emerging, and endeavoured to help to create, in the wake of the disaster of the war of 1870 and the Commune. The modern state is not opposed to, but is to be the principal agency of, the advancement of the moral individualism embodied in the ideals of the Revolution of the eighteenth century. As Durkheim sought to show in *The Division of Labour*, 'moral individualism' and 'utilitarianism' are not to be identified with each other. While in 1893 he believed it necessary to devote a lengthy section of the above work to a critical repudiation of utilitarianism, particularly in its Spencerian version, by 1898 he was clear that 'the practical philosophy of Spencer . . . hardly has any supporters any longer', and that there was little need to 'combat an enemy which is in the process of quietly dying a natural death'.[63] Moral individualism is a creation of society – and, more specifically, of the collective effervescence of the 1789 Revolution and its immediate aftermath – and hence derives its force from the authority of society; as such it is quite distinct from the 'egoism' of the 'isolated' or 'pre-social' individual of utilitarian theory.

In these terms, Durkheim attempted to distance his position from three streams of thought – 'individualism' (in the form of utilitarianism), revolutionary 'socialism', *and* 'conservatism'. *The Division of Labour* already exposes the essential flaw in the conservatism of the Catholic apologists: moral individualism is the emergent form of moral ideal in modern society, and there can be no return to the sort of moral order characteristic of previous ages (even in the guise of the hierocratic society of Comte's *Positive Polity*). But Durkheim drew upon important elements of this tradition of thought, just as he did upon each of the others. He owed certain of his key concepts to this source, as Marx owed certain of his to Hegel; but, like Marx, he attempted to apply them in such a way as to effect a critique of the very stream of thought from which they originally derived. Durkheim's work, in other words, originates in an attempt to synthesize, and thereby to transcend, each of these three traditions of thought bequeathed from the earlier part of the nineteenth century; and thus is most appropriately regarded as an attempt to *rethink the foundations of liberalism* in circumstances in which the liberal individualism developed in the British 'case' (i.e. utilitarianism) was manifestly inappropriate.

Durkheim's sociology can no more be adequately understood, therefore, merely as a critique of utilitarianism, than it can be adequately understood merely as a critique of revolutionary socialism. The main problematic issue was not of 'order', but, if this term is to be used at all, the reconciliation of 'order' and 'change'. Durkheim accepted what he took to be the essential component of socialism: the need for the regulation of unfettered market relationships. But he rejected, of course, both the possibility of radically restructuring society through revolutionary means, and the correlate assumption that class conflict was the medium whereby this could be achieved; on the abstract level, he denied that the major tenets of socialism have any necessary connection with class conflict.[64] The theory of anomie, plainly, is of primary significance in Durkheim's rejection of both utilitarianism and socialism. But the remedy for anomie, he made clear, does not consist in the reapplication of traditional forms of moral discipline – as is suggested in conservative thought. Anomie, in other words, is a social condition which is contingent upon the transitional character of the contemporary age: it results from the fact that the changes necessary to complete the institutionalization of moral individualism have not yet come to fruition. This is the general theoretical counterpart of his more concrete interpretation of the factors retarding the development of a fully-fledged 'bourgeois society' in France in the first three quarters of the nineteenth century.

If it is not useful to treat Durkheim's concerns as deriving from an overwhelming interest in the problem of order, there can hardly be said to be much validity in applying this notion to Marx, and holding that 'order' here stems from the application of 'coercion'. The notion of 'order' is an ambiguous one, and can cover such a number of potentially quite distinct sets of circumstances (absence of conflict, absence of change, prevalence of mutually compatible cultural norms, etc.) that little is to be gained from using the term unless it refers to the more narrowly defined 'Hobbesian problem' implied in at least some versions of utilitarianism. Although this has perhaps only become fully clear subsequent to the retarded publication of Marx's early writings, it is now quite evident that Marx, from the very first stages of his intellectual career, rejected the theoretical suppositions underlying utilitarianism, regarding these as an ideological expression masking the social relationships inherent in the capitalist division of labour.[65] Over the past ten years much has been written about the supposed division between integration and coercion or conflict theory, and it is not my purpose here to evaluate the usefulness of the various contributions to this discussion. Undoubtedly this division in social theory now has a life of its own; but the claims made for its parentage in the thought of Durkheim and Marx have little foundation. Whatever may be the affinities between this debate and long-standing oppositions in social philosophy, in the main the dichotomy between integration and coercion theory is an artifact of recent construction – specifically, of Parsonian structural-functionalism and its critique at the hands of Dahrendorf, Lockwood, Rex and others.[66]

An elucidation of the elements of validity in the notion of the great divide will help us more adequately to understand in what respects the standpoints of Durkheim and Marx may be contrasted with respect to 'conflict', 'coercion', and 'change'. Durkheim's sociology, as the Marxist version of the great divide insists, was undoubtedly founded in an endeavour to examine the conditions under which France could become a fully developed 'bourgeois society'. But this was more than a defence of a given *status quo* in the face of the threat of revolutionary socialism. If concern with the 'social question' was one major factor helping to shape Durkheim's thought, of no less importance was his anxiety to rebut the resurgence of conservative forces within the social structure. Like his famous contemporary in Germany, Max Weber, through taking over ideas from both socialism and conservatism, and by recombining them within a new framework, Durkheim sought to provide a systematic rationale for a bourgeois state which necessarily had to diverge from the 'classical' principles of liberalism, i.e. those which had developed in the very different context of Britain. Since the framework of development in Germany was itself very different from that of France – and the position of the liberal bourgeoisie much weaker – Weber's attempted synthesis was itself quite divergent from that created by Durkheim.[67]

Durkheim's formula for the emergence of an autonomous discipline of sociology was connected in a very immediate fashion with his attempt to assess and combine ideas contained in both socialist and conservative traditions of thought, and was quite consciously worked out by him with such an objective in view. According to Durkheim, the major intellectual precondition for the establishment of a scientific sociology was the sloughing-off of the speculative philosophy which still remained an important part of the writings of prior thinkers such as Saint-Simon and Comte. But the most significant residue of speculative philosophy in the works of these authors, according to Durkheim, was of two related kinds, each closely connected with the very social impulses which generated sociology itself. The first was the impulse towards social reform or social reorganization; the other, that towards a revitalization of religion. The former finds its most characteristic expression in the doctrines of socialism, the latter in the conservative call for a religious revival. Throughout the first three quarters of the nineteenth century, Durkheim argued, but particularly in times of social upheaval, the impetus to these three sets of ideas – socialism, religion and sociology – appears. In the works of Saint-Simon these are found in almost inextricable confusion. Comte went beyond Saint-Simon, not only in giving 'sociology' its name (which Durkheim thought to be a 'rather barbaric neologism'), but also in making a substantive contribution towards the separation of this new discipline from the other forms of thought in which it was embedded; but he failed to make this separation complete, and in the latter part of his career largely sacrificed his sociology to the religious impulse.

Durkheim's stress upon the need for drawing a very clear delimitation of the subject-matter of sociology, its aims and objectives, thus has to be understood in terms of what he perceived as the pressure to dissolve sociology within the more directly practical impulsions involved in socialism and religious revivalism. Only an autonomous, firmly established, science of sociology can actually discern and analyse what socialism and revivalism share in common and can thereby accurately diagnose the solutions to the social problems of which each of the latter are an expression. For while socialism, especially Marxist socialism, claims to be scientific, the propositions it embodies, springing from a pressing awareness of the need for social reorganization, go far beyond what can be said to be empirically verified, or even verifiable.[68] Hence Durkheim's frequent emphasis upon the necessarily modest and cautious nature of sociological investigation, and his attempt to preserve the 'positive' character of Comte's sociology in a new form; in spite – or, as this analysis has tried to demonstrate, because of – its restricted and scientific character, sociology really holds the key to the practical understanding of the 'modern crisis'.

Durkheim was thus led to establish a precise definition of the field of sociology, and to insist upon the limitation of sociological investigations to restricted and clearly bounded problems. But the very ambitiousness of the context which led him to construct this new sociological perspective placed sociology in an impossibly paradoxical situation; for no 'neutral', circumscribed discipline of sociology could come to grips with the problems which stimulated Durkheim's writings, and most of his works range very much more broadly than is consistent with his own methodological doctrine.[69] In terms of the separation of sociology from ('speculative') social philosophy, Durkheim's writings hardly mark the clear-cut line of demarcation claimed by their author. It seems, in fact, to have been a characteristic of each successive generation of social thinkers throughout the nineteenth century to hold that, whereas the works of their forerunners were speculative or ideological, or both, their own writings were grounded in empirical reality and thus scientific in character. This was said by Saint-Simon of the eighteenth-century philosophers; by Comte and Marx of Saint-Simon (among others); and by Durkheim of all of these.

What validity remains, then, in the notion of the great divide? A full discussion of this matter would demand an assessment of the question of how far, in sociology, intellectual advance comparable to that found in the natural sciences is possible, something which goes far beyond the scope of this paper. It can hardly be disputed that the sociological programme which Durkheim set himself made it possible for him to illuminate a variety of diverse problems in sociology and social philosophy. But this is not the same as breaking with the general frames of thought and analysis which guided his precursors. In this regard, there are perhaps two principal respects in which Durkheim's sociology marks a new point of departure from the social thought of his predecessors; one is intellectual, the other refers to the social context of his thought. The first concerns his abandonment of unilinear evolutionism and his use of materials drawn from cultures outside Europe.[70] Each of the previous thinkers whose works formed an important part of Durkheim's intellectual horizon were mainly bounded by the European experience; indeed, their very willingness to set out 'universal' schemes bears witness to this. Although Durkheim did not abandon evolutionism altogether, his use of anthropological studies within a comparative framework marks the beginning of the modern era in Western social thought, and made possible the variety of researches carried out under the aegis of the *Année sociologique* school by scholars originating in numerous different disciplines. The very success and prestige of this group is indicative of the progress made in the effective institutionalization of sociology as a recognized academic discipline. This is the second, and perhaps the most basic, element of validity in the notion of the great divide. It is significant that it was Durkheim's sociology, rather than other potential competitors (e.g. that of Le Play and his followers), which was the most eminently successful in this respect.[71] For Durkheim's writings offered a unique combination of a firmly-made claim to scientific respectability, together with a persuasive explication of the problems facing the retarded emergence of a mature bourgeois state.

7 Durkheim's political sociology

Durkheim's theory of politics and the state is undoubtedly the most neglected of his contributions to social theory.[1] There are perhaps two main reasons why Durkheim's political sociology has not received the attention which it demands. One is that several of the standard expositions of his work (such as Parsons's *The Structure of Social Action* and Alpert's *Emile Durkheim and his Sociology*)[2] were written before the publication of the series of lectures in which he most directly confronted the problems of political analysis (*Leçons de sociologie*, 1950).[3] A second, although related, factor in this neglect derives from the 'phases' through which the secondary interpretation of Durkheim's work has passed.[4] During his own lifetime, and for some little while after his death, Durkheim was generally seen as the originator of a radical form of 'sociological realism', which subordinates the individual to a hypostatized 'group mind'; and his political thought was widely regarded as a form of mystical nationalism.[5] Later accounts, such as those by Parsons and Alpert, provided much more sophisticated, and accurate, evaluations of Durkheim's general sociology, but these tended to direct attention away from the political content of Durkheim's writings, emphasizing other aspects of his works.

Parsons's interpretation of Durkheim has been the most influential, and the view of Durkheim's writings set out in *The Structure of Social Action* has since become something of an established orthodoxy.[6] According to this standpoint, Durkheim's thought underwent a series of profound changes over the course of his career: beginning from an initially 'positivistic'[7] position (as manifest primarily in *The Division of Labour in Society* and *The Rules of Sociological Method*), he eventually moved to one which was 'idealistic' in character. The effect of this interpretation is definitely to underplay the importance of *The Division of Labour* in Durkheim's writings. Since any examination of Durkheim's political ideas must be grounded in the theory established in that work, it follows that this tends to obscure the degree to which Durkheim's general sociology is concerned with political problems and with the nature of the modern state. This tendency has been accentuated even more forcibly by Nisbet, who has argued that, in his subsequent writings, Durkheim relinquished all of the most important theses which he had established in *The Division of Labour*:

> ... Durkheim never went back, in later studies, to any utilization of the distinction between the two types ('mechanical' and 'organic') of solidarity, nor to the division of labour as a form of cohesion, much less to any rationalization of conflict and anomie in society as mere 'pathological forms of division of labour'. The kinds of society, constraint, and solidarity dealt with in all his later works – either in theoretical or practical terms – have nothing whatsoever to do with the attributes that he had laid down for an organic and (presumably) irreversibly modern society in *The Division of Labour*.[8]

It is undoubtedly the case that Durkheim's thought did undergo significant modification and elaboration over the course of his intellectual career. But this now apparently 'orthodox' view, which sees a pronounced discrepancy between Durkheim's earlier and later works, is highly misleading. The substance of this paper, indeed, is founded upon the premise that the truth of the matter is almost completely the reverse of the view suggested by Nisbet: that Durkheim continued in his later thinking to base his works upon the distinction between 'mechanical' and 'organic' solidarity; that the existence of solidarity deriving from the division of labour was always conceived by Durkheim to be the most distinctive feature of contemporary as opposed to traditional societies; that Durkheim's treatment of 'conflict and anomie' in his later writings cannot be understood apart from his analysis of the 'pathological' forms of the division of labour; and that 'the kinds of society, constraint, and solidarity dealt with in all his later works' have everything to do with the attributes of contemporary society as formulated in *The Division of Labour*. The overall continuity between Durkheim's early and later works does not become fully apparent, however, unless considerable attention is given to his political theory. Far from being of peripheral significance to his sociology, Durkheim's political thought has an important role in his ideas; and, as I shall seek to demonstrate in a subsequent section of this paper, an appreciation of this fact allows the correction of a prevalent, but mistaken, interpretation of the main sociological problem with which Durkheim was concerned in all of his major works: the theory of moral authority.

The social and political background of Durkheim's thought

It has often been remarked that Durkheim's sociology has to be understood as a response to the shattering effects upon French society of the German victory of 1870–1.[9] But this says too much, and too little. Too much, because Durkheim's writing also has to be seen as rooted in the traditions of French positivist philosophy which stretch back to Comte, Saint-Simon, and beyond; too little because – by this very token – the social and political background to Durkheim's thought embodies important elements which were the legacy of the Revolution in the eighteenth century, and of which the events of 1870–1 were in part a direct outcome.[10] If the Revolution successfully disposed of the *ancien régime*, it also prepared the ground for certain generic social and political problems which were to haunt France for more than a century afterwards. Rather than introducing the liberal, bourgeois society which was proclaimed in its slogans, the Revolution opened up social cleavages of a chronic nature. If it was a 'successful' revolution, it was not successful enough, and produced that cycle of revolution and restoration which has dominated French history to the present day. The 1789 Revolution did not create a 'bourgeois society', if this be taken to mean one which conjoined political democracy and the hegemony of a capitalist class; throughout the nineteenth century, heavily conservative elements, centred particularly in the church, rentiers and peasantry, retained a deep-seated influence in government and society. The writings of Saint-Simon and Comte, in their somewhat variant ways, embodied and gave expression to this precarious balance of liberal and conservative influences. Both perceived this as a transitory situation, and both looked forward to a new and more 'stable' order in the future. Their divergent conceptions of this future order are among the major problematic issues which Durkheim sought to resolve in his sociology. Is the emergent form of society to be one in which there is a single 'class' of *industriels*, where equality of opportunity will prevail, and in which government is reduced to the 'administration of things', not of persons; or is it to be the hierocratic, corporate state of Comte's *Positive Polity*?

As in the writings of Max Weber, the problem, not of 'order' in a generic sense,[11] but of the form of *authority* appropriate to a modern industrial state, is the leading theme in Durkheim's work. But whereas in Germany a different combination of political and economic circumstances helped to establish a tradition of *Nationalökonomie* which led liberal scholars of Weber's generation to an overwhelming concern with 'capitalism',[12] in France the problem was posed within the context of the long-standing confrontation between the 'individualism' embodied in the ideals of the Revolution, and the moral claims of the Catholic hierocracy. Thus the Third Republic certainly came into being amid an atmosphere of crisis – and of class conflict as manifest in the Paris Commune and its repression – but, so it seemed to Durkheim and his liberal contemporaries, the disasters of 1870–1 also provided both the possibility and the necessity of at last completing the process of social and political change which had been initiated in the Revolution almost a century earlier. In his sociological works, Durkheim was not, as is often stated, concerned above all with the nature of 'anomie', but rather with exploring the complex interrelationships between the *three* dimensions of 'anomie', 'egoism' and 'individualism'. *The Division of Labour* states Durkheim's thinking on this matter, and he did not afterwards deviate from the position set out therein, although he did not fully elaborate certain of its implications until later. The most important substantive conclusion which Durkheim reached in *The Division of Labour* is that organic solidarity presupposes *moral* individualism: in other words, that 'it is wrong to contrast a society which comes from a community of beliefs (mechanical solidarity) to one which has a cooperative basis (organic solidarity), according only to the first a moral character, and seeing in the latter simply an economic grouping'.[13] The immediate source of this moral individualism, as Durkheim made clear in his contribution to the public discussion of the Dreyfus affair,[14] is in the ideals generated by the 1789 Revolution. Moral individualism is by no means the same as egoism (i.e. the pursuit of self-interest), as is posited in classical economic theory and utilitarian philosophy. The growth of individualism, deriving from the expansion of organic solidarity, is not to be necessarily equated with anomie (the anomic condition of the division of labour is a *transitory* phenomenon, which stems precisely from the fact that the formation of contracts is insufficiently governed by moral regulation).

Thus the social order which is coming into being demands the realization or *concrete implementation* of the ideals of the French Revolution.

This theory, therefore, provided a resolution of the issues separating Saint-Simon's and Comte's otherwise closely comparable views.[15] The emergent social order is certainly to be one founded in the complex division of labour entailed by modern industry – as specified by Saint-Simon; Comte was mistaken in supposing that the condition of unity in traditional societies, the existence of a strongly formed *conscience collective*, is necessary to the modern type of society.[16] But it is not to be a society in which authority will be confined to the 'administration of things', as Saint-Simon envisaged:[17] on the contrary, the division of labour in industry must be infused with *moral* controls, and these must be under the general moral guidance of the state.

Durkheim's assessment of the underlying factors in the Dreyfus affair, as well as his own active participation in it, focus these issues with great clarity. The immediate stimulus to Durkheim's discussion of the questions raised by the Dreyfus controversy was the publication of an article by Brunetière, the Catholic apologist, who accused the *dreyfusards* of fostering moral anarchy by rejecting traditional values in favour of an egoistic rationalism.[18] Durkheim replied by asserting the existence of a radical distinction between 'egoism' and 'rationalist individualism'. It is true that no society can be built upon the pursuit of self-interest; but the latter is not at all the same thing as 'individualism'. Individualism must not be identified with 'the utilitarian egoism of Spencer and of the economists'.[19] Indeed, Durkheim continued, there would be no need to attack individualism if it possessed no other representatives, for utilitarian theory is in the process of dying a natural death. Individualism is in fact quite distinct from this: it is not merely a 'philosophical construction', but is a living part of the social organization of contemporary society. It is 'that which the Declaration of the Rights of Man sought, more or less successfully, to give a formula to; that which is currently taught in our schools, and which has become the basis of our moral catechism'.[20] This is, in an important respect, the very opposite of egoism. It involves, not the glorification of self-interest but of the welfare of others: it is the morality of cooperation. Individualism, or the 'cult of the individual', is founded upon sentiments of sympathy for human suffering, a desire for equality and for justice. It in no sense derives from egoism, but is social in origin. The growth of individualism does not, therefore, intrinsically promote anomie, the decay of moral authority.

There can be no retreat to the traditional deism of the church, or to the patterns of hierocratic control associated with it. Individualism nonetheless preserves a 'religious' character, as do all moral rules. This 'cult of the individual' is the only moral form possible in an industrial society, having a highly differentiated division of labour:

> To the degree that societies become larger, and embody broader territorial areas, traditions and practices must necessarily exist in a state of plasticity and ambiguity which no longer offers as much resistance to individual differences ; thus traditions and practices are able to adapt themselves to a diversity of situations and to changed circumstances. Individual differences, being much less confined, develop more freely, and multiply ; that is to say, everyone pursues, to a greater degree, his own bent [*son propre sens*]. At the same time, because of the more advanced developments of the division of labour, each person finds himself turned towards a different point on the horizon, reflects a different aspect of the world and, consequently, the content of individual minds differs from one man to another. Thus we move little by little towards a situation, which has now almost been reached, where the members of the same social group will share nothing in common save their quality of humanness [*leur qualité d'homme*], the constitutive characteristics of the human person in general. This idea of the human person, somewhat modified according to differences in national temperament, is thus the only one which is maintained, immovable and impersonal, above the flux of particular opinions . . . nothing remains which men can love and worship in common, except man himself . . . Let us therefore use our liberties in order to seek what must be done, and in order to do it ; to soften the functioning of the social machine, which is still so harsh on men, to make available to them all possible means for the development of their faculties without obstacle, to work to finally make a reality of the famous precept: to each according to his works![21]

As Richter has pointed out,[22] Durkheim's political liberalism and his sociological defence of republicanism played a major role in the promotion of his own academic career, and in facilitating the rise of sociology as a recognized discipline in the French academic system. The opprobrium which was directed at sociology – especially from Thomist critics[23] – bears witness to the degree to which the new discipline (especially in its Durkheimian form) came to be regarded as the hand-maiden of an ascendant republicanism. The struggle for the secularization of education, of course, was an element of primary significance as a background to this: Durkheim was first appointed to the Sorbonne in 1902 as a professor of education, and in his courses on pedagogy he set out a systematic theoretical exposition of the factors which necessitated the transformation of the educational system.[24] But while it was true that the ideological complementarity between Durkheim's sociology and victorious republicanism accounts for much of the considerable influence which he and the *Année sociologique* school exerted in French intellectual circles, it would be quite misleading to imply that his assessment of concrete political issues or personalities played a significant part in shaping his sociological views. Durkheim, in Davy's phrase, always kept aloof from the *cuisine politique*;[25] he had little feeling for, or interest in, the practical problems of politics. Consequently, he never affiliated himself directly to any political party, although he maintained a close contact with his fellow *normalien* Jaurès, and both influenced and was influenced by some of the leading trends in Radical Socialism.[26]

To trace Durkheim's intellectual indebtedness to socialism is to reveal some of the most profound sources of his thought. Mauss has stated that Durkheim originally conceived the subject-matter of *The Division of Labour* in terms of an analysis of the relationship between individualism and socialism.[27] 'Socialism' here does not refer, however, to the traditions of revolutionary thought which are so richly represented in French political life from the concluding decades of the eighteenth century onwards. If Durkheim's attitudes towards other branches of socialism were less than wholly unambiguous, his views on revolutionary socialism were clear-cut and unchanging. Major social change is not brought about by political revolution. According to Durkheim, the history of France in the first two thirds of the nineteenth century bears witness to this. 'It is among the most revolutionary peoples', he wrote, 'that bureaucratic routine is often most powerful'; in such societies, 'superficial change disguises the most monotonous uniformity'.[28] Thus the class struggles which manifested themselves in 1848 and 1870–1, rather than being the harbingers of an entirely new social order,[29] bear witness to the fact that the underlying social changes (of which even the 1789 Revolution was more of a symptom than a cause) have not yet been accommodated within the general framework of modern French society. *The Division of Labour* establishes the theoretical grounding of this position, showing that the existence of class conflict derives from the fact that the transitional phase between mechanical and organic solidarity has not been completed. In reviewing Labriola's *Essais sur la conception matérialiste de l'histoire* in 1879, Durkheim made this position fully explicit. The 'sad class conflict of which we are the witnesses today' is not the cause of the *malaise* which the contemporary European societies are experiencing; on the contrary, it is secondary and derived. The transition from the traditional to the newly emergent type of social order is a protracted process, which does not 'begin' at any definite date, and which is evolutionary rather than revolutionary in character. The elimination of class conflict, therefore, does not necessitate an 'upheaval and radical reorganization of the social order', but instead demands the consolidation and absorption of the basic social and economic transformations which have already taken place.[30]

Although Durkheim seems to have been acquainted with Marx's writings at a very early stage in his intellectual career, according to his own testimony[31] he was in no way directly influenced by Marx, either in formulating his general conception of sociology and sociological method, or in arriving at the theory of social development set out in *The Division of Labour*. In France prior to the turn of the twentieth century, Marxism was not, of course, the major political and intellectual force which it was in the last two decades of the nineteenth century in Germany. The thought of Max and Alfred Weber, Sombart, Tönnies, and the other younger members of the *Verein für Sozialpolitik* was in substantial part shaped through a confrontation with Marxism.[32] Whatever the naïvetés and oversimplifications of Marx's ideas which became current in Germany, both Marx's self-professed followers and the leading critics of Marxism there possessed an understanding of Marx which was vastly more advanced than that which became diffused into French intellectual circles from the 1880s onwards. The Guesdist variety of Marxism, which held sway up until the middle of the 1890s, when translations of more sophisticated Marxist writings (such as those by Labriola) became available, was raucous and shallow. Hence, by the time Marxism made a substantial penetration into French intellectual consciousness, Durkheim had already worked out most of the essential components of his sociology.

His lectures on socialism, given at Bordeaux in 1895-6 were, however, partly stimulated by the spread of Marxism at this period;[33] some of his own students, indeed, became converted to Marxism at this time.[34] But Durkheim was, by this stage, equipped to meet with and to assimilate the challenge of Marxism in his own terms. His *Socialism* lecture-course sets out, in the face of the revolutionary Left, the same basic position which, at the height of the Dreyfus affair, was to be made against the reactionaries of the Right, and at the same time affirms the key role of sociology in the analysis and resolution of the 'contemporary crisis'. Moreover, in these lectures, Durkheim made explicit the continuity between the intellectual problems tackled by Saint-Simon and those which face the modern age. The writings of Saint-Simon, and of his followers, comprised – in a confused form – three sets of ideas: first, the conception of a scientific sociology; second, the notion of a religious revival; and third, a body of socialist doctrine. It is not by chance, Durkheim asserted, that these three sets of ideas have again come to the fore, since 'there are striking analogies between the period we have just been studying and the one in which we now live'.[35] These sets of ideas appear at first sight to be quite distinct, and even opposed to each other: in fact, each derives from the same circumstance – the 'condition of moral disorder' which prevailed before 1848, and which had been reactivated after 1870.[36] Each expresses, in a partial fashion, aspects of this 'disorder'. The religious movement arises from a felt need to control egoism, and hence to recreate a strong moral authority; it is inadequate, because it seeks to re-establish forms of ecclesiastical domination which are only appropriate to an earlier type of society. Socialism recognizes that the old order has been superseded, and that consequently traditional institutions must cede place to new forms of social organization; but it looks to purely economic transformations in order to remedy a situation of crisis which is primarily moral in character. The impetus towards sociology stems from the desire to understand and to explain the origins of the changes which are taking place. It, too, is limited because, as a scientific study, it necessarily proceeds only cautiously and slowly, while the demands of the day stimulate a desire for instant and all-embracing solutions. Nevertheless, it is clear that, in Durkheim's thinking, sociology claims a definite primacy over the other two. For while each of the others gives only a distorted picture of the modern crisis,[37] sociology is able to reveal its true nature. Sociological analysis cannot in and of itself be a substitute for the other two sets of ideas. Each has something to offer which no science can provide. But only sociology can show what those necessary elements are:

> Our conclusion therefore is that if you wish to allow these practical theories (which have not advanced much since the beginning of the century) to go forward a step, you must force yourself habitually to take account of their different tendencies and discover their unity. That is what Saint-Simon attempted. His undertaking must be renewed and in the same direction. His history can serve to show us the way.[38]

But Saint-Simon's thought contained an essential weakness: that he looked to 'industry' – that is, economic change – to supply the main remedy for the modern crisis. This emphasis was in turn transferred to subsequent branches of socialism, including that created by Marx. Marxist socialism, in common with all other forms, is a product of the social and economic changes set into motion in the late eighteenth and early nineteenth centuries in Western Europe. It is certainly a more 'scientific' type of socialism than other more idealistic strains in socialist thought – 'it has thus rendered social science more services perhaps than it received from it'[39] – but, however valid certain of its propositions and insights, its programme still rests upon a combination of purely economic measures. The principal thesis of *Capital* is that the 'anarchy of the market', characteristic of capitalism, will, under socialism, be replaced by a system in which production will be centrally regulated: 'In short, in Marxist socialism, capital does not disappear: it is merely administered by society and not by individuals.'[40] Marx's works thus conform to what Durkheim takes to be a cardinal principle of socialism: namely that the productive capacity of society is to be regulated centrally. But while this might allow the overcoming of the 'forced' division of labour (*la division du travail contrainte*), it would do nothing to reduce the moral hiatus which derives from the anomic condition of modern industry. On the contrary, it would deepen it, since it would further elevate the importance of the 'economic' at the expense of the 'moral'.

Although this is not made explicit in *Socialism*, there can be no doubt that the theory of the division of labour is basic to the differentiation between 'communism' and 'socialism', as this is formulated by Durkheim.[41] Communist ideas, which have sprung up at many diverse periods of history, advance the notion that private property is the essential source of all social evils and that therefore the accumulation of material wealth must be subject to severe restrictions. According to communist theory, the political sphere must be strictly separated from the potentially corrupting influence of economic production. Socialism, on the other hand, which has only come into being with the social and economic transformations of the late eighteenth century, is founded upon the view that the progress of human welfare depends upon the expansion of industry. The main principle involved in socialism is exactly contrary to that proposed in communist theory: socialism advocates the fusion of the political and the economic. Socialism claims, not simply that production should be *controlled* by the state, but that the role of the state should be defined in economic terms: that is, that the 'administration of things' should replace the 'administration of men'. Whereas, therefore, the aim of communism is the regulation of consumption, that of socialism is the regulation of production.[42] Thus communism, in Durkheim's understanding of the term, is a form of political protest and theory which corresponds to societies having a low division of labour. Everyone works in a like fashion, as a separate producer, and there is not a large measure of economic interdependence; consequently, the conception of the regulation of *production* cannot emerge. In the ideal society envisaged by communism, 'There is no common rule which determines relationships among the different workers, or the manner in which all these diverse activities should cooperate for collective goals. As each one does the same thing – or almost the same – there is no cooperation to regulate.'[43] The appearance of socialism, on the other hand, is only possible with the development of a differentiated division of labour, since it presupposes the idea of a (coordinated) economy of interdependent producers.

Durkheim's proposals for the revival of occupational associations (*corporations*), within the general framework of the state, have definite affinities with the solidarism of the Radical Socialists, and more broadly with the traditions of corporatism which intertwine with socialism in the history of French political theory.[44] But it would be mistaken to suppose that Durkheim developed these ideas in close and direct relation to the political interests of the solidarists, although his views did exert some considerable degree of influence over a number of major contemporary figures

associated with the movement. The solidarists advocated a programme of state intervention in economic affairs which was
roughly comparable to that proposed by the *Kathedersozialisten*
in Germany. Durkheim made the acquaintance of the writings of
the 'older generation' of the *Kathedersozialisten* at an early stage
in his career, whilst studying in Germany in 1885–6. He was
especially impressed with what he perceived in the writings of
Schmoller, Wagner and others as an attempt to break away from
utilitarianism in political and social theory. They showed that, in
utilitarian theory, 'the collective interest is only a form of personal
interest', and 'altruism is merely a concealed egoism'.[45] Neither
society nor the state can be understood except as moral agencies:
no society exists where economic relationships are not controlled
by the regulative force of custom and law. Thus measures involving state intervention in economic life must be clothed in a moral
and legal framework. The emphasis upon the moral role of the
modern state, which is the ultimate guarantor of just contractual
relations, finds a place in *The Division of Labour*: 'There is,
above all, an agency upon which we are tending to become increasingly dependent: this is the state. The points at which we are
in contact with it multiply as do the occasions when it is entrusted
with the duty of reminding us of the sentiment of common
solidarity.'[46] The first edition of *The Division of Labour* already
contained a fragmentary analysis of the role of the occupational
associations.[47] But a much fuller exposition is given in the preface
to the second edition of the book in 1902. The connections are
clear between Durkheim's call for an expansion of the functions
of the occupational associations, and the analysis of the anomic
division of labour contained in the work. The occupational system
is in an anomic condition in so far as moral regulation is absent
at the 'nodal' points of the divisions of labour – the points of
'intermesh' between the different occupational strata. The main
function of the occupational associations is to provide the appropriate moral coordination at these points, and thus to promote
the operation of organic solidarity.

Durkheim's ideas on the role of the occupational associations,
which he worked out in detail in the latter part of the 1890s, were
formulated in close relationship to the development of his thinking on the state. While *The Division of Labour* allowed Durkheim
to elucidate some of the major problems, as he perceived them,
in the legacy of Saint-Simon and Comte, it left aside the problem

of the state as a system of political power. The work simply
assumes an inverse correlation between the advance of the division
of labour and the diminishing of state absolutism: 'the place of
the individual becomes greater and the governmental power
becomes *less absolute*'.[48] But Durkheim later came to see this
position as an oversimplified one, which failed to come to terms
with some of the central issues which the social philosophy of the
late eighteenth and early nineteenth centuries had left unresolved.
The tradition of French thought on the matter, which Durkheim
saw as rooted primarily in Rousseau,[49] fails to examine the institutions which mediate between the state and the individual. If the
state directly represents the 'will of the people', then it tends to
become 'merely a carbon-copy of the life underlying it. It does
no more than translate what individuals think and feel, in a
different notation.' It is precisely this situation which has characterized French political history throughout the nineteenth century,
and it explains the alternating phases of revolution and absolutist
dictatorship through which the French polity has passed. 'The
state does not move of its own power, it has to follow in the wake
of the obscure sentiments of the multitude. At the same time,
however, the powerful means of action it possesses makes it
capable of exerting a heavy repression over the same individuals
whose servant, otherwise, it still remains.'[50] In these conditions
it seems as though all is change. But this is only superficial: the
bewildering flux of events on the political level masks a deep
stagnation in the rest of society. A democratic order, therefore,
which is capable of implementing the ideals comprised in the 'cult
of the individual', must depart from the contemporary form of
the French political system. The 'paradox', which Rousseau
'wrestled with in vain', of the fact that the state must rest upon
common moral sentiments and yet play an active part in promoting genuine social change, can be resolved if the occupational
associations are given an intermediary role in the electoral system.
Durkheim thus proposed that the regionally based electoral system
should be abandoned, arguing that regional differences in culture
and interests were becoming increasingly eradicated by the
advance of industrialization. The main differences today stem
from the diversification of the division of labour, and these are
not bound to regional variations:

. . . nowadays, the links that bind each one of us to a particular spot in
an area where we live are extremely weak and can be broken with the

greatest ease . . . Professional life, on the other hand, takes on increasing importance, as labour goes on splitting up into divisions. There is therefore reason to believe that it is this professional life that is destined to form the basis of our political structure. The idea is already gaining ground that the professional association is the true electoral unit, and because the links attaching us to one another derive from our calling rather than from any regional bonds of loyalty, it is natural that the political structure should reflect the way in which we ourselves form into groups of our own accord.[51]

Durkheim's portrayal of the moral character of the state, and his version of democratic republicanism, gave minimal importance to the external relationships of the modern nation-state. Although Durkheim rejected Spencer's contention that industrial society necessarily tends to be pacific in character, he none the less emphasized that there is no intrinsic incompatibility between the republican state and the progress of international harmony. The ideals of moral individualism, at their most abstract level, refer not to the citizens of any particular nation, but to mankind in general. Consequently, it is probable that the future will see an evolution towards the decline of national differences, and that the expansion of the division of labour in the international context will eventually lead to the formation of a supra-national community. At the time of the writing of *The Division of Labour*, Durkheim thought he discerned a definite movement towards the creation of a European community, quoting Sorel in order to substantiate this judgement.[52] This optimistic perspective, of course, contrasted sharply with the subsequent deterioration of the relationships between the major powers which culminated in the First World War. Although Durkheim, together with most other intellectuals of his generation, experienced the outbreak of the war with a profound sense of tragedy and shock, he did not abandon the notion that it 'is the tendency of patriotism to become, as it were, a fragment of world patriotism'.[53] This is made clear in the various patriotic pamphlets which Durkheim wrote during the war.[54] These have often been dismissed as mere exercises in propaganda, but in fact they stand in close relationship to his theory of the state. The main point in the most important of Durkheim's wartime publications, *L'Allemagne au-dessus de tout,* is that German militarism rests upon a 'pathological' form of mentality which is a kind of 'collective anomie'. This phenomenon results from 'a certain manner of conceiving the state, its nature and its role',[55] which Durkheim found to be expressed in a clearly defined way in the thought of Treitschke. Treitschke, according to Durkheim, is not an original thinker, but a writer whose works represent the ideas and sentiments of the collectivity, and thus contain 'all the principles which German diplomacy and the German state has daily put into practice'.[56]

For Treitschke the state is the highest value, can accept no limits to its power, and must ultimately pursue its aims by warfare: constant struggle between nation-states is an inevitable characteristic of the modern world. According to his conception, the power of the state is the criterion in terms of which all other values are to be judged; but the state itself is not a moral entity. This is a 'pathological' form of national patriotism, in Durkheim's analysis, because it treats the state purely as a system of power, which recognizes no intrinsic limits to its hegemony. But, as in the case of the individual, the state cannot exist as an amoral being which acknowledges no constraints upon the expansion of its ambitions. Treitschke's conception of the state is based upon a fallacious view of the relationship between state and society. According to him, 'there is a difference in nature . . . between the individual and the state'.[57] This is a standpoint which perpetuates the Hegelian notion of the state as existing on an utterly different plane from that of life in civil society, and which readily serves to legitimize an autocratic tyranny. To admit the sovereignty of the state, internally and in external relations, Durkheim concluded, does not at all entail acceptance of such a view: the sovereignty of the state is 'relative', both to the internal moral structure of civil society – 'a multitude of moral forces which, although not possessing a rigorous juridical form and organization, are none the less real and efficacious' – and to the morals of international relations, 'the attitudes of foreign peoples'.[58] Although German imperialism must be defeated militarily, it is by its very nature an unstable phenomenon, and is incompatible with the moralization of international relations which characterizes the modern world: 'There is no state which is not incorporated into the broader *milieu* formed by the totality of other states, that is to say, which is not part of the great human community . . .'[59]

Examination of Durkheim's writings on the growth of moral individualism, on socialism, and on the state, in the context of the social and political issues which he saw as confronting the Third Republic, shows how mistaken it is to regard him as being primarily 'conservative' in his intellectual standpoint.[60] The proponents of this view[61] have recognized Durkheim's liberalism in politics, but have sought to show that the most important intellectual parameters of his sociology were derived from those traditions of French social philosophy (especially the so-called 'counter-reaction' to the French Revolution) which emphasized 'cohesion' rather than 'conflict', 'order' rather than 'change', and 'authority' rather than 'freedom'. 'Conservatism' here means, in Coser's words, 'an inclination to maintain the existing order of things or to re-enforce an order which seems threatened'.[62] As a description of Durkheim's concerns, however, this is quite one-sided. Not the defence of the 'order' against change, but the objective of *achieving* change is what Durkheim sought to promote. The point is that France in the first two thirds of the nineteenth century, while manifesting various periods of apparently rapid political 'change', in fact remained basically stable: the socio-economic transformations necessary to further the transition to a modern industrial order had not been realized.

The structure and substance of Durkheim's political sociology

The formula which identifies Durkheim with a 'conservative' intellectual standpoint has been heavily reinforced by the view which holds that his thought underwent dramatic modification in the course of his career: for the interpretation which minimizes the importance of *The Division of Labour* in his writings also serves to underplay the significance which he attributed to the historical element in sociology.[63] Durkheim always stressed that 'history is not only the natural framework of human life; man is a product of history'.[64] This emphasis gives a clear continuity to his life's work, within the evolutionary scheme set out in *The Division of Labour*. But the 'orthodox' viewpoint, such as presented by Parsons and by Nisbet, places most weight upon Durkheim's functionalism, conceived in terms of an abstract and a-historical relationship between the individual and society. In these terms the fundamental theorem in Durkheim's sociology appears to be that of the need for a *consensus omnium* in society, to counter the Hobbesian 'war of all against all' which constantly threatens to destroy social order. If, however, the whole of Durkheim's writings are seen in terms of the historical framework of the movement from mechanical to organic solidarity, then the resultant picture is quite different: a guiding theme of Durkheim's work is the depth of the *contrast* between traditional forms of society and the modern social order. This contrast, according to Durkheim, has not been adequately understood by those forms of social theory which, in the earlier part of the nineteenth century, have grasped the significance of the fact that the traditional order has gone forever. Both utilitarians and socialists have mistakenly proceeded by separating the 'moral' character of traditional society from the 'economic' basis of the modern type. The crucial problem facing sociology is that of defining what are the social forms capable of realizing the ideals of freedom and equality generated by the transition from the traditional order. The dilemma which Durkheim faced, and which was clarified – but not fully resolved – in *The Division of Labour*, stemmed, therefore, from his conviction that, while 'the defenders of the old economic theories are mistaken in thinking that regulation is not necessary today', 'the apologists of the institution of religion are wrong in believing that yesterday's regulation can be useful today'. [65] The work which Durkheim undertook on primitive religion, culminating in *The Elementary Forms of the Religious Life*, allowed the solution of this dilemma in terms of a more elaborate theory of authority. The functional theory of religion advanced in *The Elementary Forms* has to be understood in relation to Durkheim's explicit statement that,

. . . the importance we thus attribute to the sociology of religion does not in the least imply that religion must play the same role in present-day societies that it has played at other times. In a sense, the contrary conclusion would be more sound. Precisely because religion is a primordial phenomenon, it must yield more and more to the new social forms it has engendered.[66]

What *The Elementary Forms* demonstrates is not that 'religion creates society',[67] but that the collective representations embodied in religion are the expression of the *self-creation* of human society. The force of religiosity is thus a symbolic consciousness of the capabilities of human society to dominate and to change the world. Read as a *genetic*, and not simply as a functional theory, *The Elementary Forms* provides the foundation for an understanding of the processes which have led to the emergence of moral individualism. As Max Weber demonstrated in a different context, the advance of rationalistic individualism is grounded in the 'irrationalism' of sacred symbols: all forms of thought, including science, have their origins in religious representations. In an important, but neglected work,[68] Durkheim details some of the elements of this process in the history of the European societies. Christianity in general, and Protestantism in particular, are the proximate source of the ideals which later became transferred to the political sphere in the French Revolution. The Christian ethic, Durkheim sought to show, broke in a radical way with the pagan religions of Rome, by focusing its emphasis upon the 'internal' state of the soul, rather than upon the 'external' world of nature. For the Christian, 'virtue and piety do not consist in material procedures, but in interior states of the soul'; of the 'two possible poles of all thought, nature on the one hand, and man on the other', it is 'around the second that the thought of the Christian societies has come to gravitate . . .'[69]

Clarification of the origins and nature of moral individualism made possible for Durkheim a clear elucidation of the differences between 'individualism' and 'egoism' – differences which, although already fundamental in *The Division of Labour* and *Suicide,* remained in some degree ambiguous until after 1895. The theory which subsequently was set out in *The Elementary Forms* is organized in terms of a duality between the 'sacred' and the 'profane' which cross-cuts the more conventional distinction between the 'sacred' and the 'secular'. Any ideal which is a collective product has, *ipso facto,* a sacred character in these terms, and hence possesses the twin aspects of all morality: it is 'as if surrounded by a mysterious barrier which keeps violators at arm's length'[70] – i.e. imbues men with positive sentiments of respect and commitment – and it carries the notion of duty or obligation. It follows that the process of 'secularization' (meaning by this the decline of traditional deism), although a progressive trend within modern societies, does not entail the disappearance of the 'sacred': on the contrary, the freedom of men from the repressive moral controls of former times is dependent upon the continuing 'sacred' quality of the ideals which comprise moral individualism. Freedom cannot, however, be identified with the liberation from all moral controls (as utilitarians and socialists assert); acceptance of the moral regulation of the 'cult of the personality' is the *condition* of freedom:

. . . rights and liberties are not things inherent in man as such . . .
Society has consecrated the individual and made him pre-eminently
worthy of respect. His progressive emancipation does not imply a
weakening but a transformation of the social bonds . . . For man freedom consists in the deliverance from blind, unthinking physical forces;
this he achieves by opposing against them the great and intelligent force
which is society, under whose protection he shelters.[71]

There is in Durkheim's writings no yearning for a former age,
no wistful search for the revitalization of the stability of the past.
There can be no reversion to the social forms of earlier types of
society, and neither, in Durkheim's eyes, would this be a desirable
prospect if it were possible. In traditional society men are subject
to the tyranny of the group: individuality is subordinated to the
pressure of the *conscience collective*. The expansion of the division
of labour, and the weakening of the *conscience collective*, are the
agencies of the escape from this tyranny; but the dissolution of the
old moral order threatens the individual with another tyranny,
that of his own inexhaustible desires. An individual can only be
free if he is an autonomous actor, capable of mastering and of
realizing his impulses.[72] The distinctions between 'anomie', and
'egoism' and 'individualism' are thus of key importance. The sort
of modern social order represented by the utilitarians and socialists
is one built upon the supposed mutuality of individual egoisms.
But no form of society, traditional or modern, could exist on this
basis. The common error of these authors, therefore, is to
assimilate 'egoism' and 'individualism': these derive from essentially different sources. Moral individualism is a product of
human society, the outcome of a very long period of social
evolution. Egoism, on the other hand, is anchored in the needs
and desires of the pre-social individual. This opposition between
the egoistic inclinations of the individual and the moral products
of society, according to Durkheim, is expressed in religious
thought in the distinction between the body and the soul. The
body is the source of sensation, and of appetites which are 'necessarily egoistic';[73] the soul, by contrast, is a primitive representation
of the concepts and moral rules which are created by society. The
child begins life as an egoistic being, whose needs are defined
purely in terms of personal sensory wants. These become overlaid
with modes of thought and moral ideals which are taken from
society: the developed individual always has an egoistic side to his
personality, at the same time as he is a social being.

If 'individualism' is to be separated from 'egoism', it is also to be stringently distinguished from 'anomie'. While a (hypothetical) society formed out of the conjunction of individual egoisms would be one of moral anarchy or anomie, this is most definitely not the case in a society founded upon moral individualism within a differentiated division of labour. On the contrary, the condition of anomie which prevails within certain sectors of contemporary societies derives from the *lack* of institutionalization of individualism – as Durkheim made clear in his reply to Brunetière during the course of the Dreyfus affair. This institutionalization, according to the premises established in *The Division of Labour*, must involve the formation of integrating links between the political and economic orders: the progression towards a more just distribution of functions (i.e. the elimination of the forced division of labour) under the general guidance of the state, and the moralization of economic relationships through the occupational associations. There are, therefore, the closest of ties between Durkheim's theory of moral authority and his analysis of the modern political system.

The conception of the 'political', Durkheim pointed out, is one which has only come into being with the development of the modern form of society, since it presupposes a differentiation between government and the governed which does not exist in more primitive societal types. A 'political society' for Durkheim, however, is not to be defined purely in terms of the existence of constituted authority in a grouping: a family, for example, is not a political society, even though it may possess an individual or group in authority, such as a patriarch or a council of elders. An additional criterion is necessary. This is not to be found in the characteristic of the fixed territorial area; unlike Weber, Durkheim rejected this as of critical importance. Rather it is to be discerned in the degree of complexity in social organization: a political society is one which manifests a clear-cut authority division, but which is composed of a plurality of kinship groups, or of larger secondary groups. A political society does not necessarily possess a state: a 'state', in Durkheim's terminology, refers to an administrative staff or officialdom which is formally entrusted with the function of government.[74]

According to the thesis of *The Division of Labour*, the development of society towards increasing internal differentiation produces the progressive emancipation of individual thought and action from subordination to the *conscience collective*. *Prima facie* this would appear to lead to a paradox: for if the growth in the division of labour is associated with the expansion of the self-determination of the individual, it also goes hand in hand with a widening of the powers of the state to subject the individual to its authority. In fact this is no paradox, because it is the state which, in the modern type of society, is the institution which is concerned with the implementation and the furtherance of individual rights. In *The Division of Labour*, just as he saw a direct correlation between the advance of social differentiation and the development of the state, Durkheim also conceived of a direct relationship between the growth of the division of labour and the decline of coercive sanctions.

> Similarity between individuals gives rise to juridical rules which, with the threat of repressive measures, impose uniform beliefs and practices upon all . . . The division of labour produces juridical rules which determine the nature and the relations of divided functions, but whose violation calls forth only restrictive measures without any expiatory character.[75]

Later Durkheim came to see that 'kinds of society should not be confused with different types of states',[76] and that the coercive powers possessed by the state apparatus can vary in some degree independently of the level of the development of the division of labour. In *Deux lois de l'évolution pénale*,[77] written at the turn of the century, Durkheim presented a systematic and cogent analysis of the implications of this position. The coercive sanctions which have existed in different types of society can be classified along two partially independent dimensions: the 'quantitative' and the 'qualitative'. The first refers to the intensity of punishment for deviation from a norm or a law, the second to the modality of punishment (i.e. death versus imprisonment, for example). The intensity of sanctions varies in relation, not only to the level of development of the division of labour, but also in relation to the centralization of political power. We can thus establish a 'law of quantitative variation', which holds that, 'The intensity of punishment is greater to the degree that a society belongs to a less advanced type, and that the central power is of a more absolute character'.[78]

There is, according to Durkheim, an intrinsic connection between how far 'all of the directive functions of society (are) in the same hands', and the degree of absolute power wielded by government. What determines the existence, or otherwise, of absolutism is not, as Spencer held, the number of functions exercised by the state, but how far there are other sources of institutional power which can act as a counterweight to that possessed by the state.[79] It follows from this – and Durkheim made this one of the cornerstones of his exposition of the nature of democratic government – that the extension of the directive influence of the state, which is a 'normal' characteristic of contemporary societies, does not in itself lead to a growth in state absolutism. Conversely, it does not follow that, where the state only has a relatively limited range of operations, it cannot be absolute in character: indeed, this is often the case. It is not the degree of absolutism of state power, but the range of activities engaged in by the state which varies directly with the division of labour:

. . . for the degree of development of the regulative organ simply reflects the development of collective life in general in the same way as the dimensions of the nervous system of the individual differ according to the importance of organic connections. The directive functions of society are thus only rudimentary when other social functions are of the same nature ; and the relation between the two hence remains the same . . . Nothing is simpler than the government of certain primitive kingdoms ; nothing is more absolute.[80]

As society moves, therefore, towards increasing complexity, it does not necessarily result in a decline in the repressive character of punishment: if this is accomplished, as it may be, by a heightening of state absolutism, it would cancel out the effects of the expansion of the division of labour. The relationship between societal and political development is a complex one.

The 'law of quantitative variation' refers only to the intensity of punitive sanctions. This can be complemented by a 'law of qualitative variation', concerning modalities of punishment: this law states that there is a direct relationship between the level of societal development and the use of deprivation of liberty as a mode of punishment. Imprisonment for criminal activity is almost unknown in primitive societies; and it is only amongst the peoples of Western Europe (since the latter part of the eighteenth century) that it has become the primary type of sanction. This can be explained in the following way. Imprisonment is absent from the penal system of the less developed societies because responsibility

is collective: when a crime is committed, the demand for repara-
tion falls not upon the culpable individual, but upon the whole
clan group. But with the development of more complex forms of
society, and the increasing emergence of organic solidarity
founded upon cooperative interdependence in the division of
labour, responsibility becomes individualized, and the concept of
punishment of the individual through imprisonment makes its
appearance.

The most important point in this analysis is that, while maintaining the basic standpoint of *The Division of Labour*, it faces
squarely the previously neglected problem of political power, and
more specifically the problem of coercive power, in society. The
theme, so strongly developed in *The Division of Labour*, that the
tyranny of the *conscience collective*, through the growth of
organic solidarity, is gradually dissolved in favour of a cooperative
order, is affirmed: the 'normal' tendency of the advancing complexity of society is to produce both a decline in the intensity of
coercive sanctions, and to 'individualize' punishment through
imprisonment. But the nature of political power in a given form
of society cannot simply be treated as a 'consequence' of changes
on the level of 'infrastructure'. The discussion in *Deux lois de
l'évolution pénale* makes abundantly clear how far Durkheim
was, in his insistence upon the continuing relevance of the 'sacred'
in contemporary society, from minimizing the contrast between
traditional religion and the moral character of the modern order.
For what gives rise to the heavy dominance, in the less developed
forms of society, of repressive sanctions, is the fact that crime is
interpreted as an offence against the collectivity, and therefore as
a *religious* transgression. It is crime against strongly held collective
values, against 'transcendent beings', and 'the same act which,
when it concerns an equal, is simply disapproved of, becomes
blasphemous when it relates to someone who is superior to us;
the horror which it stimulates can only be assuaged by violent
repression'. This 'religious' quality is appropriated by the absolutist
state, and is what enables it to legitimate the use of coercive
power: offences against the state are treated as 'sacrilege, and
hence, to be violently repressed'.[81]

If the political structure of society is not, at least in any simple
manner, 'determined' by the level of complexity of the division of
labour, then the status of democratic republicanism in the modern
social order is, in an important sense, problematic. What are the

conditions which provide for the implementation of a democratic political order? Durkheim's answer to this question effects a neat tie with his treatment of the role of the occupational associations in the division of labour. The state becomes absolutist to the degree to which secondary groupings, which intervene between the state and the individual, are not strongly developed: in modern society, these groupings are the occupational associations. The family, Durkheim argued, is of declining significance in this respect, and must cede place to the *corps intermédiares*, the occupational associations. He rejected the traditional theory of democracy, according to which the mass of the population 'participate' in the exercise of government. For Durkheim, this is a situation which is only possible in a society which, according to his own definition, is not a 'political' society. Such a conception of democracy cannot be sustained:

> We must therefore not say that democracy is the political form of a society governing itself, in which the government is spread throughout the *milieu* of the nation. Such a definition is a contradiction in terms. It would be almost as if we said that democracy is a political society without a state. In fact, the state is nothing if it is not an organ distinct from the rest of society. If the state is everywhere, it is nowhere. The state comes into existence by a process of concentration that detaches a certain group of individuals from the collective mass . . . If everyone is to govern, it means in fact that there is no government . . . If we agree to reserve the name democracy for political societies, it must not be applied to tribes without definite form, which thus far have no claim to being a state and are not political societies.[82]

Government, by definition, must be exercised by a minority of individuals. 'Democracy', therefore, must concern the relationship between the differentiated political agency, or the state, and the other institutional structures of society: more specifically, according to Durkheim, how far there is an interplay of communication between state and society. Where the citizens are regularly informed of the activities of the state, and the latter in turn is aware of the sentiments and wishes of all sectors of the population, then a democratic order exists. A democratic system thus presupposes a balance between two opposed tendencies: on the one hand, that in which the state directly reflects the 'general will', and on the other in which the absolutist state, 'closed in upon itself', is cut off from the people. Each of these conditions tends to inhibit the effective occurrence of social change. As has been indicated previously, the first, in Durkheim's view, produces a situation in which only superficial change can take place. In the second case, although it might appear as though the political power wielded by the state would allow the possibility of bringing about radical social transformation, this is not in fact the case: such states 'are indeed all-powerful against the individual and this is what the term "absolute" means, as applied to them . . . But against the social condition itself, against the structure of society, they are relatively powerless.'[83] In a democratic order, however, the pace of change can be advanced, because the conduct of social life assumes a more 'conscious' and 'controllable' character. Democratic government makes it possible for many aspects of social organization previously dominated by unthinking custom or habit to become open to effective intervention on the part of the state. In a democratic order, the state does not simply express the sentiments held in a diffuse fashion among the population, but is often the origin of new ideas: it leads society as well as being led by it. The extension of the activities of the state, whereby it penetrates into many spheres of society formerly controlled by custom or tradition – in the administration of justice, in economic life, in science and the arts – is therefore certainly not to be identified as necessarily leading to the autocratic domination of state over society. On the contrary, it is just this phenomenon which permits the active interplay between the 'government consciousness' and the views and feelings of the mass. A democracy, therefore, has two primary characteristics: the existence of close, and two-way, communication between government and governed; and the increasing extension of the contacts and ties of the state with other sectors of the society. But these characteristics do not imply that the state 'merges' with society. Rather, they presuppose the existence of a differentiated political agency: this is what saves a society from being the 'victim of traditional routine'.[84]

The occupational associations play a vital role in both of these respects. Since they are the intermediaries between the state and the individual, they are a principal medium whereby the expanding range of activities of the state are channelled to the rest of society, and they also thereby facilitate communication between state and the less organized levels of the society. It is thus the occupational associations which are of primary importance in checking two divergent possibilities whereby democracy can be undermined: the emergence of an autocratic state, separated from the people, and the 'absorption' of the state by the society. This is the reason why it is desirable that the occupational associations should intervene in the electoral process between electorate and government: 'These secondary groups are essential if the state is not to oppress the individual: they are also necessary if the state is to be sufficiently free of the individual . . . They liberate the two confronting forces, whilst linking them at the same time.'[85] In this analysis, even if it is partly latent, there is a theory of bureaucracy. A bureaucratic state, in which officialdom possesses the real power – and thereby, through adherence to bureaucratic routine, effectively promotes the maintenance of the *status quo* – is more likely to arise where the state is weak than where it is strong. In an absolutist state, although the officialdom may be used as the instrument of the domination of a ruler or an oligarchy, it is not the officials who dominate. But, as in France, where the state tends to become 'absorbed', this situation of apparent 'democracy' actually conceals a bureaucratic domination. In modern societies, where the hold of traditional customs and beliefs has been largely dissolved, there are many avenues for the display of critical spirit, and changes of opinion and mood among the mass of the population are frequent. Where government simply 'reflects' this, the outcome is a constant vacillation in the political sphere, and because of this dearth of active leadership, power devolves upon the officialdom: 'Only the administrative machine has kept its stability and goes on operating with the same automatic regularity.'[86]

A democratic society therefore, according to Durkheim, is a society which is 'conscious of itself'. On analogy with an organism, one can say, as Durkheim frequently did, that the state is the 'brain' – the conscious, directive centre – which operates, via the intermediary organs, within the complex nervous system of a diffentiated society. Thus a democratic order enjoys the same relative superiority over other societies as the self-conscious being does over an animal whose behaviour is unreflective or instinctive. Durkheim placed considerable emphasis upon the 'cognitive' as opposed to the 'active' significance of the state. In particular, the state makes articulate and furthers the moral aims and sentiments embodied in the diffuse *conscience collective*.[87] This is important to the understanding of Durkheim's conception of moral authority as it exists in modern societies. The state within a democratic polity is the main agency which actively implements the values of moral individualism; it is the institutional form which replaces that of the church in traditional types of society. But only when it tends towards absolutism does the moral authority of the state approach that characteristic of earlier societal types, in which the individual, 'absorbed, as he was, into the mass of society . . . meekly gave way to its pressures and subordinated his own lot to the destinies of collective existence without any sense of sacrifice'.[88] The specific role of the democratic state is not to subordinate the individual to itself, but in fact to provide for his self-realization. This is not something which can occur (as is held in the theories of the utilitarians and socialists) when the operations of the state are kept to a *minimum*. The self-realization of the individual can only take place in and through his membership of a society in which the state guarantees and advances the rights embodied in moral individualism.

Of course, for Durkheim, discipline, in the sense of the control of egoism, is an essential characteristic of all moral authority. But, according to his analysis, the view which equates discipline *inherently* with the limitation of human self-realization is fallacious. All forms of life-organization, both biological and social, are controlled by defined, regular principles; by this very fact the mere existence of any type of society presupposes the regulation of behaviour according to moral rules. Certainly the moral authority characteristic of traditional forms of society, or of autocratic states, is inherently repressive, denying any great range of possibilities of self-development to the individual; but the moral regulation of the modern society and state is the very condition of the individual's self-realization, and his freedom. Durkheim's theory of moral authority is thus far from being the rationale for authoritarianism which it is often portrayed as being.[89] The sort of misinterpretation which presents Durkheim's conception of moral authority in this way tends to derive again from the failure to inject the historical element into his analysis, and from the supposition that there are close parallels between Durkheim's position and that of Hobbes on the relationship between the individual and society in the modern order. According to this view, Durkheim's theory of moral authority rests upon the premise that man is 'naturally' a refractory being, and so must be rigidly restrained by society.[90] In fact, however, Durkheim criticized Hobbes on precisely this point. Hobbes's error was to stand outside of history, by positing a 'state of nature', and thereby to assume that there is a 'break in continuity between the individual and society': this results in the notion that 'man is thus naturally refractory to the common life; he can only resign himself to it when forced'.[91]

In Durkheim's usage, even the category of 'egoism' is historical in nature. Egoism is certainly anchored in the biological or 'pre-social' needs and sensations of the individual organism; but these organic needs of the infant become overlaid with other motivations. Egoism and moral individualism, as Durkheim constantly stressed, derive from inherently opposed sources: the one from the appetites of the organism, the other from the collective activity of the group. But, while opposed in origin, and thus always potentially in tension with each other, the growth of moral individualism nevertheless acts to expand the range of egoistic inclinations. This is why, in modern society, egoism and anomie are intimately linked; this reflects the very advance in the variety of motives and sensibilities of individuals which is the outcome of a long process of social development. Egoism and anomie are not closely tied in a biologically 'given' fashion: the hypothetical savage in a pre-societal 'state of nature' would be an egoistic being, but not an anomic one, since his needs would be bound to biologically given limits – just as is the case with the infant.

'Our very egoism' is thus, according to Durkheim, 'in large part a product of society'. Moral individualism involves values which stress the dignity and worth of the human individual *in abstracto*; and individuals apply these to themselves as well as to others, and hence become more sensitive both to the feelings and needs of others and to their own. 'Their griefs, like our own, are more readily intolerable to us. Our sympathy for them is not, accordingly, a mere extension of what we feel for ourselves. But both are effects of one cause and constituted by the same moral state.'[92] The characteristic problems facing the constitution of moral authority in the modern age derive from this confrontation of egoism and moral individualism, from the fact that 'it is wholly improbable that there will ever be an era in which man is required to resist himself to a lesser degree, an era in which he can live a life that is easier and less full of tension', and that 'all evidence compels us to expect our effort in the struggle between the two beings within us to increase with the growth of civilization'.[93] These are problems of a pluralistic society, in which the despotism of the moral authority of traditional types of social order has been broken. The moral authority characteristic of traditional societies, founded upon a poverty of individuality and repressive discipline, is wholly inappropriate in modern, highly differentiated society.

The critical evaluation of Durkheim's political thought

In this paper I have stressed the central role of Durkheim's political thought in his sociology as a whole. Consequently any attempt at a critical assessment of his political ideas must be placed within a broader evaluation of his writings in sociology and social philosophy. The 'orthodox' interpretation of Durkheim readily delivers him up to a number of apparently conclusive criticisms, such as that he emphasized the importance of cohesion or *consensus* in society to the almost total exclusion of conflict; that he failed to develop a theory of institutions, because he concentrated above all upon the relationship between society and the individual, neglecting intermediate structures; that he displayed a lack of concern with the role of political power, since he was overwhelmingly interested in the nature of moral ideals; and that 'he did not duly appreciate the import of social innovation and social change because he was preoccupied with social order and equilibrium. . . .'[94] While each of these accusations contains an element of truth, none of them can be sustained in the sweeping fashion in which they are frequently made. Those who interpret Durkheim's work as being essentially concerned with a 'conservative' 'inclination to maintain the existing order of things'[95] – and such a view, although implicit, is as much contained in Parsons's basically sympathetic account of Durkheim's writings as it is in those of other authors, such as Coser or Zeitlin, who are heavily critical of Durkheim – have inevitably tended to present a misleading picture of Durkheim's position on each of these dimensions.

Both in political temper and in sociological conviction, Durkheim was an opponent of revolutionary thought. Evolution, not revolution, provided the framework for his conception of social change: he frequently emphasized that significant change only takes place through the cumulation of long-term processes of social development. His refusal to see in class conflict the mechanism which would generate a radical social transformation separated him conclusively from Marxism and from any other type of revolutionary activism. But to say this is not at all to say that he neglected the phenomenon of social conflict, or of class conflict, or that he sought to accommodate them to his theoretical position by denying the reality of the aspirations of the working class. His constantly echoed assertion that 'the social problem' (i.e., the problem of class conflict) cannot be solved through purely economic measures, because of the 'instability' of human appetites, has to be read against his equally emphatic stress upon the basic changes in the economic order which have to be made to complete the institutionalization of moral individualism. The reality behind the occurrence of class conflict is the new desire for self-realization and equality of opportunity of those in the lower socio-economic strata: this cannot be repressed but demands ultimately the abolition of all economic and social barriers to 'external equality', to 'everything that can even indirectly shackle the free unfolding of the social force that each carries in himself'.[96] Like Marx, Durkheim anticipated the emergence of a society in which class conflict would be eliminated, and where the element of coercion in the division of labour would be eradicated. But it is wholly mistaken to regard this as a scheme which absolved Durkheim from a concern with conflict. Indeed, the reverse is nearer to the truth: that the starting-point of his sociology was an attempt to analyse the sources of the conflicts which have characterized the expansion of industrialism.

Since the publication of *Leçons de sociologie*, it has become impossible to maintain that Durkheim gave no attention to intermediate institutions in society. He once defined sociology as the 'science of social institutions',[97] and it is evident that this was in fact central to his thought. *Leçons de sociologie* makes it particularly clear, however, that a profound transformation of the institutional organization of traditional forms of society is a necessary concomitant of the transition from mechanical to organic solidarity; the relationship between the state and the *corporations* is seen to be fundamental to the modern social order. It is in these terms that Durkheim sought to tackle the question of political power. Although it can hardly be granted that he dealt satisfactorily with the nature and sources of political power, it is quite clearly not the case that he merely ignored the issues posed by it. Finally, as I have emphasized throughout this paper, not only is it fallacious to hold that 'he did not duly appreciate the import of social innovation and social change', but it is not possible to understand the main themes in his work without locating it within the scheme of social development, set out in *The Division of Labour*, which underlay all of his major writings. In one of his earliest works, a dissertation on Montesquieu, Durkheim established his position on this point. Montesquieu, he showed, 'fails to see that every society embodies conflicting factors, simply because it has gradually emerged from a past form and is tending towards a future one'.[98]

Durkheim frequently asserted that sociology should, at some point, find its justification in practice: that a sociology which had no relevance to practical problems would be a worthless endeavour. It is one of the major tasks of sociology to determine the nascent directions of change which a society at any given time is experiencing, and to show which trends 'should' be fostered as the coming pattern of the future. This closure between the 'is' and the 'ought' Durkheim sought to achieve in terms of his distinction between the 'normal' and 'pathological', conceived on analogy with health and disease in the organism. The theory set out in *The Division of Labour* is founded upon this conception: the work was conceived by Durkheim to show that the ideals of moral individualism correspond to the 'social needs' engendered by the growth of mechanical solidarity – that these ideals are 'normal' to the modern type of society, and hence are to be protected and promoted. No aspect of Durkheim's writings has been more universally rejected than his notion of normality and pathology, and rightly so: even if it were possible to determine 'scientifically' whether or not a given moral norm were a 'necessary' element in the functioning of a particular society, it is altogether another thing to hold this *ipso facto* to be 'desirable'. The questions at issue here are not to be resolved by any sort of appeal to the criteria of health and disease in biology: medicine, in this respect, is a technology to be applied in pursuit of given values. In spite of – or perhaps because of – the fact that the conception of normality was integral to Durkheim's work, he never fully clarified his position in this respect. In his most systematic formulation of the principle, in *The Rules of Sociological Method*, he definitely attempted to establish scientific criteria for the verification of ethical ideals, rejecting the view that 'science can teach us nothing about what we ought to desire'.[99] But, in replying later to critics of these views, he appeared to retract his earlier formulation, indicating that ethics and sociology are concerned with two 'different spheres', and claiming that 'we ask simply that ethical constructions should be preceded by a science of morality which is more methodical than the ordinary speculations of so-called theoretical ethics'.[100]

Durkheim's ambiguity on this matter is reflected in his failure to deal in an explicit manner with the relationship between sociological analysis and political intervention in the interests of securing practical social change. As Marx realized,[101] this demands a dialectical conception of the dual character of knowledge as a means of knowing the world, and at the same time as a mode of changing it. When pursued to its logical consequence, this leads to a stress upon the directly *political* role of sociology. But, although. Durkheim wished to relate sociology to practical concerns, he also sought to advance a conception of the 'neutral' character of sociological analysis as a 'natural science of society'. Although this was no doubt reinforced by his personal characteristics and his disdain for the squabbles of party politics, his general aloofness from politics was certainly supported by this position. The result was that, in practice, the relevance of sociology to the achievement of real social change remained obscure. Durkheim attempted to escape from this difficulty by placing stress upon the 'partial' character of sociological knowledge: the emphasis that the advance of sociology is slow and painstaking, because it must conform to the rigorous criteria of scientific validation. Since the needs of life in an everyday social and political context require immediate decisions and policies, the relevance of the 'scientific' knowledge of the sociologist has definite limitations. But his own writing, often dealing with the broadest issues of social organization and social change, belies this sort of modest prescription – as, indeed, does the more abstract analysis of the 'therapeutic' role of sociology in diagnosing what is 'normal' and what is 'pathological' at given stages of societal evolution.

In Durkheim's writings this uneasy tension between theory and practice finds expression in a constant tendency, as Bendix has noted,[102] to shift from the analytical to the optative. Durkheim's discussions of extant reality frequently slide into a portrayal of what he expects to be the case in the future, because of what is supposedly entailed by the 'normal' conditions of functioning of a society or social institution. Thus the development and strengthening of the occupational associations is due to occur because this is demanded by the 'normal' operation of the division of labour. This analysis is not based upon an empirical demonstration that there is a discernible trend towards the emergence of such *corporations*: it derives from the attempt to implement the notion that the functionally necessary supplies the criterion of what is desirable – in this case, that 'the absence of all corporative institution creates . . . a void whose importance it is difficult to exaggerate'. As with all of Durkheim's attempts to diagnose 'normality', this barely avoids degenerating into crude teleology: the 'evil', the 'malady *totius substantiæ*' of the anomic division of labour, calls into being the 'remedy' of the development of the *corporations.*[103]

The shortcomings of Durkheim's writings in these very general respects are undoubtedly related to inadequacies in his conceptual treatment of the state and political power. While it is not the case that he 'ignored' the problem of power, or more specifically the role of force, in society, it is true that he established the basic framework of his thought, in *The Division of Labour*, before he developed a systematic analysis of the state and politics. His subsequent exposition of the partial 'independence' of state power only effected a restricted modification of the theory of the division of labour. While this enabled him to deal more adequately with the existence of coercive power it failed to deal with a really consequential point: what are the *conditions* which generate the development of an absolute state? The analyses given in *Leçons de sociologie* and *Deux lois de l'évolution pénale* leave this as a residual factor: Durkheim nowhere undertook to show what *determines* the degree to which the state is able to 'separate itself' from society. He continually underlined the point that every form of state, weak or strong, is rooted in civil society, and nourished from it; but he failed to analyse in any detail at all the nature of these connections. Consequently there is in Durkheim's writings no systematic treatment of the mechanisms of legitimation in politics.[104] Political power is implicitly assumed to be an outcome of a pre-established moral ascendancy of the state: the more transcendent or 'religious' the moral basis of the state, the more absolute its power. But this conception allows no means of dealing with the tension between legitimation and power which is of crucial importance in all political systems: power, and force, in other words, are frequently *means* for the creation of values by dominant strata.

In this Durkheim certainly remained a prisoner of the main intellectual sources in which his thought is steeped. The concept of the state which he employed is a clear indication of this, and while he used it to attempt to break away from Comte's treatment of the state, his own conceptual formulation actually here resembles that of Comte.[105] The state is defined as the 'organ of social thought', the 'ego' of the *conscience collective*. Durkheim specifically rejected the notion that the state is primarily an executive agency. The main task of the state is to be 'a special organ whose responsibility it is to work out certain representations which hold good for the collectivity'; the 'true meaning' of the state 'consists not in exterior action, in making changes, but in deliberation. . . .'[106] His treatment of democracy, of course, is intimately tied in with this conceptualization. In analysing the role of the occupational associations, he certainly saw them as 'balancing' the power of the state. But the view that an integral element in democratic government is the sharing of power, as he made fully explicit, is to him not a viable one. He rejected not only the classical conception of 'direct democracy', but also what has today come to be called the 'theory of democratic élitism'. A minority must govern, in any developed society, and it makes little odds how this minority comes to power: the activities of an aristocracy might often conform more closely to the will of the people than that of an elected élite. The difference between a system in which 'the governing minority are established once and for all', and one in which 'the minority that carries the day may be beaten tomorrow and replaced by another' is only 'slight'.[107] Democracy, for Durkheim, thus becomes a matter of the interplay of sentiments and ideas between government and mass; his discussion of democratic government contains no developed examination of the functioning of political parties, or of parliament, or of the franchise, and indeed these considerations are regarded as of purely minor significance.

The weaknesses inherent in this viewpoint are nowhere more clearly exposed than in Durkheim's discussion of the German state in *L'Allemagne au-dessus de tout*. As has been indicated previously, the weight of Durkheim's theoretical perspective directed his thinking towards asserting the basic compatibility, in the modern world, between national ideals, patriotism, and the growth of a pan-national European community. Characteristically, his response to the growth of German militarism – since the latter fell outside the expectations generated by his standpoint – was to treat it as a 'pathological' phenomenon. This 'pathology' is explained by Durkheim as a 'moral disorder' which is manifest

Durkheim's political sociology 269

in a grandiosity of national ambition such as is revealed in the ideological writings of Treitschke. The effect of Durkheim's analysis, however, is to consider power *itself* only from the moral aspect, in terms of the immoderate emphasis which Treitschke places upon the supremacy of the state. In point of fact, German militarism can only be properly interpreted in terms of the structural properties of the nineteenth-century German state – of the leading part played by Prussian military strength in securing the political unification of the country, and the continued domination of the landowning élite in government. These made Germany into a 'power-state', as Max Weber well understood, and it is, of course, no accident that Weber's conceptualization of the state, which eschews any possibility of defining the state in moral terms, places primacy upon just those aspects which Durkheim underplayed: the successful claim to monopoly of the legitimate deployment of force, and the existence of fixed territorial boundaries.[108]

Unlike Weber, Durkheim undeniably belongs to those traditions of nineteenth-century social thought which subordinate the state to society.[109] While he rejected the notion of the 'disappearance' of the state, and held instead that an expansion of the purview of the state is inevitable in modern society, he did not substantially break with the assumption that it is the movement of the 'infrastructure' which is of decisive significance in analysing social change. 'Infrastructure' here, of course, refers to the division of labour. In assessing Durkheim's theory of the division of labour in relation to his political sociology, it is important to evaluate what he shared in common with socialism (as he defined it).

Although Parsons has claimed that, according to his own definition of these terms, Durkheim's political sociology marks him out as being closer to 'communism' rather than 'socialism',[110] it is surely evident that the reverse is true. Communism, for Durkheim, expresses the constantly reappearing, but ultimately futile, hope that human egoism can be eradicated: it is thus essentially both a-historical and unrealizable. Socialism, on the other hand, according to Durkheim, is an expression of the consciousness that radical changes have and are occurring in contemporary societies, and that these changes have brought about a condition of crisis which presses for resolution. This consciousness is filtered by the social circumstances of which it is an expression. That is to say, it reflects a condition of society in which economic relationships have come to dominate social life; hence it assumes that the remedy for the modern crisis must be purely economic. The flaw in all socialist doctrines is that they fail to see that the resolution of the crisis must entail moral reorganization, whereby the primacy of the 'economic' over the 'social' will be readjusted in favour of the latter.[111] But they are correct in holding that regulation of the capitalist market is necessary. Although Durkheim repudiated the possibility of reorganizing capitalism by revolutionary means, it is an integral part of his ideas that the forced division of labour, the exploitative relationship of capital and wage-labour, must be eliminated. This is to be accomplished by the disappearance of the inheritance of property:

> Now inheritance as an institution results in men being born rich or poor; that is to say, there are two main classes of society, linked by all sorts of intermediate classes: the one which in order to live has to make its services acceptable to the other at whatever the cost; the other class which can do without these services, because it can call upon certain resources . . . as long as such sharp class differences exist in society, fairly effective palliatives may lessen the injustices of contracts; but in principle, the system operates in conditions which do not allow of justice.[112]

The abolition of inherited property is a process which is to take place through the action of the state. Although Durkheim was not entirely unambiguous on this point, it seems that he did not envisage the abolition of private property as such,[113] but rather that differentials in possession of property should be entirely determined by differences in the services which men render to society. Functional importance in the division of labour is to govern property rights. This is a 'work of justice' which has to be accomplished if the morality of individualism is to have regulative force in modern society: the advance of moral individualism is incompatible with a social order in which class situation determines from birth an individual's position in the occupational structure. Thus there is an intrinsic connection between the elimination of the 'forced' division of labour and the amelioration of the 'anomic' division of labour. What is required in order to reduce anomie is not simply the imposition of regulation upon the existing market system: this would only lead to an intensification of class conflict. 'It is not sufficient that there be rules . . . for sometimes the rules themselves are the cause of evil.'

The morality of organic solidarity demands major economic changes, which create a system in which there is a free or 'spontaneous' ordering of individuals in the division of labour, such that no 'obstacle, of whatever nature, prevents them from occupying the place in the social framework which is compatible with their faculties'.[114]

Seen in this light, it is hardly justified to argue that Durkheim's theory of the division of labour neglects the existence of interest conflict in modern societies. While it envisages the future development of an order in which such conflict will be, if not eliminated altogether, radically reduced, it is no different in this respect to that stream of thought which is generally taken to be the main source of 'conflict theory': Marxism. The real weaknesses in Durkheim's theory at this point derive from his failure, as noted previously, to work out the conditions under which the division of labour is linked to definite types of political formation. Thus, according to him, the elimination of the 'forced' division of labour is to be accomplished under the general patronage of the state. That basic changes of this sort might not be possible without a radical *transformation* of the existing system of political power is not seriously considered. It is just this premise, by contrast, which is built into Marx's conception: the class relations of the market are focused and stabilized by the capitalist state. No basic change in the class structure, in property relations, is capable of being achieved through the existing political apparatus: that is to say, apart from political change of a profound nature.

Conclusion

Durkheim's sociology was rooted in an attempt to re-interpret the claims of political liberalism in the face of a twin challenge: from an anti-rationalist conservatism on the one hand, and from socialism on the other. Each of these constituted major traditions in French social thought, and each of them, in the early part of the nineteenth century, represented a response to the legacy of the French Revolution. Durkheim borrowed elements from both in an attempt to transcend them through a revitalized liberal republicanism which would fully realize the structural changes in society which had been promised, but not achieved, by the Revolution. What has been remarked of Jaurès is an apt and exact description of Durkheim's viewpoint: he was concerned with, 'not the negation but the completion of the bourgeois Republic, the extension of the Rights of Man from the political to the economic and social spheres'.[115]

8 The 'individual' in the writings of Emile Durkheim

During his lifetime, Durkheim's methodological writings were notoriously subject to controversy, and his 'sociologism' was widely condemned. These early critiques, often involving quite inaccurate versions of Durkheim's views, have long since ceded place to critical interpretations of Durkheim's writings which are founded upon a more adequate understanding of the themes and the dilemmas inherent in his sociology.[1] None the less, it is arguable that we still await a treatment which fully explores the strengths and weaknesses of Durkheim's method. One main reason for this is that most secondary interpreters of Durkheim have failed to connect his *analytical* discussion (and rejection) of individualism as a methodological approach to social theory, with his *developmental* conception of the emergence of individualism as a morality brought into being by the growth of the differentiated division of labour. It is commonly accepted – and, indeed, he himself stressed this very strongly – that Durkheim's methodological ideas must be evaluated in relation to their concrete implementation in his more empirical works. But this is generally taken to mean showing how successfully or otherwise he 'applied' his methodological views in his other studies. I wish in this essay to establish a reciprocal relationship between Durkheim's substantive discussion of the development of individualism and his abstract formulations of sociological method. Durkheim is often regarded as being fervently 'anti-individualist'. But in fact his works contain a vigorous defence of individualism – understood in a specific way. In other words, Durkheim's writings represent an attempt to detach 'liberal individualism', regarded as a conception of the characteristics of the modern social order, from 'methodological individualism'.[2]

It is necessary, of course, to specify the main senses in which the term 'individualism' appears in Durkheim's writings. In his very earliest works, such as his long review article devoted to a study of certain leading contemporary German thinkers,[3] he uses

the term indiscriminately to refer to any branch of social philosophy which accords the 'individual' some sort of definite primacy
over 'society' – whether in ethical terms (as in Kant) or in
methodological terms (as in utilitarian philosophy). But he soon
came to perceive more clearly that there is an essential difference
between these two types of 'individualist' philosophy, and the
elaboration of the precise nature of this difference became a
dominant theme in his own sociological viewpoint. Whereas utilitarian individualism must be rejected as a methodology – sociology cannot be based upon a theory which treats the individual
as a *starting-point* of analysis – ethical or 'moral individualism'
refers to a social process which is of the greatest significance in
modern society. The latter form, which Durkheim also frequently
refers to as the 'cult of the individual', is created by society: it is
this very fact which demonstrates the inadequacy of utilitarianism
as a social theory, because what it takes as its premise is actually
the outcome of a long-term process of social development.

Durkheim's discussion of the origins and nature of moral
individualism thus constitutes one major dimension of his attempt
to meet the age-old question of the relationship between the
individual and society. The general framework of this position is
set out in *The Division of Labour in Society*, but it is substantially clarified in later writings.[4] The primary question which
Durkheim sets himself in the former work is as follows:

> How is it that, at the same time as the individual becomes more
> autonomous, he depends more closely on society? How can he be at
> the same time more individuated [*personnel*] and more solidary? For
> it is indisputable that these two developments, contradictory though it
> may appear, occur in a parallel way.[5]

The formulation of the problem has become famous; its resolution, however, has frequently been represented as ambiguous by
those who have sought to render the substance of Durkheim's
argument. For it has seemed as though, while mechanical solidarity refers to a *moral* attachment between the individual and
society, organic solidarity refers to a purely economic relation –
functional interdependence within the division of labour. Thus it
appears as though it is only somewhere near the end of the work
that Durkheim perceived that organic solidarity must have a
moral underpinning in the same way as mechanical solidarity
does, and hence that there is a crucial shift in his argument from

the first to the concluding half of the book.[6] But, in Durkheim's own eyes at least, there is clearly no such transition in his thinking in the work. Some years prior to the publication of *The Division of Labour*, Durkheim made just this point in criticizing Tönnie's differentiation of *Gemeinschaft und Gesellschaft*: that, while Tönnies recognizes the moral basis of solidarity in traditional societies, his portrayal of *Gesellschaft* treats modern society in a way comparable to that of the utilitarians, as lacking the moral character of the traditional type. Where, then, is the main line of Durkheim's argument? It seems to be as follows. In mechanical solidarity each individual remains largely unconscious of his 'separateness' as an individual since, dominated by the *conscience collective*, he shares similar traits with the other members of society; the limits of his autonomy are strictly bounded. The strength of the moral integration of the *conscience collective* is directly related to the strength of the ties which attach the individual to the group: like a simple organism, such a society can shed individuals, and even whole segments of itself, without difficulty. The characteristic of organic solidarity, on the other hand, is that the attachment of the individual to the *conscience collective* is mediated by his ties to other groups: especially, of course, those created by occupational specialization in the division of labour. Durkheim was never in any doubt that these are moral ties – that is, that there is a 'non-contractual element' which governs the negotiation of contracts. The point is that this presupposes moral diversity rather than uniformity: the 'universal man' of traditional society is replaced by modern 'specialist man'. The greater autonomy which is not only allowed for, but thereby *demanded*, of the individual, however, does not detach him from society, but actually increases the strength of the reciprocal tie between them. The main issue which is not fully clarified in *The Division of Labour* is not the nature of organic solidarity itself, but the relationship between the 'morality of specialization' generated by organic solidarity, and the morality of the *conscience collective*, which becomes focussed upon the 'cult of the individual'; because Durkheim makes it clear that 'there will always remain, at the very least, this cult of the person, of individual dignity . . . which now has become the focal rallying-point for so many'.[7] What does this 'cult of the individual' refer to, and how is it compatible, as a general shared morality, with the moral specialization enjoined by organic solidarity?

While all the main elements of Durkheim's answer are present in *The Division of Labour*, he did not elaborate upon them fully until later, in the context of his subsequent appreciation of the intimate connections between religion and moral authority. In these later writings, three important characteristics of moral individualism are worked out in some detail: what the 'individual' refers to in the 'cult of the individual'; why it is a 'cult'; and what is the proximate ideological source from which it derives. 'The individual' who is the subject of the ideals embodied in moral individualism is not the concrete individual, the particular personality, but 'man' in general. The morality of the 'cult of the individual' is composed of those values given intellectual expression by the eighteenth-century philosophers and inspiring the French Revolution. These are values which emphasize the dignity and worth of 'man' in the abstract; as such, not only do they not derive from the 'egoism' of the utilitarians, but they are its direct opposite. Egoism is the pursuit of self-interest. But these values imply sentiments of sympathy for others and for human suffering.[8] Precisely because they are created by society, they have a religious quality – although, if Durkheim's definition of religion given in *The Elementary Forms* be strictly applied, it is by no means clear what corresponds to the 'church' in relation to the 'sacred' beliefs of moral individualism. Finally, it can be shown, as Durkheim indicates in *L'Evolution pédagogique en France*, that the ideals of moral individualism have their immediate origin in Protestantism, and are more generally founded upon conceptions common to all forms of Christianity.[9]

Understood in these terms, moral individualism is not merely compatible with the moral diversification of organic solidarity, but directly stimulates its development. Respect for the individual, and the concomitant demand for equality, become moral imperatives: as such, they entail that the welfare and self-fulfilment of every member of society should be sought after. Human life can no longer be contained within the narrow limits enforced in traditional society. Specialization of occupational function according to talent and capacity is the principal mode in which the (concrete) individual can realize himself. Hence the emergence and strengthening of the 'cult of the individual' progresses hand in hand with the diversification of the division of labour. Now Durkheim's theory of moral authority holds that *all* moral norms have two components: they command respect, and have a positive attraction; but they also have a 'dutiful' character, and are supported by sanctions against deviation. It does not follow from this, however, that the *form* of moral authority is everywhere the same. The moral authority of mechanical solidarity is repressive: the individual is subject to the 'tyranny of the group'. Human freedom, according to Durkheim, consists in the autonomy of individual action. This is not acquired by the dissolution of moral codes, but by the transformations implicit in the development of moral individualism:

Rights and . . . liberties are not things inherent in the nature of the individual as such. Analyse the given constitution of man, and you will find there no trace of the sacred character with which he is today invested and from which his rights are derived. He owes this character to society. It is society that has consecrated the individual, and made of him the thing to be respected above all. The progressive emancipation of the individual thus does not imply a weakening, but a transformation of the social bond.[10]

Durkheim's conception of anomie connects directly with each of the two types of 'individualism' distinguished above: in a positive sense, it provides an important reinforcement to his analysis of moral individualism; negatively it constitutes a major aspect of his critique of utilitarian philosophy. The notion of anomie, as Durkheim employs it in his writings, appears at first sight to be fairly simple in form; further investigation of it, however, discloses various overlapping strands which enter into his formulation. As an element in his critical evaluation of utilitarianism, it rests first of all upon a set of empirical observations, which seem to have constituted the mainspring of Durkheim's first appreciation of its significance.[11] These observations concern the proposition that there is no direct correlation and, under certain circumstances, an inverse correlation, between the growth of economic prosperity and the advance of human happiness. The evidence from the analysis of suicide rates provides the clearest empirical index of this. In an early study of suicide, Durkheim noted that, if human wants are not simply 'given', but are plastic, then the rising capacity of society to provide for the needs of its members may in turn generate new needs, and thereby increase the gap between wants and their satisfaction.[12] This conclusion is affirmed in *The Division of Labour*. The theoretical side of this, however, remained obscure until the publication of *Suicide*. In that work, the empirical observations (concerning, for example, the rising rate of suicide with the advance of material civilization, and the relation between suicide and socio-economic position within the occupational system) are drawn together in terms of a coherent theoretical analysis. Durkheim's discussion of anomie in *Suicide* is far from unambiguous, but one major point can be gleaned from it. There is an essential distinction between biological needs and those which are engendered by society. The former are fixed in their *object* and in their *limits*: these two aspects may vary independently in the case of socially produced needs. That is to say, whereas biological needs are specific in what they demand of motivated action (e.g. hunger: food) and in their point of satiation (there are given organic reactions which reduce appetite in relation to the intake of nourishment), neither of these is necessarily fixed in a determinate fashion in the case of socially created needs or desires. The importance of the differentiation between these two aspects is never clearly brought out in any of the discussions of anomie which appear at various places in Durkheim's work: as will be shown below, it is a source of certain basic difficulties in his writings. For the present, however, it is sufficient to note the significance of this theoretical position for the critique of utilitarianism. This critique is also twofold. First, the human wants cannot be taken as givens, but are socially created and thus historically variable. Second, and equally important: that the creation of wants does not automatically produce the circumstances which make possible their realization. This latter point became focal to Durkheim's critical assessment of socialist doctrines. Socialism is superior to utilitarianism in recognizing that human wants are not simply 'contained' in the individual, but are socially created; however it shares with utilitarianism the notion that society does not have to intervene in the satisfaction of needs. According to socialist theory, production thus has to be regulated, but consumption must be freed from social control.

The positive connections between the conceptions of moral individualism and anomie, apart from the early formulation in *The Division of Labour*, were nowhere explicitly stated in any detail by Durkheim, and thus have tended to be among the most frequently misunderstood parts of his writings. As I have tried to show elsewhere, faulty interpretation of Durkheim on this matter has helped to sustain two of the most prevalent misrepresentations of Durkheim's sociology in the secondary literature: that which

see →
p. 223
× p. 230

sees his work as primarily concerned with an abstract 'problem of order', and the closely related view of his writings as advancing a heavily authoritarian theory of moral discipline.[13] If there is a basic opposition in all of Durkheim's work, it is not that of social integration (normative control) versus social disintegration (lack of normative regulation: anomie), but, as with virtually all leading social thinkers of his time, that of 'traditional' versus 'modern' society, with all the profound social transformations which this latter distinction implies. It does not seem to have been generally appreciated that there is necessarily an historical dimension to Durkheim's treatment of anomie: this is integral to the very conception of 'socially generated need', but it is also important in regard to the second aspect of anomie, that of *provision* for wants. In the traditional social order, human faculties and needs are kept to a low level, and therefore are readily provided for. The dominance of the *conscience collective* plays a role in each of these respects: on the one hand, by restricting the development of 'individualism' – the liberation of the individual personality – and, on the other, by setting strict limits to what may legitimately be striven for by an individual in a given social position. The process of evolution away from traditionalism both increases the level of individuation and at the same time undermines the fixed moral boundaries characteristic of previous ages. It is these *twin* developments which create the important theoretical problem – which Durkheim seeks to resolve in terms of his analysis of the emergence of moral individualism. Anomie, therefore, is a phenomenon specific to the modern order (as is indexed by the documentation of the growth of anomic suicide in *Suicide*); it is to be understood in relation to individuation and moral individualism. Although Durkheim concedes that 'a certain level' of anomie is inevitable in modern society, which is committed to rapid and continuous change, anomie as pathology is to be traced to the temporarily inadequate development of moral individualism. The upsurge of anomie found in the contemporary age is mainly centred in economic life, which has broken away from the confines of tradition, but has not yet been sufficiently penetrated by the new morality of individualism.

It might be useful at this juncture to summarize what has been said so far: 1) There are two, connected, aspects of Durkheim's discussion of the relationship between the 'individual' and 'society': a defence of the essential place of moral individualism in modern society, coupled with a disavowal that this implies acceptance of 'individualism' as developed in utilitarian philosophy, as a viable methodological basis for sociology. 2) Moral individualism is consequently quite distinct from 'egoism': the increasing range of individual autonomy (in the sense of 'individuation') is contingent upon the emergence of this 'cult of the individual', in conjunction with the other social changes entailed in the transition from mechanical to organic solidarity. 3) Both the critique of utilitarianism and the analysis of moral individualism receive an important reinforcement from the elaboration of the theory of anomie; the remedy for anomie does not consist in the re-imposition of traditional, repressive moral discipline, but the further advance of the liberal morality of individualism.

With these points in mind, it is possible to turn to Durkheim's critique of 'methodological individualism', as set out in his discussion of 'social facts' in *The Rules of Sociological Method*. Like the rest of the work, much of this is bluntly polemical: while its impact upon the reader is correspondingly powerful and convincing, the positive elements in the exposition of the characteristics of social facts are in fact difficult to unearth. As in his analysis of the difference between egoism and moral individualism, there are two conceptions of the 'individual' implied in what he has to say: but whereas in the former case he himself specifies the nature of the distinction, in his treatment of social facts this is not clearly brought out. This time it is a distinction between the concrete, flesh-and-blood individual, on the one hand, and the abstractly conceived 'social actor' on the other. The concrete individual is necessarily, of course, the 'carrier' of society: remove all human organisms, and there is no society. In holding that social facts are 'external' to the individual, Durkheim has in mind the concrete individual; there is no role for sociology as an independent discipline if we accept the utilitarian premise. But the manner in which this is expressed is such that it is hardly surprising that Durkheim has been accused of an illegitimate reification of the 'social'. A similar ambiguity arises in relation to the second criterion which he applies: that of 'obligation' or 'constraint'. If Durkheim's 'individual' is the 'concrete individual', then his analysis of the 'constraining' character of social facts in *The Rules* is, to say the least, unsatisfactory; for other phenomena 'external' to the concrete individual share the same character – such as those given in the geographical environment. Social facts would be merely residual, placed 'outside' the individual and resistant to his will.[14] But it is evident that Durkheim does not wish to hold this. Social facts are distinct from those of the physical world, because 'they consist in ideas and actions'.[15] In what sense, then, are social facts 'constraining'?

Much hangs on the answer to this question, of course, since it has been commonly accepted, even by those generally sympathetic to Durkheim's viewpoint, that his stress upon the constraining nature of social facts leaves no place for the social actor as a conscious willing agent. In *The Rules*, Durkheim offers two sorts of example to support his argument – without clearly recognizing the difference between them:

> If I attempt to contravene legal rules, they react against me in such a way as to prevent my act if that is possible; or to annul or re-establish it in its normal form if this can be done after it has been carried out; or to demand expiation if there is no way of repairing what has been done . . . Moreover, constraint is no less effective if it is indirect . . . If I am an industrialist, nothing prevents me from working with the procedures and methods of a hundred years ago: but if I do so, I shall surely be ruined.[16]

In the examples mentioned in the first part of the quotation, law and custom, constraint involves moral obligation (supported by sanctions). In those given in the second part, constraint does not involve any sort of immediate moral commitment but only factors which comprise a 'factual' element in the horizon of the social actor. Thus the industrialist who ignores certain technical requisites of production fails to prosper. If Durkheim realized the full significance of this distinction at the time at which he wrote *The Rules*, he gave little sign of it, and it is clear that he tended to identify social facts primarily as moral obligations. Later, he became more clearly aware of the importance of the difference between these two sorts of social 'constraint', seeing that the moral sanction is different in character from the constraining factor which is present in the other type. The feature of moral sanctions is that they are not intrinsic to the act which is sanctioned: they cannot be deduced from the properties of that act itself. The same act which is morally reprehensible in one type of society, for instance, may be tolerated or even actively encouraged in another. This is not the case with the consequences which stem from failure to adhere to prescriptions or practices which are not moral obligations.[17] Here the 'constraint' is an undesired consequence which follows automatically from the transgression of the rule – as in the case of the industrialist who fails to observe the rules of efficient business practice.

The distinctive character of moral obligation has two implications for Durkheim's sociology. One is that the content of moral obligations varies in different forms of society; the second is that, according to the theory of anomie, moral obligation not only sets limits to human action, but also focuses it and gives it defined aspiration. Each of these actually indicates, in a differing way, that 'obligation' is not to be identified with 'restriction' *tout court*, as might be suggested by Durkheim's habit of using 'obligation', 'constraint', and even, occasionally, 'coercion' as interchangeable terms. To be sure, moral obligations are always constraining in the sense that deviation produces sanctions: but the degree to which acceptance of obligation is 'restrictive' upon the actor is contingent upon the moral form in question. The moral obligations involved in the 'cult of the individual' confer increased autonomy of action, as compared to the rigid discipline of traditional society. This is possible precisely because moral codes define the content of human motivation, at least with regard to socially generated needs. While Durkheim no doubt did not achieve complete clarity on the latter point until after he had written his account of the nature of social facts in *The Rules*, he does specifically point out in the book that his understanding of moral obligation diverges from the 'constraint' of Hobbes and Rousseau, who neglect the 'spontaneous' character of moral life. These thinkers, according to Durkheim, assume that there is a dislocation between society and its component individuals: the human being is treated as naturally hostile to social life. Society, therefore, can only exist if men are compelled, by the action of the state, to adapt themselves to it. Their views contrast with those of the utilitarians, who see social life as a spontaneous phenomenon. In the first conception, 'constraint' is seen as fundamental to social life, but is considered as a purely 'external' sort of coercion. The second standpoint eliminates constraint, in any form, from the operation of society. His own position, Durkheim says, comprises elements of each of these, and also rejects both: there is no contradiction in holding that social life is both 'constraining' and 'spontaneous'.

These considerations are surely enough to suggest that Durkheim may be absolved from the cruder type of criticism which has frequently been directed against his methodological writings: that he accords society 'objective' reality only at the expense of denying any reality to the active subject. Nor is there much substance in the equally common assertion that Durkheim's work should be ranged with that of those thinkers (mainly of a broadly 'conservative' persuasion) who hold that there is an inherent antinomy between man and society, such that the continuation of social life depends upon the strict repression of individual desires. He clearly recognizes that what the (concrete) individual is, depends upon 'internalized' norms which are, in part, the *condition* of freedom of action. But his treatment of this matter involves definite inconsistencies. This can be seen quite plainly in his various discussions of 'egoism'. In his earlier writings, 'egoism' has reference to the utilitarian model of self-interest. In Durkheim's view, this presupposes a 'pre-social' man, and his critique of this conception in *The Rules* takes this as its foil. But he evidently soon came to perceive that according to the position which he had taken in criticizing utilitarian individualism, egoism itself must be a product of sociology. That is to say, that there can be socially created self-interest. He even gives a specific illustration of this. Moral individualism, he emphasizes, does not derive from egoism: but the growth of moral individualism none the less produces, as an offshoot, an expansion in the range of egoistic inclinations:

Undoubtedly pity for others and pity for ourselves are not foreign to one another, since they progress or decline in tandem ; but the one does not derive from the other. There exists a tie of common origin between them, because they both originate in, and are only different aspects of, the same state of the *conscience collective*. They both express the way in which the moral value of the individual has come to be esteemed. Any social judgement which is collectively valued is applied to others at the same time as to ourselves ; their person, like our own, becomes more highly valued in our eyes, and we become just as sensitive to what affects everyone individually as to what affects us particularly . . . Thus it is the case that even the sentiments which seem to belong most directly to the personal makeup of the individual depend upon the causes which go beyond him! Our egoism itself is, in large part, a product of society.[18]

Yet, in other writings, Durkheim reverts to a conception of 'egoism' which counterposes it in a direct way to social learning as if the two are necessarily mutually exclusive. Man, he argues, everywhere conceives of himself as *homo duplex*, as being composed of two beings, which are usually represented in religious thought as the body and the soul.[19] This corresponds to a psychological division between sensations, on the one side, and concepts and moral activity on the other. Sensations and sensory needs, according to Durkheim, are necessarily egoistic, because they originate from, and refer to, conditions of the biological organism. Conceptual thought and moral activity are 'impersonal'; they are social products, and do not 'belong' to any particular person who uses them. These, therefore, are two opposed aspects of personality. They are not merely separate from one another, but are in constant conflict. 'Egoism' is thus identified solely with the 'pre-social', and is portrayed as wholly foreign to the 'penetration of the individual by society'.

The implications of this will be further discussed below. But it is worth pointing out that a similar inconsistency appears in various other parts of Durkheim's writings, which have reference to the connection between the 'biological' and the 'social' components of personality. An example may be given from his work on suicide.[20] The main thesis which Durkheim develops in *Suicide* is that the suicide rate, as compared with particular cases of suicide, 'constitutes in itself a new fact, *sui generis*, which has its own unity and individuality', and has to be explained sociologically.[21] To this end, he develops his typology of the social factors underlying observed differences in suicide rates. To hold that the suicide rate can only be explained in sociological terms does not mean, however, he goes on to say, that there is no place for psychological studies of suicide. It is the role of the psychologist to examine the particular characteristics which cause one man, rather than another, to kill himself, when placed in a given set of social circumstances: not everyone who is exposed to a situation of anomie actually commits suicide. While this may be a neat division of tasks between sociology and psychology, it is a clearly inadequate position, because it implicitly assumes that the traits of the 'suicidal personality' are formed outside of society. The (social) factors which cause a certain *rate* of suicide are presented by Durkheim as separate from those relevant to the aetiology of the individual case. But this would only be so if it were true that the characteristics of suicidal personality were 'pre-social': i.e. settled in the biological constitution of the organism. In fact, Durkheim accepts that this is not the case, showing that the 'individual type' of suicide is strongly influenced by the 'social type'. If this be admitted, however, the explanatory model which Durkheim sets up in the book is immediately defective. It follows that there is a complicated interplay between society and personality in the aetiology of rates of suicide: the social conditions which he treats as simply acting 'directly' upon 'suicide-prone' individuals also must have an influence in *producing* that 'suicide-proneness' as a complex of personality characteristics.

Enough has been said this far to indicate that, although Durkheim's attempt to detach moral from methodological individualism is perhaps more subtle than has been assumed by many of his critics, what results is a brittle synthesis and essentially an unsatisfactory one. The ambiguities, and the very serious deficiencies, which run through his works, however, have to be understood in the light of this attempt. As happens so often with a writer whose works are strongly polemical in tone, ultimately he was unable to abandon certain of the very premises of which he was most critical in the writings of his opponents. In this paper I have given most prominence to Durkheim's critique of utilitarian individualism, but this was not his only target of attack. A second tradition of thought that he sought to evaluate critically, while also being strongly influenced by it, was that of 'idealist holism'. A variety of substantively quite different doctrines, of course, may be subsumed under such a rubric. But the most important element in these doctrines which formed a negative frame of reference for the development of Durkheim's thought was the notion that a 'universal' moral consensus is the condition of the existence of society, of whatever type. As Durkheim attempted to show in *The Division of Labour*, this is a mistaken view. While this is indeed the condition of unity in traditional society, moral diversity is the necessary concomitant of the modern societal type. If modern society is, and must be, a moral order, it is distinct from the traditional form. In developing this standpoint, as is plainly evident in his early critical articles and reviews, Durkheim was, in a certain sense, positively influenced by utilitarianism, especially as it was adapted by such writers as Spencer. These authors at least recognize that the character of modern social life is distinctively different from the life of man in traditional society, and their version of 'individualism' gives expression to this awareness. In exploring the insufficiencies of utilitarian individualism, however, Durkheim borrowed heavily from the other school of thought, asserting that moral ideals are irreducible to individual motivations or interests.

Along the *historical* dimension, therefore, Durkheim leans partly upon utilitarianism in rejecting the conception of the relationship between the individual and society implicit in holistic idealism – that the individual is merely a 'microcosm' of society. This may be, in a sense, an apt characterization of the situation in traditional society, in mechanical solidarity, but it is quite inappropriate to the modern order, in which 'the individual personality develops with the division of labour'.[22] This shows, of course, that idealism is *methodologically* wanting. The individual in society is not simply a passive imprint of social forms, but an active agent. But, even while he recognizes this, he relies upon the holistic standpoint in working out his critique of utilitarian individualism. From each of these two aspects, historical and methodological, this rests upon the proposition that society is not a creation of the (pre-social) individual, but exists 'prior' to him and moulds him. How, then, is it possible that the (concrete) individual is an active agent? It is at this point that the two dimensions, the historical and the methodological, in Durkheim's thought diverge. The answer which he reaches via his study of the evolution of solidarity, and his analysis of moral conduct more generally, is that it is possible because the cognitive and motivational personality of the individual is shaped by social learning. He is not just moulded by society; the active orientation of his conduct is framed by 'internalized' moral norms. But there is a second answer, to which his thought constantly tends to revert, and which is undoubtedly a derivative of his preoccupation with utilitarianism. This is that whatever is actively willed by the individual is a 'pre-social' impulsion. In other words, in seeking to reject utilitarianism, Durkheim tends to deal with it in its own terms. Society cannot be conceived as the outcome of pre-formed individual wills – because society makes, and must make, demands upon the individual which are foreign to his own wishes. Hence we reach the position that there is irremediable conflict between the ('egoistic') inclinations of the individual, and the moral commands which society enjoins upon him.

Durkheim never managed adequately to reconcile these two strands of his thought, and this is reflected in several of the ambiguities noted previously. Thus his discussion of social facts in *The Rules*, as has been mentioned, shifts from one meaning of 'individual' to another. His discussion easily lends itself to the interpretation that social facts are empirically 'external' to individual conduct, and exert a constraining force over that conduct which is of the same kind as that produced by geographical or climatic forces. The same kind of enforced polarization between the 'internal' and the 'external' appears in Durkheim's use of *argumentuum per eliminationem* in *Suicide*.[23] Various sorts of 'external' or 'pre-social' factors (e.g. the influence of climate) are eliminated separately as explaining observed differentials in suicide rates. These include the influence of inherited insanity. Now the assumption that this is an 'external' factor is acceptable if it be granted that insanity is wholly inherited, and thus is built into the constitution of the organism. But Durkheim explicitly points out that this is not so: social factors have a definite role in the aetiology of mental disorder. The insight is, however, allowed to remain undeveloped. Yet, as has been indicated above, Durkheim at no time wished to advance what he calls at one juncture the 'absurd notion' that society is 'external' to the individual in the same sense as the geographical environment is; and most of his argument in *The Rules* is only understandable if his 'individual' is the 'concrete individual'.

A similar point may be made about the concept of anomie. It has already been shown that, in Durkheim's formulation, the concept involves two components, which tend to be assimilated in his own use of it. One of these refers to the degree to which human action is provided with definite objectives; the other concerns how far these ends are *realizable*. The distinction is a fundamental one, yet Durkheim glosses over it. It is easy to see how closely this is tied in to the ambiguity in his treatment of social facts. In so far as one uses the concept of anomie as referring primarily to the first element, the lack of coherent norms which provide firm objectives for a man to strive for, one is talking of the 'concrete individual'. This is certainly the type case in most of Durkheim's abstract discussion of anomie. But many of the examples of anomie which he applies in his more empirical analyses (e.g. in relation to class conflict) actually concentrate upon the second element: the objectives of conduct may be clearly defined, but cannot be *attained*. In such cases his argument again tends to slip back into a direct opposition to the utilitarian position: utilitarian theory is mistaken because an external limitation (which can only come from society) must be placed upon individual desires. It might be pointed out that Durkheim's illustrations often refer to cases of *biological* drives: e.g. that 'an insatiable thirst cannot be quenched'.

Durkheim's failure to utilize the distinction between the two aspects of anomie is a source of some of the most basic flaws in his sociology. As the more recent literature employing the notion of anomie demonstrates, the concept takes on quite divergent theoretical applications according to which aspect is emphasized. If anomie is taken to refer mainly to 'normlessness' – the first aspect – then it tends to support a standpoint emphasizing the dimension of 'meaning'/'lack of meaning' in individual conduct.[24] The end result of this is likely to be a position which, implicitly or otherwise, treats social conflict as 'pathological' – that is to say, which links conflict to 'deviance' produced by 'imperfect socialization'. Although, as I have argued elsewhere,[25] it is quite mistaken to hold that Durkheim regards all social conflict in this way, there are obviously strong elements of this viewpoint in his writings. If the other aspect is emphasized,[26] on the other hand, it tends to lead to a conception of 'normative strain', rather than 'normlessness'. Here the objectives of conduct may be quite clear to the actor, and there is not the strong overtone of irrationality which appears to characterize the conduct of the individual where the first aspect is stressed. The importance of this conception, then, is that it allows a much greater scope for conceptualizing conflicts which derive from divisions of interest in society. Durkheim undoubtedly minimizes the significance of this form of conflict in his writings. There are two respects in which it is possible to claim that a given objective is not 'realizable'. One is that there exist barriers in a society which prevent its realization. This *may* mean that it cannot be achieved – that it involves some good which, in any conceivable form of society, is simply impossible of attainment; or it may mean that its realization demands some kind of *change* in the existing organization of society. This perspective certainly has a substantial place in Durkheim's writings. Thus he emphasizes that, in order to overcome the class conflict which characterizes modern industry, social change (involving principally the removal of blockages upon equality of occupational opportunity) is necessary. But there is another sense in which an objective may be said to be 'unrealizable', and Durkheim continually reverts to this – for reasons explained above – in his anxiety to refute the utilitarian position. This is where the objective in question has no limits: the insatiable appetite. We can now grasp more clearly the significance of another ambiguity which has been referred to in a previous part of this paper, concerning Durkheim's treatment of moral obligation and 'factual' constraint. Although he did not seem to attach any importance to this distinction in *The Rules*, he did later recognize that moral constraint is quite different in character from the 'factual' consequences of actions. But he only elucidates one dimension of this difference – the difference in the nature of the sanction involved. He fails to consider the theoretical significance of the possibility that moral obligations *themselves* may be 'factual' elements in the horizon of the acting individual. A person (or a group) may acknowledge the existence of the obligations, and take account of them in orienting his conduct, without feeling any strong commitment to them. Such action is not necessarily 'criminal', in the sense of directly flouting the moral prescriptions in question. But it rests neither solely upon fear of the sanctions which would be invoked as punishment for transgression, nor solely upon moral commitment. While Durkheim accepts that there are varying degrees of attachment to moral norms,[27] he has no place for this in his theoretical analysis of the nature of moral obligation. Nor is there any recognition of the differential 'interpretation' of moral norms.

These inadequacies can also be seen at the level of Durkheim's historical analysis and, indeed, partly derive from that analysis. It is perhaps significant that Durkheim has been called both a 'materialist' and an 'idealist'. The first label, so it has been thought, can be readily applied to his standpoint as expressed in *The Division of Labour*. In that work he argues that

[Civilization] is itself a necessary consequence of changes which take place in the volume and density of societies. If science, art and economic activity develop, it is as a result of a necessity imposed on men; it is because there is no other way for them to live in the new conditions in which they are placed. From the moment that the number of individuals among whom social relations are established reaches a certain point, they can only sustain themselves if they specialize more, work more, and stimulate their mental capacities; and from this general stimulation there inevitably results a higher level of culture. From this point of view, civilization thus appears, not as a goal which moves people by the hold that it exerts over them, not as a good perceived and desired in advance, which they strive to create as fully as possible. Rather, it is the effect of a cause, the necessary result of a determinate state of affairs.[28]

K

290 Studies in Social and Political Theory

The apparent theme of such statements is that the transformation of society from mechanical to organic solidarity is wholly a matter of changes in the social 'infrastructure'; that the changes which occur in the character of moral conduct are simply 'effects' of these 'causes'. The perspective developed in *The Elementary Forms* seems to contrast markedly with this. In the latter work, so it would appear, Durkheim treats moral ideals as the *force dirigeante* in social life. It is mainly by reference to this work that he has been regarded as advancing an 'idealist' position. Thus it seems as though, if one follows through the stages of his intellectual career, he begins from a 'materialistic' standpoint, and moves later towards a view which is directly opposed to that which he initially adopted. In fact, however, throughout his writings Durkheim frequently and specifically denies that he wishes to adopt either of these positions. In *The Division of Labour*, for example, the section which has just been quoted is immediately followed by the assertion that 'a mechanistic conception of society does not exclude ideals', and that 'it is mistaken to suppose that this conception reduces man to a mere inactive witness of his own history'. On the other hand, while his later writings are full of statements such as 'society is the ideal', he is always careful to insist that such propositions must be interpreted to mean that ideals are *creations* of human society, not 'given' forces which determine social conduct. This is, after all, the main proposition developed in *The Elementary Forms*, and Durkheim himself evidently still considered that his critics would regard it as another version of his earlier 'materialism'. Near the end of the book, he takes pains to make clear that this is not what he is proposing: there is, he emphasizes, an active interplay between the *conscience collective* and its 'infrastructure'.

But he never solved the problems which the analysis of this interplay presents and, where he discusses social change, it is often as if there are two quite independent sets of processes going on: those in the 'infrastructure', on the one hand, and those in the sphere of moral ideals on the other. This is undoubtedly one reason which explains the apparent 'break' in the argument in *The Division of Labour*, mentioned earlier. The only direct connections which Durkheim was able to establish between the expansion of the division of labour and the changing nature of the *conscience collective* are those whereby the influence of the latter is *weakened*. It is not at all clear why its content should become changed: what factors promote the emergence of the 'cult of the individual'? Even in the theory developed in *The Elementary Forms*, the origin of the content of religious beliefs remains obscure. These beliefs are created in the fervour of collective ceremonial. But sacred beliefs, while framed in terms of categories ('space', 'time', etc.) which are formed upon the characteristics of society, are basically 'random': any object may become sacred, and there is, applying Durkheim's theory, a practically infinite range of potential primitive classifications. Durkheim's sociology lacks any systematic theoretical treatment of the social mechanisms which mediate the relationship between infrastructure and *conscience collective*.

The reasons for this touch upon weaknesses in Durkheim's thought which have not been explored in this paper. But the analysis given earlier is certainly of basic importance here: for it helps to show how it is that, as a result of the theoretical impasse in which his thought became wedged, he was unable to deal in a satisfactory way with *socially generated* interests, and more especially with conflicts which stem from opposition of such interests.

Durkheim on social facts

An indication of the elements of Durkheim's programme for sociology was already given in Durkheim's first published article. Sociology, Durkheim held, can emerge as an independent science through a conceptual revamping of Comtean positivism: Comte was certainly on the right lines, but he failed to follow his own methodological prescriptions and to break away from the speculative philosophy of history.[29] Durkheim explicitly refused to call himself a 'positivist', and was very critical of some features of Comte's social-philosophical writings, but he never deviated from his self-appointed task, stated in the opening pages of *The Division of Labour*, of providing the means of studying social life 'according to the method of the positive sciences'.[30] The principal work

292 Studies in Social and Political Theory

in which such a method is set out was bitterly attacked when it first appeared, and it has hardly shed much of its controversial character since then. The passing of time, and the efforts of later scholars, have allowed us to see how poorly some of Durkheim's critics understood his arguments, but have also demonstrated that the latter are nevertheless themselves highly unsatisfactory as a plausible analysis of the subject-matter and proper objectives of sociology. Notwithstanding the fame which it has achieved, I think it possible to claim that *The Rules of Sociological Method* is the weakest of Durkheim's major works: the principles set out therein were mainly received ideas, stated in a new form perhaps, but gaining most of their force from the polemical ardour with which they were advocated and the attractive simplicity of their presentation.

Sociology, Durkheim says, is the study of social facts. But in this there is already a confusion of more than purely terminological significance. A 'fact' is a proposition about the world, which can be said in some sense to be 'true', or at least 'open to test', not an element or an aspect of that world itself.[31] Durkheim often uses the term to refer to the latter rather than to the former, without apparently noticing the difference between them. Thus in introducing the first chapter of *The Rules* entitled 'What is a social fact?',[32] he moves straight from mentioning what one might call 'facts about society' ('Each individual drinks, sleeps, eats, reasons; and it is to society's interest that these functions be exercised in an orderly manner') to the elements which could be said to compose that society (illustrated by the social obligations involved in the fulfilment of contracts). The elision both expresses major shortcomings in Durkheim's epistemology and is consequential for his attempt to characterize the distinctive qualities of 'social facts'. On the epistemological level, Durkheim's writings show an uncritical acceptance of a crudely empiricist stance, albeit one well in accord with the thrust of much nineteenth-century social thought, according to which the natural and social worlds can be described in a theory-free observation language as immediately accessible to the senses. As regards his characterization of 'social facts', the consequence is that he recognizes no difference between the position of the *social actor* who is confronted by society as a 'facticity', and that of the sociological observer who seeks to encompass the latter in his analyses.

Durkheim's endeavour to elucidate the distinctive properties of the subject-matter of sociology contains what has become one of the most well-known, and oft-quoted, passages in his work, which it will however do no harm to quote briefly again:

There is in every society a certain group of phenomena which may be differentiated from those studied by the other natural sciences. When I fulfil my obligations as brother, husband, or citizen, when I execute my contracts, I perform duties which are defined externally to myself and my acts, in law and in custom. Even if they conform to my own sentiments and I feel their reality subjectively, such reality is still objective, for I did not create them, I merely inherited them through my education.[33]

Society is 'external' to the individual, and exerts 'constraint' (for which he uses the words *contrainte* or *coercition* interchangeably) over him.[34] Social institutions confront the individual member of society not merely as external 'facts', which he must take account of in his action: they are constraining forces which, in Durkheim's words, 'impose themselves upon him, independent of his individual will'.

But this presentation of the characteristics of 'social facts' confuses some vital distinctions. 'External' can be used, and was used by Durkheim, with regard to the following ideas. First, that in studying social life the sociological observer should, or must, base his analysis only upon the externally visible components of the actions of others. This might loosely be said to imply a sort of behaviourism, according to which 'introspection' is to be eschewed as a source of information relevant either to the description or the explanation of social conduct. We must approach the identification and classification of social facts, Durkheim says in one place, in terms of their 'external characteristics' and in this, according to him, the sociologist proceeds much in the same manner as the physicist. Thus 'it is a rule in the natural sciences to discard those data of sensation that are too subjective'; just as the physicist 'substitutes, for the vague impressions of temperature and electricity, the visual registrations of the thermometer or electrometer', so in sociology we must substitute, for the 'inner' data of sensation and consciousness, what is externally observable.[35] Social facts, according to Durkheim, lend themselves more readily to objective representation to the degree that their separation from the individual facts expressing them is more complete. If studied on the level of day-to-day events, or seen from the perspective of its participants, social life appears as in a constant state of flux; the scientific observer can penetrate this only if he first of all considers social activity in those forms in which it has become institutionalized or 'crystallized', and which therefore have an existence independent of or 'external to' the particular persons who are their carriers at any one point in time. Thus formalized legal codes are the external expression of types of moral regulation, and provide the most appropriate means of studying the latter. 'A legal regulation is what it is, and there are no two ways of looking at it.'[36]

The relevance of this to the precept that social facts should be treated as 'things' is obvious enough; but the thing-like character of social facts also appears in the two other senses of 'externality' which can be discerned in Durkheim's account, although these themselves are not methodological principles and concern pro-perties attributed to social phenomena as such. One of these is the sense in which Durkheim wished to say that the social world is independent of, or external to, human consciousness in a way akin to the world of nature. The distinctive quality of a 'thing' in *this* connotation is that it has an empirical reality independent of human activity; the material world would continue to exist quite apart from whether human beings are around or not. Plainly social facts cannot be external to human consciousness in pre-cisely this way, but Durkheim is constantly drawn to this non-sensical proposition because of the conceptual muddles in his discussion. Moreover this use of 'thing' has no logical connection with the one that is the focus of Durkheim's attention in the third sense in which he talks about the externality of social facts. In this sense, 'social facts' are external to the members of society because they have the property of being refractory to the human will: 'the most important characteristic of a "thing" ', Durkheim proposes, 'is the impossibility of its modification by a simple effort of the will . . . a mere act of the will is insufficient to produce a change in it'.[37] Now while it is true that the things which exist in the external reality of the natural world have the quality of being 'refractory to the human will', it is of course not true that the reverse necessarily holds. Social phenomena are neither 'external' to human consciousness in this way, nor are they 'thing-like'; if, therefore, they are resistant to the human will this is in a fashion distinct from that characteristic of objects in the physically external world.

These conceptual inadequacies clearly have repercussions in Durkheim's treatment of the origins of the constraining power of social facts. Although it is one of the main themes of the argument in *The Rules* that society exerts constraint over the actions of its members, Durkheim's discussion contains a major ambiguity – as he himself subsequently realized. Consider some of the examples which he gives of the situations in which the coercive influence of society may make itself felt: not using the legal currency in financial transactions; not using up-to-date technical methods in production for the competitive market; not paying one's debts; not carrying out one's duties as a parent or husband. The nature of the 'constraint' or 'coercion' which might make itself felt in these various cases differs. In the first two examples mentioned, the constraints which operate derive from the circumstance that, if the given action is not carried out in a particular way, a definite consequence follows, as it were, mechanically – if a manufacturer persists in using plant which has an output of only a third of that of his rivals for a similar investment cost, he is going to be driven out of business. If someone tries to use children's imitation money to make a purchase in a shop, he will very probably come away empty-handed. The constraining influences which operate here are indeed similar to those which may affect a person in his relation to the 'factual' world, the world of nature, even if their operation presupposes the existence of a society. The constraining element is in a definite sense parallel to that involved in, say, failing to observe precautions in drinking water which might be contaminated. It cannot be said that there is any (moral) *obligation* upon the individual to take such precautions, even though it may be reasonable to suppose that it is in his interest to do so. In the other instances quoted above, some sort of obligation is necessarily involved, even though the individual may flout it, deliberately or inadvertently.

When, in his later writings, he became more clearly aware that his original discussion of these matters was unsatisfactory, Durkheim tried to establish a basis for distinguishing 'utilitarian' from 'moral' sanctions. The characteristic feature of moral obligation is that its transgression calls forth a sanction (formalized punishment in the case of law, ostracism, ridicule, etc., in the case of customary norms) which has no definite connection with the transgressing act as such. In the contravening of utilitarian prescriptions, by contrast, the undesired consequence which forms the constraining element follows directly from the nature of the act itself. Thus, in an example which he gives, while 'murder', and the sanctions which are applied against murderers, are defined in terms of moral norms – not all forms of killing other people are criminal acts – contravening principles of hygiene has consequences that apply universally, regardless of whatever society one happens to be a member. In the first instance the constraint is social (i.e. moral), in the second it is not. But this is misleading, and is connected to mistakes that are inherent in many of Durkheim's writings, not simply those that are directly concerned with methodological questions. For by identifying the 'utilitarian' type of action with conduct which risks 'technical' (i.e., in Durkheim's idea, 'non-social') sanctions, Durkheim fails to see that such action *may be oriented to moral norms* in a way that is directly comparable to how a person acts when, say, seeking to avoid drinking water which might be contaminated. This is a mistake that many later authors have also made, but it is one which is inexcusable. For the result is that it becomes difficult to analyse certain forms of orientation to established moral codes that are decisively important in social life. Thus it is very often the case that conformity to such a code (or law) is not based upon a person's acceptance of it *as a moral obligation*, but upon his recognition that he faces some undesirable consequences if he fails to conduct himself in the appropriate manner. Something of an opposite circumstance to this occurs in a case in which a person feels very strongly committed to a particular ideal, but believes that current practice is based upon a misinterpretation of it – such as frequently occurs in religious movements which are directed towards revitalizing an existing church. These considerations are important because they bear directly upon the prevalence of conflict and power in social life.

In so far as 'social facts', as Durkheim would have it, imply moral imperatives, which have some hold over the consciences of members of society, they may, through the stimulus of guilt, for instance, have a 'coercive' hold over human conduct; but the compliance of those who are either indifferent to the prescribed practices, or who actively question their legitimacy, is commonly secured through the coercive measures which *some are able to apply against others.*

9 A theory of suicide

Research into suicide as a social and psychological phenomenon dates back to the late eighteenth century. Few other types of human act can have attracted the same measure of continuous interest on the part of students in several disciplines: sociology, psychology, psychiatry and medicine. H. Rost's *Bibliographie des Selbstmords,* published in 1927, lists well over 3000 items in the main European languages, and today the total must be more than twice as many as this.[1] So far as the sociological literature is concerned, Durkheim's *Suicide* has long been, and continues today to be, the outstanding work. What has made the book pre-eminent is not the empirical materials upon which it is based, nor the statistical methods used to assemble and analyse them, all of which were made familiar by others previously; rather it is the consistency and force with which these are marshalled to document Durkheim's conception of sociological method. But the work was from the outset controversial, serving to give new focus to well-established debates in the literature on suicide. Critics objected in particular to Durkheim's attempt to treat suicide rates as 'social facts', and to his apparent disregard of the intentional or 'meaningful' character of suicide as a freely undertaken act.[2]

Such critiques have been repeated in some more recent analyses of Durkheim's work. The most notable and ambitious of these is that set out by Douglas in his *The Social Meanings of Suicide* (1967), and in the opening part of this essay I shall concentrate upon the issues which he raises in respect of Durkheim's views, and his strategy for resolving them.[3]

Douglas's critique of Durkheim

According to Douglas, certain 'metaphysical ideas' dominate the nineteenth-century literature on suicide. These are essentially common-sense notions, taken over by academic writers on the

...ect, and they pervade Durkheim's work just as they do that of ...e many authors who preceded him. The most important of such metaphysical ideas are the following. First, that 'social actions are in some way caused (or motivated) by meanings held by the individual and shared by other members of the society'; second, that, as observers, we know the 'meanings of other individuals' actions' in an unproblematic way; third, that 'meaningful social actions . . . are just as subject to counting and quantitative analyses as are physical objects and properties'.[4] These ideas were accepted, largely implicitly, both by those, like Durkheim, who favoured the statistical study of suicide as a general phenomenon, and those who opposed such an approach in favour of a case-study method. The former added to such implicit ideas a range of more explicit propositions, namely, that the stability of official statistics on suicide from year to year shows that they are reliable and valid; that such stability also demonstrates the operation of some sort of laws affecting the behaviour of those committing suicide; and that these laws can be explained in terms of 'a reasonably small set of highly abstract social meanings [called the "social system" or the "social structure"] which are the causes of specific patterns of social actions such as suicide rates; and the only valid sociological theory of such patterns (or suicide rates) will be one in terms of states of this set of abstract meanings'.[5]

Douglas's critique of Durkheim is based on the thesis that most of these ideas, both those implicitly taken over as common-sense assumptions and those explicitly applied as a theory of suicide, must be either discarded altogether or radically revised. They crystallize, according to Douglas, into two sets of problems. One concerns the status of official suicide statistics and their application in social research; the other concerns how the meanings of suicidal actions are to be determined and described by those interested in explaining them.

There are strong reasons, Douglas argues, to doubt the trust which Durkheim, and many authors both before and after him, have placed in official suicide statistics as reliably expressing the incidence of suicide. The identification of a death as 'suicide' in the published statistics depends upon the application of 'social meanings' shared by the officials involved. Suicide, in Western culture, is regarded as 'an unnatural way of dying', and in common with other 'unnatural' causes of death, is subject to *ex post facto* examination by doctors, police, coroners and other officials.[6] What appears as a 'suicide' in the official data is the result of a potentially complicated process of inference and the application of common-sense notions on the part of those involved in this process. Though it may be generally agreed that an 'intention to die' is in some way a necessary characteristic of what distinguishes 'suicide' from other causes of death, there is likely to be considerable vagueness and difference between those in different regions or countries about what constitutes adequate grounds for inferring a person's intentions, and about what other defining features are presupposed by 'suicide'. 'It is clear', Douglas says, 'that coroners do in fact use different *operational* definitions of suicide. Moreover, different coroners' offices use very different *search procedures* in trying to get evidence for their decisions about categorizations of causes of death. These two facts must lead us to expect that suicide statistics are incomparable even within each local area.'[7]

There are also a range of other factors which compromise the reliability of official statistics on suicide. In most countries, suicide is recognized to be a stigma upon the family, and hence there are bound to be pressures against categorizing deaths as suicide. We might presume that such pressures are most pervasive and effective among those groups which, in Durkheim's terms, are most 'integrated' in society. Thus it may be that Durkheim's findings can be explained simply in terms of systematic differences in procedures of categorizing suicides. Whether or not this is the case could only be shown by detailed study of the assumptions, beliefs and procedures of those involved with the events and decisions whereby a death becomes a 'case of suicide'. Even this 'will only tell us what the official suicide rates are and what they are not'; it 'will not necessarily tell us much about the real-world suicidal phenomena'.[8]

Here we come to the second theme of Douglas's critique: that Durkheim draws upon unacknowledged common-sense assumptions in referring to suicide and its causes, and 'did not clearly see the need for any scientific method of determining and analysing meanings'.[9] The various statistical associations which Durkheim sought to establish in *Suicide* are 'made sense of' only because the author relies upon common-sense knowledge to provide their meaning. The generalization: 'the rate of suicide is inversely related to the degree of integration of religious communities', for example, presumes some kind of association in meaning between the two elements, 'suicide' and 'the degree of integration', which is not spelled out, much less studied directly. For 'social integration' can influence suicide only in so far as it is expressed in meaningful action, since that is what suicide necessarily is. If Durkheim did not grasp this, it is because his insistence that social facts have to be treated as 'things' led him to imply that the causal connections involved in sociological generalizations operate in the same sort of way as those in nature; this emphasis coexists in an unresolved antinomy with his recognition of the distinctively moral (therefore 'meaningful') character of social phenomena.[10] In sum, Durkheim and others who have adopted the same sort of approach that he did

. . . have no scientific means of determining and analysing social meanings in terms of real-world events that can be objectively observed and replicated because they have denied all epistemological value to such forms of data. They must, however, have social meanings to explain the suicide rates. Consequently, they must use their common sense ideas . . . about the meanings of certain categories. Being unconstrained by any methods of observation for arriving at such meanings, they use their common-sense ideas to impute those meanings to the category which their abstract theories have predicted.[11]

The remedy, therefore, is to study the social meanings of suicide in detail, and within the context of the events surrounding the suicidal act. This should be done by employing a kind of hierarchical method, involving first of all the 'exact recording of all verbal and non-verbal communicative acts involved in a case of suicide'. Following this, the observer would conduct a preliminary analysis of 'the patterns of invariant *linguistic items*' used in such a setting – including not just the terms 'suicide', 'suicidal' themselves, but a whole range of others: 'disillusionment', 'despair', 'hopelessness', etc. The next procedure would be to classify the ways in which these are employed by the actors in their interactions with each other, and relate them to broader features of the 'social situation'. Only then would it be appropriate to entertain the possibility of establishing 'a more general theory relating meanings to each other and to actions'.[12] At the present time, the formulation of such general theories has to be deferred, because the detailed empirical study which has to precede them has not yet been undertaken.

We do already know enough, however, to say that not only the term 'suicide' itself but many other linguistic expressions connected with its use, in Western culture at least, have a variety of meanings. 'Suicide', Douglas says, is both an 'essentially problematic' and 'situationally problematic' notion. In other words, just as there is variability in the general common-sense understanding of 'suicide' in different groups or different societies, so the meanings of 'suicide' in the context of suicidal acts are influenced by the particular interactions that occur. What Douglas calls the 'abstract' meanings of suicide thus differ from its 'situated meanings'. 'Abstract meanings' of suicide, within which he includes such notions as Durkheim's 'egoistic' or 'anomic suicide', hence cannot be used to predict or explain suicide. This 'is a denial', Douglas concludes, 'of the fundamental assumption of most general theories in sociology today'.[13]

An assessment

There are undoubtedly major elements of Douglas's work that have to be accepted, as does his overall theme that Durkheim's methodological stance and his theoretical conclusions have to be criticized in a rather basic fashion. I shall return to this shortly, when I sketch in an evaluation of Durkheim's theory. For the moment, however, let me concentrate upon the shortcomings of Douglas's own account, which are surely as considerable as those of Durkheim. I shall list these as a number of points.

1) Douglas's analysis of the use of official statistics in studying suicide is ambiguous in its conclusions, hesitating between a moderate and a more radical stance. He tends to lump together two types of criticism of the use of such statistics which actually have different implications. One is the thesis that official suicide rates are an inaccurate, perhaps even a completely misleading, index of the incidence of suicide. He devotes some considerable space to discussing the influence of factors relevant to this: such factors include, for example, variations in procedures used in different areas to identify a death as 'suspicious' and therefore warranting investigation as being a potential suicide, pressures applied by families to get a death classified as other than the outcome of suicide, etc. The implication of these is that officially calculated suicide rates may be misleading, but they are in principle *corrigible*: the notion of a suicide rate as such is not impugned, only the official representation of such a rate. The remedy then would be to use other, carefully organized methods

of classifying deaths to see how far their results are similar to those produced in the official statistics. Some studies of this sort have in fact been carried out by various authors: one means of trying to do this, for example, is for researchers to investigate in detail every death occurring within a given period of time in a community, comparing the rate then calculated with the officially registered one.[14] Douglas, however, more than hints at acceptance of another, more radical view of suicide statistics which, if adopted, makes any discussion of factors such as dissimulation, etc., redundant. According to this second view, the very notion of a 'suicide rate', of a statistical distribution of the incidence of suicide, is an error and has to be abandoned altogether. As Douglas expresses this in one place, 'There is no such thing as one definite, necessarily valid (socially meaningful) "suicide rate". This whole idea of a given, necessarily valid (or invalid) "suicide rate" for a Western society is a complete misconception of the meaningful nature of "suicide" in Western societies, *even* if one is only concerned with the categorizations made by officials.' The reason given for this is the 'essentially problematic nature of the social meanings of suicide'.[15]

2) The term 'meaning' does far too much work in Douglas's discussion, covering various distinct phenomena that have to be separated in the analysis of social action. Douglas on numerous occasions throughout his work uses 'social meanings of suicide' as equivalent to the following aspects of suicidal acts or the study of such acts: actors' intentions or purposes for their action; their reasons for their action; their motives for their action; the moral norms or ideals to which action may be oriented; the concepts and generalizations ('common-sense meanings') which lay actors use in their day-to-day conduct; and the concepts and generalizations which sociologists use in describing or analysing such conduct.

3) Douglas provides no satisfactory account of the relation that is supposed to exist between the latter two senses of 'meaning', i.e. between lay concepts and the concepts employed in social science. He consistently rejects 'positivism', but his own view of how general concepts and theories should be developed in the social sciences seems to be a quasi-positivistic one. We first of all have to study 'everyday meanings' in empirical detail, and from such observations construct theories. The terms involved in the theories thus formulated, Douglas appears to believe, must directly reflect

the ambiguities and diffuseness of lay concepts: there must be a relation of isomorphy between 'situated meanings' and 'abstract meanings', or otherwise the latter are mistakenly expressed.

4) Douglas holds that the causal influences involved in the events leading to suicide operate solely through the 'meaningful' character of the conduct of the actors involved in the situation, where 'meaningful action' is taken to refer to 'intentional action'. But this is not so, and limits his analysis as seriously as Durkheim's was limited by his attempt to eschew any reference to intentions altogether. There are three major respects in which the causal explanation of suicide (or any form of 'meaningful action') escapes such limits: in regard of the unacknowledged social conditions of action, the unintended consequences of action, and unconscious motivating elements in action.[16] Where Douglas does mention motives, he stresses he is concerned with them 'only as they appear in the statements of social actors involved in suicidal phenomena: that is . . . the imputations of motives made by the actors themselves'.[17]

These weaknesses in Douglas's arguments restrict the effectiveness of his critique of Durkheim and his attempt to suggest a new mode of approach to the study of suicide. Let me therefore offer a rather different critical gloss on Durkheim's theory of suicide, drawing where relevant upon similar themes to those developed by Douglas, but also preparing the way for a theory which will avoid the ambiguities or difficulties just noted. For sake of brevity, this also can be expressed as an enumerated series of comments.

1) Durkheim wanted *Suicide* to be an exemplification of the fruitfulness of his views on sociological method. If it is this, it also provides as clear an indication as one could wish for of the failings of his methodological system. The theory set out in *Suicide* is a deterministic one, which allows no space for suicidal acts as rationalized action: that is to say, as conduct carried out for reasons reflexively applied by the agents involved.

2) This is of course closely related to Durkheim's determined attempt to write out actors' intentions as of any relevance to the notion of suicide.[18] Thus he defines suicide as any act carried out by an individual that results in his death, where he knows that the act will have that result – thereby excluding intention or purpose formally from his conceptualization of the object of his study. But this definition papers over the distinction between 'doing something knowing it will produce a particular result', and 'doing

something intending to produce that result', a distinction that has to be preserved if a theory of suicide is to admit the causal relevance of the rationalization of action.[19]

3) The fact that Durkheim's account in *Suicide*, and his formulation of sociological method more generally, lacks a theory of action (in the sense which I have ascribed to that term elsewhere)[20] has the consequence that he identifies 'social structure' with constraint – although, as Douglas points out, the causal effects whereby social structures impel individuals to self-destruction remain obscure. In place of the equation of 'structure' and 'constraint' we should substitute a revised notion of the former concept as both the medium and the outcome of the generation of interaction in social systems: as both enabling and constraining.

4) The preceding point is connected to Durkheim's tendency to infer directly from macrostructural conditions of a society as a whole to individual behaviour in linking suicide rates to 'egoism', 'anomie', etc.[21] He gives virtually no attention to the more immediate nexus of social relations surrounding the suicidal act: the 'situated meanings', as Douglas calls them, of suicide. But it is precisely here that the circumstances typically involved in suicidal acts can most directly, and most profitably, be studied.

5) Durkheim accepts the role of psychological theory in the explanation of suicide, as complementary to his sociological explanation of patterns in suicide rates. But: *a*) His interpretation of the relation between psychological and sociological explanation is inadequate. According to him, the latter serves to identify the social conditions governing the suicide rate, while the former identifies the particular individuals, or types of individuals, who kill themselves in those conditions. Thus it is the task of sociological analysis to determine the influence of a situation of anomie on suicide; a psychological theory will explain why person A commits suicide in such circumstances, whereas B, C, D . . . do not. This, however, would only be a satisfactory viewpoint if it were the case that the origins of 'suicide-proneness' in personality were purely biological, i.e. independent of social conditions. As Durkheim himself admits at one point, they are not: the social circumstances which he treats as acting 'directly' to produce a given suicide rate also therefore are likely to affect socialization processes, and thereby the incidence of 'suicidal personalities'. *b*) Durkheim's account of the psychology of suicide is very limited, and offers little in the way of hypotheses about the dynamics of

motivation that might be involved. Hence we have to look to other sources to attempt to develop such hypotheses.

6) Durkheim concerns himself almost solely with completed suicide, mentioning attempted suicide only in passing. But it is probably much more fruitful to study completed suicide in relation to 'suicidal behaviour' as a whole, including within this 'unsuccessful' suicide attempts, gestures, threats, and other forms of self-punitive act. The importance of this can easily be brought out in relation to point 4 above. The events leading up to a suicidal act, and the social context in which it occurs, may involve various sorts of contingency that influence whether or not, for instance, a verbal threat of suicide becomes anything more than that. Particularly important, as will be described further below, is the fact that suicide attempts commonly involve a strong 'risk-taking' element: the individual's survival depends upon contingencies such as the response of others to verbal warnings issued prior to the attempt being carried out.

There still remain two problems raised by Douglas's criticisms of Durkheim: the question of the significance of suicide statistics, and the more embracing issue of the relation between lay concepts and those coined by social scientists in the characterization and explanation of suicide. I distinguished previously two types of critique of the use of suicide statistics, as indicating rates of suicide, suggested in Douglas's discussion. The first creates no particular theoretical difficulties, although it is obviously highly consequential for the evaluation of the mode of research adopted by Durkheim and many others. It seems reasonable to conclude so far as matters of differential reporting, dissimulation, etc., go, that official suicide rates should be only used in research, if at all, with much more circumspection than Durkheim sought to apply them. On the other hand, if it be accepted that officially published rates are in principle corrigible, then there is no reason on *a priori* grounds to discount the results of studies that employ them: the evidence from such studies could not be regarded as conclusive documentation of the theories advanced, but might indicate that these theories are plausible and worth examining further in the light of other evidence. What, then, of the more radical view that the notion of a 'suicide rate' makes no sense, since the term 'suicide' has no commonly accepted, precisely formulated meaning in lay usage? The answer is that such a view is founded upon an erroneous idea of the relation between lay and social-science concepts, supposing that the latter must reflect the diffuseness or ambiguities of the former. This is simply not so. While, as I again have argued in some detail elsewhere, the concepts employed in the social sciences are necessarily connected to lay concepts, in ways that can be specified, it does not follow that they have to be isomorphic in their logical form: it is possible, and necessary, to attempt to give precision to what is inexact in ordinary language, and to discuss ambiguity unambiguously.[22] The variability in lay meanings of the term 'suicide', and related terms, does not compromise the idea of a precisely delimited rate of suicide; nor should the theorist be obliged to avoid offering a clearly delimited definition of 'suicide' on the basis that those whose behaviour is referred to by the term do not apply it in such a way. Any further discussion of this issue would go beyond the bounds of this paper.

We now have prepared the ground required for formulating an approach to the theory of suicide, or suicidal behaviour more generally understood, that can draw upon Durkheim's study while seeking to avoid the difficulties created by the framework he adopted. In sum, such a theory should involve the following elements: a discussion of suicidal behaviour as rationalized action, reflexively monitored by the actor; an analysis of the motivational components involved in such behaviour; and an examination of the structural conditions of this behaviour, especially in the context of the nexus of social relationships in which the action occurs. The problem is to connect these together in a coherent scheme. Before sketching in how such a scheme might be constructed, however, a digression is necessary in respect of what is lacking in Durkheim's analysis: a theory of motivation relevant to suicidal acts.

Psychological aspects of suicide

The most significant theory of suicide which has been developed in psychology, and almost the only theory which goes beyond common-sense observations, is based on the psychoanalytic theory of depression.[23] In his original formulation of the theory, Freud draws an illuminating comparison between depressive states and grief produced by the death of a loved person. When such a person dies, or is suddenly removed through some other cause, the individual has to withdraw his emotional ties to that person and develop new ones elsewhere. This cannot be done immediately, and emotional energy is typically withdrawn from the external world and incorporated into the ego; the individual continues to identify with an introjected image of the other, and much interest in the external world is correspondingly lost. Now all love relations involve some ambivalence, and the individual has a fund of repressed hostile feelings about the object. The bereaved individual unconsciously feels he has been abandoned by the lost object: the aggressive feelings which this stimulates become the focus of the previously existing reservoir of hostile impulses. Feelings of dejection and lack of interest in life are based upon the retroflexion of these hostile impulses against the introjected object in the ego.

Both grief and depression originate in feelings stimulated by another person which become redirected against the self. However, while grief is a normal process of adjustment to the death of a loved one, in some individuals the tendency to depression is chronic. The key to differences between grief and states of depressive disorder is that 'melancholia is in some way related to an object-loss which is withdrawn from consciousness, in contradistinction to mourning, in which there is nothing about the loss which is unconscious . . . (in grief) it is the world which has become poor and empty; in melancholia it is the ego itself'.[24] The depressive individual is characterized by an abnormally rigid and punitive super-ego, which causes him to refer hostile impulses back against himself. The stronger the super-ego, the greater the tendency to invert hostile feelings, stimulated by others, against the self. The frustrations generating these aggressive impulses are not confined to actual object-loss, but 'extend for the most part beyond the clear case of loss by death, and include all those situations of being slighted, neglected or disappointed, which can import opposed feelings of love and hate into the relationship or reinforce an already existing ambivalence . . .'[25] The self-accusations and feelings of worthlessness which characterize depression are thus sentiments which really refer to another person, and are stimulated by the real or imagined behaviour of another or others. The reason for the close connection between depression and suicide is now evident: suicide represents an extreme on a range of possible forms of self-aggression, which extends from relatively minor forms such as verbal self-deprecation to actual self-destruction.[26] Suicide presupposes a highly ambivalent object-relationship, in which the ego directs against itself 'hostility which relates to an object and which represents the ego's original reaction to objects in the external world. . . . In the opposed situations of being most intensely in love and of suicide the ego is overwhelmed by the object, though in totally different ways.'[27]

The main deficiency of the theory is that empirically the correspondence between depression and suicide is not complete. There appears to be no strict continuum between the self-deprecations which typically characterize depression, and actual physical self-aggression: people suffering from extreme states of depressive disorder are not necessarily more prone to suicide than those experiencing an isolated depressive mood which is traceable to some defined precipitating event. Thus, while there is an intimate connection between depression and suicide, it is by no means established what are the specific characteristics of those depressive states producing direct attempts at self-destruction. It seems probable, however, that one factor of considerable importance is the conscious and unconscious symbols surrounding the idea of death: suicidal acts are likely to accompany depression when death is invested with an instrumental significance – as a 'magical' solution to problems, or a weapon that can be used to secure a desired end.[28]

In spite of its partial character, the psychoanalytic theory of depression is, as a theory of suicide, simple and powerful. Many cases of suicide seem to fit within this general framework. Suicide is probably almost universally preceded by some form of depression, and depressive disorder is far more commonly associated with suicide than are any of the other commonly acknowledged types of mental disorder. On the other hand, it is not difficult to find cases which do *not* fit easily within such a pattern. The difference between the following two summary case-histories is illustrative: the first seems to fit the character type and life-history which would be expected according to the theory, while the second does not.

Case 1. Suicide attempt (Method: barbiturate poisoning)
G.S. lost her father when she was 3. Her mother spent several periods in mental hospitals, during which time G.S. was cared for by relatives. G.S. was stated to be moody and withdrawn, and had no close friends. At the age of 25 she married: her husband left her seven months later, and this precipitated her suicide attempt.

Case 2. Suicide (Method: hanging)

T.W. was the son of a successful advertising executive. His childhood was apparently uneventful. T.W. had poor results at school, but his father, who was determined that he should 'do well', got him a job as a management trainee in his firm. He married at 22, and had three children, aged 2, 3 and 5 at the time of his death. He was a sociable individual, and had a close circle of friends. Apparent precipitating cause of suicide: his application for promotion to a higher grade was rejected.

Even in these two very short case-histories, several differences are evident. G.S. lost a parent at an early age, and her relationship with her mother was rather unstable. As a person, she was withdrawn and friendless. Her suicide attempt was precipitated by an object-loss – the departure of her husband. T.W., on the other hand, had no apparent disruption in his relationships with his parents in childhood. His family life was, to outward appearances at least, happy. He was sociable and had many friends. The suicide attempt of G.S. followed the breaking of an important love relationship; T.W.'s suicide followed a failure to achieve a desired objective.

In Freud's analysis of depression, an indication is given of a type of suicide rather different from that which is directly covered in the standard theory. Freud mentions that a psychological equivalent for the frustrating object can be a 'highly cherished ideal' which becomes unobtainable.[29] Other writers have also linked suicide with 'failure' and a 'sense of inferiority', but little attempt has been made to set up a psychological type which might embrace such cases of suicide more easily than the conventional theory is able to do. There are, however, concepts and ideas in the repertoire of psychoanalytic theory which can provide the basis of such a type.

In his initial formulation of the 'superstructure' of the ego, Freud used the term 'ego-ideal'. He later distinguished the ego-ideal from the super-ego, and by far the greater bulk of writing in psychoanalysis has been devoted to the latter. The positive goals and objectives which individuals strive for nevertheless clearly form a highly important sector of personality, as has always been stressed in academic psychology. The super-ego and ego-ideal, as Piers has pointed out, can be regarded as having different generic sources and different integrative tasks in personality; and each may be a partially independent source of tension and anxiety.[30]

The ego-ideal, which 'is in continuous interaction with the conscious and unconscious awareness of the ego's potentialities', is the critical agency besides the super-ego which governs the individual's self-esteem.[31]

Overwhelming concern with the importance of the super-ego in psychoanalysis is connected, Piers has suggested, with a corresponding over-emphasis upon guilt at the expense of other forms of tension which may frequently play an important role in personality. If guilt can be conceived as deriving from a tension between super-ego and ego, a second major source of anxiety can be differentiated as stemming from friction between ego-ideal and ego. *Shame* is anxiety generated when the goals and self-conception embodied in the ego-ideal diverge from the actual performance of the ego.

It seems plausible to hypothesize that, just as in many cases of suicide guilt is the dominant source of motivation to the act, in others shame may be the main mobilizing energy. Most persons presumably maintain a fairly high degree of 'fit' between the position and the attainments of the ego, and the demands and conception of self set by the ego-ideal. In some circumstances, however, the ego-ideal may impose demands which can come to place great strain upon the capabilities of the ego to achieve an identity which will satisfy them. Such individuals will be abnormally vulnerable to shame anxiety and must constantly be sensitive to validation of their worth from the external world. Any change in their external circumstances would threaten the insecure position of the ego *vis-à-vis* the ego-ideal. This is particularly true if the ego-ideal is at the same time both demanding *and* non-specific, i.e. if the individual internalizes powerful motivations which are not linked to defined absolute goals, but which demand that he should continually prove himself worthier than, or superior to, others, or which produce in him a general 'restlessness'. The condition for the development of such a demanding ego-ideal is that the child is exposed to generalized shame-oriented techniques of socialization, such that he is teased, ridiculed, or even ignored, rather than scolded or threatened for his misdemeanours. These imply to the child that he is 'not good enough' and constantly menace him with feelings of inferiority and worthlessness. At the back of shame there is, as Piers puts it, not fear of hatred (punishment) but fear of contempt, or 'death by emotional starvation'.[32]

In such a pattern, masochistic tendencies are based upon shame.

Frustration generated by disjunction between ego-ideal and ego provides the basis for aggression turned against the 'inadequate' ego-identity. In suicidal behaviour connected with this type, the self-destructive act represents an attempt to destroy the unsatisfactory ego which has shown itself incapable of acquiring an identity adequate to the ego-ideal. Suicide probably in most cases follows a long-term cumulative process: there are various psychological mechanisms whereby the ego can temporarily protect or shelter itself from overweaning demands of the ego-ideal. The individual may, for example, continually project his hopes into the future, convincing himself that others will one day appreciate his true worth, or that one day he will be a success. The rebuttal which finally precipitates suicide may be an apparently minor one.[33] There are many clinical descriptions of suicide in the literature which seem to fit within this hypothetical framework. Hendin, for example, describes the case of a lawyer who was not doing well in his career, and who made a suicide attempt:

His dreams under hypnosis were of the most elemental kind. In one instance they revealed him running to catch a boat and just missing it. In his associations 'missing the boat' symbolized the low opinion which he had of his entire career. His legal ambitions were excessive and he found it impossible to compromise with his grandiose success fantasies. The aggressiveness which stemmed from his grandiosity interfered with his actual performance, a constellation frequently observed in male patients with extremely high and rigid standards for themselves. What is seen as failure causes an enormous amount of self-hatred, and suicide amounts to a self-inflicted punishment for having failed.[34]

Now there are good reasons to suppose that the unconscious motivational sources of suicide are connected with fantasy gratifications which do not represent death as an end to existence.[35] The unconscious objective of suicide in which shame is the dominant mobilizing anxiety thus might be seen as the replacement of the unsatisfactory ego-identity by a new identity more consonant with the demands of the ego-ideal – the re-birth of the ego in a new guise. Since this in fact entails the destruction of the existing identity, we might regard this type as 'more genuinely suicidal' than suicide in which guilt is the dominant anxiety. Using Menninger's trichotomy of suicidal motivations,[36] we could hold that the former type is governed primarily by the 'wish to die', while in the latter type the 'wish to kill' and the 'wish to be killed' are the dominant impulses.

A theory of suicide

An endeavour now has to be made to show how such an account of the psychological dynamics of suicide can be connected to a theory which recognizes the social conditions relevant to the explanation of suicidal behaviour, but also treats the latter as the outcome of rationalized processes of action. While the details of such an account have to be fairly speculative, its general form does not stand or fall upon their particular validity.

In reference to contemporary societies, Durkheim distinguished two types of suicide, egoistic and anomic (altruistic suicide supposedly being primarily characteristic of traditional social orders, with a fourth type, fatalistic suicide, being alluded to only in passing). The terms 'egoism' and 'anomie' are strongly embedded in the general perspectives of Durkheim's sociology, and I shall not employ them here. Moreover since, as many subsequent writers have pointed out,[37] they are not always clearly distinguished by Durkheim, any use that may be made of the ideas that they express should treat them as 'pure types', rather than as a descriptive classification. Durkheim's analysis moves, as most nineteenth-century statistical studies of suicide did, on the level of trying to connect very general characteristics of societies with the distribution of suicide, and does so in a deterministic way. Neither of these emphases, as I have indicated above, is acceptable. While it is no doubt the case that the incidence and nature of suicidal behaviour in a society is influenced in important ways by overall traits of that society, we must show how these are expressed in the more concrete forms of interaction in which actors are implicated: and we have to consider such interaction as actively sustained by those concerned, rather than as mechanically determined. Durkheim's 'egoistic' and 'anomic suicide' are not so much types of suicide, as types of social condition in which suicide is relatively common. In so far as there is a clearly discernable difference between these types, the first suggests the importance of *social isolation* in the origins of suicide, while the second might be said to relate to *moral isolation*. Neither of these is easily defined, but I shall use the first to refer to the detachment of individuals from close and stable organized social relations with others; by the second I shall mean their separation from morally binding commitments which relate directly to the enactment of day-to-day life.

Now each of these clearly reflects aspects of the overall society, and the social changes which transform it. Both are obviously promoted by the development of large-scale urban communities and the expansion of geographical mobility; and by the spread of bourgeois values stressing individualism and personal initiative in the major institutional spheres. Thus, for example, values which emphasize romantic love as a basis for marriage thereby place the onus on each individual to search out and win a partner through his own efforts. Moreover, as contrasted with systems in which arranged marriages are customary, there are only relatively few duties and obligations in respect of a wider circle of relatives which stem from the marital role itself. Such factors, however, as I have mentioned previously, do not only operate 'directly' to influence suicide rates, but are mediated through socialization processes that govern personality development. This is crucial to the *reproduction* of social or moral isolation: depressive or 'suicide-prone' persons are likely to be involved in what I shall call a 'deteriorating spiral' of interaction, in a manner which I shall try to explicate below. A scheme of the elements involved can be portrayed as follows:

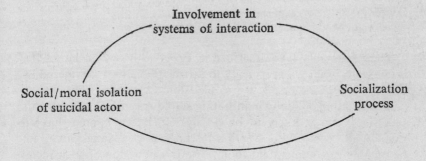

I use the term 'socialization' here to refer not just to the development of personality from infancy to maturity, but to mean a continuous interchange between the personality of the actor and his social relations with others. The social or moral isolation of the actor can be understood neither as the outcome merely of 'external' social circumstances (in Durkheim's sense), or of the traits of his personality, nor even of the conjunction of these two if they are treated as if they have separate origins. Rather these are mutually connected in the structuration of interaction, as reflexively monitored by the actor: the actor helps to create his own social milieu at the same time as he is created by it.

Let me now try to expand upon this scheme, by sketching in a typology which connects my prior discussion of the psychology of suicide to the differentiation of social isolation and moral isolation. I shall suggest that this latter differentiation can be tied in to the characteristics of 'suicide-prone' personality types to yield two forms of 'deteriorating spiral' of interaction involved in suicidal behaviour.

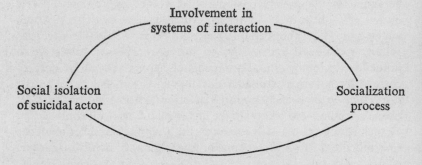

Involvement in systems of interaction

Social isolation of suicidal actor

Socialization process

Motivational source: punitive super-ego (guilt)
Suicidal behaviour=aggression against introjected object
(predominance of 'wish to kill' + 'wish to be killed')

The personality type described in Freud's theory of depression is characterized by a propensity to introvert feelings stimulated by the conduct of others. It seems plausible to suppose that such a person will find difficulty in initiating stable emotional attachments to others, and is likely to be highly dependent upon a limited number of established relations, while at the same time not being able easily to sustain them. The reproduction of such social ties is likely to be particularly unstable where such an individual moves in a social context in which, for example, personal initiative and responsibility for action are strongly sanctioned normatively. Thus, to continue the instance mentioned before: in a system where the formation of courtship–marriage relationships is largely left up to each individual, the kind of person who is most disadvantaged in finding a mate (and keeping him or her once found) is precisely the one who is already very dependent upon his pre-existing attachments, normally with a parent or parents, and who finds it difficult to form or sustain close affective relations with others – while at the same time having a strong need for such relations. A variety of contingent events, in such circumstances of unstable social reproduction, but especially the death, abandonment, or fear of abandonment by a loved one, can set into play a deteriorating spiral of events in which the individual's demands alienate others, causing him to withdraw further or perhaps increase the demands he makes upon them, thus accentuating his separation from them, and so on. This indicates perhaps how difficult it would be to measure 'social isolation' quantitatively,[38] since the experience of isolation, or frustrated dependency, may occur within what is nominally a closely defined relationship with another or others: but the individual is unable to make of the relationship a stable and satisfying tie. Such a situation may indeed result when a highly dependent individual has made the transition from the parental family into a marriage relationship.

It is important to note that, in Freud's theory, depression and the suicidal act have an intrinsically social nature. Depression and suicide, which in obvious respects go together with withdrawal from the social world, are also seen to represent hostile impulses directed towards *others*. The depressive state, which appears simply to entail a retraction from social life, is at the same time in an inverted sense aimed at others. The pattern of dependency which goes hand in hand with the tendency to depression means, as various psychoanalytic authors have tried to show in detail, that suicidal behaviour represents *both* an aggressive impulse towards the other(s), turned back against the self, and also an attempt to regain the affection of the object.[39] It is both a hostile act, and an appeal for love and forgiveness, having the form of expiation. Thus Fenichel writes that suicidal acts are

. . . desperate attempts to enforce, at any cost, the cessation of the pressure of the superego. They are the most extreme acts of ingratiatory submission to punishment and to the superego's cruelty; simultaneously they are also the most extreme acts of rebellion, that is murder – murder of the original objects whose incorporation created the superego, murder, it is true, of the kind of Dorian Gray's murder of his image. This mixture of submission and rebellion is the climax of the accusatory demonstration for the purpose of coercing forgiveness: 'Look at what you have done to me; now you have to be good again.'[40]

A suicidal act of this sort represents an expiatory attempt at or appeal for reintegration within a relationship or a group. Suicide here, then, is a more inherently social phenomenon than even Durkheim supposed.

The possible permutations of hostile and expiatory motives appear to be many. In some instances, 'revenge' appears to be a main motivation; others are more obviously an 'appeal for help'. In virtually all cases the presumption must be that suicidal behaviour has some unconscious reference to the objects who were the original identifications from which the super-ego was formed: the parental figures. Hendin observes:

> The act of dying itself can be conceived as pleasurably incorporated into the reunion fantasy. Most frequently the emphasis is not placed upon the dying but upon the gratification to follow with the mood in such reunion dreams being quite pleasant. In the overwhelming majority the gratification is of an extremely dependent variety, either directly with parental figures or with wives, husbands or siblings substituting as parents.[41]

It seems normally the case that unconscious elements strongly influence motivation such that, on the level of intentional action, the suicidal act is rationalized only in a diffuse way: it is common for people who survive such acts to say afterwards that they 'weren't really sure what they were doing', or even quite often that they 'didn't really want to die'.[42] *Risk-taking* is a prominent feature of many suicidal acts: the individual in a very real sense stakes his life on securing an adequate response from others.[43] In most cases, this seems to be directed at a specific object upon whom the actor's dependency needs are focused. Sometimes the appeal for love may be aimed at a different object from the introverted hostility: the individual simultaneously rejects one object and appeals to another. In still other instances, the appeal for response from others may be non-specific; a person may perpetrate a suicide attempt, for example, in a public place. There is no doubt that some suicide attempts or threats are consciously intended as a sanction to influence others in a desired direction, and are clearly rationalized as such by the actor concerned. It appears evident enough (although it is not universally the case) that in such circumstances the suicidal act is unlikely to be a 'serious' attempt: that is, the person is likely to adopt a method in which little risk of death is involved, perhaps even staging a sham performance altogether.

It seems clear that a range of factors[44] may intervene in what

I have called the deteriorating spiral of events that leads up to a suicide attempt. Suicidal behaviour of the kind being discussed here is in a fundamental way introjected aggression against other objects; the process of deterioration of social relations in which the individual is involved will be crucially influenced by the contingent responses of others in succeeding phases. Thus many people contemplating a suicide attempt give some prior verbal warning of their intention, sometimes phrased in a light-hearted way, or otherwise cryptically expressed.[45] If the warning is heeded, and an appropriate response is forthcoming, the sequence of events potentially culminating in a suicidal act may be arrested at quite an early stage. Such warnings are sometimes repeated in a more urgent and direct fashion immediately prior to a suicide attempt, and may be bound-in by the actor to its risk-taking character. For example, a person may telephone a friend just before, or even after, taking an overdose of drugs; if the friend is in, and if he responds quickly, the individual is saved the full consequences of his act. This makes it apparent how much of a misnomer it is to speak of as 'unsuccessful attempts at suicide' those suicidal acts which do not eventuate in death. The contrary is just as near the truth: the individual's survival is proof of the success of his action. In suicidal behaviour of this type there may be, in what is psychologically a highly significant sense, no 'wish to die'. As Menninger writes: 'Anyone who has sat by the bedside of a patient dying from a self-inflicted wound and listened to pleadings that the physician save a life, the destruction of which had only a few hours or minutes before been attempted, must have been impressed by the paradox that one who has wished to kill himself does not wish to die! '[46] In the light of what has been said previously, however, this no longer appears as paradoxical – nor is it simply the result of the individual 'changing his mind' as a result of his encounter with death.

The sociological significance of suicidal behaviour does not terminate with the suicide attempt itself, regardless of whether or not this produces the individual's death. This is plain enough in cases of 'unsuccessful' attempts. Studies of the latter show that suicide attempts do appear to have a 'shock' effect on relatives and friends, stimulating the sort of responsiveness which the actor may have been seeking. Even the fact that the person is placed in a hospital ward, and some special attention paid to him by medical or social workers, may go some way towards achieving this objective, combined with the expiatory catharsis of the suicidal act itself.[47]

I shall now turn to the connections between moral isolation and suicide, using the same general theoretical scheme, but suggesting that suicidal behaviour involved here may be of a different sort to that just described.

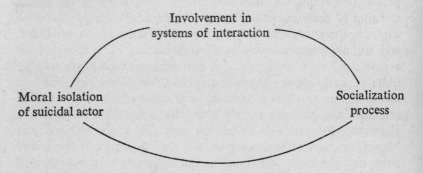

Motivational source: demanding ego-ideal (shame)
Suicidal behaviour = aggression against inadequate ego-identity
(predominance of 'wish to die')

The second type of 'suicide-prone' personality described previously is one in which shame rather than guilt is the dominant mobilizing motivational force. This type of person is likely to have difficulty in sustaining morally satisfying transactions with the normative framework of the surrounding social world. Any generalized social conditions promoting the instability of such transactions will influence his propensity to suicidal behaviour. These conditions undoubtedly include some of those classified generically by Durkheim as 'anomie'. Day-to-day life in contemporary Western society has become largely stripped of moral legitimation, apart from that derived from competitive economic success; the chronic tendency to crisis manifested by the system as a whole no doubt finds expression on a more concrete level in the tensions and anxieties of a morally tenuous 'adjustment' to the exigencies of good or ill-fortune.

The deteriorating spiral of events precipitating a suicidal act here is likely to contrast in important respects with that discussed previously, with regard to the social nexus involved as well as the connections between motivation and the rationalization of action.

The theory of depression and suicide associated with the first type involves the introjection of hostile impulses stimulated by others, and a principal characteristic of the depressive state is withdrawal. Where guilt is not the dominant tension, however, the characteristics of depressive states produced by and helping to give rise to the degenerating sequence of events resulting in a suicide attempt are likely to be quite different. This was in fact recognized by Durkheim in his discussion of the 'individual forms' of egoistic and anomic suicide. Egoistic suicide is characterized by 'a condition of melancholic languor which relaxes all the springs of action'. Anomic suicide, by contrast, where it is traceable to some sudden and radical reversal, derives from 'anger and all the emotions customarily associated with disappointment'. In more chronic cases, it is the act of those 'who, having no complaint to make of men or circumstances, automatically weary of a palpably hopeless pursuit, which only irritates rather than appeases their desires. They turn against life in general and accuse it of having deceived them.'[48] These latter descriptions are not too far removed from the syndrome sometimes identified as 'anxiety depression'. This pattern is generally not accompanied by the withdrawal characteristics found in classical depressive states; rather there is a more 'active' anxiety focused upon perceived inadequacies of performance or attainment. A typical instance is described by one observer as follows:

Occasionally the whole clinical picture seems dominated by anxiety, a point mentioned by some writers. This was demonstrated in a case seen recently by me: a man aged forty-four who fairly suddenly developed numerous anxiety symptoms following a difficult time in his business in which he had worked excessively hard. In addition, he experienced headaches of the tension type, and gave a good description of what was in fact a degree of retardation, and complained of early waking. Throughout his illness he denied being depressed, and indeed he did not strike one as being so to any appreciable degree . . . He described himself as normally placid and good-natured, and he was in effect a little obsessional and unbending. He had always been a very hard worker and a successful planning executive in business.[49]

Such an individual may continue to sustain established social relationships with others, even if these become subject to strain; he may, in fact, hide his anxieties from others as far as possible, for to show them might reinforce his feelings of inferiority or worthlessness. Compared to the type of suicidal behaviour discussed previously, suicidal acts in these circumstances are less likely to be preceded by the person giving warnings of the impending attempt. If life seems empty to him, it is not because he is separated from necessary contacts with others, but because his activity is directed to aspirations which do not accord with the identity he has achieved. This type of suicidal behaviour, like the first, presumably has an 'internal object reference', founded upon parental identifications. But here the expiatory character of 'vindication through self-punishment' is transformed into a more thorough-going overthrow of the ego-identity. As Lynd suggests, shame demands a change in the self, rather than offering the possibility of atonement or appeal: 'Unlike guilt [shame] . . . is – in specific terms – irreversible. "In shame there is no comfort but to be beyond all bounds of shame." '[50] If the underlying motives in the first type of suicidal behaviour are ones such as 'revenge' upon or 'reunion' with others, in this type they are those of 'rebirth' or 'starting anew'. As in the former type, the relation between unconscious motives and the conscious rationalization of conduct is likely to be a variable one. But it may be that even in instances where a suicidal act is carried out in a carefully reasoned way, as where a person suffering from a serious and painful illness decides to put an end to his existence by his own hand, unconscious fantasy motives operate.

Conclusion: suicide and attempted suicide

Since these are offered as abstract types, many actual cases of suicidal behaviour may involve elements of both; and the typology may not in any case be comprehensive enough to be usefully applied to all forms of suicide. Nevertheless, it seems reasonable to conclude that suicidal acts which approximate to the second type are more likely to show a higher proportion of completed to ('unsuccessful') attempted suicide than are those which are closer to the first. This implies that *methods* of attempting suicide are important features of the overall pattern of action involved – something which Durkheim and others have denied.[51] In types of suicidal act which have the expiatory objective of coercion of/ appeal to others, the individual is likely to dramatize his plight by choosing a risk-taking method of suicide which provides some opportunity for others to respond in the desired fashion. The taking of a drug which has a progressive comatose effect, for example, is one such method. In suicide by shooting, hanging or drowning, on the other hand, unless the person very deliberately arranges the situation so as to make the act ineffective, death is more immediate and inevitable. The typology might thereby help illuminate aspects of the differences between attempted and completed suicides. In most sociological studies of suicide authors have based their ideas, like Durkheim did, on surveys of completed suicide, the implication being that 'failed' suicide attempts are the same in all significant respects. But, while all forms of suicidal behaviour are influenced by contingent events intervening between the attempt itself and its outcome, there seems strong evidence to support the notion that most attempted suicides differ in important respects from most completed suicides. A high proportion of suicide attempts are made in situations where the intervention of others is inevitable or probable, and where this must be known to the person who makes the attempt.[52] A man threatens to jump from a building overlooking a busy street, for example, rather than choosing a deserted height equally near by. Follow-up studies of attempted suicides indicate that only a small proportion of those who attempt suicide actually kill themselves at a later date. Even allowing for the difficulties involved in the calculation of suicide rates, there are several notable differences in the relative distribution of completed and attempted suicide that seem fairly reliably established. Attempted suicide seems to be much more common than completed suicide. Male rates of suicide appear to outrank female rates by a ratio of two or three to one; but women apparently attempt suicide several times more frequently than men. Suicide rates probably increase with advancing age; but rates of attempted suicide seem to be highest in the 20–40 year age-group.[53]

L.

The suicide problem in
French sociology

It is not always recognized today how far Durkheim's *Suicide* was indebted to the works of earlier authors on the topic.[54] Suicide was the subject of extended debate even in the eighteenth century.[55] Most eighteenth-century works on suicide were concerned with the moral implications of the suicidal act, but towards the end of the century writers began to turn their attention to discussing the significance of the apparently rapidly rising suicide rates in Europe,[56] and out of this a more statistical concern with the determinants of suicide began to develop.

One of the earliest comprehensive investigations of suicide was made by Falret in his *De l'hypocondrie et du suicide* (1822).[57] Falret examined at some length both 'internal causes' of suicidal tendencies in the individual, which he attributed principally to certain forms of inherited mental disorder, and 'external causes' producing variations in suicide rates between different groups.[58] *De l'hypocondrie et du suicide* was followed by a proliferation of works on suicide by French, German and Italian writers. Perhaps the most influential of these were those by Guerry (1833), Lisle (1856) and Legoyt (1881) in France, Quételet (1835, 1848) in Belgium, Wagner (1864) and Masaryk (1881) in Germany, and Morselli (1879) and Ferri (1883) in Italy.[59] There were many others. In terms of sheer bulk of material, suicide was probably one of the most discussed social issues of the nineteenth century.[60] By the time at which Durkheim wrote, a substantial number of empirical correlations had been established linking suicide rates with a range of social factors. Later writers confirmed Falret's contention that suicide rates tend to rise during periods of rapid social change and in times of economic depression;[61] and that rates vary positively with socio-economic position, being highest in professional and liberal occupations, and lowest among the chronically poor.[62] The fact that suicide rates are higher in urban localities than in rural areas was extensively documented.[63] Some writers claimed to have shown that suicide rates co-vary with crime rates, but are inversely related to rates of homicide.[64] Wagner was perhaps the first to identify clearly a direct relationship between rates of suicide and the religious denominations of Protestantism and Catholicism, but this was quickly substantiated by later investigation.[65] It was widely shown that suicide rates vary by sex, age and marital status; as well as by time of the year, day of the week, and hour of the day.[66]

Some writers gave prominence to racial and climatic factors in accounting for differential suicide rates. Most, however, questioned this type of explanation, and looked instead to social causes. Quételet placed great emphasis, as Durkheim later did, on the relative stability of suicide rates from year to year in comparison with other demographic data,[67] attempting to interpret differences between suicide rates in terms of variations in the 'moral density' of society. Many writers attributed the general rise in suicide rates to the dissolution of the traditional social order and the transition to industrial civilization, with its concomitants of increasing 'rationality' and individualism – an explanation close to that later elaborated by Durkheim.[68]

Most of the early-nineteenth-century investigations of suicide took for granted a close relationship between suicide and mental disorder. The notion that suicide derived from 'miserable insanity'[69] was clearly in part a survival of the belief that suicide is of diabolical inspiration, a view which, under the impress of the church, held sway until some way through the eighteenth century. The theory that suicide is always associated with some form of mental disorder was, however, given its most definitive formulation in Esquirol's classic *Maladies mentales* (1838).[70] 'Suicide', asserted Esquirol, 'shows all the characteristics of mental disorders of which it is in fact only a symptom.'[71] In this view, since suicide is always symptomatic of mental illness, it is to the causes of the latter that the student of suicide must turn in order to explain the phenomenon. The nature and distribution of mental disorder in any population determine the distribution of suicide in that population.

The question of how far, and in what ways, suicide is related to mental disorder became a major problem occupying writers on suicide during the latter half of the nineteenth century, and was discussed at some length by Durkheim.

The originality and vitality of Durkheim's work did not lie in the empirical correlations contained in *Suicide*: all of these had been previously documented by other writers. Durkheim took a great deal of material directly from the works of Legoyt, Morselli and Wagner, and used Öttingen's *Die Moralstatistik* extensively as a source of data.[72] Where Durkheim's work differed decisively was in the attempt to explain previous findings in terms of a coherent sociological theory. Previous writers had used a crude statistical methodology to show relationships between suicide rates and a variety of factors: Durkheim developed this technique in order to support a systematic sociological explanation of differential suicide rates. He was by no means the first to propose that suicide rates should be explained sociologically;[73] but no writer before Durkheim had presented a consistent framework of sociological theory which could bring together the major empirical correlations which had already been established.

The basic contention made by Durkheim in *Suicide* is that problems relating to the analysis of suicide rates can be separated in a clear-cut fashion from those relating to the psychology of the individual suicide. The suicide rate of a society or community 'is not simply a sum of independent units, a collective total, but is itself a new fact *sui generis*, with its own unity, individuality and consequently its own nature. . . .'[74] The factors governing the distribution of suicide are 'obviously quite distinct' from those determining which *particular* individuals in a group kill themselves.[75] Having rejected inherited insanity, psychological imitation, race and various 'cosmic' factors as possible determinants of the distribution of suicide, Durkheim located these determinants in aspects of social structure, distinguishing three main types of suicide: egoistic, anomic and altruistic. Strictly speaking, these are not types of suicide, but types of social structure producing high rates of suicide. Egoism refers to a low level of 'integration' in social structure; anomie to a dearth of regulative norms in society. Egoistic and anomic suicide are the predominant types in modern society.

Durkheim used the analysis of suicide explicitly as a platform for the vindication of his sociological method. He did not limit himself, moreover, to delineating a sociological analysis of suicide rates, but tended to argue as if the role of psychology in the explanation of suicide would be a subordinate one.[76] In a general way Durkheim's polemic was aimed against Tarde and other 'reductionist' schools of social thought.[77] More specifically, however, Durkheim's argument was also directed at Esquirol and other representatives of the view that suicide rates could be explained directly in terms of the distribution of mental disorder.

The publication of *Suicide* stimulated divergent reactions in France. Durkheim's immediate disciples were prepared to adopt the text as a model of sociological method. Others, particularly in the field of psychology, were equally ready to reject entirely the claims for sociology advanced in the book. Most psychologists and psychiatrists continued to be heavily influenced by the 'psychiatric thesis', stemming from the position established by Esquirol, in relation to suicide. This thesis entailed the following four propositions: 1) suicide is always the product of some psychopathological condition;[78] 2) the causes of suicide must thus be sought in the causes of the relevant types of mental disorder; 3) these causes are biological rather than social;[79] 4) sociology can therefore make little if any contribution to the analysis of suicide.

The foundations were thus laid for a controversy which, although part of a broader conflict between Durkheim's advocacy of sociology as an autonomous discipline and the resistance of its detractors, did not become fully developed until the period following the First World War, after the death of Durkheim himself.

The first major assault on Durkheim's position was launched in 1924 by de Fleury, a psychiatrist, in his *L'Angoisse humaine*.[80] Following broadly the theoretical standpoint established by Esquirol, and supporting his argument with case-history material, de Fleury reiterated that suicide is always derivative of mental disorder, the causes of which are biopsychological rather than social. Suicidal tendencies, he concluded, are found mainly in persons suffering from cyclical depressive disorder (cyclothymia). This type of affective disorder, stated de Fleury, depends upon inherited characteristics of temperament: the disposition to suicide is biologically 'built into' such individuals. The tendency to states of morbid depression, moreover, according to de Fleury, develops largely independently of the objective circumstances of the individual. It is of little consequence, therefore, whether the individual is integrated into a group or not. While fluctuations in suicide rates can possibly be linked in a very crude way to social or economic changes, their role in the aetiology of suicide is even then only a secondary one: such changes may only serve to partially 'cluster' the suicides of individuals who would in any case kill themselves at a later date. The state of morbid anxiety into which depressive individuals periodically lapse, wrote de Fleury, 'is, in the immense majority of cases, the only cause of suicide'.[81]

In 1930 Halbwachs published *Les Causes du suicide,* a work

intended to review, in the light of later statistics, the conclusions reached by Durkheim thirty years earlier.[82] Halbwachs claimed confirmation in detail of Durkheim's generalizations relating suicide rates to family structure[83] and religious denomination.[84] However, he emphasized that it is illegitimate to use, as Durkheim did, statistical relationships of this sort independently as if each had a separate significance. The influence of family life, for instance, cannot, argued Halbwachs, be detached from 'a much broader social milieu'.[85] The same is true of the religious factor. In France, for example, the more strongly Catholic groups tend to be also the most conservative and 'traditional', and have a strongly integrated family structure. It is not possible to separate the specifically religious practices from the broader community of which they are one part. According to Halbwachs, several of the factors which Durkheim isolated as producing a high suicide rate combine in the characteristics of modern urban life. Halbwachs provided an extensive comparative analysis of suicide rates in urban and rural areas indicating that, in general, rates are highest in large towns.[86] Reviewing Durkheim's propositions regarding suicide and social change through an examination of the relationship between fluctuations in the business index and suicide in Germany during the period 1880–1914, Halbwachs confirmed that suicide rates do tend to rise during economic crises. The increment in the rate does not, however, take place only at the lowest point of a trough, but is spread over the whole phase of the depression. Durkheim's thesis that rates of suicide rise during periods of marked economic prosperity was not substantiated: on the contrary, during such periods suicide rates tend to decline.[87]

Although his statistical analysis is generally supportive of Durkheim's, Halbwachs rejected the typology of egoism and anomie proposed by Durkheim.[88] In Halbwachs's own theory, suicide is attributed directly to the 'social isolation' of the suicidal individual. Suicide rates are high in social structures promoting the detachment of individuals from stable relationships with others – as is the case, according to Halbwachs, in urban communities.[89] Halbwachs discussed in some detail the psychiatric thesis advanced by de Fleury. According to Halbwachs, only a minority of suicides are associated with a recognizable form of mental disorder;[90] and these, he claimed, are not incompatible with his theory. 'Normal' suicides in Halbwachs's theory may become detached from relationships with others as a consequence of many factors, which include many of the 'motives' popularly offered for suicide – such as failure in business, unrequited love, chronic illness, etc. But 'pathological' suicides also derive from the social isolation of the suicidal individual: it is precisely those mental disorders producing 'a failure of adaptation between the individual and his *milieu*'[91] which culminate in suicide. In both 'normal' and 'pathological' suicides, Halbwachs concluded, the 'true' cause of the suicide is a social *lacuna* which surrounds the individual suicide. In reaching this conclusion, although questioning Durkheim's analysis in several respects, Halbwachs reaffirmed the validity of the sociological approach to suicide: suicide is primarily a social phenomenon.[92]

Those who were favourable to the psychiatric thesis found Halbwachs's arguments unconvincing. Courbon, for example, reviewing Halbwachs's book, accused the latter of an incompetent assessment of the relevance of psychopathology to suicide. Courbon repeated that suicide derives universally from pathological anxiety and depression and that these are 'through their purely biological nature' as completely independent of social factors as are colour of eyes or reaction time.[93] In his *Psychologie pathologique du suicide* (1932), Delmas summed up the views of the psychiatric school on the question of suicide, and made an explicit attempt to destroy the sociological standpoint of Durkheim and Halbwachs.[94] Social factors cannot possibly play a significant role in the aetiology of suicide, argued Delmas, since suicide takes place in such small proportion to any population. It sounds impressive to say that one country A has a suicide rate of 450 (per million) per year, while another country B has a rate of only 50. But invert these proportions, and we have a comparison of the following order: 999,550 (per million) per year *do not* commit suicide in country A, while 999,950 do not commit suicide in country B. The proportional difference between those who do not commit suicide is very small indeed. How could we say that there exist general social factors which 'protect' 999,950 in every million in country B, whereas only 999,550 are 'protected' in country A?[95]

Using the same psychiatric classification as de Fleury, Delmas repeated that the 'fundamental cause' of suicide[96] is pathological depression; and that the tendency to depressive states develops largely independently of the external situation of the individual. Endogenous changes, according to Delmas, produce with advancing age more profound and protracted states of melancholic anxiety: this, he claimed, rather than any changes in the social position of the ageing individual, is the major factor behind the common observation that suicide rates tend to rise with increasing age. The same can be said, he concluded, of other apparent direct causal relationships between suicide and social phenomena. If suicide rates are higher among unmarried than among married people, it is because depressives tend not to marry. It is the endogenous process of depression which is aetiologically crucial; the vast majority of suicides 'are exclusively the result of a biopsychological mechanism into which nothing social enters. . . .'[97]

In *Le Suicide* (1933) Blondel finally attempted to reconcile the *thèse psychiatrique* with the *thèse sociologique*.[98] According to Blondel, in 'normal' suicides the social situation of the suicidal individual is a crucial determinant; the depressive personality, however, is born with a constitutional tendency towards pathological depression, and this is the 'deep-lying cause' of his suicide. Although the role of social factors in the aetiology of cyclothymic suicides is less central than in 'normal' suicides, in both cases there is nevertheless an interaction between the social and the non-social.[99] This view was endorsed by several other writers.[100] Dombrowski, for example, in his *Les Conditions psychologiques du suicide* (1929) had stressed that the controversy could only be resolved by examining the interplay between psychological and social factors.[101] Psychopathological states, he suggested, produce in certain individuals a *Minderwertigkeit* which promotes a 'disharmony' in social relationships, thus leading to the social isolation of the individual emphasized by Halbwachs as the 'true' cause of suicide.[102]

Little further progress in the resolution of the controversy was made before the intervention of the Second World War, and since the war suicide has not received the same amount of attention as a test problem in French sociology.[103] This is partly due to a pronounced shift in the predominant character of French social thought generally. Until the period immediately preceding the Second World War, sociology in France remained firmly set in the theoretical cast moulded by Durkheim. Although some of Durkheim's most able followers were killed in the First World War, several of the prominent figures (such as Halbwachs) survived and dominated the sociological scene up to 1940.

In the late nineteen-thirties, however, particularly under the leadership of Gurvitch, theoretical sociology in France began to come increasingly under the influence of German phenomenology.[104] In his *Essais de sociologie* (1939) Gurvitch propounded a detailed series of criticisms of the fundamental tenets of Durkheim's sociology, attempting to expose certain of the major theoretical questions with which Durkheim had concerned himself as 'pseudo-problems' – problems falsely posed.[105] One such 'pseudo-problem' involves the debate over 'society' and 'the individual'. Both Durkheim and Tarde, Gurvitch emphasized, while engaging in a protracted polemic with each other, made a false opposition between society and the individual; there is, in fact, a constant 'reciprocity' between the 'individual' and the 'social'. In an article published in 1952, Bastide took up again the suicide controversy within the framework laid down by Gurvitch, arguing that the controversy hinged upon the same mistaken conception of the relationship between society and the individual.[106] The psychiatric thesis states that suicide is an 'individual' matter, since it depends mainly upon 'internal' biopsychological mechanisms, and that consequently the study of suicide is a psychological rather than a sociological matter. But this argument only has any weight if we accept the ontological realism of a dichotomy between society and the individual. To admit that psychology can properly contribute to the analysis of suicide does not mean that suicide, in certain aspects – particularly as a demographic phenomenon – cannot be studied sociologically; conversely, to accept that social factors play a role in the aetiology of suicide does not entail the exclusion of other factors as having causative force.[107]

The suicide controversy in French sociology is of interest not only because of the direct content of the argument. Tracing the origins of the dispute allows some insight into the historical 'depth' which an intellectual controversy may have: the issues involved in the debate were already set out, and not in a radically different guise, in the early nineteenth-century literature on suicide. Through the agency of Durkheim, however, the analysis of suicide became a critical issue in the struggle to establish sociology as a recognized academic discipline in France. This was, of course, largely due to Durkheim's own stage-management; as Lévi-Strauss remarks, 'the clash occurred on the ground Durkheim had himself chosen: the problem of suicide'.[108]

Durkheim's interest in suicide as a research problem was a direct development from his concerns in *The Division of*

Labour.[109] But two other factors lay behind his selection of suicide as a topic for a comprehensive investigation. First, the very volume of work which had already been carried out by previous writers apparently provided an abundant source of data which would be used to develop a systematic sociological analysis of suicide. Second, suicide appears to be wholly 'an individual action affecting the individual only. . .'[110] The demonstration of the relevance of Durkheim's sociological method to the analysis of an apparently purely 'individual' phenomenon had a particular significance in the context of the dispute with Tarde over the nature of social reality. *Suicide* supposedly represents a vindication of Durkheim's thesis that social facts can be studied as 'realities external to the individual'[111] as against Tarde's position that the subject-matter of sociology consists in 'the sum of consciousness in individuals'.[112] The character of the subsequent suicide controversy cannot be fully understood apart from the broader dispute between Durkheim and Tarde. As Gurvitch has shown, the Durkheim–Tarde debate depended in part upon a largely fruitless argument about the primacy of the 'social' over the 'individual'. The degree of interdisciplinary rivalry which became manifest in the suicide controversy was in substantial part the acceptance of the same misconceived ontological dichotomy.

The major substantive issue separating the *thèse sociologique* from the *thèse psychiatrique* concerns the 'pathological' nature of suicide. In one sense this question is easily resolved; since suicide is in all societies statistically a rare phenomenon, considered in terms of deviation from the majority, suicide is necessarily an 'abnormal' act. But the real problems are the extent to which suicide must be explained in terms of factors producing recognized forms of 'mental disorder' (itself now recognized as a problematic notion) and the relationship of *these* to social factors. There is no systematic evidence to support the contention that suicide is universally associated with identifiable forms of mental illness.[113] It is probable that most suicides are preceded by some form of depression: but only in a minority of cases is this part of a recurrent pathological depressive disorder.[114] Moreover, only a small proportion of individuals suffering from depressive disorder actually attempt or commit suicide.[115] Empirically, therefore, the *thèse psychiatrique* has not been borne out by later research.

The question of the relationship between suicide and mental disorder served, however, as a cloak for the real theoretical problem in the French suicide controversy: the relevance of sociology to the explanation of suicide. As has been indicated, the dispute depended at least partly upon a misconception shared by both sides and integral to the Durkheim–Tarde debate: that suicide is 'fundamentally' either a 'social' or an 'individual' phenomenon.[116] It would be facile, however, to dismiss the core of the dispute as a 'pseudo-problem'. The relationship between social and psychological factors in the aetiology of suicide is a focal problem in suicide theory, and one which bears directly upon the analysis of other phenomena which can be construed in terms of rates (e.g. homicide, crime and delinquency, or divorce).

It was Delmas's contention that, since suicide is statistically infrequent in relation to the total population of a society, social factors cannot play a significant role in its aetiology. The only necessary implication of this argument, in fact, is that sociology cannot furnish a *complete* explanation of suicide since only a small proportion of those in, for example, a loosely integrated community actually kill themselves. But to pose the question: why are suicide rates *so small*? does allow a clearer insight into the error of Durkheim's supposition that the explanation of incidence,[117] as a psychological problem, can be conceptually and methodologically separated from the sociological analysis of suicide rates. In Durkheim's conception, optimally integrated social structures 'protect' their component individuals against suicide; in loosely integrated structures, or in states of anomie, the members of the group are less 'protected'. In the former conditions, suicide rates will be low; in the latter, rates will correspondingly increase. The question of why individual A commits suicide – why A is a suicidal personality – while B, in an identical social situation, does not, is, according to Durkheim, a psychological matter, and not relevant to the explanation of rates: in an economic depression, for example, it will be A, rather than B, who commits suicide. However, to ask: why are rates so small?, which is clearly a central question in the aetiology of any rate, is to ask: why are most of the population 'B's rather than 'A's? Such a question, the answer to which depends upon an understanding of the factors producing suicidal propensities in the individual, is directly relevant to an explanatory assessment of suicide rates. The factors governing the distribution of suicide in a community cannot therefore be usefully considered in isolation from those determining why individual A commits suicide while individual B does not, i.e., apart from the study of suicidal personality. Durkheim's position is given a spurious plausibility by the assimilation of an ideographic question (why did this *particular* individual A commit suicide?) to the more important general psychological problem (why does a particular *type* of individual commit suicide?). The answer to the first question depends partly upon the investigation of strictly idiosyncratic factors in the particular suicide's life-history; the answer to the second question entails a generalized psychological theory of suicidal personality.

10 'Power' in the writings of Talcott Parsons

As the most eminent modern representative of functionalism, Talcott Parsons has been consistently attacked for his neglect of issues of conflict and power.[1] It is therefore of some interest that Parsons should have devoted a number of his more recent writings to a discussion of power and related phenomena, explicit reference to which is conspicuous by its relative absence in the bulk of his earlier works.[2]

Parsons's work on power involves a conscious modification of his previous views, where he accepted what he calls the 'traditional' view of power. This newer theory of power is an attempt to develop a set of concepts which will overcome what he sees as important defects in the 'traditional' notion. One of the first places where Parsons explicitly confronted these issues was in a review article of C. Wright Mills's *The Power Elite*, published in 1957. There Parsons proffered a variety of criticisms of Mills's book, but also took issue with the conception of power which he saw as underlying Mills's work. Mills's thesis, Parsons argued, gains weight from a 'misleading and one-sided' view of the nature of power, which Parsons labelled the 'zero-sum' concept of power. That is, power is conceived to be possessed by one person or group to the degree that it is not possessed by a second person or group over whom the power is wielded. Power is thus defined in terms of mutually exclusive objectives, so that a party is conceived to hold power in so far as it can realize its own wishes at the expense of those of others. In terms of game theory, from which the phrase 'zero-sum' is taken, to the degree that one party wins, the other necessarily loses. According to Parsons, this tends to produce a perspective from which all exercise of power appears as serving sectional interests.[3] Parsons then went on to suggest that power is more adequately conceived by analogy with a non-zero-sum game: in other words, as a relation from which both sides may gain.

Power, Parsons proposed, can be seen as being 'generated' by a social system, in much the same way as wealth is generated in the productive organization of an economy. It is true that wealth is a finite quantity, and to the degree that one party possesses a proportion of a given sum of money, a second party can only possess the remainder; but the actual amount of wealth produced varies with the structure and organization of different types of economy. In an industrial society, for example, there is typically more for all than in an agrarian one. Power similarly has these two aspects, and it is the collective aspect which is most crucial, according to Parsons, for sociological analysis. Parsons summed up his objections to Mills's views as follows:

> . . . to Mills, power is not a facility for the performance of function in, and on behalf of, the society as a system, but is interpreted exclusively as a facility for getting what one group, the holders of power, wants by preventing another group, the 'outs', from getting what it wants. What this conclusion does is to elevate a secondary and derived aspect of a total phenomenon into the central place.[4]

Much of the substance of Parsons's later writings on power consists of a reaffirmation of this position, and an elaboration of the analogy between power and money.[5] The parallels which Parsons develops between the two are based upon the supposition that each has a similar role in two of the four 'functional sub-systems' of society which Parsons has distinguished in previous works. Power has a parallel function in the polity (goal-attainment subsystem) to that of money in the economy (adaptive subsystem). The main function of money in the modern economy is as a 'circulating medium': that is, as a standardized medium of exchange in terms of which the value of products can be assessed and compared. Money itself has no intrinsic utility; it has 'value' only in so far as it is commonly recognized and accepted as a standard form of exchange. It is only in primitive monetary systems, when money is made of precious metal, that it comes close to being a good in its own right. In a developed economy, precious metal figures directly only in a very small proportion of exchange transactions. The sense in which the economy is 'founded' upon its holdings of gold is really a symbolic and an indirect one, and gold forms a 'reserve' to which resource is made only when the stability of the economy is for some reason threatened.

Power is conceived by Parsons as a 'circulating medium' in the same sense, 'generated' primarily within the political subsystem as money is generated in the economy, but also forming an 'output' into the three other functional subsystems of society. Power is defined, therefore, as 'generalized capacity to serve the performance of binding obligations by units in a system of collective organization when the obligations are legitimized with reference to their bearing on collective goals'.[6] By 'binding obligations' Parsons means the conditions to which those in power, and those over whom power is exercised, are subject through the legitimation which allows them that power; all power involves a certain 'mandate', which may be more or less extensive, which gives power-holders certain rights and imposes on them certain obligations towards those who are subject to their power. The collective goals rest upon the common value-system, which sets out the major objectives which govern the actions of the majority in a society. Thus American society is, according to Parsons, characterized by the primacy of values of 'instrumental activism', which entails that one main 'collective goal' of the society is the furtherance of economic productivity.

Just as money has 'value' because of common 'agreement' to use it as a standardized mode of exchange, so power becomes a facility for the achievement of collective goals through the 'agreement' of the members of a society to legitimize leadership positions – and to give those in such positions a mandate to develop policies and implement decisions in the furtherance of the goals of the system. Parsons emphasizes that this conception of power is at variance with the more usual 'zero-sum' notion which has dominated thinking in the field. In Parsons's view, the net 'amount' of power in a system can be expanded 'if those who are ruled are prepared to place a considerable amount of trust in their rulers'. This process is conceived as a parallel to credit creation in the economy. Individuals 'invest' their 'confidence' in those who rule them – through, say, voting in an election to put a certain government in power; in so far as those who have thus been put into power initiate new policies which effectively further 'collective goals', there is more than a zero-sum circular flow of power. Everybody gains from this process. Those who have 'invested' in the leaders have received back, in the form of the effective realization of collective goals, an increased return on their investment. It is only if those in power take no more than 'routine' administrative decisions that there is no net gain to the system.

Power is thus for Parsons directly derivative of authority: authority is the institutionalized legitimation which underlies power, and is defined as 'the institutionalization of the rights of "leaders" to expect support from the members of the collectivity'.[7] By speaking of 'binding obligations', Parsons deliberately brings legitimation into the very definition of power, so that, for him, there is no such thing as 'illegitimate power'. As Parsons expresses it:

. . . the threat of coercive measures, or of compulsion, without legitimation or justification, should not properly be called the use of power at all, but is the limiting case where power, losing its symbolic character, merges into an intrinsic instrumentality of securing compliance with wishes, rather than obligations.[8]

In line with his general approach, Parsons stresses that the use of power is only one among several different ways in which one party may secure the compliance of another to a desired course of action. The other ways of obtaining compliance should not be regarded, Parsons stresses, as forms of power; rather it is the case that the use of power (i.e., the activation of 'binding obligations') is one among several ways of ensuring that a party produces a desired response. Parsons distinguishes two main 'channels' through which one party may seek to command the actions of another, and two main 'modes' of such control, yielding a four-fold typology. Ego may try to control the 'situation' in which alter is placed, or try to control alter's 'intentions'; the 'modes' of control depend upon whether sanctions which may be applied are positive (i.e. offer something which alter may desire), or negative (i.e. hold out the threat of punishment):

1) Situational channel, positive sanction: the offering of positive advantages to alter if he follows ego's wishes (*inducement*, e.g. the offering of money).
2) Situational channel, negative sanction: the threat of imposition of disadvantages if alter does not comply (the use of *power*: in the extreme case, the use of force).
3) Intention channel, positive sanction: the offering of 'good reasons' why alter should comply (the use of *influence*).
4) Intention channel, negative sanction: the threat that it would be 'morally wrong' for alter not to comply (the appeal to *conscience* or other moral commitments).[9]

There is, Parsons points out, an 'asymmetry' between positive and negative sanctions. When compliance is secured through positive sanctions, because there is some definite reward, the sanctions are obvious. But, in the case of negative sanctions, compliance entails that the sanction is not put into effect; the operation of negative sanctions is generally symbolic rather than actual. In most cases where power is being used, there is no overt sanction employed (instances where force is used, for example, are relatively rare in the exercise of power). It is quite misleading, Parsons emphasizes, to speak of the use of power only when some form of negative sanction has actually been used: some writers who take the 'zero-sum' notion of power tend to do this, speaking of 'power' only when some form of coercion has been applied. As Parsons says:

[When things are 'running smoothly'] to speak of the holder of authority in these circumstances as not having or using power is, in our opinion, highly misleading. The question of his capacity to coerce or compel in case of non-compliance is an independent question that involves the question of handling unexpected or exceptional conditions for which the current power system may or may not be prepared.[10]

It is particularly necessary to stress, Parsons argues, that possession and use of power should not be identified directly with the use of force. In Parsons's view, force must be seen as only one means among several, in only one type among several, modes of obtaining compliance. Force tends to be used in stable political systems only as a last resort when other sanctions have proved ineffective. Again using the analogy between money and power, Parsons draws a parallel between centralization of state control over gold, and state monopoly over the instruments of organized force in 'advanced and stable' societies. In the economy, there sometimes occur deflations, in which loss of confidence in the value of money leads to increasing reliance upon gold reserves in order to maintain the stability of the economy. In a similar way, Parsons holds, 'power deflation' can occur when a progressive decrease of confidence in the agencies of political power develops. Such a 'loss of confidence' produces increasing reliance by such agencies upon force to preserve political integration. In both the economic and political case, the undermining of the confidence which is the foundation of money and of power produces a 'regression' towards a 'primitive' standard.[11]

In the subsequent discussion, my principal interest will be to comment on Parsons's analysis of power as such. I shall not attempt to assess in any detail the accuracy of the parallels which Parsons attempts to specify between the polity and economy as 'functional subsystems' of society. If Parsons's conceptual scheme, and the assumptions which underlie it, cannot satisfactorily handle problems of power, then many of these 'parallels' must in any case be declared either invalid or misleading.[12]

Parsons's critique of the 'zero-sum' concept of power does contain a number of valuable contributions and insights. There is no doubt that Parsons is correct in pointing out that the 'zero-sum' concept of power sometimes reinforces a simplistic view which identifies power almost wholly with the use of coercion and force. Such a perspective tends to follow from, although it is not at all logically implied by, the Weberian definition of power, which has probably been the most influential in sociology. In Weber's familiar definition, power is regarded as 'the chance of a man or of a number of men to realize their own will in a communal action even against the resistance of others who are participating in the action'.[13] Such a definition tends to lead to a conception of power relations as inevitably involving incompatible and conflicting interests, since what is stressed is the capacity of a party to realize its *own* (implicitly, sectional) aims, and the main criterion for gauging the 'amount' of power is the 'resistance' which can be overcome.

As Parsons correctly emphasizes, this can be extremely misleading, tending to produce an identification of power with the sanctions that are or can potentially be used by the power-holder. In fact, very often it is not those groups which have most frequent recourse to overt use of coercion who have most power; frequent use of coercive sanctions indicates an insecure basis of power. This is particularly true, as Parsons indicates, of the sanction of force. The power position of an individual group which has constant recourse to the use of force to secure compliance to its commands is usually weak and insecure. Far from being an index of the power held by a party, the amount of open force used rather is an indication of a shallow and unstable power base.

However, to regard the use of force in itself as a criterion of power is an error which only the more naive of social analysts would make. It is much more common to identify the power held by a party in a social relation with the coercive sanctions it is *capable* of employing against subordinates if called upon to do so – including primarily the capacity to use force. Again Parsons makes an important comment here, pointing out that a party may wield considerable power while at the same time having few coercive sanctions with which to enforce its commands if they are questioned by subordinates. This is possible if the power-holding party enjoys a broad 'mandate' to take authoritative decisions ceded or acquiesced in by those subject to the decisions – i.e., if those over whom the power is exercised 'agree' to subject themselves to that power. In such circumstances, the party in power depends, not on the possession of coercive sanctions with which it can override non-compliance, but sheerly upon the recognition by the subordinate party or parties of its legitimate right to take authoritative decisions. The latter in some sense acquiesce in their subordination. Thus when subordinates 'agree' to allow others to command their actions, and when at the same time those who receive this 'mandate' have few coercive sanctions to employ if their directives are not obeyed, then there exists a situation of power not based upon control of means to coerce. It is because of such a possibility that Parsons emphasizes that the question of 'how much' power a party holds, and the question of what sanctions it is able to bring into play in case of disobedience, are analytically separable. And it must be conceded that lack of capacity to command a defined range of sanctions does not necessarily entail a lack of power; the 'amount' of power held by a party cannot be assessed simply in terms of the effective sanctions it is able to enforce if faced with possible or actual non-compliance.[14] At the same time, it should be pointed out that the 'amount' of power wielded in any concrete set of circumstances, and the effective sanctions that can be used to counter non-compliance, are usually closely related. Studies of all types of social structures, from small groups up to total societies, show that power-holders usually do command or develop sanctions which reinforce their position: in any group which has a continued existence over time, those in power face problems of dissensus and the possibility of rebellion. The very fact of possession of a 'mandate' from those subordinated to a power relation allows the dominant party to use this 'good will' to mobilize sanctions (even if only the scorn, ridicule, etc., of the conforming majority) against a deviant or potentially deviant minority. If a power-holding party does not possess sanctions to use in cases of disobedience, it tends rapidly to acquire them, and can in fact use its power to do so.

What Parsons is concerned to point out, then, is that the use of power frequently represents a facility for the achievement of objectives which *both* sides in a power relation desire. In this sense, it is clear that the creation of a power system does not *necessarily* entail the coercive subordination of the wishes or interests of one party to those of another. Nor is the use of power inevitably correlated with 'oppression' or 'exploitation'. Quite clearly, in any type of group, the existence of defined 'leadership' positions does 'generate' power which may be used to achieve aims desired by the majority of the members of the group. This possibility is, of course, envisaged in classic Marxist theory, and in most varieties of socialist theory, in the form of 'collective' direction of the instruments of government.

As Parsons recognizes, this kind of power is necessarily legitimate, and so he makes legitimacy part of his very definition of power. Parsons thus rejects the frequently-held conception that authority is a 'form' of power, or is 'legitimate power'. This is again a useful emphasis. To regard authority as a 'type' of power leads to a neglect of its principal characteristic: namely that it concerns the *right* of a party to make binding prescriptions. Authority refers to the legitimate position of an individual or group, and is therefore properly regarded as a *basis* of power (for Parsons, the only basis of power), rather than as a kind of power. It is precisely the confusion of the forms with the bases of power which causes Parsons to specify a very restricted definition of power. Authority is no more a form of power than force is a form of power.

A further valuable aspect of Parsons's analysis is the introduction of a typology of compliant behaviour. It is still quite common for social analysts naively to assert or to assume that conformity to any specific course of social action is founded *either* on 'internalization' of appropriate moral values *or* upon some form of coercion. This tendency is strong in the works both of those who follow Parsons and those who are highly critical. The isolation of various modes of securing compliance does allow for other mechanisms of conformity. The importance of the typology is diminished by the lack of any attempt to specify how these different ways of securing compliance are related together in social systems. Nevertheless, within the general context of Parsonian theory, this typology has some significance, marking a more definite recognition of the role of non-normative factors in social action.[15]

But there are other respects in which Parsons's discussion of power shares some of the basic difficulties and deficiencies of his general theory, and is at least as one-sided as the conception which he wishes to replace. Parsons is above all concerned to emphasize that power does not necessarily entail the coercive imposition of one individual or group over another, and he does indeed point to some valuable correctives for the mainstream of sociological thinking on problems of power. But what slips away from sight almost completely in the Parsonian analysis is the very fact that power, even as Parsons defines it, is always exercised *over* someone! By treating power as necessarily (by definition) legitimate, and thus *starting* from the assumption of consensus of some kind between power-holders and those subordinate to them, Parsons virtually ignores, quite consciously and deliberately, the necessarily hierarchical character of power, and the divisions of interest which are frequently consequent upon it. However much it is true that power can rest upon 'agreement' to cede authority which can be used for collective aims, it is also true that interests of power-holders and those subject to that power often clash. It is undoubtedly the case that some 'zero-sum' theorists tend to argue as if power differentials *inevitably* entail conflicts of interest, and produce overt conflicts – and fail to give sufficient attention to specifying the conditions under which no conflict of either type is present. But it is surely beyond dispute that positions of power offer to their incumbents definite material and psychological rewards, and thereby stimulate conflicts between those who want power and those who have it. This brings into play, of course, a multiplicity of possible strategies of coercion, deceit and manipulation which can be used to either acquire, or hold on to, power. If the use of power rests upon 'trust' or 'confidence', as Parsons emphasizes, it also frequently rests upon deceit and hypocrisy.[16] Indeed this is true of all social life; all stable social action, except perhaps for all-out total war, depends upon some kind of at least provisional 'trust' – but this very fact makes possible many sorts of violations and rejections of 'confidence'. *L'enfer c'est les autres.* 'Deceit' and 'mistrust' only have meaning in relation to 'trust' and 'confidence': the former are as ubiquitous a part of social life as the latter are, and will continue to be as long as men have desires or values which are exclusive of each other, and as long as there exist 'scarce resources' of whatever kind. Any sociological theory which treats such phenomena as 'incidental', or as 'secondary and derived', and not as structurally intrinsic to power differentials, is blatantly inadequate. To have power is to have potential access to valued scarce resources, and thus power *itself* becomes a scarce resource. Though the relationships between power and exploitation are not simple and direct, their existence can hardly be denied.

Parsons escapes dealing with such problems largely through a trick of definition, by considering only as 'power' the use of authoritative decisions to further 'collective goals'. Two obvious facts, that authoritative decisions very often do serve sectional interests and that the most radical conflicts in society stem from struggles for power, are defined out of consideration – at least as phenomena connected with 'power'. The conceptualization of power which Parsons offers allows him to shift the entire weight of his analysis away from power as expressing a relation *between* individuals or groups, towards seeing power solely as a 'system property'. That collective 'goals', or even the values which lie behind them, may be the outcome of a 'negotiated order' built on conflicts between parties holding differential power is ignored, since for Parsons 'power' assumes the prior existence of collective goals. The implications of this are clearly demonstrated in Parsons's short book, *Societies*, in which he tries to apply some of these ideas to social change in actual historical settings. Social change in its most general aspect, Parsons makes clear, is fundamentally cultural evolution – i.e., change in values, norms and idea-systems. And the basic *sources* of change are to be traced to changes in cultural values, and norms *themselves*, not to any sort of 'lower-level' factors, which at the most exert a 'conditioning' effect on social change. In spite of various qualifications and assertions to the contrary, Parsons's theory, as he applies it here, comes down to little more than a kind of idealist orthodoxy. History is moved, societies change, under the guiding direction of cultural values, which somehow change, independently of other elements in the structure of social systems, and exert a 'cybernetic control' over them. This is hardly consonant with Parsons's conclusion that 'once the problem of causal imputation is formulated analytically, the old chicken and egg problems about the priorities of ideal and material factors simply lose significance'.[17] There is a great deal of difference between the sort of interpretation of social and historical change which Parsons presents in *Societies*, and one which follows a Marxist standpoint. Parsons's account is based very largely upon an examination of value-systems, and changes in them, and displays practically no concern with non-normative factors as causative agencies in their formation, maintenance and diffusion. As in Parsons's more general theoretical expositions, such factors are formally recognized as of some importance, but no systematic discussion of the interplay between them and values is presented. As a consequence, Parsons tends to argue as if to show that some kind of logical relationship or 'fit' between a specific value, norm, or pattern of behaviour, and some more general value or set of values, constitutes an 'explanation' of the former. This is characteristic also of Parsons's theoretical analysis of power and social change. Thus, for example, at one point in his discussion of political power, he traces 'political democracy' – i.e., universal franchise – to 'the principle of equality before the law', which is a 'subordinate principle of universalistic normative organization', as if this were to explain why or how universal franchise came into being.

In Parsons's conceptualization of power there is one notion which has an explicitly dynamic reference: that of 'power deflation'. This does at least make a conceptual *niche* in the Parsonian system for the possibility of social revolution.[18] It is characteristic, however, that this concept depends upon the prior assumption of consensual 'confidence' in the power system. Power deflation refers to a spiralling diminution of 'confidence' in the agencies of power, so that those subordinate to them come increasingly to question their position. Parsons does not suggest any answers to why power deflations occur, except to indicate that once they get under way they resemble the 'vicious circle' of declining support characteristic of economic crisis. Now the parallel with economic deflation, in the terms in which Parsons discusses it, shows clearly that he conceives the process as basically a psychological one, which is a kind of generalization of the picture of deviance presented in *The Social System*. Power deflation is deviance writ large and in so far as it is focused on legitimate authority.[19] Thus the possibility of explaining power deflation in terms of the mutual interaction of interest-groups is excluded. The opportunity for theoretically tying such factors to the mechanics of power deflation, via the typology of means of obtaining compliance, is left aside. The parallels which Parsons is determined to pursue between the polity and the economy serve, in fact, to separate political and economic processes from one another. That economic and other 'material' factors themselves play a key part in power deflation is ignored because Parsons is above all concerned to show how the polity and economy are 'analytically' similar, not how they intertwine. Parsons's many discussions of the relationships between sociology and economics, including his and Smelser's *Economy and Society*, are all stated in terms of highly formal typological categories, and rarely suggest any substantive generalizations linking the two. Parsons's method is well illustrated by the entirely abstract character of his typology of modes of securing compliance. A distinction is made between 'inducement' and 'power'. The rationale for the distinction is that these can be considered parallel 'media' in the subsystems of the economy and the polity. Now such a typological distinction might be useful, but the important sociological problem is to apply it. How do inducement and power operate as systematic properties of societies or other social structures? Obviously inducement is often a *basis* of power; and the reverse also may frequently be true – a person or group holding power is often in a position allowing access to various forms of inducement, including the offer of financial reward. The relationship between 'positive' and 'negative' sanctions may be quite complicated as they actually operate in social systems. Thus inducements, offering some definite rewards in exchange for compliance, always offer the possibility of being transformed into negative sanctions; the *withholding* of a reward represents a punishment, and represents a definite form of coercion. But Parsons makes no attempt to draw out such possibilities and apply them to the analysis of power deflation, and in view of this, the process of power deflation is conceived purely as one of psychological 'loss of confidence' in the existing system.

Perhaps it is significant that Parsons makes very little mention of what factors produce 'power inflation' – i.e., the process whereby 'confidence' in a power system is *developed and expanded* in societies. It is just in this area that some of the most crucial problems in the study of power lie, and where conflict and coercion may play a major part. In Parsons's treatment of power, coercion and force are pictured as along the end of the line of a progression of corrective sanctions which can be applied to counter any tendency towards power deflation. Force is the sanction which is applied when all else has failed. It is only when the system shows a lack of 'confidence' that open use of power becomes frequent. Thus, Parsons argues, stable power systems are only based indirectly, or 'symbolically', on the use of force. But in power 'inflation', coercion and force may be the foundation of a consensual order in quite a different way. The history of societies shows again and again that particular social forms are often at first implemented by force, or by some other form of definite coercion, and coercive measures are used to *produce* and reinforce a new legitimacy. It is in this sense that power can grow out of the barrel of a gun. Force allows the manipulative control which can then be used to diminish depen-dence upon coercion. While this has been in previous ages probably only in part the result of conscious manipulation, in recent times, through the controlled diffusion of propaganda it can become a much more deliberate process. But whether deliberate or not, it is not only the fact that stable power systems rest upon stable legitimation of authority which is the key to the analysis of power but, as the 'zero-sum' theorists have always recognized, just how legitimation is *achieved*. Through defining power as the activation of legitimate obligations, Parsons avoids dealing with the processes whereby legitimacy, and thereby authority and power, are established and maintained. Consensus is assumed, and power conceived to be derivative of it; the determinants of the consensual basis of power are regarded as non-problematic.

This means also that Parsons tends to accept the operations of authority at their face-value, as if all 'obligations' of importance were open, public, and legitimate. But it is an accepted fact of political life that those who occupy formal authority positions are sometimes puppets who have their strings pulled from behind the scenes. It is in the hidden processes of control that some of the crucial operations of power in modern societies are located. By defining power as 'the activation of *legitimate* obligations' Parsons would seem to have to classify those processes as not involving 'power'. But the puppeteers behind the scenes may be the people who hold real control, and it is not a helpful concept of power which does not allow us to explore the often compli-cated relations which pertain between the 'unrecognized' or illegitimate, and the legitimate, in systems of power.

This may not necessarily stem from Parsons's definition of

power *per se*, since it could be held that those who are *in fact* 'activating legitimate obligations' are those who are using the individuals in formal authority positions as a front – that it is the men behind the scenes who really control those 'legitimate obligations', and thus who really hold 'power'. But, at any rate, Parsons's own analysis shows an ingenuous tendency to see nothing beyond the processes which are overt. Parsons's account of how political support is derived, for example, is given in terms of a *prima facie* comparison between government and banking:

. . . political support should be conceived of as a generalized grant of power which, if it leads to electional success, puts elected leadership in a position analogous to a banker. The 'deposits' of power made by constituents are revocable, if not at will, at the next election . . .

Thus those in positions of political power have the legitimized right to 'use' the power 'granted' to them by the electorate in the same way as a banker can invest money deposited with him. Parsons is presumably only arguing that these two processes are 'analytically' parallel, and would no doubt recognize the many substantive differences between them. But nevertheless his anxiety to develop formal similarities between the polity and economy, and correspondingly between money and power, seems to have blinded him to the realities of political manipulation.

It is apparent that Parsons's treatment of power, while marking in a few respects a greater formal recognition of the role of 'interests' in social action,[21] in the main represents a strong retrenchment of his general theoretical position as set out in *The Social System*. Power now becomes simply an extension of consensus, the means which a society uses to attain its 'goals'. But this is surely inadequate. We must assert that power extends as deeply into the roots of social life as do values or norms; if all social relationships involve normative elements, so also do all social relationships contain power differentials.

Remarks on the theory of power

In the 'normative functionalism' of Durkheim and Parsons, the concept of interest tends to be conceived of only in relation to a traditional dichotomy of the individual and society, rather than as concerning divisions between groups within the social totality. Thus this type of social theory finds difficulty in allowing a conceptual space for the analysis of power as the instrument of sectional group interests. Power is conceived as the 'power of society' confronting the individual. While this type of theory, as is shown in Durkheim's political writings, can yield an account of the domination of the state over civil society, it cannot conceive of society itself as a system of power founded in entrenched divergencies of interest. However, the notions that power is not adequately treated as being a fixed quantum, and that it has no necessary tie with the existence of conflict, are important. But neither is dependent upon the sort of formulation of the concept that Parsons gives. The 'expandable' character of power actually has no logical connection with its conceptualization as directed to the achievement of 'goals' of the collectivity. It is possible, and indeed necessary, to sustain the substance of Parsons's critique of the zero-sum conception of power without following the same route that he does in developing a reconstruction of the notion.

In the theory of structuration, power is recognized as an integral element in the reproduction of systems of interaction; but it can also be shown, in an even more basic way, that power is a logical component of the idea of 'action' itself. I wish to claim that we can distinguish a broad and narrow sense of the term power, and that these parallel the differentiation between 'action' and 'interaction', where the latter refers to mutually oriented forms of conduct between two or a plurality of actors. Action or agency implies the intervention (or refraining) of an individual in a course of events in the world, of which it would be true to say that 'he could have done otherwise'. Defined in this way, action involves the application of 'means' to secure outcomes, these outcomes constituting the intervention in the on-going course of events. Let us now define power as the use of resources, of whatever kind, to secure outcomes. Power then becomes an element of action, and refers to the *range* of interventions of which an agent is capable. Power in this broad sense is equivalent to the *transformative capacity* of human action: the capability of human beings to intervene in a series of events so as to alter their course. In this sense, power is closely bound up with the notion of *Praxis,* as relating to the historically shaped, and historically mutable, conditions of social and material existence.

The production and reproduction of interaction of course involves power as transformative capacity: but in interaction we can distinguish a narrower, 'relational' sense of power, since action taken with intentions of securing particular outcomes then involves the responses, or the potential behaviour, of others (including their resistance to a course of action that one party wants to bring about). Power here is domination, but it would be quite mistaken to suppose, as zero-sum theories of power suppose, that even in this narrower sense the existence of power logically implies the existence of conflict, whether that latter term is taken to mean opposition of interest or actual struggle of some sort between two or more combatants. It is precisely the concept of interest that is most immediately linked to those of conflict and solidarity. The use of power is frequently accompanied by struggle; this is not because of a logical relation between the two, but because of a lack of coincidence of actors' interests in circumstances of the application of power. (In saying this, I do not want to propose the view that people are always aware of what their interests are, although the identification of interests on the part of the theorist always involves the imputation of wants to those persons. Nor do I want to claim either that division of interest always leads to open conflict, or conversely that the existence of such conflict *ipso facto* presupposes division of interest.) The concept of interest has to be understood as a metatheoretical one. That is to say, it has to be freed from any association with human needs in a state of nature, or for that matter with any unique connection to class divisions in society. The first leads to a situation in which interest is conceived solely in reference to the interests of the 'individual' as opposed to those of 'society' (or the state). The second, on the other hand, as expressed in certain readings of Marx, carries the implication that, with the transcendence of classes, divisions of interest in society thereby disappear. While we must recognize that particular interest oppositions may always be transcended by social transformation, this is altogether distinct from the presumption that divisions of interest in a society may be superseded altogether.

The same point applies to domination. Specific forms of domination, as historically located systems of power, are in every instance open to potential transformation. Since power, according to the theory of structuration, is held to be intrinsic to all interaction, there can be no question of transcending it in any empirical society. It would be possible to develop a model of emancipation based upon the achievement of equality of power in interaction. But taken alone, this would be quite inadequate. For it does not come to terms with the significance of power, in the guise of transformative capacity, as the medium of the realization of collective human interests. From this aspect, freedom from domination in systems of interaction appears as a problem of the achievement of rationally defensible forms of authority.

References

Some US editions, where available, are indicated in square brackets: [   ].
The pagination of US and UK editions may differ.

Introduction: some issues in the social sciences today

1. See 'Positivism and its critics', pp. 29–89.
2. E. Husserl, *The Crisis of European Sciences and Transcendental Phenomenology*, Evanston, 1970; cf. also K.-O. Apel, *Transformation der Philosophie*, Frankfurt, 1971, 2 vols.
3. *New Rules of Sociological Method*, London [New York], 1976, pp. 148 ff.
4. For a slightly different formulation, cf. 'Functionalism: *après la lutte*', pp. 128–9.
5. Thomas Kuhn, *The Structure of Scientific Revolutions*, Chicago, 1970.
6. 'Functionalism: *après la lutte*', pp. 96–129.
7. In German, these terms normally appear in noun form, with the first letter capitalized. I have, however, followed the practice of printing '*verstehen*' with a small '*v*', not just because this particular word has by now become semi-Anglicized, but because this helps to emphasize the processual character of 'understanding'.
8. cf. 'Habermas's critique of hermeneutics', pp. 135–64.

9. 'Positivism and its critics', pp. 29–89; 'Functionalism: *après la lutte*', pp. 96–129; 'Notes on the theory of structuration', pp. 129–34; 'Hermeneutics, ethnomethodology, and problems of interpretative analysis', pp. 165–78.

10. I offer a more detailed exposition of social reproduction in 'Notes on the theory of structuration', pp. 129–34; cf. also 'Remarks on the theory of power', pp. 347–9.

11. This point is made in Göran Therborn, *Science, Class and Society*, London, 1976, p. 164.

12. *The Class Structure of the Advanced Societies*, London, 1973.

13. cf. 'The "individual" in the writings of Emile Durkheim', pp. 273–91.

14. Emile Durkheim, *The Division of Labour in Society*, London, 1964 [Glencoe, 1947]; 'Durkheim's political sociology', pp. 235–72.

15. Talcott Parsons, 'Equality and inequality in modern society, or social stratification revisited', *Sociological Inquiry*, vol. 40, 1970.

16. cf. my *Politics and Sociology in the Thought of Max Weber*, London, 1972; and 'Marx, Weber and the development of capitalism', pp. 183–203.

17. 'Marx and Weber: problems of class structure', pp. 203–7.

18. Wolfgang Mommsen, *Max Weber und die deutsche Politik, 1890–1920*, Tübingen, 1959; cf. also ' "Power" in the writings of Talcott Parsons', pp. 333–46.

19. Parsons, *The Structure of Social Action*, Glencoe, 1949, pp. 6 ff.

20. cf. 'Four myths in the history of social thought', pp. 208–34.

21. Harry Elmer Barnes, *An Introduction to the History of Sociology*, Chicago, 1948 (later, abridged edition 1967) contains forty-seven essays on 'the period from Comte to Sorokin', but has no essay on Marx. From 1948 to 1967 six editions of the book were published, and according to the editor 'the book has served as a standard reference in the field' (p. vii, 1967 edition).

22. cf. 'Four myths in the history of social thought,' pp. 208–34.

23. See, for example, Martin Shaw, *Marxism versus Sociology*, London, 1974; cf. T. B. Bottomore, *Marxist Sociology*, London, 1976.

24. Louis Althusser, *For Marx*, London, 1969 [New York, 1970], pp. 32 ff. and *passim*; also, however, *idem, Eléments*

d'auto-critique, Paris, 1974; Parsons, op. cit., pp. 6 ff.

25. cf. Weber's comments on 'revolutionary experiments' in a letter to Lukács, quoted in Mommsen, op. cit., p. 303.

26. cf. my *Politics and Sociology in the Thought of Max Weber.*

27. Georg Lukács's *Die Zerstörung der Vernunft,* Berlin, 1955, tries to set this in the context of a general relapse of German social philosophy into irrationalism.

28. cf. 'Durkheim's political sociology', pp. 235-72.

29. *Capitalism and Modern Social Theory,* Cambridge (UK) [New York], 1971, pp. 199 ff.

30. Therborn's *Science, Class and Society* is a much more sober and accurate work in this respect than many others, claiming Marxism to be a science, but not overplaying its dominance in late nineteenth-century social thought.

31. See, e.g., the famous 'Afterword to the second German edition' of *Capital,* vol. I, London, 1970.

32. *The New Science of Giambattista Vico,* Ithaca, 1968.

33. Jürgen Habermas, *Knowledge and Human Interests* [Boston, 1971], London, 1972, pp. 71 ff. and *passim.*

34. F. Gibson Winter, *Elements for a Social Ethic,* New York, 1966; cf. also Zygmunt Bauman, *Toward a Critical Sociology,* London, 1976.

35. cf. 'Positivism and its critics', pp. 29-89.

36. cf. 'Habermas's critique of hermeneutics,' pp. 135-64.

37. cf. 'Max Weber on facts and values', pp. 89-95.

1 Positivism and its critics

1. The influence of Saint-Simon over Marx is a matter of some controversy in itself. For a systematic treatment, see Georges Gurvitch, 'La sociologie du jeune Marx', in *La Vocation actuelle de la sociologie,* Paris, 1950.

M

354   *Notes to pages 32–43*

2. Herbert Marcuse, *Reason and Revolution*, London, 1955 [Boston, 1960], p. 341.

3. *Cours de philosophie positive*, vol. 1. (*Philosophie première*), Paris, 1975, pp. 21 ff.

4. ibid., p. 21.

5. ibid., pp. 28-9.

6. ibid., vol. 2 (*Physique sociale*), p. 139.

7. ibid., pp. 139–40.

8. cf. John Stuart Mill, *Auguste Comte and Positivism*, Ann Arbor, 1961, pp. 125 ff.

9. *Cours de philosophie positive*, vol. 1, pp. 44 ff.

10. See Herbert Spencer, *Reasons for Dissenting from the Philosophy of M. Comte*, Berkeley, 1968; Mill comments on this, op. cit., pp. 5 ff.

11. cf. Kurt H. Wolff, *Emile Durkheim* et al., *Essays on Sociology and Philosophy*, New York, 1964.

12. Durkheim and Fauconnet, 'Sociologie et sciences sociales', *Revue philosophique*, vol. 55, 1903.

13. Mill, op. cit., p. 59.

14. Durkheim, *The Elementary Forms of the Religious Life*, New York, 1965, pp. 170 ff; (with M. Mauss) *Primitive Classification*, London [Chicago], 1963.

15. Durkheim, *The Rules of Sociological Method* [Glencoe, 1950], London, 1964, p. 14.

16. ibid., pp. 48 ff.

17. For a full-scale biography of Mach, see John T. Blackmore, *Ernst Mach, his Work, Life and Influence*, Berkeley, 1972.

18. cf. Jürgen Habermas, *Knowledge and Human Interests* [Boston, 1971], London, 1972, pp. 74 ff.

19. *Cours de philosphie positive*, vol. 2, pp. 16 ff.

20. Ernst Mach, *The Analysis of Sensations*, Chicago, 1914, pp. 37 ff.

21. Mach, *Erkenntnis und Irrtum*, Leipzig, 1917, p. vii.

22. *The Analysis of Sensations*, op. cit., p. 369.

23. cf., *inter alia*, Victor Kraft, *The Vienna Circle*, New York, 1953. Mach's theories also attracted the attention of prominent literary figures. Hofmannsthal, the poet, attended Mach's lectures, believing that if the world consists only of our sensations, it can be described more directly and thoroughly in poetry than in science. Robert Musil began his career as a philosopher, actually writing a doctoral thesis on Mach, before turning to the novel form.

24. A. J. Ayer *et al.*, *The Revolution in Philosophy*, London, 1956.

25. Rudolf Carnap, 'Intellectual autobiography', in Paul Arthur Schilpp, *The Philosophy of Rudolf Carnap*, La Salle, 1963, pp. 12 ff.

26. Stephen E. Toulmin, 'From logical analysis to conceptual history', in Peter Achinstein and Stephen F. Barker, *The Legacy of Logical Positivism*, Baltimore, 1969, pp. 31 ff. Carnap later wrote on this point, 'when we were reading Wittgenstein's book in the Circle, I had erroneously believed that his attitude towards metaphysics was similar to ours. I had not paid sufficient attention to the statements in his book about the mystical, because his feelings and thoughts in this area were too divergent from mine' (op. cit., p. 27).

27. Herbert Feigl, 'The origin and spirit of logical positivism', in Achinstein and Barker, op. cit., p. 5.

28. cf. Carnap's Preface to the second edition of *The Logical Structure of the World*, London [Los Angeles], 1967.

29. A. J. Ayer, 'Editor's introduction', in *Logical Positivism*, Glencoe, 1959, p. 8.

30. Carnap, *The Logical Structure of the World*.

31. Carnap, 'Intellectual autobiography', op. cit., p. 52.

32. Carnap, 'Psychology in physical language', in Ayer, *Logical Positivism*, p. 197.

33. cf. Richard von Mises, *Positivism, a Study in Human Understanding*, Cambridge (Mass.), 1951, pp. 80 ff.

34. Richard Bevan Braithwaite, *Scientific Explanation*, Cambridge (UK) [New York], 1968, p. 51.

35. cf. Carnap, 'The methodological character of theoretical concepts', in Herbert Feigl and Michael Scriven, *The Foundations of Science and the Concepts of Psychoanalysis*, Minneapolis, 1956.

36. Herbert Feigl, 'The "orthodox" view of theories: some remarks in defence as well as critique', in M. Radner and S. Winokur, *Minnesota Studies in the Philosophy of Science*, vol. 4, Minneapolis, 1970.

37. Carl G. Hempel and P. Oppenheim, 'Studies in the logic of explanation', *Philosophy of Science*, vol. 15, 1948.

38. Hempel, 'Deductive-nomological vs. statistical explanation', in Herbert Feigl and Grover Maxwell, *Scientific Explanation, Space, and Time*, Minneapolis, 1962.

39. Hempel, 'The function of general laws in history', in

356   *Notes to pages 51–62*

Aspects of Scientific Explanation, New York, 1965, pp. 240–1.

40. Carnap, 'Intellectual autobiography', op. cit., p. 24.

41. Otto Neurath, 'Sociology and Physicalism', in Ayer, *Logical Positivism*, p. 283; see also Neurath, *Foundations of the Social Sciences, International Encyclopaedia of Unified Science*, vol. 2, Chicago, 1944.

42. Neurath, 'Sociology and Physicalism', op. cit., p. 299.

43. Paul F. Lazarsfeld and Morris Rosenberg, 'General introduction', in *The Language of Social Research*, New York, 1955, pp. 2 ff.

44. Ernest Nagel, *The Structure of Science*, London [New York], 1961, p. x.

45. ibid., p. 484.

46. ibid., pp. 468–9.

47. Hans L. Zetterberg, *On Theory and Verification in Sociology*, Totawa, 1966.

48. ibid., pp. 46 ff. Compare Hubert M. Blalock Jr., *Theory Construction*, New Jersey, 1969, pp. 2 ff. and 10 ff.

49. ibid., pp. 81 and 85.

50. ibid., pp. 102–3.

51. Hempel, 'The logic of functional analysis', in Hempel, op. cit.

52. ibid., p. 317.

53. ibid., p. 325.

54. cf. Popper's autobiographical article in Paul Arthur Schilpp, *The Philosophy of Karl Popper*, La Salle, 1974.

55. See, e.g., Popper, 'Science: conjectures and refutations', in *Conjectures and Refutations* [New York, 1968], London, 1972, pp. 34–7.

56. ibid., p. 37.

57. *The Logic of Scientific Discovery*, London [New York], 1972, pp. 41 ff.

58. See, e.g., 'Two faces of common sense', in *Objective Knowledge*, Oxford, 1973, pp. 57 ff. For a critical discussion of Popper's use of Tarski's theory of truth, see Susan Haack, ' "Is it true what they say about Tarski?" ', *Philosophy*, vol. 51, 1976. On 'verisimilitude', see David Miller, 'Popper's qualitative theory of verisimilitude', *British Journal for the Philosophy of Science*, vol. 25, 1974.

59. Thomas S. Kuhn, *The Structure of Scientific Revolutions*, Chicago, 1970, p. 1.

60. ibid., p. 126.

61. cf. Kuhn, 'Reflections on my critics', in Imre Lakatos and Alan Musgrave, *Criticism and the Growth of Knowledge*, Cambridge (UK) [New York], 1970, p. 248.

62. cf. Kuhn, 'Second thoughts on paradigms', in Frederick Suppe, *The Structure of Scientific Theories*, Urbana, 1974. For Popper's most recent reflections on similar issues, see Popper, 'The rationality of scientific revolutions', in Rom Harré, *Problems of Scientific Revolution*, Oxford [New York], 1975.

63. Max Weber, *The Methodology of the Social Sciences*, Glencoe, 1949, pp. 13 ff.

64. cf. my *Politics and Sociology in the Thought of Max Weber*, London, 1972.

65. Marcuse, op. cit., pp. 6 ff.

66. Max Horkheimer, *Eclipse of Reason*, New York, 1974, p. 5.

67. Horkheimer, 'Der neueste Angriff auf die Metaphysik', *Zeitschrift für Sozialforschung*, vol. 6, 1937.

68. Jürgen Habermas, *Knowledge and Human Interests* [Boston, 1971], London, 1972, pp. 43 ff.

69. Max Horkheimer and Theodor W. Adorno, *Dialectic of Enlightenment*, New York, 1972.

70. Adorno, *et al.*, *The Positivist Dispute in German Sociology*, London, 1976 (first published in German in 1969). A new controversy has now appeared, crossing some of the lines of the first, in which followers of Popper have moved to the offensive in launching an attack on the 'politicization of science'. (For a discussion, see Ralf Dahrendorf, 'Die Unabhängigkeit der Wissenschaft', *Die Zeit*, 21 May 1976; and reply by Lobkowicz in the same issue.)

71. Popper, 'The logic of the social sciences', *The Positivist Dispute . . .*' p. 102.

72. Habermas, 'Analytical theory of science and dialectics', ibid., p. 142.

73. William W. Bartley, *The Retreat to Commitment*, London, 1964.

74. cf. Habermas, *Knowledge and Human Interests*, pp. 301 ff.

75. Hans Albert, 'Behind positivism's back?', in Adorno, *et al.*, op. cit., pp. 246 ff. cf. also Albert, *Traktat über kritische Vernunft*, Tübingen, 1968.

76. Popper, 'Reason or revolution?', in Adorno *et al.*, op. cit., p. 299.

77. Lakatos, 'Falsification and the methodology of scientific research programmes', in Lakatos and Musgrave, op. cit., pp. 106 ff; cf. Lakatos, 'Changes in the problem of inductive logic', in *The Problem of Inductive Logic*, Amsterdam, 1968.

78. Kuhn, 'Reflections on my critics', op. cit., pp. 256 ff.

79. Lakatos, op. cit., p. 121. cf. also footnote 4, p. 122 and p. 137, where 'verification' is reintroduced, albeit reluctantly.

80. Mary Hesse, 'Positivism and the logic of scientific theories', in Achinstein and Barker, op. cit., p. 96.

81. Dudley Shapere, 'Notes toward a post-positivistic interpretation of science', ibid.

82. ibid., p. 127.

83. See, *inter alia*, W. O. Quine, *From a Logical Point of View*, Cambridge (Mass.), 1953; *Word and Object*, Cambridge (Mass.), 1960; *Ontological Relativity and Other Essays*, New York, 1969; Hesse, *The Structure of Scientific Inference*, London [Los Angeles], 1974.

84. cf. Pierre Duhem, *The Aim and Structure of Physical Theory*, Princeton, 1954; *To Save the Phenomena*, Chicago, 1969.

85. Hesse, *The Structure of Scientific Inference*, pp. 175 ff.

86. ibid., pp. 4–5.

87. cf. my *New Rules of Sociological Method*, London [New York], 1976, pp. 142 ff.; cf. also Israel Scheffler, *Science and Subjectivity*, Indianapolis, 1967, pp. 80 ff.

88. Karl-Otto Apel, *Hermeneutik und Ideologiekritik*, Frankfurt, 1971; Bryan Wilson, *Rationality*, Oxford, 1970 [New York, 1971].

89. cf. Kuhn, 'Second thoughts on paradigms', in Suppe, op. cit.

90. Hesse, *The Structure of Scientific Inference*, pp. 57 ff.

91. cf. the Austin–Strawson debate, in George C. Pitcher, *Truth*, New Jersey, 1964.

92. Hesse claims that this standpoint is consistent with Tarski's 'semantic conception' of truth.

93. Hans-Georg Gadamer, *Truth and Method*, London [New York], 1975, pp. 55 ff.

94. Theodore Abel, 'The operation called *Verstehen'*, *American Journal of Sociology*, vol. 54, 1948; Carl Hempel, 'On the method of *Verstehen* as the sole method of philosophy', *The Journal of Philosophy*, vol. 50, 1953.

95. Abel, op. cit.

96. Gadamer, op. cit.; cf. also *Kleine Schriften*, Tübingen, 1967.

97. cf. my *New Rules of Sociological Method*, pp. 148 ff.

98. Abel, op. cit.

99. cf. John G. Gunnell, 'Political inquiry and the concept of action: a phenomenological analysis', in Maurice Natanson, *Phenomenology and the Social Sciences*, Evanston, 1973.

100. For a definition of 'determinism' here, see my *New Rules of Sociological Method*, p. 85.

101. Talcott Parsons, *The Structure of Social Action*, Glencoe, 1949.

102. *New Rules of Sociological Method*; Alfred Schutz, *The Phenomenology of the Social World* [Evanston, 1967], London, 1972.

103. The idea of 'structure', of course, appears in many varying contexts in modern thought. There are obvious contrasts between the mode in which the term is used in 'structural-functionalism' on the one hand, and 'structuralism' on the other. For relevant surveys, see Raymond Boudon, *The Uses of Structuralism*, London, 1971 [New York, 1974]; Jean Piaget, *Structuralism*, London [New York], 1970; Peter M. Blau, *Approaches to the Study of Social Structure*, New York, 1975.

104. cf. the analysis offered in my 'Functionalism: *après la lutte*', pp. 96–129.

Max Weber on facts and values

105. cf. Hanna Feinchel Pitkin, *Wittgenstein and Justice*, Berkeley, 1972, pp. 220 ff.

106. Weber, ' "Objectivity" in social science and social policy', in *The Methodology of the Social Sciences*, Glencoe, 1949, pp. 51–2 and 54.

107. ibid., p. 57.

108. cf. my *Politics and Sociology in the Thought of Max Weber*, London, 1972.

109. W. D. Hudson, *The Is/Ought Question*, London, 1969 [New York, 1970].

110. J. R. Searle, 'How to derive "ought" from "is" ', in Hudson, op. cit.; *Speech Acts*, Cambridge (UK), 1969 [New York, 1970], pp. 54 ff.

111. Searle, 'Deriving "ought" from "is": objections and replies', ibid.

112. Searle, 'How to derive "ought" from "is" ', op. cit., p. 263.

113. For various relevant discussions, see John H. Schaar, 'Reflections on authority', *New American Review*, vol. 8, 1970; Pitkin, op. cit., pp. 280 ff; Wolfgang J. Mommsen, *Max Weber und die deutsche Politik 1890–1920*, Tübingen, 1959; Jürgen Habermas, *Legitimation Crisis*, Boston, 1975, pp. 97 ff.

114. Weber, *Economy and Society*, New York, 1968, vol. I, pp. 212 ff.

115. Pitkin, op. cit., pp. 280–82. The implications of this for Weber's sociology of law are traced through beautifully in M. Albrow, 'Legal positivism and bourgeois materialism: Max Weber's view of the sociology of law', *British Journal of Law and Society*, vol. 2, 1975.

116. Schaar, op. cit., p. 283.

117. Searle, *Speech Acts*, pp. 194–5.

118. cf. my *New Rules of Sociological Method*, pp. 50–1.

119. cf. Pitkin, op. cit., p. 234; cf. also Charles Taylor, 'Neutrality in political science', in Peter Laslett and W. G. Runciman, *Philosophy, Politics and Society*, Oxford [New York], 1967, pp. 48 ff. Consider in this regard the sort of statement that frequently appears in Weber's writings: 'The dignity of the "personality" *lies in the fact* that for it there exist values about which it organizes its life.' The *Methodology of the Social Sciences*, op. cit., p. 55 (italics not in original).

2 Functionalism: *après la lutte*

1. Some of the more well-known contributions are collected in N. J. Demerath and Richard Peterson, *System, Change, and Conflict*, New York, 1967. For convenience's sake, I shall quote from this wherever possible.

2. See, for instance, Piotr Sztompka, *System and Function*, New York, 1974.

3. The use of biological notions was more than analogical in

the writings of the 'organicists' in the closing decades of the nineteenth century. Lilienfeld is perhaps the best example.

4. Some recent critical analyses have definitely tended to exaggerate the extent to which structural-functionalism, and more particularly Parsons's ideas, dominated American sociology. Quite apart from the continuing anti-theoretical tendencies in American sociology, against which Parsons fought, symbolic interactionism was always, and still is, a pervasive influence; Parsons's writings were widely shrugged off as obscure or tendentious (and not only by radical opponents such as C. Wright Mills).

5. Robert K. Merton, 'Manifest and latent functions'; Ernest Nagel, 'A formalization of functionalism with special reference to its application in the social sciences', both in Demerath and Peterson, op. cit.

6. Arthur Stinchcombe, *Constructing Social Theories*, New York, 1968.

7. E.g., Pierre L. van den Berghe, 'Dialectic and functionalism: toward a synthesis', in Demerath and Peterson, op. cit.

8. cf. also Nagel's 'Concept and theory formation in the social sciences', in *Science, Language, and Human Rights*, Philadelphia, 1952; and Carl G. Hempel, 'The logic of functional analysis', in *Aspects of Scientific Explanation*, New York, 1965.

9. 'Classical social theory and the origins of modern sociology', *American Journal of Sociology*, vol. 81, 1976.

10. *New Rules of Sociological Method*, London [New York], 1976.

11. This is clear throughout the text; cf., however, especially the footnote to p. 43.

12. For a typical discussion of purposive action within orthodox functionalism, see Sztompka, op. cit., pp. 112 ff.

13. Emile Durkheim, *Suicide* [Glencoe, 1951], London, 1952, p. 44.

14. cf. Peter Winch, *The Idea of a Social Science*, London, 1963 [New Jersey, 1970], pp. 110–11; more particularly, Alasdair MacIntyre, 'The idea of a social science', in Bryan Wilson, *Rationality*, Oxford, 1970 [New York, 1971], pp. 124–5.

15. Such a differentiation holds only on the logical level: many actual instances of suicidal behaviour do not involve a clearly formulated 'wish to die', but a confusion of this with other motives. This in no way compromises the point, however.

16. cf. Hempel, op. cit.

17. cf. Ronald Philip Dore, 'Function and cause', in Demerath and Peterson, op. cit., pp. 412–13.

18. D. F. Aberle *et al.*, 'The functional prerequisites of a society', in Demerath and Peterson, op. cit., pp. 324 and 326.

19. ibid., pp. 323 and 327.

20. ibid., p. 319.

21. For surveys of the use of 'structure' see, *inter alia*, Jean Piaget, *Structuralism*, London [New York], 1970; Raymond Boudon, *The Uses of Structuralism*, London, 1971 [New York, 1974].

22. The quotation is from Radcliffe-Brown, 'On the concept of function in social science', now in *Structure and Function in Primitive Society*, London [Glencoe], 1952.

23. cf. Walter Buckley, *Sociology and Modern Systems Theory*, Englewood Cliffs, 1967; for a more detailed discussion, Jürgen Habermas and Nikolas Luhmann, *Theorie der Gesellschaft oder Sozialtechnologie?*, Frankfurt, 1971.

24. cf. Ludwig von Bertalanffy, 'General System Theory', in Demerath and Peterson, op. cit.; also Buckley, op. cit.

25. cf. Charles Taylor, 'Interpretation and the sciences of man', *Review of Metaphysics*, vol. 25, 1971.

26. See Talcott Parsons, *Societies: Evolutionary and Comparative Perspectives*, Englewood Cliffs, 1966.

27. Claude Lévi-Strauss, 'Réponses à quelques questions', *Esprit*, vol. 11, 1963.

28. For amplification of this analysis, see my *New Rules of Sociological Method*, op. cit., Chapter 3.

29. For Parsons's discussions of such issues in the context of evolution, see *Societies: Evolutionary and Comparative Perspectives*; 'Evolutionary universals in society', in *Sociological Theory and Modern Society*, New York, 1967.

30. Kingsley Davis, 'The myth of functional analysis as a special method in sociology and anthropology', in Demerath and Peterson, op. cit.

31. My *New Rules of Sociological Method*.

32. cf. Alvin Gouldner, 'Reciprocity and autonomy in functional theory', in Demerath and Peterson, op. cit., pp. 156 ff.

33. David Lockwood, 'Social integration and system integration', in George K. Zollschan and W. Hirsch, *Explorations in Social Change*, London, 1964 [Cambridge (Mass.), 1975].

34. See John O'Neil, *Modes of Individualism and Collectivism*, London [New York], 1973.

35. In any of the senses in which this can be understood. See my 'The "individual" in the writings of Emile Durkheim', pp. 273–91.

36. Nicos Mouzelis, 'Social and system integration: some reflections on a fundamental distinction', *British Journal of Sociology*, vol. 25, 1974.

37. Most notably, in the present generation, Habermas.

Notes on the theory of structuration

38. cf. T. G. Bever and D. T. Langendoen, 'The interaction of speech perception and grammatical structure in the evolution of language', in Robert R. Stockwell and Ronald K. S. Macaulay, *Linguistic Change and Generative Theory*, Bloomington, 1972.

39. My *New Rules of Sociological Method*, pp. 88 ff.

40. Karl Marx, *Capital*, London, 1970, vol. I, p. 572.

41. Etienne Balibar, 'On reproduction', in Louis Althusser and Etienne Balibar, *Reading Capital*, London, 1970, pp. 263–4.

42. Ludwig Wittgenstein, *Philosophical Investigations*, Oxford, 1972 [New York, 1973], S217 ff. and *passim*.

43. Many philosophers have suggested that it is useful to distinguish between 'constitutive' and 'regulative' rules. But it can be shown that all social rules have 'constitutive' and 'regulative' aspects, as is suggested indeed by the common root which 'rule' and 'regulate' share. cf. Max Black, 'The analysis of rules', in *Models and Metaphors*, Ithaca, 1962.

44. Peter Winch, *The Idea of a Social Science*, London, (new edition) [New York], 1970. cf. my *New Rules of Sociological Method*, pp. 44 ff.

45. cf. O. R. Jones, *The Private Language Argument*, London, 1971.

46. *New Rules of Sociological Method*, pp. 104 ff.

47. Harold Garfinkel, *Studies in Ethnomethodology*, Englewood Cliffs, 1967.

48. Alfred Schutz, *Collected Papers*, The Hague, 1967, 2 vols.; Alfred Schutz and Thomas Luckmann, *The Structures of the Life-World* [Evanston, 1973], London, 1974.

49. For a recent critique of semiology, see Dan Sperber, *Rethinking Symbolism*, Cambridge (UK), 1975.

50. Winch, op cit., pp. 58–62.
51. cf. 'Remarks on the theory of power', pp. 129–34.

3 Habermas's critique of hermeneutics

1. In saying this, I do not ignore Bradley and Green, nor the influence of Collingwood in history. But 'British Hegelianism' was quite short-lived, and through the influence of Moore and Russell British philosophy recovered its continuity with Hume and his successors. The 'second revolution' in British philosophy, largely due to the later Wittgenstein, has no doubt created a climate more favourable to a renewed sympathy with these traditions.

2. See 'Hermeneutics, ethnomethodology, and problems of interpretative analysis', pp. 165–78.

3. cf. Paul Ricoeur, *Husserl: an Analysis of his Phenomenology*, Evanston, 1967.

4. Hans-Georg Gadamer, *Truth and Method,* London [New York], 1975.

5. Peter Winch, *The Idea of a Social Science,* London, 1958 (new edition, London [New York] 1970); 'Understanding a primitive society', *American Philosophical Quarterly*, vol. 1, 1964. Habermas's views on Winch appear in *Zur Logik der Sozialwissenschaften*, Tübingen, 1967, pp. 134 ff.; on Wittgenstein, see also the brief comments in Habermas, *Philosophisch–politische Profile*, Frankfurt, 1971, pp. 141–6.

6. See various papers collected together in Ernest Gellner, *Cause and Meaning in the Social Sciences,* London [Boston], 1973; also *Legitimation of Belief,* Cambridge, 1974 [New York, 1975].

7. Gellner, *Words and Things,* London, 1968.

8. *Zur Logik der Sozialwissenschaften,* pp. 3 ff.

9. Jürgen Habermas, *Knowledge and Human Interests* [Boston, 1971], London, 1972, p. 4.

10. Habermas, *Toward a Rational Society,* London [Boston],

1971, pp. 91 ff. *Knowledge and Human Interests,* pp. 196 ff. See also *Zur Rekonstruktion des Historischen Materialismus,* Frankfurt, 1976, pp. 34 ff.

11. *Knowledge and Human Interests,* p. 308.

12. ibid., p. 310.

13. cf. 'Between philosophy and science: Marxism as critique', in *Theory and Practice* [Boston, 1973], London, 1974.

14. It is worth remarking upon the massive revival of concern with psychoanalysis that has attended the thesis that Freud's theories can be treated as expressing a 'depth hermeneutics' in which language, and its deformations, are at the centre. Psychoanalysis until quite recently has been more influential in the United States than elsewhere, and has characteristically been moved in the direction of an 'ego psychology'. Authors such as Habermas, Lorenzer, Lacan and Derrida, however, are much more interested in the reformulation of classical psychoanalytic concerns with the id, repressions, and the unconscious.

15. 'Wahrheitstheorien', in Helmut Fahrenbach, *Wirklichkeit und Reflexion, zum sechzigsten Geburtstag für Walter Schulz,* Pfüllingen, 1973; 'Was heisst Universalpragmatik?', in Karl-Otto Apel, *Sprachpragmatik und Philosophie,* Frankfurt, 1976. For an English version of some of the latter, see 'Some distinctions in universal pragmatics', *Theory and Society,* vol. 3, 1976.

16. 'Wahrheitstheorien', op. cit., p. 219. However, Habermas also holds that all speech has a 'double structure', such that non-constative speech acts have an implicit propositional content, which can be made explicit. cf. 'Some distinctions in universal pragmatics', op. cit., pp. 156-8.

17. ibid., p. 221.

18. 'Was heisst Universalpragmatik?', op. cit., p. 174.

19. The continuity can be discerned in a paragraph in *Zur Logik der Sozialwissenschaften,* where Habermas connects labour with 'external nature', language with inter-subjectivity (subsequently differentiated into 'intelligibility' as an overarching notion, and 'practical discourse') and domination with the repression of 'inner nature'.

20. 'Wahrheitstheorien', op. cit., p. 245. According to Habermas, the forms of discourse connect to 'cognitive schemata' of the sort described by Piaget. Such schemata also provide the basis of a speculative theory of evolution, which Habermas regards as essential to 'rethinking historical materialism'. This is

366 Notes to pages 146–54

at the centre of his current preoccupations, but falls outside the scope of my discussion here.

21. 'Was heisst Universalpragmatik?', op. cit., p. 213.

22. 'Wahrheitstheorien', op. cit., pp. 252 ff.

23. ibid., p. 264, footnote 43.

24. ibid., p. 260.

25. *Legitimation Crisis,* Boston, 1975. There is by now a very large critical literature, mostly in German, dealing with Habermas's writings. Moreover, Habermas's interchanges with Gehlen, Gadamer and Luhmann have also generated secondary controversies. I shall not cite much of this literature directly. Among the more important items are: Habermas *et al., Hermeneutik und Ideologiekritik,* Frankfurt, 1971; Habermas and N. Luhmann, *Theorie der Gesellschaft oder Sozialtechnologie?,* Frankfurt, 1971; Rüdiger Bubner *et al., Hermeneutik und Dialektik,* Tübingen, 1970. For a useful survey in English, see Fred R. Dallmayr, 'Critical Theory criticised: Habermas' *Knowledge and Human Interests* and its aftermath', *Philosophy of the Social Sciences,* vol. 2, 1972; a fairly full bibliography appears in *Cultural Hermeneutics,* vol. 2, 1975 (special issue on hermeneutics and critical theory).

26. cf. the various contributions in M. Radner and S. Winokur, *Minnesota Studies in the Philosophy of Science,* vol. 4, Minneapolis, 1970.

27. Habermas now seems to acknowledge this more clearly, but does not make much of it. cf. 'Was heisst Universalpragmatik?', op. cit., p. 186.

28. cf. Gadamer: 'From the hermeneutical standpoint, rightly understood, it is absolutely absurd to regard the concrete factors of work and politics as outside the scope of hermeneutics. . . . The principle of hermeneutics simply means that we should try to understand everything that can be understood.' 'On the scope and function of hermeneutical reflection', *Continuum,* vol. 8, 1970.

29. *New Rules of Sociological Method,* London [New York], 1976, pp. 88 ff.

30. *Zur Logik der Sozialwissenschaften,* p. 178. Italics in original.

31. *New Rules of Sociological Method,* pp. 118 ff.

32. In his discussion of universal pragmatics, Habermas says he accepts Searle's 'principle of expressibility', according to which

every speech act can be specified as a statement; but this principle seems compromised in a basic way by the idea of 'indefinite elaboration' as formulated in the writings of Garfinkel, and in a similar way in those of Ziff.

33. *Knowledge and Human Interests*, p. 313.

34. ibid., p. 314.

35. cf. Gadamer: 'I cannot share the claims of critical theory that one can master the impasse of our civilization by emancipatory reflection . . .', 'Hermeneutics and social science', *Cultural Hermeneutics,* vol. 2, 1975, p. 315.

36. *Knowledge and Human Interests*, p. 310. One should perhaps point out that Habermas's relation to Hegel has occupied many of his critics, some of whom (like me) think he remains too much of an Hegelian, others of whom accuse him of not being Hegelian enough. The highly eclectic character of Habermas's writings is no doubt partly responsible for such debates.

37. Habermas has recently acknowledged, in a new edition of *Theory and Practice,* that he has, 'in the works collected together here and also in later works, often used the idea of a human species, which constitutes itself as the subject of world-history, in an uncritical way'. *Theorie und Praxis,* Frankfurt, 1971, p. 289.

38. *New Rules of Sociological Method*, pp. 110 ff.

39. 'Introduction: some difficulties in the attempt to link theory and practice', in *Theory and Practice*, op. cit.

40. William Sargant, *Battle for the Mind,* London, 1956 [New York, 1957].

41. Gadamer, 'Replik', in K.-O. Apel, *Hermeneutik und Ideologiekritik,* Frankfurt, 1971.

42. This thesis is further affirmed in *Legitimation Crisis*.

43. 'A postscript to *Knowledge and Human Interests'*, *Philosophy of the Social Sciences,* vol. 3, 1973, p. 169.

44. cf. T. A. McCarthy, 'A theory of communicative competence', *Philosophy of the Social Sciences,* vol. 3, 1973, p. 149. McCarthy makes the point, but subsequently defends what he calls a 'weaker' version of Habermas's consensus theory.

45. Habermas at one point hints that it may be possible to rehabilitate a correspondence notion of truth in the context of his approach. cf. 'Wahrheitstheorien', op. cit., p. 247.

46. *Zur Rekonstruktion des Historischen Materialismus.*

4 Hermeneutics, ethnomethodology and problems of interpretative analysis

1. Hans-Georg Gadamer, *Wahrheit und Methode,* Tübingen, 1960; Peter Winch, *The Idea of a Social Science,* London, 1958 (new edition, London [New York], 1970); Paul Ricoeur, *De l'interprétation: essai sur Freud,* Paris, 1965.
2. Most of the views in this paper are discussed in a more detailed way in my *New Rules of Sociological Method,* London [New York], 1976.
3. cf. Gibson Winter, *Elements for a Social Ethic,* New York, 1966, pp. 9 ff.
4. For a good, short, discussion in English, see William Outhwaite, *Understanding Social Life,* London, 1975; a longer account appears in Gerard Radnitsky, *Contemporary Schools of Metascience,* Göteborg, 1970, vol. 2.
5. Theodore Abel, 'The operation called *Verstehen',* American *Journal of Sociology,* vol. 54, 1948; Ernest Nagel, 'On the method of *Verstehen* as the sole method of philosophy', *The Journal of Philosophy,* vol. 50, 1953.
6. Emmanuel A. Schegloff and Harvey Sacks, 'Opening up closings', *Semiotica,* vol. 8, 1973; Alan Blum, *Theorising,* London [New York], 1974; Peter McHugh *et al., On the Beginning of Social Enquiry,* London [Boston], 1974.
7. cf. *New Rules of Sociological Method,* pp. 118 ff.
8. Karl-Otto Apel, *Analytic Philosophy of Language and the Geisteswissenschaften,* Dordrecht, 1967; Jürgen Habermas, *Knowledge and Human Interests* [Boston, 1971], London, 1972; *Theory and Practice* [Boston, 1973], London, 1974; A. Lorenzer, *Sprachzerstörung und Rekonstruktion,* Frankfurt, 1970.

Max Weber on interpretative sociology

9. Max Weber, 'Roscher und Knies und das Irrationalitätsproblem', in *Gesammelte Aufsätze zur Wissenschaftslehre,* Tübingen, 1968.

10. *Economy and Society,* New York, 1968, vol. I, p. 4.
11. ibid., pp. 5, 8, and 11.

5 Marx, Weber and the development of capitalism

1. George Lichtheim, *Marxism, an Historical and Critical Study,* London [New York], 1964, p. 385.
2. These include the 'Critique of Hegel's Philosophy of Right'; 'Economic and Philosophical Manuscripts'; the complete text of *The German Ideology*; and other smaller articles, letters and fragments. These were all published for the first time between 1927 and 1932, in *Marx-Engels Gesamtausgabe (MEGA).*
3. Marx did not, of course, use this term, which originated with Engels; but it has become conventional to use it also to refer to Marx's writings on the interpretation of historical development.
4. *A Contribution to the Critique of Political Economy,* Chicago, 1904.
5. David Koigen's *Ideen zur Philosophie der Kultur* (Munich and Leipzig, 1910) was one of the first attempts to stress the importance of the 'young' Marx. In common with most authors who have stressed the divergencies between Marx and Engels, Koigen laid emphasis upon the significance of Hegelian thought upon the whole of Marx's works. But the most influential work along these lines published before *MEGA* was Georg Lukács's *Geschichte und Klassenbewusstsein,* Berlin, 1923. In this article I shall refer to the more accessible French edition: *Histoire et conscience de classe,* Paris, 1960. Lukács was among the first to understand the possibility of assimilating Weber's studies within a truly dialectical Marxist standpoint; cf. especially pp. 142 ff. and 267 ff.
6. In this article I shall follow the terminological practice suggested by Rubel, calling those views which I attribute to Marx

himself 'Marxian', terming 'Marxist' ideas adopted by professed
followers of Marx. I shall similarly use 'Marxism' in a very
broad sense to refer generically to the latter group.

7. cf. Karl Löwith, 'Max Weber und Karl Marx', *Archiv für
Sozialwissenschaft und Sozialpolitik*, vol. 67, 1932, part I, pp. 58 ff.

8. See, for example, Weber's discussion of bureaucracy and
political power in 'Parliament and government in a reconstructed
Germany', reprinted as an Appendix to the English edition of
Economy and Society, New York, 1968, vol. 3, pp. 1381–469.

9. The best study of the development of the SPD available in
English is Günther Roth, *The Social Democrats in Imperial
Germany*, New Jersey, 1963. cf. also Werner Sombart, *Der prole-
tarische Sozialismus*, Jena, 1924, 2 vols., esp. vol. 1, pp. 333 ff.,
and vol. 2, pp. 9-95. Birnbaum's discussion of the views of Marx
and Weber on the rise of capitalism is one of the most incisive
analyses which has been made of these issues. But Birnbaum
does not separate out the various dimensions which Weber's
attack upon 'historical materialism' embraced; consequently, he
tends to fluctuate between the conclusions that Weber's work
'made explicit what Marx left implicit' (p. 133), and that Weber
considerably modified Marx's theoretical position by refuting the
notion that 'ideas are simply reflections of social position and
exercise no independent effects on historical development' (p.
134). 'Conflicting interpretations of the rise of capitalism: Marx
and Weber', *British Journal of Sociology*, vol. 4, 1953, pp. 125–41.

10. 'Contribution to the critique of Hegel's Philosophy of
Right' (1844), in T. B. Bottomore, *Karl Marx, Early Writings*,
New York, 1964, pp. 57-9; cf. also George Lichtheim, op. cit.,
pp. 51–4.

11. cf. also Engels's views as set out in his 'Der Status quo in
Deutschland', *Werke*, 4, pp. 40–57.

12. The *Communist Manifesto* announces: 'the bourgeois revolution in Germany will be but the prelude to an immediately
following proletarian revolution'.

13. cf. Marx's article in the *Deutsche Brüsseler Zeitung* of the
18 November 1847; *Werke*, 4, pp. 351 ff. For a more extended
analysis, see Engels, *Germany: Revolution and Counterrevolution*,
London, 1933 [revised edition, New York, 1969].

14. cf. Karl Demeter, 'Die soziale Schichtung des deutschen
Parlamentes seit 1848', *Vierteljahrschrift für Sozial- und Wirtschaftsgeschichte*, vol. 39, 1952, pp. 1–29. For the attitudes of

liberals towards equal suffrage, cf. Walter Gagel, *Die Wahl-rechtsfrage in der Geschichte der deutschen liberalen Parteien, 1848–1918*, Düsseldorf, 1958.

15. Particularly significant in separating the development of the labour movement in Germany from that in Britain was the fact that in Germany, until relatively late on, the working-class was without the franchise. cf. Roth, op. cit. pp. 32 ff. and *passim.*

16. cf. Hans Kelsen, *Marx oder Lassalle,* Darmstadt, 1967.

17. Eduard Bernstein, *Evolutionary Socialism,* London, 1909 (second edition [New York, 1961], London, 1963). For a short description of Bernstein's role in relation to the Social Democratic Party, see Christian Gneuss, 'The precursor: Eduard Bernstein', in Leopold Labedz, *Revisionism,* London [New York], 1962, pp. 31–41.

18. It might be pointed out here that the consequences of the German victory of 1870–71 were equally fraught with significance for the sociological perspective of Durkheim. cf. Melvin Richter, 'Durkheim's politics and political theory', in Kurt H. Wolff, *Emile Durkheim et al., Essays on Sociology and Philosophy,* New York, 1964, pp. 171 ff. For a discussion in relation to German intellectual traditions, see Fritz K. Ringer, *The Decline of the German Mandarins,* Cambridge (Mass.), 1969, pp. 81 ff.

19. cf. Wolfgang J. Mommsen, *Max Weber und die deutsche Politik: 1890–1920,* Tübingen, 1959, pp. 103 ff.; cf. also Raymond Aron, 'Max Weber und die Machtpolitik', *et seq.,* in *Max Weber und die Soziologie heute,* Tübingen, 1965.

20. 'Der Nationalstaat und die Volkswirtschaftspolitik', *Gesammelte politische Schriften,* Tübingen, 1958, pp. 1–25. See also Johannes Winckelmann, *Max Weber, Staatssoziologie,* Berlin, 1966.

21. cf. also Durkheim's analysis of Treitschke in *L'Allemagne au-dessus de tout,* Paris, 1915.

22. Weber made this remark at a meeting of the *Verein für Sozialpolitik.* See 'Diskussionsreden auf den Tagungen des Vereins für Sozialpolitik', in *Gesammelte Aufsätze zur Soziologie und Sozialpolitik,* Tübingen, 1924, pp. 394 ff., and especially pp. 408–9.

23. 'Parliament and Government in a reconstructed Germany', p. 1453.

24. Weber also offered a number of technical economic objec-

tions to the operation of a planned economy, in the form in which most socialists at that time conceived of such an economy. cf. *Economy and Society*, vol. 1, pp. 65–8; and pp. 100–107.

25. 'Parliament and government in a reconstructed Germany', p. 1453. For Weber's views on Russia, cf. 'Russlands Übergang zur Scheindemokratie' in *Gesammelte politische Schriften*, pp. 192–210.

26. cf. 'Das neue Deutschland', *Gesammelte politische Schriften*, pp. 472–5. For an accurate interpretation of some of the schisms splitting the Social Democrats during the First World War see J. P. Nettl, *Rosa Luxemburg*, London [New York], 1966, vol. 2.

27. e.g., Sombart. See, for example, his *Der moderne Capitalismus*, particularly vol. 1; Sombart of course, even early on in his career, was far from being an orthodox 'Marxist'. On the relationship between Sombart, Marx, and Weber, cf. Talcott Parsons, 'Capitalism in recent German Literature: Sombart and Weber', *The Journal of Political Economy*, vol. 36, 1928, pp. 641–61; and vol. 37, 1929, pp. 31–51. On Weber and Michels, cf. Roth, op. cit., pp. 249–57.

28. cf. Weber's discussion of Stammler's book on historical materialism and law; 'R. Stammlers "Überwindung" der materialistischen Geschichtsauffassung', in *Gesammelte Aufsätze zur Wissenschaftslehre*, Tübingen, 1951, pp. 291–359.

29. cf. Weber's letter to his mother of 8 July 1884, in *Jügendbriefe*, Tübingen, n.d., pp. 121 2. It is worth noting that Weber was impressed by his reading David Strauss's *Das Leben Jesu* (1835) at an early age; the same work had played a prominent part in the development of Marx's views as a member of the 'Young Hegelians'. cf. David McLellan, *The Young Hegelians and Karl Marx*, London [New York], 1969, pp. 2–9, and *passim*.

30. cf. Roth, 'Introduction' to *Economy and Society*, vol. 1, pp. lxx–lxxi.

31. See Karl Kautsky, *Karl Marx' ökonomische Lehren*, Stuttgart, 1887; and, subsequently, his *Der Ursprung des Christentums*, Stuttgart, 1908.

32. cf. *The Protestant Ethic and the Spirit of Capitalism*, New York, 1958, especially pp. 194–8. For an account of the background to Weber's views on religion, see Paul Honigsheim, 'Max Weber: his religious and ethical background and development', *Church History*, vol. 19, 1950, pp. 2–23.

33. cf. Weber: 'Der Sozialismus', in *Gesammelte Aufsätze zur Soziologie und Sozialpolitik*, pp. 504 ff.

34. cf. Weber's outline of *Erwerbsklassen*, in *Economy and Society*, vol. 1, p. 304.

35. Although this is set out in most detail in his more technical essays on method, Weber's basic epistemological position is formulated in a brilliantly concise fashion in 'Science as a vocation', in H. H. Gerth and C. Wright Mills, *From Max Weber: Essays in Sociology*, New York, 1958, pp. 129–56.

36. See Weber's remarks on Marx's concepts in ' "Objectivity" in social science and social policy', in *The Methodology of the Social Sciences*, p. 103 and *passim*.

37. Weber discussed the notion of evolutionary 'stages' in some detail in relation to a problem which also preoccupied Marx, and more particularly, Engels: the question of the development of Germanic tribal society in relation to the decline of Rome and the organization of medieval feudalism. cf. Weber, 'Der Streit um den Charakter der altgermanischen Sozialverfassung in der deutschen Literatur des letzten Jahrzehnts', in *Gesammelte Aufsätze zur Sozial- und Wirtschaftsgeschichte*, Tübingen, 1924, pp. 508–56.

38. The phrase comes from Weber's contribution to a meeting of the German Sociological Association, reported in 'Geschäftsbericht und Diskussionsreden auf den deutschen soziologischen Tagungen', in *Gesammelte Aufsätze zur Soziologie und Sozialpolitik*, p. 456.

39. 'Objectivity in social science and social policy', p. 68. Weber nevertheless spoke of the *Communist Manifesto* as 'a scientific achievement of the first rank' in 'Der Sozialismus', pp. 504–5.

40. *Economy and Society*, vol. 1, p. 63. For Weber's earlier formulation of the concept of the 'economic', see 'Objectivity in social science and social policy', p. 64.

41. 'Objectivity in social science and social policy', p. 65.

42. Marx, *The Poverty of Philosophy*, Moscow, n.d., p. 92. (The quotation in the text is Weber's version of the Marxian original.) For Weber's distinction between 'economy' and 'technology' see *Economy and Society*, vol. 1, pp. 65–7.

43. 'Geschäftsbericht und Diskussionsreden auf den deutschen soziologischen Tagungen', p. 450.

44. *Economy and Society*, vol. 2, pp. 928 ff.

45. Collected together as *Gesammelte Aufsätze zur Wissenschaftslehre,* Tübingen, 1968 (third edition).

46. cf. Shils's 'Foreword' to *The Methodology of the Social Sciences,* pp. vii–viii.

47. 'Science as a vocation', p. 153.

48. Much of the dispute over Weber's objectives in the book stems from neglect of Weber's published replies to his early critics. cf. his 'Antikritisches zum Geist des Kapitalismus', *Archiv für Sozialwissenschaft und Sozialpolitik,* vol. 20, 1910; and his 'Antikritisches Schlusswort', ibid., vol. 31.

49. The most definite evidence for the continuity of Marx's thought is the draft version of *Capital.* This was published in 1939, but did not become generally available until 1953 as *Grundrisse der Kritik der politischen Ökonomie,* Berlin, 1953. For an analysis of some of the phases in the development of differing 'interpretations' of Marx since the turn of the century, see Erich Thier, 'Etappen der Marxinterpretation', *Marxismusstudien,* 1954, pp. 1–38.

50. 'Theses on Feuerbach', in Loyd D. Easton and Kurt H. Guddat, *Writings of the Young Marx on Philosophy and Society,* New York, 1967, p. 402 (Thesis 9).

51. Ludwig Feuerbach, *The Essence of Christianity,* London, 1853.

52. This phrase was, of course, originally used by Engels to refer to Marx's relation to Hegel. cf. Engels, 'Ludwig Feuerbach and the end of classical German philosophy', *Selected Works,* London, 1950, vol. 2, p. 350.

53. 'Theses on Feuerbach', loc. cit., p. 400 (Thesis 1).

54. 'Preface to *A Contribution to the Critique of Political Economy',* in Marx and Engels, *Selected Works,* vol. 1, pp. 328–9.

55. cf. Thesis 7 in 'Theses on Feuerbach', loc. cit., p. 402.

56. *The German Ideology,* Moscow, 1968, pp. 38–9.

57. ibid., p. 61.

58. 'Theses on Feuerbach', loc. cit., p. 402 (Thesis 6).

59. cf., for example, 'The Civil War in France', in *Selected Works,* vol. 1, pp. 429–40.

60. *Grundrisse,* pp. 375–413; the relevant sections are mostly included in an English translation of a small section from the work – E. J. Hobsbawm, *Pre-capitalist Economic Formations,* London, 1964; Weber's discussion of Rome is to be found in 'Die

sozialen Gründe des Untergangs der antiken Kultur', in *Gesam-melte Aufsätze zur Sozial- und Wirtschaftsgeschichte,* pp. 289–311. In the subsequent part of this paper I do not deal with the discrepancies between Marx's discussion of 'the Asiatic mode of production', and Weber's analysis of China and India. It has often been stated that Weber's views upon the emergence of rational capitalism in the West can only be fully understood in the light of his writings on the various 'world religions'. This is undeniably true. It is, however, quite misleading to regard these writings, as many have, as a form of *ex post facto* experiment which 'tests' the 'independent' influence of ideology upon social development. What Weber shows is that *both* the content of the religious ethics he discusses *and* the specific combination of 'material' circumstances found in Europe, China and India differ. (Thus, for example, Weber laid stress upon the ease of communications in Europe, the peculiar economic and political independence of the European city, plus various other 'material' conditions in terms of which Europe differed from China and India.) These material and ideological factors form a definite, interrelated 'cluster' in each case: the material conditions cannot therefore simply be treated as a 'constant' against which the 'inhibiting' or 'facilitating' influence of religious ideology as a 'variable' can be determined.

61. *Pre-capitalist Economic Formations,* p. 84.

62. *Grundrisse,* p. 740.

63. Marx pointed out also that while the use of money was widespread in antiquity, only in certain trading nations did it become essential to the economy; in Rome, the monetary system came to be fully developed only during the period of the disintegration of the economy. *Grundrisse,* pp. 23–4. Compare Engels's discussion of Rome, in his 'The origin of the family, private property and the state', in *Selected Works,* vol. 2, pp. 270–8.

64. See the discussion of Stirner's *Der Einzige und sein Eigentum* in *The German Ideology,* pp. 143 ff.

65. Ibid., p. 151. Weber, on the other hand, stressed that Christianity has always been primarily a religion of the urban artisanate. See *Economy and Society,* vol. 2, pp. 481 ff.

66. 'Contribution to the critique of Hegel's Philosophy of Right', in *On Religion,* p. 50. Marx only briefly alluded to the significance of the ideological content of Calvinism. (See, for

example, *Capital*, vol. 1, p. 79.) Engels, on various occasions, discussed Calvinism at greater length.

X 67. 'Economic and Philosophical Manuscripts', in Bottomore, op. cit., pp. 168 ff.; see also Löwith, op cit., pp. 77 ff.

68. *Grundrisse*, p. 313. cf., on the 'universalizing' character of money, Georg Simmel, *Philosophie des Geldes*, Leipzig, 1900. Weber remarked of Simmel's book, that 'money economy and capitalism are too closely identified, to the detriment of his concrete analysis' (*Protestant Ethic*, p. 185). Marx also noted the significance of a phenomenon which Weber later discussed at great length – the fact that Roman law played an important role in the formation of bourgeois society. cf. *Grundrisse*, p. 30; and p. 916.

69. 'Economic and Philosophical Manuscripts', p. 171; cf. Avineri, op. cit., pp. 110–11.

70. *Grundrisse*, pp. 133–4.

71. Marx and Engels, *The Holy Family*, Moscow, 1956.

72. Letter to the Editor of *Otyecestvenniye Zapisky*, 1877, *Selected Correspondence*, London, 1934, p. 355. (I have modified the translation.)

73. Marx, of course, realized that political structures could vary to a considerable degree independently of class interests. (See, for example, his letter in *Letters to Kugelmann*, London, n.d., p. 23.) Marx saw that the most developed society in economic terms, England, had a less complex state than Germany or France. The English state, Marx wrote in 1885, was 'an archaic, time-worn and antiquated compromise between the bourgeoisie, which rules over all the various spheres of civil society in reality, but *not officially*, and the landed aristocracy which rules *officially*'. 'Die britische Konstitution', *Werke*, 11, p. 95.

74. Gerth and Mills, op. cit., p. 47.

75. *Grundrisse*, p. 428. Marx, however, noted that the case of the army and that of the capitalist organization differed in that the professional soldier was not hired in order to produce surplus value.

76. *Anti-Dühring*, Moscow, 1962; *Dialectics of Nature*, Moscow, 1954.

77. It would perhaps be nearest to the truth to say, in Laski's words, 'That the two men had, as it were, evolved in common a joint stock of ideas which they regarded as a kind of intellectual bank account upon which either could draw freely'. Harold J.

Laski, 'Introduction to *The Communist Manifesto*, New York, 1967, p. 20.

78. The phrase is Lukács's, op. cit., p. 20. cf. MacIntyre's remarks on Kautsky, Bernstein and Lukács, in Alasdair MacIntyre, *Marxism and Christianity*, London, 1969, pp. 95 ff.

79. Engels, in fact, disclaimed the writings of some of his intellectual disciples who were actually only drawing the logical implication of the main themes of *Anti-Dühring*. His attempt to escape the theoretical impasse to which his views led is given in his statement, 'According to the materialist conception of history, the determining element in history is *ultimately* the production and reproduction in real life. More than this neither Marx nor I have ever asserted' (Engels to Bloch, 21 September 1890, in *Selected Correspondence*, p. 475). Marx had earlier, of course, also felt compelled to comment ironically that he 'was not a Marxist'.

80. On Marx's theory of bureaucracy, see Avineri, op. cit., pp. 48 ff.

81. *Protestant Ethic*, p. 181.

82. Herbert Marcuse, 'Industrialization and capitalism in the work of Max Weber', in *Negations, Essays in Critical Theory*, London, 1968 [Boston, 1969], p. 223.

Marx and Weber: problems of class structure

83. H. H. Gerth and C. Wright Mills, *From Max Weber: Essays in Sociology*, New York, 1958, p. 47.

84. cf. Dieter Lindenlaub, *Richtungskämpfe im Verein für Sozialpolitik*, Wiesbaden, 1967.

85. Max Weber, *Economy and Society*, New York, 1968, vol. 2, p. 927.

86. ibid., p. 928.

87. Weber, *General Economic History* [New York, 1961], London, 1966, pp. 208–9.

88. *Economy and Society*, op. cit., vol. 1, p. 305.

89. For a slightly different formulation, cf. *The Class Structure of the Advanced Societies*, London [New York], 1973, p. 86.

90. ibid., p. 99. I hope this will make clear that the arguments I set out in *The Class Structure of the Advanced Societies* are not to be characterized as 'Weberian', either in the narrow sense that they employ a similar notion of class to that of Weber, or in the

wider connotation that they presuppose acceptance of Weber's philosophical and methodological views. Several critical discussions of the book, especially those emanating from more dogmatic Marxist authors, have seriously – almost wilfully – misrepresented my position in these respects.

6 Four myths in the history of social thought

1. Talcott Parsons, *The Structure of Social Action*, New York, 1937 (second edition, 1949).
2. Parsons actually distinguishes two strands in utilitarianism: that associated with Hobbes, and the postulate of a 'natural identity of interests', originating with Locke. The latter became the dominant theme in economic theory.
3. See particularly C. B. Macpherson, *The Political Theory of Possessive Individualism* [New York, 1962], London, 1964, pp. 19 ff.
4. My 'Introduction' to *Emile Durkheim: Selected Writings*, Cambridge (UK) [New York], 1972.
5. See my 'Durkheim as a review critic', *Sociological Review*, vol. 18, 1970, pp. 188–91.
6. Parsons, op. cit., pp. 310 ff.
7. For a more detailed discussion of this matter, see 'Durkheim's political sociology', pp. 235–72.
8. *The Division of Labour in Society* [Glencoe, 1947], London, 1964, pp. 374 ff.
9. 'Durkheim's political sociology', pp. 235–72.
10. See Durkheim's remarks on Hobbes, in *The Rules of Sociological Method* [Glencoe, 1950], London, 1964, pp. 121 ff.
11. cf. Coser: 'The problem of order preoccupied Durkheim from his earliest writings to the last pages of the *Introduction à la morale*, a paper he wrote shortly before his death.' Lewis A.

Coser, 'Durkheim's conservatism and its implications for his sociological theory', in Kurt H. Wolff, *Emile Durkheim et al., Essays
on Sociology and Philosophy*, New York, 1964.

12. Marion M. Mitchell, 'Emile Durkheim and the philosophy
of nationalism', *Political Science Quarterly*, vol. 46, 1931.

13. cf. Melvin Richter, 'Durkheim's politics and political
theory', in Wolff, op. cit.

14. Robert A. Nisbet, 'Conservatism and sociology', *American
Journal of Sociology*, vol. 58, 1952; *Emile Durkheim*, Englewood
Cliffs, 1965; *The Sociological Tradition*, London, 1967; Coser, op.
cit.; Irving M. Zeitlin, *Ideology and the Development of Socio-
logical Theory*, Englewood Cliffs, 1968. Comparison of Nisbet's
Sociological Tradition with the writings of von Hayek and
Salomon, of a generation ago, provides an instructive contrast in
motives and styles of intellectual history.

15. Nisbet, *The Sociological Tradition*, pp. 12–13.

16. Nisbet, *Emile Durkheim*, pp. 23–5.

17. 'Les études de science sociale', *Revue philosophique*, vol.
22, 1886; 'La science positive de la morale en Allemagne', ibid.,
1887 (in three parts); 'Le programme économique de M. Schäffle',
Revue d'économie politique, vol. 2, 1888.

18. See Durkheim's review of Simon Deploige, *Le conflit de la
morale et de la sociologie, Année sociologique*, vol. 12, 1909–12.
Here Durkheim rejects Deploige's accusation that his works were
'made in Germany'.

19. Charles Renouvier, *La science de la morale*, Paris, 1869.

20. Nisbet, *Emile Durkheim*, p. 28.

21. For a fuller account, see my 'The "individual" in the writings of Emile Durkheim', pp. 273–91.

22. 'L'individualisme et les intellectuels', *Revue bleue*, vol. 10,
1898, p. 9.

23. An attempt which was also made, as the subsequent publications of the 'early writings' have made clear, by Marx in the
earlier part of the nineteenth century.

24. An exception is Robert N. Bellah, 'Durkheim and history',
American Sociological Review, vol. 24, 1959. But Bellah does not
set out to show how far this shows the necessity of re-examining
the conventional interpretations of the main themes of Durkheim's work.

25. See, for example, Zeitlin, op. cit., pp. 234 ff. Nisbet's
analysis of this matter is much more sophisticated than that of

most of those who have focused upon Durkheim's 'conservatism'. See *Emile Durkheim*, pp. 49 ff.

26. This was undeniably Freud's view, and therefore creates considerable difficulties for the 'left' Freudians who wish to employ Freud's conceptions to reach a very different standpoint to that taken by the master. The obvious way out of the problem is to 'relativize' Freud by holding that certain of Freud's 'universal' attributes of human society were in fact specific to the Western bourgeois society in which he lived. See Herbert Marcuse, *Eros and Civilization*, New York, 1955, pp. 117 ff., and *passim*.

27. cf. my 'The "individual" in the writings of Emile Durkheim', pp. 273–91.

28. Parsons has elaborated this in a more technical manner, in relation to the transcendance of 'positivism'. See Parsons, op. cit.

29. *Education and Sociology*, Glencoe, 1956, p. 89. (I have modified the translations.)

30. Andrew F. Henry and James F. Short, 'The sociology of suicide', in Edwin Schneidman and Norman L. Farberow, *Clues to Suicide*, New York, 1957, p. 58.

31. cf. my 'The suicide problem in French sociology', pp. 322–32.

32. See Paul F. Lazarsfeld, 'Notes on the history of quantification in sociology', *Isis*, vol. 52, 1961.

33. 'Sociologie et sciences sociales', *Revue philosophique*, 1886, p. 469.

34. Letter to Davy, quoted in George Davy, 'Emile Durkheim', *Revue française de sociologie*, vol. 1, 1960, p. 10.

35. *The Rules of Sociological Method*, op. cit., pp. 47–75.

36. See Durkheim's own remarks in *Socialism*, New York, 1962, pp. 283–5.

37. Ralf Dahrendorf, *Class and Class Conflict in Industrial Society*, Stanford, 1959, p. 159. It should be noted, however, that the 'problem of order' is defined here in a less specific, and a more ambiguous, way than it is understood by Parsons.

38. John Horton, 'The dehumanisation of anomie and alienation', *British Journal of Sociology*, vol. 15, 1964; and 'Order and conflict theories of social problems as competing ideologies', *American Journal of Sociology*, vol. 71, 1965–6.

39. cf. my *Capitalism and Modern Social Theory*, Cambridge (UK) [New York], 1971, pp. 14 ff. and 224–32.

40. T. B. Bottomore, *Karl Marx, Early Writings*, New York, 1964, pp. 147 ff.

41. *Socialism*, New York, 1962, p. 240.

42. For a useful discussion, see Stephen Lukes, 'Alienation and anomie', in Peter Laslett and W. G. Runciman, *Politics, Philosophy and Society* (Third Series), Oxford [New York], 1967.

43. See John Rex, *Key Problems of Sociological Theory*, London, 1961 [New Jersey, 1970]. It is important to emphasize that most writers represent the distinction between integration and coercion theory in ideal-typical form, holding that most social theories involve at least certain elements of both.

44. *Capitalism and Modern Social Theory*, pp. 205–23.

45. ibid., pp. 206 ff.

46. I do not deal with the methodological issues involved here. But it might be mentioned that the problems here are not as clear-cut as is sometimes assumed. Durkheim's stress upon the 'objective' character of social phenomena finds a counterpart in Marx's 'objectification'.

47. See Durkheim's review of Labriola, *Essais sur la conception matérialiste de l'histoire* in *Revue philosophique*, vol. 44, 1897.

48. 'Introduction à la morale', *Revue philosophique*, vol. 89, 1920, p. 89.

49. Thus Nisbet, for example, emphasizes the continuity of social thought over the whole of the nineteenth century. Parsons has specifically questioned the interpretations given in the former's *The Sociological Tradition*; see his discussion of the work in the *American Sociological Review*, vol. 32, 1967, pp. 640–43.

50. Parsons usually only seems to reply to his critics elliptically. See, for example, the various remarks *à propos* scattered throughout his various papers in *Ideology and Modern Society*, New York, 1970.

51. *Emile Durkheim*, p. 28.

52. This is most obviously true of Nisbet's *The Sociological Tradition*, which, while noting the significance of the reactions to the 'two great Revolutions', proceeds to treat those reactions as disembodied systems of 'unit-ideas'. Parsons's *The Structure of Social Action* is, of course, quite a different case, since it was never intended to be anything like an 'historical' account. However, Peel's recent comment here is not at all irrelevant to Parsons's concerns: 'If we ask why Durkheim wrote about the

causes of suicide and the religion of the Australian aborigines, or why Weber and Pareto made so much of their respective concepts of bureaucracy and élite, we should not look first at the deficiencies of the then current, but immanently developing, "theory of society"; but the novel features of their own societies, so different from that which had produced Spencer and provided Marx with so much of his subject matter.' J. D. Y. Peel, *Herbert Spencer: The Evolution of a Sociologist*, London [New York], 1971, p. 240.

53. Colette Capitan, 'Avant-propos' to Bonald, *Théorie du pouvoir politique et religieux*, Paris, 1966, p. 10.

54. In this connection it is instructive to compare the attitudes of the 'young' and 'mature' Hegel. cf. Georg Lukács, *Der junge Hegel*, Zürich, 1948.

55. A. V. Dicey, *Law and Public Opinion in England*, London, 1962, p. 7. For a survey of some of the nineteenth-century English 'conservatives', see Benjamin Evans Lippincott, *Victorian Critics of Democracy*, Minneapolis, 1938.

56. cf. especially J. W. Burrow, *Evolution and Society*, Cambridge [New York], 1968.

57. See Alan J. Milne, 'The idealist criticism of utilitarian social philosophy', *Archives européennes de sociologie*, vol. 8, 1967.

58. Sometimes 'utilitarianism' has been so broadly interpreted as to be almost meaningless. Thus Gouldner speaks of utilitarianism, or 'utilitarian culture', 'not as a technical philosophy but as a part of the popular, everyday culture of the middle class'. Alvin W. Gouldner, *The Coming Crisis of Western Sociology* [New York, 1970], London, 1971, pp. 61–2.

59. cf. Kenneth D. Barkin, *The Controversy over German Industrialization, 1890–1902*, Chicago, 1970; for a broader discussion, Alexander Gerschenkron, *Economic Backwardness in Historical Perspective*, Cambridge (Mass.) [London], 1962.

60. Arthur Mitzman, 'Anti-progress: a study in the Romantic roots of German sociology', *Social Research*, vol. 33, 1966.

61. *Professional Ethics and Civic Morals*, p. 99.

62. ibid., pp. 105–6.

63. 'L'individualisme et les intellectuels', p. 8.

64. *Socialism*, pp. 58–62.

65. T. B. Bottomore, *Karl Marx, Early Writings*, New York, 1964, pp. 147 ff.

66. Most of those involved in the debate seem to have followed

Parsons in identifying the Simmelian question 'How is society possible?' with the resolution of the 'problem of order'; but, as I have indicated, this is not justified, since the terms involved in the form in which the 'problem of order' is posed already prejudice the solution.

67. cf. my *Politics and Sociology in the Thought of Max Weber*, London, 1972.

68. See Durkheim's review of Labriola's *Essais sur la conception matérialiste de l'histoire*, in my *Emile Durkheim: Selected Writings*, Cambridge [New York], 1972, pp. 159–62.

69. See 'Durkheim's political sociology', pp. 235–72.

70. cf. Gouldner, op. cit., who speaks of the 'atrophying of social evolutionism in both Emile Durkheim's work and in Max Weber's, and its replacement by comparative study' (p. 117).

71. cf. Terry N. Clark, 'Emile Durkheim and the institutionalisation of sociology in the French university system', *Archives européennes de sociologie*, vol. 9, 1968.

7 Durkheim's political sociology

1. See, however, Reinhard Bendix, 'Social Stratification and the Political Community', *Archives européennes de sociologie*, vol. 1, 1960, pp. 181–210; Melvin Richter, 'Durkheim's Politics and Political Theory', in Kurt H. Wolff, *Emile Durkheim et al., Essays on Sociology and Philosophy*, London, 1964, pp. 170-210; and Erik Allardt, 'Emile Durkheim: sein Beitrag zur politischen Soziologie', *Kölner Zeitschrift für Soziologie und Sozialpsychologie*, vol. 20, 1968, pp. 1–16.

2. Talcott Parsons, *The Structure of Social Action*, New York, 1937 (second edition, New York, 1949); and Harry Alpert, *Emile Durkheim and His Sociology*, New York, 1939.

3. Translated into English under the title of *Professional Ethics and Civic Morals*, London, 1957.

4. Compare the treatment of Marx in Erich Thier, 'Etappen

der Marxinterpretation', *Marxismmusstudien*, 1954, pp. 1–38.

5. See, for example, Marion M. Mitchell, 'Emile Durkheim and the Philosophy of Nationalism', *Political Science Quarterly*, vol. 46, 1931, pp. 87–106.

6. cf. my 'Durkheim as a review critic', *Sociological Review*, vol. 18, 1970, pp. 188–91.

7. Parsons's usage of this term is somewhat unusual. See *The Structure of Social Action* (second edition), pp. 60–69.

8. Robert A. Nisbet, *Emile Durkheim*, Englewood Cliffs, 1965, p. 37. My first parenthesis. cf., however, Allardt: op. cit., p. 1. Parsons does not deny that, as he puts it, 'The Division of Labor contains, in germ, almost all the essential elements of Durkheim's later theoretical development . . .', op. cit., p. 308.

9. Richter, loc. cit., pp. 171–2.

10. See my *Capitalism and Modern Social Theory*, Cambridge (UK) [New York], 1971, Chapter 14. Cobban remarks: 'A revolution had laid the foundations of an intensely conservative society, nor is this difficult to understand. The classes which consolidated their victory in the Revolution were the peasant proprietors in the country and the men of property in the towns, neither with any vision beyond the preservation of their own economic interest, conceived in the narrowest and most restrictive sense.' Alfred Cobban, *A History of Modern France*, Harmondsworth [New York], 1968, vol. 2, p. 219.

11. Parsons, op. cit., p. 307 and *passim*.

12. See the important analysis given in Chapter 14 of Dieter Lindenlaub: *Richtungskämpfe im Verein für Sozialpolitik*, Wiesbaden, 1967, pp. 272–384; also my *Politics and Sociology in the Thought of Max Weber*, London, 1972. As Friedrich Neumann remarked in 1911: *'Ungefähr so wie der Französe sein Thema hat: was ist die grosse Revolution, so haben wir durch unser Nationalschicksal für lange Zeit unser thema bekommen: was ist der Kapitalismus.'* Quoted in Lindenlaub, p. 280.

13. E. Durkheim, *The Division of Labor in Society*, Glencoe, 1964, p. 228. (I have modified the translation in this and certain other quotations in subsequent parts of the paper.)

14. E. Durkheim, 'L'individualisme et les intellectuels', *Revue bleue*, vol. 10, 1898, pp. 7–13. A translation appears in Steven Lukes, 'Durkheim's "Individualism and the Intellectuals"', *Political Studies*, vol. 17, 1969, pp. 14–30.

15. In saying this, of course, I do not wish to hold that Saint-

Simon and Comte were the only important intellectual influences exerting an important positive influence over Durkheim: other, more immediate influences were Renouvier, Fustel de Coulanges, and Boutroux.

16. cf. Alvin W. Gouldner: 'Introduction' to Durkheim's *Socialism and Saint-Simon*, London, 1952 [Kent, Ohio, 1958], pp. 13–18.

17. cf., on this point, Durkheim's interpretation of the final phase of Saint-Simon's career, as manifest in the latter's *Nouveau christianisme*, in ibid., pp. 229 ff.

18. See Lukes, loc. cit., pp. 15–19.

19. 'L'individualisme et les intellectuels', loc. cit., p. 7.

20. ibid., p. 8.

21. ibid., pp. 11 and 13.

22. Richter, loc. cit., pp. 172 ff.

23. See, for example, Simon Deploige, *Le Conflit de la morale et de la sociologie*, Paris, 1911. Durkheim reviewed the book in the *Année sociologique*, vol. 12, 1909–12. For an earlier exchange of letters between Deploige and Durkheim, see the *Revue néo-scolastique*, vol. 14, 1907, pp. 606–21.

24. See, above all, E. Durkheim, *L'Evolution pédagogique en France*, Paris, 1969 (first published, in two volumes, in 1938).

25. Georges Davy, 'Emile Durkheim', *Revue de métaphysique et de morale*, vol. 26, 1919, p. 189.

26. cf. J. E. S. Hayward, 'Solidarist Syndicalism: Durkheim and Duguit', *Sociological Review*, vol. 8, 1960, parts 1 and 2, pp. 17–36 and 185–202.

27. Marcel Mauss, Introduction to the first edition of *Socialism*, p. 32.

28. E. Durkheim, *Moral Education*, Glencoe, 1961, p. 137.

29. cf. K. Marx, 'The Civil War in France', in *Selected Works*, Foreign Languages Publishing House, Moscow, 1958, vol. 1, p. 542.

30. E. Durkheim, Review of Antonio Labriola's *Essais sur la conception matérialiste de l'histoire*, *Revue philosophique*, vol. 44, 1897, pp. 649 and 651.

31. ibid., pp. 648–9.

32. See Lindenlaub, op. cit.

33. Sorel played an important part in this; for his evaluation of Durkheim, see 'Les théories de M. Durkheim', *Le Devenir social*, vol. 1, 1895, pp. 1–26 and 148–80.

N

34. Mauss, loc. cit., p. 34.

35. *Socialism*, p. 283.

36. ibid., p. 284.

37. 'Socialism is to the facts which produce it what the groans of a sick man are to the illness with which he is afflicted, to the needs that torment him. But what would one say of a doctor who accepted the replies or desires of his patient as scientific truths?' ibid., p. 41.

38. ibid., p. 285.

39. ibid., p. 40.

40. ibid., p. 90. For further discussion of Durkheim's evaluation of Marx, see my *Capitalism and Modern Social Theory*, Chapter 13.

41. ibid., pp. 39–79.

42. ibid., pp. 70–1.

43. ibid., p. 71.

44. See Hayward, op. cit.

45. E. Durkheim, 'La science positive de la morale en Allemagne', *Revue philosophique*, vol. 24, 1887, part 1, p. 38.

46. *The Division of Labour*, p. 227.

47. 'Where restitutive law is highly developed, there is an occupational morality for each profession . . . There are usages and customs common to the same order of functionaries which no one of them can break without incurring the censure of the corporation.' ibid., p. 227.

48. *The Division of Labour*, p. 220.

49. E. Durkheim, *Professional Ethics and Civic Morals*, pp. 98 ff.

50. ibid., pp. 98 and 99.

51. ibid., pp. 102–3.

52. *The Division of Labour*, pp. 280–82; also pp. 405–6.

53. *Professional Ethics and Civic Morals*, p. 75.

54. See Durkheim and E. Denis, *Qui a voulu la guerre?*, Paris, 1915; and E. Durkheim, *L'Allemagne au-dessus de tout*, Paris, 1915.

55. *L'Allemagne au-dessus de tout*, p. 7.

56. ibid., p. 5.

57. ibid., p. 22.

58. ibid., p. 7.

59. ibid., p. 45.

60. cf. Richter, loc. cit., pp. 201–2.

61. See especially Robert Nisbet, 'Conservatism and Sociology', *American Journal of Sociology*, vol. 58, 1952, pp. 165–75, and *The Sociological Tradition*, London [New York], 1967; and Lewis A. Coser, 'Durkheim's Conservatism and its Implications for his Sociological Theory', in Wolff, op. cit., pp. 211–32.

62. Coser, loc. cit., p. 212.

63. See my *Capitalism and Modern Social Theory, passim.*

64. E. Durkheim, 'Introduction à la morale', *Revue philosophique*, vol. 89, 1920, p. 89.

65. E. Durkheim, *Suicide* [Glencoe, 1951], London, 1952, p. 383.

66. E. Durkheim, Preface to the *Année sociologique*, vol. 2, 1897–8, in Wolff, op. cit., pp. 352–3.

67. H. Stuart Hughes, *Consciousness and Society*, New York, 1958, p. 285.

68. *L'Evolution pédagogique en France.*

69. ibid., p. 323.

70. *Moral Education*, p. 10.

71. E. Durkheim, *Sociology and Philosophy*, London [Glencoe], 1953, p. 72.

72. 'to be free is not to do what one pleases; it is to be master of oneself . . .' E. Durkheim, *Education and Sociology*, Glencoe, 1956, p. 89.

73. 'The Dualism of Human Nature and its Social Conditions', in Wolff, op. cit., p. 327.

74. *Professional Ethics and Civic Morals*, pp. 47–8.

75. *The Division of Labour*, p. 226.

76. E. Durkheim, *Montesquieu and Rousseau*, Ann Arbor, 1960, p. 33.

77. E. Durkheim, 'Deux lois de l'évolution pénale', *Année sociologique*, vol. 4, 1899–1900, pp. 65–95.

78. ibid., p. 650.

79. ibid., pp. 67–8.

80. ibid., p. 69.

81. ibid., pp. 88 and 93.

82. *Professional Ethics and Civic Morals*, pp. 82–3.

83. ibid., p. 87.

84. ibid., p. 89.

85. ibid., pp. 96 and 106.

86. ibid., p. 106.

87. ibid., p. 51.

88. ibid., p. 56.

89. See, for example, John Horton, 'The De-humanisation of Anomie and Alienation', *British Journal of Sociology*, vol. 15, 1964, pp. 283–300; and Irving M. Zeitlin, *Ideology and the Development of Sociological Theory*, New Jersey, 1968, pp. 241 ff. Zeitlin speaks of 'a conservative and authoritarian ideology that dominated (Durkheim's) entire sociological system' (p. 241).

90. Horton, op. cit.; cf. Aron who says, 'From the outset Durkheim posits man motivated and dominated by his natural egoism – Hobbes's man with unlimited desires and consequently a need for discipline'. Raymond Aron, *Main Currents in Sociological Thought*, London [New York], 1968, vol. 2, p. 86.

91. E. Durkheim, *The Rules of Sociological Method* [Glencoe, 1950], London, 1964, p. 121.

92. *Suicide*, p. 360. There are major unresolved difficulties in Durkheim's writings on this point, however, analysed in my 'The "individual" in the writings of Emile Durkheim', pp. 273–91.

93. 'The Dualism of Human Nature and its Social Conditions', loc. cit., p. 339.

94. Coser, loc. cit., pp. 211–12. cf. Parsons, '(Durkheim) was almost wholly concerned with what Comte would have called "social statics" ', op. cit., p. 307.

95. Coser, loc. cit., p. 212.

96. *The Division of Labour*, p. 377.

97. *The Rules of Sociological Method*, p. lvi.

98. *Montesquieu and Rousseau*, p. 59.

99. *The Rules of Sociological Method*, p. 47.

100. Review of Deploige, p. 327.

101. See particularly the brief but deservedly famous 'Theses on Feuerbach', in Loyd D. Easton and Kurt H. Guddat, *Writings of the Young Marx on Philosophy and Society*, New York, 1967, pp. 400–402.

102. Bendix, op. cit., pp. 184 ff.

103. *The Division of Labour*, p. 29.

104. cf. my ' "Power" in the Recent Writings of Talcott Parsons', pp. 333–46.

105. cf. Aron, op. cit., pp. 82 ff.

106. *Professional Ethics and Civic Morals*, pp. 50–1.

107. ibid., p. 78.

108. For background material on Weber's conception of the state, see my *Politics and Sociology in the Thought of Max Weber.*

109. See Sheldon S. Wolin, *Politics and Vision* [Boston, 1960], London, 1961.

110. Parsons, op. cit., p. 341; but cf. Richter, loc. cit., p. 208.

111. The publication of Marx's early writings has, however, made it apparent that this thesis of Durkheim's is erroneous, at least as applied to Marx. Marx was primarily concerned with the alienative dominance of economic relationships under capitalism: the regulation of the market was to Marx a means, not an end. See my *Capitalism and Modern Social Theory*, Chapter 15.

112. *Professional Ethics and Civic Morals*, p. 213.

113. 'A limitation to the right of disposal is in no way an attack on the individual concept of property – on the contrary. For individual property is property that begins and ends with the individual.' ibid., pp. 216–17.

114. *The Division of Labour*, pp. 374 and 377.

115. Robert Wohl, *French Communism in the Making, 1914–1924*, Stanford, 1966, p. 9.

8 The 'individual' in the writings of Emile Durkheim

1. Perhaps the best of the earlier studies of Durkheim is Roger Lacombe, *La méthode sociologique de Durkheim*, Paris, 1926.

2. This point is mentioned by Steven Lukes in introducing his translation, Durkheim's 'Individualism and the Intellectuals', *Political Studies*, vol. 17, 1969.

3. 'La science positive de la morale en Allemagne', *Revue philosophique*, vol. 24, 1887, 3 parts.

4. cf. my article, 'Durkheim's political sociology', pp. 235–72.

5. *De la division du travail social*, Paris, 1960, p. xliii. (All translations are mine.)

6. See, for example, Robert A. Nisbet, *Emile Durkheim*, Englewood Cliffs, 1965, p. 37 and *passim*.

7. *De la division du travail social*, p. 396.

8. 'L'individualisme et les intellectuels', *Revue bleue*, vol. 10, 1898, pp. 7–13, translated in S. Lukes, loc. cit.

9. *L'Evolution pédagogique en France*, Paris, 1938, republished 1969. See, for example, pp. 322–3.

10. *Sociologie et philosophie*, Paris, 1924, p. 106.

11. The term 'anomie' first appears in Durkheim's writings in his review (1887) of Guyau's *L'Irréligion de l'avenir*. The latter author uses the term, however, in a sense closer to Durkheim's conception of moral individualism.

12. 'Suicide et natalité: étude de statistique morale', *Revue philosophique*, vol. 26, 1888, pp. 446–63.

13. See my *Capitalism and Modern Social Theory*, Cambridge (UK) [New York], 1971, Chapters 8 and 15; and my 'introduction' to *Emile Durkheim: Selected Writings*, Cambridge [New York], 1972.

14. Parsons, however, makes too much of this. See Talcott Parsons, *The Structure of Social Action*, Glencoe, 1949, pp. 350–3.

15. *Les Règles de la méthode sociologique*, Paris, 1950, p. 8.

16. ibid., p. 7.

17. *Sociologie et philosophie*, op. cit., pp. 60–2.

18. *Le Suicide*, Paris, 1930, p. 411.

19. 'Le Dualisme de la nature humaine et ses conditions sociales', *Scientia*, vol. 15, 1914, pp. 206–21, translated in K. Wolff, *Emile Durkheim et al. Essays on Sociology and Philosophy*, London [New York], 1964.

20. See 'The suicide problem in French sociology', pp. 322–32.

21. *Le Suicide*, p. 8.

22. *De la division du travail social*, p. 399.

23. This is, of course, reinforced by other aspects of Durkheim's methodology which I do not discuss in this paper: such as the 'rule' that 'an effect can only have one cause'.

24. This is the aspect given most prominence by Parsons. See especially *The Social System*, London, 1951, p. 39.

25. 'Introduction' to *Emile Durkheim: Selected Writings*.

26. cf. R. K. Merton, 'Social structure and anomie', in *Social Theory and Social Structure*, Glencoe, 1963.

27. See, for example, *Sociologie et philosophie*, pp. 56–7.

28. *De la division du travail social*, p. 327.

Durkheim on social facts

29. 'Les études de science sociale', *Revue philosophique*, vol. 22, 1886, pp. 78–9.

30. *The Division of Labour in Society*, London, 1964, p. 1.

31. cf. Strawson, 'Facts are what statements (when true) state; they are not what statements are about'. P. F. Strawson, 'Truth', in George Pitcher, *Truth*, New Jersey, 1964, p. 38.

32. *The Rules of Sociological Method* [eighth edition, Glencoe, 1950], London, 1964, p. 1.

33. ibid.

34. cf. 'The "individual" in the writings of Emile Durkheim', pp. 273–91.

35. *The Rules of Sociological Method*, p. 44.

36. ibid., p. 45.

37. ibid., pp. 28–9.

9 A theory of suicide

1. H. Rost, *Bibliographie des Selbstmords*, Augsburg, 1927; an earlier bibliography is given in E. Motta, *Bibliografia del suicidio*, Bellinzona, 1890; a later one is in N. L. Farberow and E. S. Shneidman, *The Cry for Help*, New York, 1961.

2. cf. 'The suicide problem in French sociology', pp. 322–32.

3. Jack D. Douglas, *The Social Meanings of Suicide*, Princeton, 1967; 'The sociological analysis of social meanings of suicide', *Archives européennes de sociologie*, vol. 7, 1966.

4. 'The sociological analysis . . .', op. cit., pp. 252–4.

5. ibid., p. 255.

6. *The Social Meanings of Suicide*, p. 228.

7. ibid.

8. ibid., p. 230.

9. 'The sociological analysis . . .', op. cit., p. 262.

10. *The Social Meanings of Suicide*, pp. 58 ff.

11. 'The sociological analysis . . .' op. cit., p. 264.

12. ibid., p. 265.

13. *The Social Meanings of Suicide*, p. 339.

14. cf. Jack P. Gibbs, 'Suicide', in Robert K. Merton and Robert A. Nisbet, *Contemporary Social Problems*, New York, 1966, p. 287.

15. 'The sociological analysis . . .', op. cit., p. 267.

16. cf. 'Functionalism: *après la lutte*', pp. 96–129.

17. *The Social Meanings of Suicide*, pp. 257–8.

18. Discussed by Douglas on pp. 378 ff. of *The Social Meanings of Suicide*.

19. Alasdair MacIntyre, 'The idea of a social science', *Aristotelian Society Supplement*, vol. 41, 1967.

20. *New Rules of Sociological Method*, London [New York], 1976, pp. 71 ff. and *passim*.

21. This point was made very forcibly by one of Durkheim's early critics, Achille-Delmas. cf. 'The suicide problem in French sociology', pp. 322–32.

22. *New Rules of Sociological Method*, pp. 148 ff.

23. S. Freud, *Mourning and Melancholia* (standard edition), London, 1955, vol. xvii; also *The Ego and the Id* (standard edition), vol. xix. A description of psychoanalytic ideas on suicide is given in D. D. Jackson, 'Theories of suicide', in E. S. Shneidman and N. L. Farberow, *Clues to Suicide*, New York, 1957, pp. 11–21. Throughout this article I have used the term 'depression' generically in a very wide sense, to include both neurotic and psychotic depression. While there are several partially distinct psychoanalytic theories of depression, I have confined the account mainly to Freud's classical statement of the nature of melancholia, since the other theories are basically elaborations of the ideas set out there.

24. S. Freud, *Mourning and Melancholia*, p. 246.

25. ibid., p. 251.

26. cf. K. Menninger, *Man against Himself*, New York, 1938.

27. S. Freud, *Mourning and Melancholia*, p. 252.

28. cf. C. W. Wahl, 'Suicide as a magical act', in Shneidman and Farberow, op. cit., pp. 22–30.

29. S. Freud, *Mourning and Melancholia*, p. 245.

30. In this analysis I have followed the basic distinctions set out by Piers. See Piers and M. B. Singer, *Shame and Guilt*, Springfield, 1953. There is no space here to discuss Parsons's

treatment of guilt and shame, which in some respects strikingly resembles that set forth in this paper. Parsons seems however to follow the 'guilt-internal, shame-external' notion. See T. Parsons and R. F. Bales, *Family Socialisation and Interaction Process*, London, 1956.

31. ibid., pp. 23 ff. It should, of course, be understood that the 'super-ego' and 'ego-ideal' are 'ordering constructs' and not in any sense discrete 'entities'. We cannot today be satisfied with the logical form which Freud himself attributed to the concepts which he used to describe unconscious mental processes, as Lacan, Lorenzer and others have shown.

32. ibid., p. 16. Most psychoanalysts, following Freud, have regarded shame as being linked specifically to fear of genital exposure, and thus to anxiety over bodily 'appearance' more generally. The phenomenon of shame is, in fact, much more pervasive than this in human experience. That this is so is shown by the frequency with which 'feeling ashamed' and synonymous phrases (e.g. 'feeling humiliated') occur in the course of everyday speech. While anthropologists have pointed to the importance of shame as a social and psychological mechanism in traditional and primitive societies, little has been written of shame in West European societies. Indeed some anthropologists have sought to contrast the 'guilt cultures' of Western Europe with 'shame cultures'. But, although shame may have a more 'external' aspect in societies in which tight formalized standards of expected punishment prevail, the phenomena of shame and shaming are ubiquitous. Shame is evidently closely related to embarrassment, which may be nothing more than a mild sense of shame. Both shame and embarrassment stem from a questioning of the appropriateness of an identity which an individual is attempting to maintain. The more deep-rooted nature of shame is indicated by the fact that, while we can 'be embarrassed *for* another', we are 'ashamed *of* another': in the second instances, the behaviour of the other casts a slur upon *ourself*, while in the first we feel in an empathic way that he is showing himself in a bad light. cf. E. Goffman, *The Presentation of Self in Everyday Life*, New York, 1959 [London, 1969], pp. 58 ff., and *Stigma*, Englewood Cliffs, 1963 [London, 1970]. cf. also K. Reizler, 'Comment on the social psychology of shame', *American Journal of Sociology*, vol. 48, 1943, pp. 457–65.

33. Menninger describes cases of suicide following the most trivial of setbacks. cf. K. Menninger, op. cit., pp. 35–6.

N*

34. H. Hendin, *Suicide and Scandinavia*, New York, 1965, p. 26.

35. These two sets of fantasy meanings are not, of course, entirely exclusive. cf. H. Feifel, 'Some aspects of the meaning of death', in Shneidman and Farberow, op. cit., pp. 50–7.

36. Menninger, op. cit., pp. 23–71.

37. e.g. Barclay Johnson, 'Durkheim's one cause of suicide', *American Sociological Review*, vol. 30, 1965.

38. See, for example, Peter Sainsbury, *Suicide in London*, London, 1955.

39. cf. S. Rado, 'Psychodynamics of depression from the aetiological point of view', *Collected Papers*, New York, 1956, vol. 1.

40. Otto Fenichel, *The Psychoanalytic Theory of Neurosis* [New York, 1945], London, 1946, p. 400.

41. Hendin, op. cit., p. 24.

42. E. Stengel, *Suicide and Attempted Suicide* [New York], London, 1964, pp. 77 ff.

43. cf. E. Stengel, op. cit.; J. Cohen, *Behaviour in Uncertainty*, London, 1964.

44. James M. A. Weiss, 'The gamble with death in attempted suicide', *Psychiatry*, vol. 20, 1957.

45. Eli Robins *et al.*, 'The communication of suicidal intent', *American Journal of Psychiatry*, vol. 115, 1959.

46. Menninger, op. cit., p. 65.

47. E. Stengel and N. G. Cook, *Attempted Suicide*, London, 1958, pp. 114 ff.

48. Emile Durkheim, *Suicide* [Glencoe, 1951], London, 1952, pp. 278 and 286.

49. E. Beresford Davies, *Depression*, Cambridge, 1964, pp. 22–3.

50. H. M. Lynd, *On Shame and the Search for Identity*, London, 1958 [New York, 1970], p. 50.

51. Menninger, op. cit., pp. 54 ff.

52. Stengel and Cook, op. cit., pp. 119–21.

53. E. S. Shneidman and N. L. Farberow, 'Statistical comparisons between attempted and committed suicides', in Shneidman and Farberow, op. cit., pp. 28–9.

The suicide problem in French sociology

54. E. Durkheim, *Le Suicide*, Paris, 1897. All further references are to the English translation: *Suicide* (trans. J. A. Spaulding and G. Simpson), London, 1952.

55. A description of some of these works can be found in L. G. Crocker, 'The discussion of suicide in the eighteenth century', *Journal of the History of Ideas*, 13 January 1952, pp. 47–52.

56. See, for example, J. Dumas, *Traité du suicide*, Amsterdam, 1773, p. 2.

57. J. P. Falret, *De l'hypocondrie et du suicide*, Paris, 1822.

58. ibid., pp. 5–6.

59. A. M. Guerry, *Essai sur la statistique morale de la France*, Paris, 1833; E. Lisle, *Du suicide*, Paris, 1856; A. Legoyt, *Le Suicide ancien et moderne*, Paris, 1881; A. Quételet, *Sur l'homme et le développement de ses facultés* (2 vols.), Paris, 1835; *Du système social et des lois qui le régissent*, Paris, 1848; A. Wagner, *Die Gesetzmässigkeit in den scheinbar willkürlichen menschlichen Handlungen*, Hamburg, 1864; T. G. Masaryk, *Der Selbstmord*, Vienna, 1881; E. Morselli, *Il suicidio*, Milan, 1879; E. Ferri, *L'omicidio-suicidio*, Turin, 1883. Studies of suicide published in English borrowed extensively from the French and German writers: F. Winslow, *The Anatomy of Suicide*, New York, 1882; W. W. Westcott, *Suicide*, London, 1885.

60. A partial bibliography of works up to 1889 can be found in E. Motta, *Bibliografia del suicidio*, Bellinzona, 1890; a fuller bibliography is included in H. Rost, *Bibliographie des Selbstmords*, Augsburg, 1927.

61. See, for example, Lisle, op. cit.

62. In his statistical analysis of suicide in London, for example, Jopling echoed the conclusions of other writers in finding rates to be highest among the 'upper and middle classes'. R. T. Jopling, *Statistics of Suicide*, London, 1852, p. 9.

63. As early as 1840, in cognizance of the differential distribution of suicide between urban and rural areas, Cazauvieilh made a specific study of suicide in rural areas in France, showing some exceptions to the general rule that suicide rates are highest in urban areas. See J. B. Cazauvieilh, *Du suicide*, Paris, 1840, pp. 2–3 and ff.

64. See, for example, A. Corre, *Crime et suicide*, Paris, 1891; Ferri, op. cit.

65. cf. Masaryk, op. cit., pp. 141–241.

66. The most thorough statistical analysis of these factors is given in Morselli, op. cit.

67. 'Not only are suicides, each year, of almost the same quantity; but, separating rates for groups in terms of the instruments used, we find the same constancy.' Quételet, *Du système social et des lois qui le régissent*, p. 88.

68. cf. esp. Masaryk, op. cit. The very earliest objective studies of suicide at the turn of the nineteenth century linked rising suicide rates to weakening religious beliefs and customs. A typical discussion is given in A. Brierre de Boismont, *Du suicide et de la folie-suicide*, Paris, 1856, ch. 4, pp. 352–89.

69. The phrase is taken from S. Miller, *The Guilt, Folly and Sources of Suicide*, New York, 1805, p. 14.

70. E. Esquirol, *Des maladies mentales*, Paris, 1838, 2 vols.

71. ibid., vol. 1, p. 639.

72. A. von Öttingen, *Die Moralstatistik*, Erlangen, 1882.

73. Most writers recognized a division of the causes of suicide into two types: 'the external or social, and the internal or personal'. O'Dea, op. cit., Preface, pp. v–vi.

74. Durkheim, op. cit., p. 46.

75. ibid., p. 51.

76. ibid., esp. bk. 3, ch. 1.

77. Tarde's characteristic point of view is clearly enunciated in his *Etudes de psychologie sociale*, Paris, 1898.

78. Many psychologists took a less extreme view than this. Viallon, for example, after a survey of the problem, concluded that 'insanity is the most important, but not the exclusive, cause of suicide'. Viallon, 'Suicide et folie', *Annales médico-psychologiques*, 25, July–August, 1901 (pt. 1), p. 22.

79. Esquirol himself did allow that social factors play a certain role in the aetiology of mental disorder and, consequently, suicide. cf. Esquirol, op. cit., pp. 526 ff.

80. M. de Fleury, *L'Angoisse humaine*, Paris, 1924. Prior to de Fleury's book, Bayet's important historical survey of suicide appeared, written from a broadly sociological standpoint, and explicitly indebted to Durkheim. A. Bayet, *Le Suicide et la morale*, Paris, 1922.

81. De Fleury, op. cit., p. 79.

82. M. Halbwachs, *Les Causes du suicide*, Paris, 1930.

83. ibid., pp. 197–239. Halbwachs made an important survey of

variations in modes of suicide registration in different countries in Europe, concluding that international comparisons of suicide rates can only be made with great caution. See pp. 19–39.

84. ibid., pp. 241–86.
85. ibid., p. 238.
86. ibid., pp. 266 ff.
87. ibid., pp. 362–74.
88. Halbwachs distinguished between suicide and self-sacrifice. The latter category of self-destruction (which takes in most of Durkheim's type of altruistic suicide), according to Halbwachs, is so different from 'individualized' suicide, that it is impossible to fit the two usefully within the same explanatory framework. ibid., pp. 451–80.
89. Halbwachs's theory, however, is a logical development of Durkheim's. Durkheim was more concerned to outline types of social structure producing high rates of suicide. Halbwachs said little about the broad structural conditions promoting the detachment of individuals from stable social relationships.
90. Serin carried out an intensive study of 450 cases of suicide in Paris, identifying about two-thirds of them as associated with some form of psychopathological condition. S. Serin, 'Une enquête médico-sociale sur le suicide à Paris', *Annales médico-psychologiques*, 2, November 1926, pp. 536–62. Halbwachs, however, questioned her results, claiming that only a minority of her cases could be properly identified as 'pathological' in character. Halbwachs, op. cit., pp. 381 ff.
91. ibid., p. 426.
92. ibid., p. 448. In other publications Halbwachs tried to show the relevance of sociology to the explanation of psychological functions. *Les Cadres sociaux de la mémoire*, Paris, 1952, developed the thesis that memory has been only treated by psychologists as a function of the 'isolated individual' whereas in fact memory is essentially a social phenomenon. An ambitious survey of social motivation was attempted in B. Raynaud, M. Halbwachs *et al.: Analyse des mobiles dominants qui orientent l'activité des individus dans la vie sociale*, Paris, 1938, 2 vols.
93. P. Courbon, review of Halbwachs's *Les Causes du suicide*. *Annales médico-psychologiques*, new series 1, March 1931, p. 322.
94. F. Achille-Delmas, *Psychologie pathologique du suicide*, Paris, 1932.
95. ibid., pp. 49 ff.

96. Delmas separated off 'true' suicide from other kinds of self-destruction. Suicide of a sacrificial nature, suicide prior to the termination of a fatal illness, and the suicide of psychotics are all examples of 'pseudo-suicide'. 'True' suicide, according to Delmas, involves the possibility of choice of life or death on the part of the individual: ibid., pp. 87 ff. This closely echoes a distinction made almost a century before by Falret (op. cit., pp. 3–5).

97. ibid., p. 234.

98. Ch. Blondel, *Le Suicide*, Strasbourg, 1933. Immediately prior to the publication of Blondel's book, Bonnafous made a spirited defence of the *thèse sociologique* in a review article of Delmas's work. M. Bonnafous, 'Le suicide: thèse psychiatrique et thèse sociologique', *Revue philosophique*, vol. 115, May–June 1933, pp. 456–75.

99. Blondel, op. cit., pp. 119 ff. See also Blondel's discussion in his *Introduction à la psychologie collective*, Paris, 1927, ch. 4, pp. 90–104.

100. For example, B. Abderrahman, *Du suicide émotif et suicide non pathologique* (M.D. thesis), Paris: Rodstein, 1933; P. Friedman, 'Sur le suicide', *Revue française de psychoanalyse*, vol. 8, 1935, pp. 106–48.

101. C. Drombrowski, *Les Conditions psychologiques du suicide* (M.D. thesis), Geneva, 1929.

102. ibid., p. 32.

103. The only important objective study of suicide to be published in France since the war is G. Deshaies, *La Psychologie du suicide*, Paris, 1947. The suicide controversy was also discussed by Deshaies in 'Les doctrines du suicide', *L'Evolution psychiatrique*, January–March 1952, pp. 41–54. A number of philosophical works concerned with suicide have been published in France in recent years. Probably the most well-known is A. Camus's *Le Mythe de Sisyphe*, Paris, 1942. Among the latest discussions of this type are L. Meynard, *Le Suicide*, Paris, 1958; and Touraine, *Le Suicide ascétique*, Paris, 1960.

104. A useful overall survey of the development of sociology in France is given in C. Lévi-Strauss, 'French sociology', in G. Gurvitch and W. E. Moore, *Twentieth Century Sociology*, New York, 1945, pp. 503–37. See also J. Stoetzel, 'Sociology in France; an empiricist view', in H. Becker and A. Boskoff, *Modern Sociological Theory*, New York, 1957, pp. 623–57.

105. G. Gurvitch, *Essais de sociologie*, Paris, 1939, pp. 141–2.

The same essay is reprinted, with minor alterations, in G. Gurvitch, *La Vocation actuelle de la sociologie*, Paris, 1950. Gurvitch's work is not without its critics. Cuvillier has been perhaps the most outspoken. See particularly A. Cuvillier, *Introduction à la sociologie*, Paris, fifth edition, 1954, ch. 4, pp. 84–124; and *Où va la sociologie française?*, Paris, 1953.

106. R. Bastide, 'Le suicide du nègre brésilien', *Cahiers internationaux de sociologie,* vol. 12, 1952, pp. 72–90. See also his 'Sociologie et psychologie', in G. Gurvitch, *Traité de sociologie*, Paris, 1962, pp. 71 ff.

107. ibid., p. 89.

108. C. Lévi-Strauss, op. cit., p. 509.

109. The continuity is evident in an article Durkheim wrote on the demography of suicide, published eleven years before his major study: 'Suicide et natalité: étude de statistique morale', *Revue philosophique*, vol. 26, November 1888, pp. 446–63.

110. Durkheim, *Suicide*, p. 46.

111. ibid., pp. 37–8.

112. Quoted by Durkheim, ibid., p. 311.

113. cf. E. Stengel and N. G. Cook, *Attempted Suicide*, London, 1958, p. 14.

114. There is considerable division between psychiatrists over the role of somatic factors in depressive disorders. A good discussion of this problem is given in R. W. White, *The Abnormal Personality*, New York, 1956, pp. 523–43. Psychiatry in Britain and America has generally tended to allow a lesser role to heredity and constitution in mental disorder than in France. As Pichot remarks: 'The French psychiatric tradition has always been strongly constitutionalist . . .' P. Pichot, 'France', in L. Bellak, *Contemporary European Psychiatry*, New York, 1961, p. 15.

115. See H. J. Walton, 'Suicidal behaviour in depressive illness', *British Journal of Mental Science*, vol. 104, July 1958, pp. 884–91.

116. See also R. Duchac, *Sociologie et psychologie*, Paris, 1963, pp. 17 ff.

117. See T. Parsons, *The Structure of Social Action*, Glencoe, 1937, p. 324.

10 'Power' in the writings of Talcott Parsons

1. See, for instance – one among many – Ralf Dahrendorf, *Class and Class Conflict in Industrial Society*, Stanford, 1959.

2. The most important of these recent publications are: 'On the concept of political power', *Proceedings of the American Philosophical Society*, vol. 107, 1963, pp. 232–62; 'Some reflections on the place of force in social process', in Harry Eckstein, *Internal War*, Glencoe, 1964; 'On the concept of influence', *Public Opinion Quarterly*, vol. 27, 1963, pp. 37–62; 'The political aspect of social structure and process', in David Easton, *Varieties of Political Theory*, Englewood Cliffs, 1966. See also an earlier paper: 'Authority, legitimation and political action', reprinted in *Structure and Process in Industrial Societies*, Glencoe, 1960, pp. 170–98. Parsons's review of Mills's book, entitled 'The distribution of power in American society', can be found in the same volume, pp. 199–225.

3. Thus Mills, in Parsons's view, shows a '. . . tendency to think of power as presumptively illegitimate; if people exercise considerable power, it must be because they have somehow usurped it where they had no right and they intend to use it to the detriment of others'. 'The distribution of power in American society', loc. cit., p. 221.

4. ibid., p. 220.

5. Parsons stresses that this analysis of power marks a shift from the views set down in *The Social System*, where he states he still accepted the 'traditional' (i.e., the 'zero-sum') conception. This also means that his view of what constitutes 'political science' has also changed; whereas previously in *The Structure of Social Action* he accepted the idea that political science is a synthetic discipline, it now becomes seen as a relatively autonomous analytical discipline on a par with economics.

6. 'On the concept of political power', p. 237.

7. 'Authority, legitimation and political action', p. 181.

8. 'On the concept of political power', p. 250.

9. 'Some reflections on the place of force in the social process'.

This typology obviously links up with the functional subsystems of society. As in most of Parsons's schemes involving the four 'functional subsystems', a regressive set of subclassifications is possible for each of the four 'media' of interaction. In the case of 'influence', for example, the pattern would look like this:

(I=integration; GA=goal-attainment; A=adaptation; PM=pattern-maintenance)

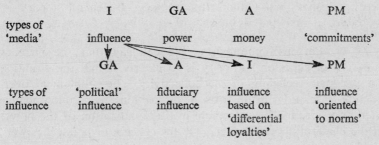

	I	GA	A	PM
types of 'media'	influence	power	money	'commitments'
	GA	A	I	PM
types of influence	'political' influence	fiduciary influence	influence based on 'differential loyalties'	influence 'oriented to norms'

10. 'Some reflections on the place of force in the social process', p. 52.

11. ibid., pp. 63 ff.

12. These parallels are discussed in Coleman's commentary on Parsons's paper on influence, loc. cit., pp. 63 ff.

13. Hans H. Gerth and C. Wright Mills, *From Max Weber*, New York, 1958, p. 180.

14. cf. some of Michael Crozier's comments in 'Pouvoir et organisation', *European Journal of Sociology*, vol. 5, 1964, pp. 52–64.

15. Parsons claims these concepts 'bridge the gap between the normative and factual aspects of the system in which they operate'. 'On the concept of influence', p. 45.

16. In commenting on Parsons's article on influence, Raymond Bauer writes: 'In advertising, in courtship, in all our relations, there is without doubt a large amount of nontruth, or irrelevance masking as relevant truth. The disparity between this circumstance and Parsons's position should not be regarded as a contradiction, but rather as a subject of investigation.' 'Communication as a transaction: a comment on "On the concept of influence"', loc. cit., p. 84. It is certainly true that deceit pre-

supposes trust, but there is also a sense in which trust presupposes deceit. Neither has any meaning without the other, and to say that social life 'rests' upon the first is just as true, and misleading, as to say that it depends upon the second. If trust is 'expansionable', so is deceit; trust and deceit feed upon and intertwine with, one another.

17. *Societies: Evolutionary and Comparative Perspectives*, Englewood Cliffs, 1966, p. 115.

18. cf. the attempt by Johnson to use some of Parsons's concepts together with others to produce a general theory of revolution. Chalmers Johnson, *Revolutionary Change*, Boston, 1966.

19. cf. Parsons's comment: 'We can say that the primary function of superior authority is to clearly define the situation for the lower echelons of the collectivity. The problem of overcoming opposition in the form of dispositions to non-compliance then arises from the incomplete institutionalization of the power of the higher authority holder.' 'On the concept of political power', p. 243.

20. 'On the Concept of Political Power', p. 254.

21. Parsons has always recognized in principle the essential linkage between values and interests. See, for example, the discussion in one of his earliest articles: 'The place of ultimate values in sociological theory', *International Journal of Ethics*, vol. 45, 1935, pp. 282–316. In a much later publication, Parsons remarks, presumably with reference to Lockwood: 'I do not think it is useful to postulate a deep dichotomy between theories which give importance to beliefs and values on the one hand, and to allegedly 'realistic' interests, e.g. economic, on the other. Beliefs and values are actualized, partially and imperfectly, in realistic situations of social interaction and the outcomes are *always* codetermined by the values and the realistic exigencies . . .' 'Authority, legitimation and political action', p. 173. There is clearly a sense in which 'values' are prior to 'interests': to have an 'interest', an individual or group must have some kind of selective motivation, which presumes in turn some kind of 'value'. But this is very different from saying that in an *explanatory* sense values are necessarily prior to interests. And this is precisely what the whole of Parsons's theory is predicated upon. Parsons's recognition of the role of non-normative interests has not led to a systematic theoretical treatment of the interaction of values and

interests. The point is that not only are the 'outcomes in realistic situations of social interaction' codetermined by values and 'realistic exigencies', but that the latter play an (often crucial) part in the *formation* and degree of 'actualization' of values.

Acknowledgements

Chapter 9, 'A theory of suicide', is loosely based on an article originally entitled 'A typology of suicide', which appeared in the *Archives européennes de sociologie*, vol. 7, 1966, but is substantially a new paper altogether. I have made only relatively minor changes in the other articles, and wish to thank the following for giving permission to reproduce them here: Basic Books, Inc. for 'Positivism and its critics', in T. B. Bottomore and Robert Nisbet (ed.), *A History of Sociological Thought* (Forthcoming); the editor of *Social Research* for 'Functionalism: *après la lutte*', vol. 43, 1976; the editor for 'Habermas's critique of hermeneutics', in T. Freiburg (ed.), *Current Trends in European Critical Theory* (Forthcoming); Macmillan Publishing Co. and the Free Press for 'Hermeneutics, ethnomethodology, and problems of interpretative analysis', in Lewis A. Coser and Otto Larsen (ed.), *The Uses of Controversy in Sociology*, New York, 1976; the editor of *Sociology* for 'Marx, Weber and the development of capitalism', vol. 4, 1970; and for 'Power in the writings of Talcott Parsons', vol. 2, 1968, the original title of which referred to 'the recent writings of Talcott Parsons', as they then were; the editors of *Economy and Society* for 'Four myths in the history of social thought', vol. 1, 1972; the editor of the *Sociological Review* for 'Durkheim's political sociology', vol. 20, 1972; the editor of the *Archives européennes de sociologie* for 'The "individual" in the writings of Emile Durkheim', vol. 12, 1971; and the editor of *The British Journal of Sociology*, and Routledge & Kegan Paul, for 'The suicide problem in French Sociology', vol. 16, 1965.

Index